Economic History and
the History of Economics

Economic History and the History of Economics

Mark Blaug

*Professor Emeritus, University of London and
Consultant Professor of Economics, University
of Buckingham*

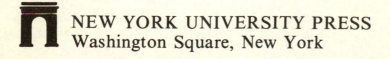

NEW YORK UNIVERSITY PRESS
Washington Square, New York

First published in the USA in 1986 by
NEW YORK UNIVERSITY PRESS
Washington Square
New York, NY 10003

Library of Congress Cataloging-in-Publication Data

Blaug, Mark.
  Economic history and the history of economics.

  Bibliography: p.
  Includes index.
  1. Economic history. 2. Economics — History.
I. Title.
HC26.B58   1986   330.9   85-29840
ISBN 0-8147-1090-5

Typeset in 10/12 point Times by Alacrity Phototypesetters,
Banwell Castle, Weston-super-Mare
and printed and bound in Great Britain by
Biddles Ltd, Guildford and King's Lynn

Table of Contents

Acknowledgements

I wish to thank the following publishers for permission to reprint: Association of Polytechnic Teachers of Economics for "Economic Methodology in One Easy Lesson" in *British Review of Economic Issues*, May 1980; Duke University Press for "Was There a Marginal Revolution?" and "Kuhn versus Lakatos, or Paradigms versus Research Programmes in the History of Economics" in *History of Political Economy*, Fall 1972 and Spring 1976; *Economic History Review* for "The Productivity of Capital in the Lancashire Cotton Industry During the Nineteenth Century" in *Economic History Review*, April 1961; John Wiley and Sons for "The Classical Economists and the Factory Acts: A Re-examination" in *Quarterly Journal of Economics*, May 1959; *Journal of Economic History* for "The Myth of the Old Poor Law and the Making of the New" and "The Poor Law Report Re-Examined" in *Journal of Economic History*, June 1963 and June 1964; *Kyklos* for "Technical Change and Marxian Economics" in *Kyklos*, 13, No. 4, 1960; Macmillan Press for "Another Look at the Labour Reduction Problem in Marx" in *Classical and Marxian Political Economy*, eds. I. Bradley and M. Howard (1982); Oxford University Press for "The Economics of Education in English Classical Political Economy: A Re-examination in *Essays on Adam Smith*, eds. A. S. Skinner and T. Wilson (1975); Revista di Politica Economica for "Ricardo e il problema della politica economica" in *Revista di Politica Economica*, 73, serie 3, fasc. 5, mag. 1983; "Entrepreneurship Before and After Schumpeter" in *Marx, Schumpeter and Keynes: A Centenary Celebration of Dissent*, eds. Suzanne Helburn and David F. Bramhall, copyright © 1968 by M. E. Sharpe, Inc. and reprinted here by permission; *Southern Economic Journal* for "Welfare Indices in *The Wealth of Nations*" in *Southern Economic Journal,* October 1959; University of Chicago Press for "The Empirical Content of Ricardian Economics" in *Journal of Political Economy*, February 1956.

Introduction

Economic history—the story of what actually happened—is intimately related to the history of economic thought—the story of what economists thought had happened and was still happening. Sometimes economists got it right and sometimes they got it wrong. The English classical economists were reformers and addressed themselves to all the outstanding policy issues of the day: population growth, welfare relief for the poor, agricultural protection, factory legislation, the public debt, etcetera. The first six chapters of this book explore that theme in some of its dimensions.

The same theme is only too obvious in the writings of Karl Marx, in which the question of technical change emerged as one of the major problems of the day. In three further chapters, the theory of technical progress in both Marx and later economists is examined in some detail.

In the 1870s, economics became professionalised and entered the modern era of marginalist thinking. The "marginal revolution" is the subject of another chapter and the aftermath of marginalism is explored in a chapter on the history of entrepreneurship.

The volume closes with a couple of chapters on unresolved issues in the history of modern economics since 1870, viewed once again in the light of changes in the institutional structure of the economies that formed the background of theorising.

THE POOR LAWS

I am very fond of my two early articles on the Old Poor Law. For one thing the first was written under the most adverse personal circumstances: I was flat on my back with a compound fractured skull and forced to rely for research material on an endless round of graduate students carrying heavy volumes to and from the library; for another the two articles were iconoclastic, created quite a stir, were frequently cited (e.g. Marshall, 1968; Poynter, 1969; Checkland, 1974) occasionally attacked at article-length (Taylor, 1969; McCloskey, 1973) and led to many invitations to address learned gatherings—all heady stuff to a young Assistant Professor making his way through the Groves of Academia. On balance, they have worn well: their findings, at least in the main, although not in all details, have been confirmed by subsequent research (Huzel, 1969; 1980; Baugh,

1975; Wellington, 1984; Boyer, 1985, 1986) and none of the recent textbooks on British economic history during the Industrial Revolution stigmatise the Old Poor Law in the lurid rhetoric that was so common in the textbooks of yesterday.

But that is not to say that I would write these essays in the same way today. The first essay combined theoretical knock-down arguments with suggestive empirical evidence. It is only in the second essay that I got down to what I now consider to be the crucial question: the actual manner in which the Old Poor Law was administered. The older writers I was attacking — the Webbs, the Hammonds, Halévy, etcetera — made the mistake of confusing Acts of Statute with the law that is actually enforced, a cardinal error in this case where the statutes left an indefinite leeway in each parish.

It is rather similar to the notion in modern macroeconomics that the effects of unemployment benefits on the willingness to work can be measured by the length of time for which benefits are paid and the ratio of benefits to wages in previous employment, the so-called "replacement ratio". But unemployment benefits are paid only to those who are involuntarily unemployed and seeking work. However in some countries (like Switzerland and Japan), the unemployed applying for benefits are required to produce firm evidence that they are actually seeking work, whereas elsewhere benefits are paid to the unemployed simply as a matter of right. It is this element of stringency or laxity in the administration of unemployment compensation, and not the replacement ratio or the duration of unemployment payments, that explains the impact of unemployment benefits on the volume of unemployment.

Of my two critics, it was McCloskey who scored most of the telling points. Taylor's main objection was that I took too narrow a view of the Old Poor Law — emphasising the rural Allowance System and neglecting the treatment of orphans, widows, the sick, the old and the disabled in urban areas — and that I arrived at far too many conclusions on the basis of too few data. But my preoccupation with allowances-in-aid-of wages was no more than a reflection of the main preoccupations of the authors of the *Poor Law Report of 1834*: contemporary opinion was indeed focused on the effects of the Old Poor Law in *rural* areas. He also convicted me of minimising the extent of indoor relief in 1802, catching a misprint in the original article whereby nearly 4,000 workhouses in 1802 appeared as a mere 400. In addition, he threw doubt on my fundamental division between Speenhamland and non-Speenhamland countries, based on a questionnaire answered by a small sample of Poor Law authorities for the 1824 Select Committee on Labourers' Wages, but neglected to mention the fact that I provided two other classifications of the countries and in any case supplied data on all the individual countries to allow the reader to form his own classification. On balance, Taylor succeeded in chipping away at some of my detail (as did Cowherd, 1978) without affecting the principal points of substance.

McCloskey, on the other hand, largely ignored my empirical evidence and instead questioned my basic theoretical analysis. He began by doubting my argument that the poor rate, being levied on farmers in proportion to the value of land they occupied, was never fully shifted to landlords in the form of lower rents because, given that the standard lease ran for 7-14 years, sharp year-to-year fluctuations in the level of the rates hindered the full adjustment of rentals to the rate burden. I cited some evidence for the county of Warwickshire where no connection was found between land rentals and rateable values under the Old Poor Law but was unable to clinch the matter because so little is known about land rentals in the crucial years 1815 to 1834. I should have cited Thompson (1907) who reports gross and net ground rents (after deducting disguised profits included in the rent figures) for two large landed estates over the whole of the nineteenth century; he shows rents per acre rising rapidly from 1801 to 1821 and rising less rapidly in the 1820s and 1830s. This suggests that the rising burden of relief payments was not shifted forward from the occupier to the landlord. Be that as it may, the purpose of McCloskey's thesis that the incidence of poor relief fell wholly on landlords rather than farmers is to argue that the system of taxation used to collect the money for poor relief had no effect on the demand for agricultural labour; the analysis of the effects of the Old Poor Law therefore can focus exclusively on what happened to the supply curve of labour.

McCloskey then went on to draw a fundamental distinction between a wage subsidy and an income subsidy and accuses me, quite rightly I now think, of never making up my mind whether the Old Poor Law was in effect a sort of negative income tax guaranteed to provide a minimum income rather than a direct supplement to earned wages. A wage subsidy would have no effect on the amount of labour supplied at a given wage rate (would leave the supply curve of labour the same as before) but would produce a larger volume of employment simply by virtue of larger total wage payments made up of a wage paid by farmers and a wage paid by the parish. But an income subsidy paid to everyone, whether working or not, will reduce the supply of labour (shift the supply curve of labour to the left) by reducing the marginal gain from work and by giving workers an alternative source of income to working; it thus raises wages but only by lowering the volume of employment. On the face of it, the Speenhamland system under the Old Poor Law looks like a guaranteed minimum wage accompanied by children allowance payments. On the other hand, as the amounts paid out in subsidy were invariably reduced as a man's earnings rose and as unemployed paupers were also subsidised if they had large families, the system amounted in fact to the guarantee of a minimum income, not a minimum wage.

If some parishes practised a wage subsidy and others an income subsidy, the two subsidies in combination might exactly offset each other, yielding an earned wage and a supply of labour identical to those yielded by a free labour market unencumbered by poor-relief payments. In any case, the two types of subsidy pull in opposite directions in respect of the incentives to work and the supply of labour and thus, McCloskey concludes, the task of assessing the economic effects of the Old Poor Law is that of estimating their separate influences. He agrees that it is difficult to tell from the evidence whether there was an employment test for eligibility both for relief in money and for relief in kind. Nevertheless, he produces two indirect and somewhat inconclusive arguments to establish the proposition that the Old Poor Law was predominantly an income subsidy, not a wage subsidy, and therefore concludes that the authors of the *Poor Law Report of 1834* must have been wrong in claiming that poor relief reduced both wages and the efforts of workers: shifting a supply curve back along a negatively inclined demand curve no doubt causes the equilibrium volume of employment to fall but only by raising the equilibrium wage rate.

The distinction between a wage subsidy and an income subsidy is illuminating and I wish that I had seen it myself in 1961/2 as clearly as I now do. I am still not convinced, however, that the Old Poor Law was effectively a system of unconditional income subsidies, although it is perfectly true that this is what it had become by 1832 when the only widespread method of giving relief was to make grants to large families for extra children. The real difficulty with McCloskey's reasoning is that it is wholly static and concerned with shifting short-run demand and supply curves for agricultural labour, whereas my argument, and indeed that of the Poor Law Commissioners themselves, was a dynamic one in the sense of being concerned with the long-run effects of the Old Poor Law when the economy has become fully adjusted to the Allowance System. Thus, the Poor Law Commissioners were not inconsistent in arguing that the Allowance System depressed wages and that the same system lessened the supply of labour; their view was that it encouraged population growth and so led to lower wages within a decade or two. They may have been wrong about the magnitude of the demographic effect but at least they were not guilty of an analytical inconsistency. Besides, the Allowance System might have depressed both wages and employment even without a stimulus to the growth of population via a fall in both the demand and supply of effort as a result of reduced incentives to work, in turn feeding back on the level of output in the long run.

My own dynamic argument, for better or for worse, was wholly different from this sort of Marshallian long-run reasoning. I was deeply influenced by Arthur Lewis's famous 1954 article on "Economic Development with Unlimited Supplies of Labour" with its analysis of the economics of "dualism", and by a spate of writings in development economics in the decade of the 1950s on "disguised unemployment" in Third World countries where wages are close to or below biological subsistence levels, so that an increase of wages raises the standard level of effort of workers by overcoming dietary deficiencies (e.g. Rao, Anschel and Eicher, 1964). Traditional marginal productivity theory cannot handle this case: once a worker's efficiency varies with wages paid, the supply of labour depends on the demand for labour, and demand-and-supply analysis breaks down. The novel feature of my analysis of the Old Poor Law, insofar as it was novel, was to treat Britain in pre-Victorian days as a Third World country, displaying all the familiar features of an underdeveloped economy with institutional devices to convert open into disguised unemployment at wages that were below the poverty line. I struggled to provide evidence of surplus rural manpower and sub-standard wages but that is not to say that I succeeded fully in showing that I had the right theoretical framework for analysing the impact of the Old Poor Law. Nevertheless, for McCloskey to have ignored my theoretical standpoint and to have proceeded as if it were a question of analysing a perfectly competitive rural labour market in full-blown stationary equilibrium was less than helpful.

I agree that generous relief payments, whether geared to earned income or not, are perfectly capable of sapping incentives to work and eroding efficiency. But the actual effect of such a system depends both on its degree of generosity and its leniency of administration. The point about the Old Poor Law was that it was administered locally by 15,000 parishes that averaged less than a thousand people with half of them containing 368 people or less; such a system provides ample safeguards against the flagrant abuse of welfare payments based on personal knowledge of welfare recipients. We come back in the final analysis, therefore, to the vital question of how the Old Poor Law was actually administered. I believe that I threw some light on that question by the statistical analysis of the volume of answers to the Poor Law Commissioners' Rural and Town Queries. The fact remains however, that it can only be settled decisively by a detailed search through parish records. It is with regret that I note twenty-four years later that little has been accomplished in this area (but see Oxley, 1974; Neumann, 1982).

However, Boyer (1985, 1986) has recently taken a step in the right direction by drawing a random sample of 329 parishes from twenty-one southern counties, using the same returns of the Rural Queries of 1832 that I analysed at the county level of aggregation. In essence, his method consists of estimating three equations explaining cross-parish variations in per capita relief expenditures, agricultural labourers' annual wage income, and the rate of unemployment. His results strongly confirmed my conjecture that poor relief expenditures in parishes varied significantly with specialisation in grain production, which in turn produced substantial seasonal unemployment, thus suggesting that a major function of outdoor relief under the Old Poor Law was to provide unemployment insurance for seasonally unemployed agricultural workers. Moreover, Boyer found little support for the fundamental hypotheses of the Poor Law Commissioners that outdoor relief caused an increase in voluntary unemployment, thus creating the very poor which the Poor Laws were supposed to relieve, no doubt because rural parishes were in fact selective in their granting of relief to able-bodied labourers. Boyer also found support for the contention of Digby (1978) — which had never occurred to me — that one reason why parish relief expenditures were positively correlated with the extent of seasonality in labour demand was that labour-hiring farmers dominated parish governments and exploited their political position by shifting part of their wage bill to other local taxpayers. On the other hand, my own favourite thesis — outdoor relief was used to supplement "substandard" wage income — was not supported by Boyer's data. In short, my "revision-ist" interpretation of the effects of the Old Poor Law is sustained but only in broad outline: I reached the right answers but, evidently, not by the right route.

THE LANCASHIRE COTTON INDUSTRY

The paper on the Lancashire cotton industry grew out of my interest in the problem of technical progress and a conviction that the literature on technical change had long overemphasised labour-saving and underem-phasised capital-saving innovations. I summed up my general argument in a later theoretical paper (Blaug, 1963) but years before that I realised that the best way to demonstrate the importance of capital-saving innovations was to show that they predominated even in the early history of the cotton industry, the first industry to undergo the process of industrialisation that was later to spread throughout the whole of manufacturing. Somewhere around 1956 or 1957 I conceived a gigantic project to study and compare the growth of the cotton industry in the nineteenth century in Britain, France and Germany. The article on the Lancashire cotton industry was the only part of the project I completed: the data for France and Germany turned out to be so poor as to defeat me.

I wove my story of the significance of capital-saving innovations in the growth of the cotton industry around an estimate of the trend in the capital coefficient or capital-output ratio. This was one of the "great ratios" of the economics of the day and was usually applied at the aggregate level for the economy as a whole. There are serious objections to the concept of an aggregate capital-output ratio, chiefly on the grounds that it has no behavioural meaning, but the concept is much less objectionable when applied at the level of an industry as I indeed applied it. Moreover, I supplemented my estimates of the capital coefficient for five benchmark years between 1834 and 1886 by estimates of the labour coefficient and by a review of the evidence on wage rates and profits in cotton. In the light of recent debates about the difficulties and indeed impossibilities of measuring capital in any meaningful way, it is amusing to note that estimating the output of the Lancashire cotton industry in the nineteenth century gave me much more trouble than estimating the value of the capital stock.

By the time I wrote this article some time in 1960, the New Economic History (known also as cliometrics) had just started its upward climb in the United States, reaching a crescendo in the early 1960s, although it was not until the late 1960s that it came to be applied to British economic history (see McCloskey, 1971). I had never heard of the New Economic History when I wrote this article and the two later ones on the Old Poor Law: like Monsieur Jourdain in Molière's *Le Bourgeois Gentilhomme* who never realised that he spoke prose, it was years later that I realised I had been unwittingly practising the New Economic History all along!

This paper on the cotton industry has fared better in some ways than my two papers on the Poor Laws, largely escaping criticism. It has been cited frequently (e.g. Deane and Cole, 1967; Crouzet, 1972; Chapman, 1972) and complemented by capital estimates for the earlier period 1770-1834 based on fire insurance valuations (Chapman, 1971). On the other hand, the idea of tracing precisely how the factor-saving pattern of technical progress altered in the course of industrial change in the eighteenth and nineteenth centuries does not seem to have been taken up in the study of other British industries.

RICARDIAN ECONOMICS

The chapter on the empirical content of Ricardian economics is a distillation of my doctoral dissertation, later published as a book with the title *Ricardian Economics: An Historical Study* (Yale University Press, 1958), and it was my first published article. It attracted little or no attention until it was attacked in a sophisticated essay by Neil de Marchi (1970). De Marchi's paper was a strange example of a critique which was designed to refute its object, while actually confirming it with additional detail — or so it seemed to be at any rate. I had argued that Ricardo's followers failed to test the accuracy of Ricardo's predictions about the declining rate of profit, the rising rental share of national income, and the constancy of even fall of real wages, even though they were in possession of statistical data that would have been perfectly adequate to undertake that task; this led some of them, and particularly John Stuart Mill, to devise a series of *ad hoc* excuses for the Ricardian system.

De Marchi argued that Ricardo committed himself under pressure to a definite length of time required to reach a long-run equilibrium — twenty-five years — and he shows that Mill gradually extended this period in successive editions of his *Principles of Political Economy* to forty and then fifty years in order to account for the failure of Ricardo's predictions to materialise. Both Ricardo and Mill were convinced of a close correspondence between their analysis and reality, partly because they thought that their axioms were grounded in fact and partly because they thought that they had actually identified the crucial economic forces. Although they did not consciously seek predictive accuracy in their statements about long-run tendencies, it is clear that both of them would have been and were surprised by the failure of these tendencies to be borne out by experience. I attribute something like duplicity to Mill on behalf of Ricardo and it is here that de Marchi parts company with me: "it was Ricardo's and Mill's greater concern with 'understanding' (explanation *ex post*) than with predictive accuracy that made them unwilling to abandon their propositions in the face of contrary facts. What has been said above goes part of the way towards showing that this preference does not represent contrived duplicity; it was rather a candid acknowledgement of the difficulty of knowing all causes in advance, and of conducting conclusive historical tests" (de Marchi, 1970). In the final analysis then only a hair's breadth separates my interpretation from that of de Marchi (see also Blaug, 1980b, pp. 73-7).

De Marchi and I agreed more often than we disagreed. Since then, Samuel Hollander has "improved" on de Marchi's critique by going so far as to argue that Ricardo never committed himself to any clear-cut prediction about any economic variable, so that the very title of my piece, "The Empirical Content of Ricardian Economics", implies a category-mistake. Hollander's thesis is argued, along with many other similarly surprising theses about the Ricardian system in a massive book, *The Economics of David Ricardo* (1979), which amounts to nothing more or less than a direct frontal assault on the entire secondary literature about Ricardo, purporting to show that everyone before Hollander got it wrong.

The final pages of the next chapter, "Ricardo and the Problem of Public Policy", attempt to explain how Hollander arrived at his bizarre conclusions. The essential message of this chapter, however, is to throw cold water on Ricardo as a policy adviser. His theories were directly aimed at the solution of the outstanding policy problem of his time, namely, the protection of agriculture, and his writings bristle with policy recommendations: to repeal the Corn Laws, to abolish the Poor Laws, to raise a levy on capital wealth, to pay off the public debt, to nationalise the note issue function of the Bank of England, and many others. All these proposals, he realised, threatened contemporary "interests" and raised profound administrative problems. Yet he never spelled out a practical programme for implementing these unpopular policies. In short, he exemplified all the weaknesses that have characterised the writings of economists on problems of economic policy right up to the present day.

THE LABOUR THEORY OF VALUE IN ADAM SMITH AND RICARDO

The chapter on "Welfare Indices in *The Wealth of Nations*" takes up a little puzzle that has caused more confusion about classical economics than any other: it is Ricardo's rejection of Adam Smith's "measure of value" as the amount of labour "commanded" in exchange, replacing it with the amount of labour "embodied" in commodities, a rejection that was endorsed by Marx and that led to the common view that Smith had confused the "measure" with the "cause" of value. Both Ricardo and Marx, however, flagrantly misunderstood Smith's intention, which was to construct an index of improvements in economic welfare. What Ricardo and Marx did was to change the question about value rather than the answer: they wanted to know the cause of variations in exchange value and that was a question which simply did not rouse Smith's interest.

This was a paper that emerged directly out of teaching the history of economic thought at Yale University: while attempting to explain Ricardo's criticism of Adam Smith to a class of students I suddenly realised that it made no sense and retired in confusion. I spent twenty-four hours rereading the relevant chapters in *The Wealth of Nations* and wrote the paper as it now stands in a few hours. Admittedly the argument is compressed and the paper, brief as it is, does not make easy reading, being a kind of verbal mathematics in prose. Nevertheless, twenty-five years later, I still believe every word of it. It was with great delight that I later read Gordon (1959), who confirmed my interpretation of Smith to the letter.

POLICY ISSUES IN CLASSICAL ECONOMICS

My doctoral dissertation on Ricardian economics took up a number of policy questions that troubled the classical economists. Some of these questions, however, raised issues that had little to do with the rise and fall of Ricardian economics and so were left out of the dissertation. One was the famous question of regulating the hours of work in factories which became a central problem of economic policy in the 1830s and 1840s. My paper on "The Classical Economists and the Factory Acts" was written in reaction to the common view of economic historians that the classical economists were unalterably opposed to the factory regulation and the less common but nevertheless prevalent view of historians of economic thought that the classical economists favoured the regulation of child labour, only disapproving of legislation for adult men and women. My reappraisal of the debate was designed to show that their views were more complex and divided than is suggested by either of the two extreme interpretations and to demonstrate that the classical economists largely ignored considerations of administrative feasibility for their concrete recommendations, thus elaborating the theme set out in the chapter "Ricardo and the Problem of Public Policy".

To this day I remain troubled by the question touched upon in its closing pages: if the steady reduction in factory hours in the nineteenth century turned out eventually to raise output per man-hour and even output per man-day, thus justifying itself as economically efficient, why is it that it required legislation to achieve this result? I suggest in the paper that it is because employers are myopic in the sense of maximising short-run profits; in addition, the pressures of competition prevent each employer from conducting experiments with shorter hours to see whether it might raise output per man. But I am not sure even now that this is the right answer to the question of whether the regulation of hours constitutes a genuine example of "market failure". Johnson (1969) and West (1983) provide further evidence on this issue without, however, coming to grips with the basic question.

In the 1960s and early 1970s, I abandoned the history of economic thought and for over a decade I worked largely in the economics of education, that is the application of economics to current questions about education and training. I always hoped that some day I would be able to bring these two interests of mine together; when invited in 1974 to contribute a paper to a collection of essays on Adam Smith, I saw my chance and the result was the paper on "The Economics of Education in Classical Political Economy". In some ways, it makes much the same point as my essay on the Factory Acts: the classical economists invariably adjusted their ideas on education (as they did their ideas on the regulation of hours) in the wake of legislative changes; instead of having an influence on policy, policy had an influence on them. But that is only one theme of the paper; another is to deny the widely held view that the classical economists originated the theory of human capital and still another is to deny the still more widely held view that they approved of the now standard belief in the principle of free but compulsory schooling. This is a long chapter, indeed the longest in the book, but the complexity of the subject warrants it and, besides, much space is taken up with a review of the bewildering interpretations of previous commentators.

MARXIAN ECONOMICS

The next two chapters, on Marx, take up aspects of Marxian economics, a subject that has always fascinated me. I have written about Marx at greater length elsewhere (Blaug, 1980b, 1985, Ch. 7) but my early essay on "Technical Change and Marxian Economics", arguing that Marx's vision of capitalism was fatally marred by the unwarranted conviction that technical progress is inherently biased in the labour-saving direction, has coloured all my subsequent thinking about the Marxian system. Needless to say, the discussion among Marxist economists of this range of questions has moved on since 1960 when my essay was written; the interested reader should consult Van Parijs (1980), which provides a useful survey of the debate over the last forty years.

"Another Look at the Labour Reduction Problem in Marx" is yet another synthesis of my interests in the history of economic thought and the economics of education. The "labour reduction problem" is an old question in Marxian economics, being the problem of whether we can in fact invoke a quantitative measure of labour-time to account for the value of commodities without resorting to differences in wages to reduce different types of labour to a single one. I was struck by the fact that the manner in which this problem was usually handled by Marxist economists bore a striking resemblance to the views of advocates of human capital theory, according to which differences in wages can largely be explained by differences in the length of schooling and on-the-job training. But "largely" is still not the same thing as "entirely" and to the extent that earnings differentials are at least in some degree due to differences in inherited or acquired talents (it matters not which), the Marxian labour-reduction problem cannot be solved. Some commentators regard this unsolved problem as the Achilles Heel of Marxian economics but I doubt that it is, or rather, it is itself a symptom of a much more serious flaw in the Marxian system, which is its inconsistent view of how labour markets work under capitalism: in Marx, occupational mobility is said to establish a uniform rate of wages for every type of labour, a proposition that is false and which Marx, having read Adam Smith, knew to be false.

THE MARGINAL REVOLUTION AND AFTER

The chapter on the marginal revolution considers the historical puzzle of the overthrow of classical economics in the 1870s and the emergence of a new kind of economics usually labelled misleadingly as "neoclassical" economics (the right term is clearly "postclassical" economics). This was a peculiar "revolution" because it took so long to make itself felt and it is not clear even today why it took place in the 1870s when it might as well have happened in the 1850s or even 1840s.

There follows a chapter on the history of the concept of entrepreneurship, or rather the strange disappearance of the entrepreneur, that central figure in the operation of a capitalist system, from the corpus of received economic doctrine. It raises a central question about the entire history of orthodox economics in the last hundred years, namely, that all the substantive findings of modern economics rest on the use of static equilibrium analysis and yet static equilibrium analysis seems to preclude fruitful discussion of such vital problems as the process of competition, the process of capital formation and the role of entrepreneurship. Economics began as *An Inquiry into the Causes of the Wealth of Nations* and yet 200 years later we have virtually abandoned that inquiry as unproductive and have taught ourselves to be content with smaller questions. Worse than that, static equilibrium analysis has furnished us with standards of rigour that cannot be met by the analysis of the dynamic problems of entrepreneurship and the competitive process, so that discussion of these questions is met with scorn almost as soon as it is started.

I do not claim to see my way out of this dilemma. But it poses a nice problem that I want to go on thinking about — so long as I can still think.

METHODOLOGY

The essay on "Kuhn versus Lakatos" has frequently been reprinted, not because it was so good — some of it is rather clumsy — but because it was the first exposition for economists of some recent developments in the philosophy of science. I extended and improved my presentation subsequently (1980b, Chs. 1, 2) but I never returned to the Lakatosian explanation of the Keynesian revolution, which I sketched in this paper. In a recent thought-provoking essay, Hands (1985) has thrown doubt on the proposition that the Keynesian revolution can be explained by Lakatos' methodology of scientific research programmes. According to Lakatos, a scientific research programme wins professional approval when it is theoretically "progressive" in the sense of predicting "novel facts" that were either unknown or at least were not themselves employed in the construction of the programme. The Keynesian revolution is one of the greatest success stories in the history of economic thought. Yet what were the novel facts predicted by Keynesian economics? Not mass unemployment, since *The General Theory* was written precisely to explain unemployment. Not the consumption function or the inverse relationship between the demand for money and the role of interest, since these concepts were used explicitly to construct the Keynesian system. Thus, Hands concludes the Keynesian programme was not "progressive" in the strict sense of Lakatos and hence the overwhelming professional acceptance of Keynesian economics in the 1930s was "irrational".

This is a striking argument that must make us think again. However, Hands fails to mention one of the central features of Keynesian economics that *may* go a long way to explain its amazingly rapid acceptance by the economics profession. It is that the Keynesian system is formulated in terms of a model whose key variables and relationships are specified in such a way as to be capable of quantitative measurement. The stimulus which *The General Theory* gave to national income accounting, incorporating Keynes' *ex post* identity of saving and investment, and to the construction of testable models of economic behaviour, is an integral feature of the Keynesian success story. I do not claim that this is a decisive answer to Hands' argument but it does suggest that he may have omitted vital elements in the story. Nevertheless, his deeper point, that professional success and failure in a subject like economics simply cannot be fitted into Lakatos' framework, cannot simply be shrugged off. As they say in America: the jury is still out on that question.

The last chapter in this collection is a lecture delivered just before the publication of my book on *The Methodology of Economics*. It attempted to present the material of the book in what I hoped would be a palatable and accessible form to undergraduates in economics, innocent of the philosophy of science. Judging by the confusing discussion that followed the lecture, it was only partly successful in accomplishing that aim.

REFERENCES

Baugh, D.A. (1975), "The Cost of Poor Relief in South-East England, 1790-1834", *Economic History Review*, 2nd Series, 28(1), February.

Blaug, M. (1963), "A Survey of the Theory of Process Innovations", *Economica*, N.S. 30 (February) repr. in *The Economics of Technological Change*, ed. N. Rosenberg (London, 1971).

—— (1980a), *A Methodological Appraisal of Marxian Economics* (Amsterdam)

—— (1980b), *The Methodology of Economics* (Cambridge)

—— (1985), *Economic Theory in Retrospect*, 4th edn. (Cambridge)

Boyer, G.R. (1985), "Economic Model of the English Poor Law circa 1780-1834" *Explorations in Economic History*, 22(1), Spring.

—— (1986) "The Old Poor Law and the Agricultural Labor Market in Southern England: An Empirical Analysis", *Journal of Economic History*, forthcoming.

Chapman, S.D. (1971), "Fixed Capital Formation in the British Cotton Manufacturing Industry", in *Aspects of Capital Investment in Great Britain, 1750-1850* eds. J.P.P. Higgins and S. Pollard (London).

—— (1972), *The Cotton Industry in the Industrial Revolution, Studies in Economic History,* ed. M.W. Flinn (London).

Checkland, S.G. and E.O.A. (1974), "Introduction" to *The Poor Law Report of 1834* (London).

Cowherd, R.G. (1978), *Political Economists and the English Poor Law* (Athens Ohio).

Crouzet, F. (ed.) (1972), *Capital Formation in the Industrial Revolution* (London).

Deane, P. and Cole, W.A. (1967), *British Economic Growth, 1688-1959*, 2nd edn. (Cambridge).

Digby, A. (1978), *Pauper Palaces* (London).

Gordon, D. F. (1959), "What Was the Labour Theory of Value" *American Economic Review*, 69, No. 2 (May).

Hands, D.W. (1985), "Second Thoughts on Lakatos", *History of Political Economy*, 17, No. 1 (Spring).

Huzel, J.P. (1969), "Malthus, The Poor Law, and Population in Early Nineteenth Century England", *Economic History Review*, 22, No. 3 (December).
    (1980), "The Demographic Impact of the Old Poor Law: More Reflections on Malthus", *Economic History Review*, 33, No. 3 (August).

Johnson, O.E. (1969), "The 'Last Hour' of Senior and Marx," *History of Political Economy*, 1, No. 2 (Fall).

Marchi, N. de (1970), "The Empirical Content and Longevity of Ricardian Economics", *Economica*, N.S. 37 (August).

Marshall, J.D. (1968). *The Old Poor Law 1795-1834*, *Studies in Economic History*, ed. M.W. Flinn (London).

McCloskey, D.N. (1971), *Essays on a Mature Economy: Britain After 1840* (Princeton, N.J.)

—— (1973), "New Perspectives on the Old Poor Law", *Explorations in Economic History*, 10, No. 4 (Summer).

Neumann, M. (1982), *The Speenhamland County. Poverty and the Poor Laws in Berkshire 1782-1834* (New York).

Oxley, G.W. (1974), *Poor Relief in England and Wales, 1601-1834* (Newton Abbott).

Poynter, J.R. (1969), *Society and Pauperism: English Ideas on Poor Relief, 1795-1834* (Carlton, Victoria).

Rao, C. H. C., Anschel, K. R. and Eicher, C. K. (1964), "Disguised Unemployment in Agriculture: A Survey", in *Agriculture in Economic Development (New York).*

Taylor, J. S. (1969), "The Methodology of the Old Poor Law", *Journal of Economic History*, 29, No. 2 (June).

Thompson, R.D. (1907), "An Inquiry into the Rent of Agricultural Land in England and Wales During the Nineteenth Century," *Journal of the Royal Statistical Society*, 70 (December).

Van Parijs, P. (1980), "The Falling-Rate-of-Profit Theory of Crisis: A Rational Reconstruction By Way of Obituary", *Review of Radical Political Economics*, 12, No. 1 (Spring).

Wellington, D.C. (1984), "The English Poor Law: A Negative Income Tax", *Atlantic Economic Journal*, 12 (4), December.

West, E.G. (1983), "Marx's Hypothesis on the Length of the Working Day", *Journal of Political Economy*, 91, No. 2 April.

Part I
Economic History

1 The Myth of the Old Poor Law and the Making of the New

No matter which authority we consult on the English Poor Laws in the nineteenth century the same conclusions emerge: the Old Poor Law demoralised the working class, promoted population growth, lowered wages, reduced rents, destroyed yeomanry, and compounded the burden on ratepayers; the more the Old Poor Law relieved poverty, the more it encouraged the poverty which it relieved; the problem of devising an efficient public relief system was finally solved with the passage of the "harsh but salutary" Poor Law Amendment Act of 1834. So unanimous are both the indictment and the verdict of historians on this question that we may forgo the pleasure of citing "chapter and verse".

The bare facts are familiar enough. Until late in the eighteenth century, public relief was largely confined to those too young, too old, or too sick to work. But in 1782 Gilbert's Act sanctioned the principle of relieving the so-called "able-bodied" without requiring them to enter the workhouse. Then, in 1795, the magistrates of Speenhamland in the county of Berkshire, responding to the exceptional rise in the price of wheat, decided to fix a "minimum standard" by supplementing earned incomes in proportion to the price of wheaten bread and the size of workers' families. The idea was soon imitated in adjoining counties, and in the following year it was ratified by Parliament. The practice of making allowances-in-aid-of-wages was almost always associated with make-work schemes which rotated the unemployed among local farmers in accordance with the rated value of their property. By divorcing earnings from the productivity of labour, the Allowance System in conjunction with the Roundsman System sapped the initiative of agricultural workers and thus contributed to the unprecedented rise in poor-relief expenditures in the years before and after Waterloo. So ran the argument of the reformers of 1834 and so runs the consensus of modern opinion.

History repeats itself, says an ancient proverb — and historians repeat each other. The standard analysis of the effects of the Old Poor Law is derived without qualification, from the *Poor Law Commissioners' Report of 1834*, that "brilliant, influential, and wildly unhistorical document", as Tawney once described it. But it was a gross exaggeration that led the

3

reformers of 1834 to characterise the Old Poor Law as "a bounty on indolence and vice" and "a universal system of pauperism". Only an incomplete theoretical analysis of the working of the Speenhamland policy and a superficial examination of the facts could have produced so one-sided an interpretation. The continued endorsement of the *Report of 1834* has seriously distorted the history of the Industrial Revolution in Britain. The Old Poor Law tried to maintain the real income of workers by tying wages to the cost of living; it provided unemployment compensation together with a scheme to promote private employment; and it coupled both of these to a family endowment plan. It is not often realised that the kind of arguments which are used to condemn the Old Poor Law *per se* would equally condemn most modern welfare legislation. Perhaps this is the intention, but even "left-wing" historians, such as the Webbs and the Hammonds, have attacked the Old Poor Law on the one hand, and, on the other, have argued that minimum-wage legislation accompanied by children-allowance payments would have been a preferable alternative to Speenhamland. But, in fact, their proposal amounts to nearly the same thing as the Old Poor Law.

The years between 1813 and the accession of Victoria have been aptly described as "the blackest period of English farming". When we put together everything we know about the causes of "agricultural distress" in those years, we will have grounds more relative than maladministration of the Poor Laws to account for the growth of relief expenditures. This is not merely an academic question. In the Victorian era, the whole of what we would nowadays call "social services" were reflected in Poor-Law expenditures. And the *Report of 1834*, with its strictures on "the old system" was revered for three generations as a canonical book, teaching that all forms of dole, charity, and relief to the unemployed are suspect, because they only induce him to breed in idleness; that least relief is best relief; and that voluntary charity is always preferable to public aid because it is somehow capable of discriminating the "deserving" poor from the "undeserving". Without the continued influence of "the principles of 1834", Mrs Jellyby is unthinkable.

I

Before looking at the empirical evidence, let us consider what results might be expected from a system of subsidising wages, considered by itself. Most historians assume without question that the Allowance System must have depressed agricultural earnings: farmers could pay less than competitive rates because the parish officers were forced to make up the deficit. But what if the guaranteed subsidy made workers less willing to supply effort?

It is elementary economics that the short-run effect of a subsidy to workers is to lessen the supply — the number of days per week offered by men, women, and children; if the supply curve of labour is positively sloped the result is that wages will *rise*. Of course, if the subsidy is tied to the size of the family, it may promote earlier marriages and more children, so that, within a decade or so, it does depress wages. To a generation drunk on Malthusian wine, the population argument seemed irrefutable. But nowadays we are inclined to treat this type of reasoning with scepticism, particularly if the subsidy is modest in amount, increases less than proportionately with each additional child, and is continuously scaled down year after year; as we shall see, all three things were true under the Old Poor Law.[1]

It is possible to argue, however, that the Allowance System depressed wages even if it did not stimulate the growth of population. A subsidy that varies inversely with earned wages, and that is what the Allowance System amounted to, gives workers no incentive to supply genuine effort. And since employers are not the only taxpayers, the system likewise deprives those who hire labour of the incentive to exact a full day's work. In consequence, productivity declines, output shrinks, and wages fall. This kind of reasoning, which for present purposes we might label Benthamite rather than Malthusian, was very common in the days before 1834. It has a distinctly modern ring: to divorce wages from their roots in the efficiency of labour must lead to a misallocation of resources.

Applied to an underdeveloped country, however, this argument must be severely qualified. The early stages of economic development are invariably characterised by "dualism": the high-wage industrial sector is largely independent of the low-wage agricultural sector. In contrast to manufacture, labour in agriculture is typically hired on a day-to-day basis and the demand for farm-workers varies sharply from season to season. Full employment may be achieved during planting and harvesting, but during slack seasons, which comprise from one-third to one-half of the calendar year, as much as half the labour force may be idle. The gradual destruction of handicraft industry due to the invasion of machine-made goods sometimes creates a pool of chronically unemployed labour even during peak seasons. The automatic market forces which would eliminate such unemployment by driving down wage rates fail to operate if wages are below the biological minimum, implying that the food intake of workers is not sufficient to permit them to supply their maximum effort per unit of time. The amount of work put forth now depends on the wages paid, rather than the other way around: lower wages would lower the consumption and hence the productivity of workers. Under these circumstances, it will pay landlords and farmers to maintain wages above competitive market-clearing levels and to devise a special scheme to eliminate open unemployment. The standard method is to disguise the manpower surplus by sharing the work out among all job-seekers with each man putting forth less effort than he is capable of supplying. Since labour costs per unit of output are now lower than they would be if the unemployed were permitted to underbid going wage rates, such institutional arrangements lead to a greater total product than would otherwise be available.[2]

With 40 per cent of the gainfully occupied population in agriculture, England in 1815 must be counted among the underdeveloped countries, displaying all the familiar features of a "dual" economy. Under the circumstances, a system of supplementing the earnings of agricultural workers so as to guarantee a "living wage" must have pulled in opposite directions. On the one hand, it reduced mortalities, particularly infant mortalities, and so depressed wages by promoting population growth. It may also have slowed down emigration to the industrial sector with similar effects. On the other hand, insofar as it repaired nutritional deficiencies, it tended to raise wages by raising the effort-level of each worker. The family-endowment features of the Speenhamland policy pulled in one direction while the use of the bread scale to determine the amount of the wage subsidy pulled in the other.

The problem of deciding which of the two forces predominated is complicated by the fact that wheat was both the principal wage-good and, in some sections of the country, the principal product of farmers demanding labour. In years of drought, when the demand for agricultural labour fell off, tending to lower wages, the price of bread soared upwards and the subsidy increased. Conversely, in years of bumper crops, wages tended to rise and the subsidy would fall as the price of bread declined. One of the significant side effects of the Allowance System, as Malthus pointed out, was to render the demand for wheat insensitive to wheat prices by stabilising the real income of agricultural workers who, if we are to believe Eden's budget studies, spent almost half of their income in wheaten bread. Thus, when wheat prices rose after a bad harvest, the total quantity of wheat sold declined less than proportionately and farmers enjoyed higher incomes than they had expected. On the other hand, a good harvest would lead to a decline both in the price of wheat and in the total receipts of farmers. So universal was this inverse association of the yield of the harvest and agricultural prosperity in this period that we may take it as a fact that the demand for wheat was then highly inelastic.

Since the poor rates were levied on the occupiers, not on the owners, of land and real estate, farmers themselves paid a major share of the rates used to finance wage subsidies. Owing to the inelastic demand for wheat, it was paradoxically true that they gained on the swings what they lost on the roundabouts. Spending on relief rose when the harvest was poor, but at such times the income of farmers was at a maximum. Conversely, when they were squeezed by falling prices and rising wages in consequence of a good harvest, the pressure on the rates was at a minimum. In other words, poor-relief spending flucturated with the income of farmers. No wonder we hear more complaints about "the onerous burdens of the poor rates" in years when inclement weather produced "agricultural prosperity"!

We must, however, take into account the possibility of a trend created by an excess of bad years over good. By putting a floor under the demand for wheat, the Old Poor Law kept up the price of bread in years of drought. In this way, a persistently unfavourable trend in rainfall or temperature could account for rising relief expenditures, irrespective of the effects of relief spending on population growth and work incentives.

To round out the analysis, we recall that allowances-in-aid-of-wages were almost always associated with the Roundsman System, modified by the use of the Labour Rate. The Poor Law authorities calculated the total wage bill of the parish and then levied the poor rate to cover this amount. Each ratepayer agreed to pay the allotted sum either in wages or in rates. By accepting his quota of the unemployed in proportion to the assessed value of his property, a farmer could be relieved of paying part of his rates. It was thought that this would encourage employment because farmers would prefer to employ more workers than they really needed rather than to pay the parish the deficiency in their allotted rates. In view of the existence of visible as well as invisible unemployment in rural districts at that time, the idea of the Labour Rate made good sense: as long as labour is in surplus, wasteful employment may well be cheaper than maintaining workers on the dole. But since employers of labour were not the only ratepayers, the system tended to discriminate against family farms and smallholders who employed little labour. We cannot say how much importance attaches to such considerations unless we know just how the rates were determined, how many workers in a parish were typically unemployed, and how far market wages stood below an acceptable minimum standard. It is time to turn to the evidence.

II

The first question is: How prevalent was the system of subsidising wages out of the rates? To answer this question at all we must perforce over-simplify. Poor Law administration before 1834 differed widely in aims and methods from place to place and from time to time. Parliamentary legislation failed to produce a national Poor Law, and throughout this period there was only a casual connection between the statute books and the administrative practices of parish officers. The 15,000 parishes in England and Wales varied in area from thirty acres to thirty square miles, in population from a few dozen to tens of thousands, and in taxable capacity from a barren common to the built-up docks of the city of London. With a system so heterogeneous, any generalisation is bound to be subject to serious qualification.

Moreover, we know next to nothing about the actual number of people relieved or about the proportions relieved inside and outside workhouses before 1834. Throughout this period, only two attempts were made to take a census of the poor. The first, in 1802, was the more thorough, showing about one million people on relief, including 300,000 children under the age of fifteen.[3] This implies that as much as 11 per cent of the population of England and Wales was then on relief, but we know that the census, unfortunately, counted more than once any "pauper" who applied for relief at two or three separate occasions in the year, a common practice at the time. Of the total number receiving aid only 8 per cent were residents of workhouses. This is not surprising, considering that there were almost 4,000 workhouses in the whole of the country, most of which were no larger than country cottages. Even where there was a workhouse in the parish, magistrates were frequently reluctant to "offer the House" which was invariably an insanitary and disorderly institution, herding together the young, the old, the sick, and the insane. The heavy reliance on outdoor relief, therefore, was as much due to a humane concern over the plight of the poor as to anything else. Even those reported to be "disabled by permanent illness" were not always forced into the workhouse, as is evidenced by the fact that their number in 1802 exceeded the number of workhouse residents. With more than 90 per cent of the pauper host receiving outdoor relief, about 55 per cent were said to be on "permanent" relief, while 35 per cent were denoted as being relieved "occasionally". This does not tell us, however, how many were entirely dependent upon parish funds and how many had their wages supplemented "permanently" or "occasionally" by the Poor Law authorities. The next census, for 1812-14, was equally vague and, furthermore, it failed to count either children under fifteen on outdoor relief or non-residents of the parish.[4]

The prevailing belief at the time was that the Allowance System was confined to the agricultural counties of the south. The *Report of 1834* made no effort to verify this assumption. The Commissioners circulated questions in the rural districts, but not all parishes were visited, and it is impossible to tell whether the replies constitute anything like a representative sample. The Commissioners never attempted to summarise their findings, and in the *Report* itself they offered a few graphic examples of the Allowance System drawn from parishes in both the south and the north, thus conveying the impression that what they admittedly called "the abuses of the south" were to be found throughout the country. Even the Webbs, in their definitive book on *The Old Poor Law*, say no more than that outdoor

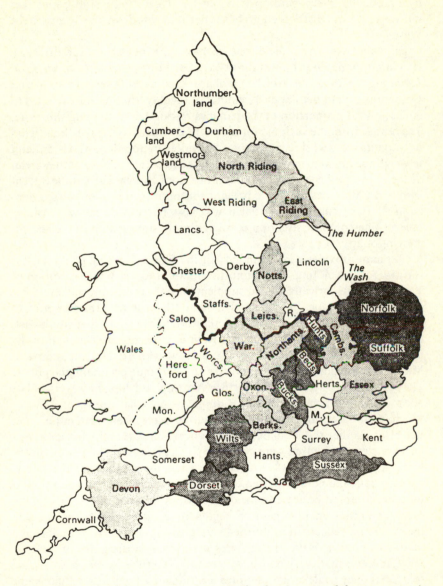

In the shaded counties, most parishes subsidised wages out of the poor rates in 1825. The system was particularly prevalent in the heavily shaded counties. The heavy line dissecting England separates the high-wage counties of the north from the low-wage counties of the south.

relief to the unemployed was "adopted, in principle, at one time or another by practically every rural parish outside Northumberland", and was universal in rural districts south of the line that runs from the Severn to the Wash.[5]

The only worthwhile evidence we have is a neglected questionnaire circulated to the Poor Law authorities in 1824 by the *Select Committee on Labourers' Wages*, to which Clapham first drew attention in 1926.[6] Unfortunately, in the slapdash manner of the day, the committee failed to indicate what proportion of the parishes responded to the questionnaire. The replies from the various counties were grouped in terms of "hundreds" or wapentakes, and since these differed widely in population, it is difficult to weigh the answers in order to arrive at an accurate picture of the spread of the Allowance System. The committee itself concluded that the Speenhamland policy was pervasive in eight southern counties, but an examination of the returns shows that it was also fairly widespread in twelve others. The complex situation is conveniently summed up in the accompanying map.

Clapham provides a fair summary of the findings, which contain a few surprises worth noting. All the northern counties, with the exception of Yorkshire, categorically denied supplementing wages from the rates. But so did all the counties in Wales and in the south-west, with the exception of some districts in Devon. Furthermore, even in the south and south-east, most of the parishes in Hampshire, Kent and Surrey, at least half of the parishes in Essex, Suffolk and Sussex, and the whole of Hertfordshire and Middlesex (including London) denied practising the Speenhamland policy. The spread of the system as far north as Nottinghamshire, however, and its adoption in the East and North Riding, is somewhat unexpected.

The committee not only inquired whether wages were paid out of rates but also whether the Roundsman System was in use and whether allowances for extra children were customary. The Roundsman System in the form of a Labour Rate was found everywhere associated with the Allowance System and never resorted to without it. It appears, however, that it was not common practice to make an extra allowance for the first child, even in counties where wages were regularly subsidised out of the rates. At the same time, all parishes admitted giving allowances to large families as a matter of course. From the answers pertaining to the grant of outdoor relief, it seems that every parish followed its own rules; some parishes gave relief in money while others confined assistance to payments in kind; some distinguished between insufficient income due to unemployment and low standard wage rates, but most did not; in some districts, no inquiry into earnings was made before granting outdoor relief; in others, only wages received during the last few weeks were taken into account. But we must remember that two-thirds of the Poor Law authorities in the country were concerned with only a few hundred families and, therefore, might be expected to be familiar with the personal circumstances of relief recipients.

What use can be made of this evidence? It is conceivable that the returns of the *Select Committee on Labourers' Wages* correctly depict the situation in 1824, but that great changes had been made since 1795. Perhaps the Allowance System was practised everywhere in 1800 or in 1815. The policy of subsidising wages met with little criticism so long as the war lasted. It was first condemned by both Commons and Lords in respective committee reports on the Poor Laws in 1817 and 1818, and the 1824 committee was designed to add ammunition to the charge. We may suppose, therefore, that fewer parishes practised outdoor relief to the able-bodied in 1824 than in previous years, and that those who persisted in the policy in 1824 must surely have made use of it before it came under attack. In other words, the eighteen counties which we have found to be Speenhamland counties in 1824 may be described as the hard core of the problem. Whatever the harmful effects of the Old Poor Law, they should be revealed by a comparison of conditions in this group of counties with all others.

III

Before proceeding to the comparison, we must ask how generously wages were subsidised. Do we have any reason to believe that wages in agriculture were below subsistence standards before the Allowance System was introduced? The first piece of evidence we have is that of the bread scale devised by the Berkshire magistrates. The Berkshire scale began with the gallon loaf at a shilling and then increased with each rise of a penny up to 2*s.*: with the loaf selling at a shilling, a single man was guaranteed a minimum weekly income of 3*s.* with an additional 1*s.* 6*d.* for each dependent; with the loaf at 2*s.*, the minimum weekly income of a single man rose to 5*s.* and the allowance for dependents to 2*s.* 6*d.* A gallon loaf of bread is 20 oz. of bread per day which was estimated, reasonably enough, to constitute a minimum ration for a man at work. The idea was that one-third of income was to be spent on bread, leaving a margin for rent, heat, clothing, and other foodstuffs. Thus, in cheap years, a family with three children was said to require an income of 9*s.* a week, spending 3*s.* on bread — a gallon loaf for the man and two loaves for his four dependents — and 6*s.* on other things. In dear years, with the gallon loaf at 2*s.* the bread allowance would double to 6*s.*, leaving a margin of 9*s.* on the notion that the prices of things in general rise by 50 per cent when the price of bread doubles.

In 1795, a single man working full time in the Midlands or the southern counties would have earned about 8*s* 6*d.* a week. Supplements in kind, which were common in rural districts, would bring this up to about 10*s*. a week. If he was unemployed, the scale allowed him 5*s*. in a dear year like 1795. If he married and had a child, his wife and he together might earn 15*s*. a week; out of work, the scale allowed him 10*s*. a week. This was hardly a temptation to marry and breed recklessly! Indeed, so modest was the Speenhamland scale that the Webbs calculated that it allowed a family with two children "about one-half of what a parsimonious Board of Guardians would today [1926] regard as bare subsistence".[7] Nevertheless, existing wage levels in agriculture frequently fell below the Speenhamland minimum. If a married man had a few children young enough to keep his wife at home, he could not possibly earn enough to support his family at the famine prices that prevailed during the Napoleonic wars. And this is precisely why the idea of a minimum-wage law as an alternative to the bread scale was rejected in 1795; if it took account of variations in the size of families, it implied a wage far in excess of prevailing rates.[8]

When the Allowance System came to be criticised in the closing years of the war, one reaction was simply to reduce the bread scale or to abandon it in favour of some loose index of food prices in general. An examination of the local scales in use in various parishes shows that they were indeed pared down everywhere, so that by 1825 they had dropped on the average by about one-third from their original level.[9] But money wages in agriculture were no higher on the average in 1825 than in 1795, and even in 1835 they still stood below the Speenhamland minimum. The Commissioners of 1834 found out to their surprise that the cost of maintaining workhouse inmates at a minimum diet sometimes exceeded the wages of agricultural workers in surrounding districts.[10]

It is clear then that the Allowance System subsidised what in fact were substandard wages. At the same time, the scale at which outdoor relief was given does not suggest that it could have devitalised the working class by offering an attractive alternative to gainful employment. Nevertheless, the bread scale tied the relief bill to the price of wheat, and its effect on the volume of relief spending shows up quite clearly: the peaks and troughs in the two coincide almost perfectly (for sources see Appendices A and B).[11]

It is apparent from the variations in the gazette price of wheat that 1811-12, 1816-17, 1823-5, and 1828-31 were years of poor harvests when both relief spending and the price of wheat rose. As we might expect the cry of "agricultural distress" was loudest in the bumper-crop years of 1813-15, 1820-2, and 1832-5, all of which show falling Poor Law expenditures.

It will be noticed that "real relief" in terms of wheat generally varied inversely with money relief up to 1834. This phenomenon might be taken as further evidence of the influence of the bread scales: the scales were so devised that they did not vary proportionately with the price of bread; hence, real relief fell in dear years and rose in cheap years. But this could well be an illusion. By itself, the inverse relationship between real and money relief tells us nothing more than that money expenditures on relief never rose or declined as fast as the price of wheat. It is easy to explain why the relief bill did not rise as fast as wheat prices: as the burden on the rates increased, the parish officers simply drew the strings together. It is not so obvious why the relief bill should have lagged behind falling wheat prices. But when one considers the inertia that characterised Poor Law administration in the period, the lag is not really surprising.

Total relief spending showed a sharp upward trend after 1795, reaching a peak in 1818, after which it declined again to a low point in 1823. In the latter part of the 1820s, the trend was upward once again. Earlier we hypothesised that the predominance of bad years over good leads to rising relief expenditures if the amount of relief given is tied to the price of wheat. We can now test this hyothesis. Out of the twenty-five years from 1793 to 1818 only 1796, 1814, and 1815 were years of abundant harvests, and as many as fourteen crops in this period were seriously deficient. In contrast, good harvests were prevalent in the decade after 1818; in particular, the yield and quality of the harvests of 1819, 1820, and 1821 were without precedent.[12] Thus, without resorting to additional considerations, it is possible to account for the sharp rise in poor-relief expenditures up to 1818 and the decline thereafter by "long waves" in climatic conditions. This

Graph 1

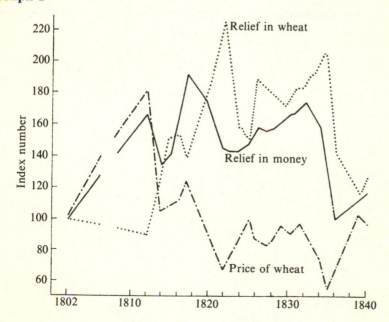

should serve to check hasty generalisations about the economic causes of a trend in the total relief bill.

IV

The amount of poor relief per head was generally higher in the eighteen counties we have designated as Speenhamland counties than elsewhere. In 1802, it averaged 12*s.* in the Speenhamland counties and 8*s.* in the non-Speenhamland counties; by 1831, the average in the first group had risen to 13*s.* 8*d.* while the average in the second group had only increased to 8*s.* 7*d.* (see Appendix A). Such figures assume, of course, that there were no variations in the accuracy of population statistics between counties, an assumption which we know to be false. Nevertheless, the pattern is so pronounced that we may ignore the shortcomings of the data. Having said this much, it must be added that there appear to be no other significant differences in the pattern of relief expenditures between the Speenhamland and the non-Speenhamland counties. For example, if we compare the rate of change of total expenditures in the two groups of counties, we discover that they varied with remarkable similarity (for sources see Appendix B).

In view of the fact that the Allowance System was almost entirely a rural problem in a particular part of the country, it is surprising to find so much coincidence between the two series. Would it make a difference if instead we grouped together the agricultural counties and contrasted their poor-relief expenditures with the non-agricultural counties? It should make a

Graph 2

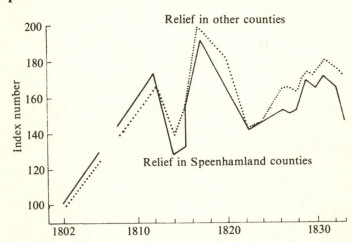

difference: while all the Speenhamland counties fall into the agricultural category, some agricultural counties are not Speenhamland counties (see Appendix C for the derivation of the series). But again, despite some differences in the amplitude of fluctuations, the peaks and troughs coincide.

Earlier we attributed increases in relief spending to the occurrence of poor harvests, and we showed that relief in agricultural counties rose and fell with the state of harvest. But, in that case, what are we to make of the fact that relief in non-agricultural counties followed so closely upon the pattern in rural areas? The explanation lies in the fact that cycles in industrial activity in this period were closely geared to fluctuations in the harvest. A markedly deficient harvest called for an increase in grain imports which put pressure on the money market, leading to a reduction in investment and employment; owing to the inelastic demand for wheat, the rise in wheat prices redistributed income from consumers to farmers; since the marginal propensity to consume of farmers was lower than that of consumers in general, the result was to lower aggregate expenditures on consumption. Conversely, an abundant domestic harvest increased the level of effective demand throughout the economy.[13] Thus, despite differences in the administration of the Poor Laws, relief spending rose and fell more or less simultaneously in all counties.

What can we learn from a graphic comparison of the two series? It appears that relief rose faster than population in all counties up to 1812, and at a fairly uniform rate. It is tempting to credit this to lax administration of relief fostered by the emergency feelings of wartime. In 1803,

Graph 3

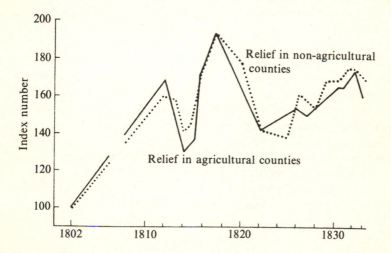

Parliament ordered parish officers to give the wives and children of militiamen a weekly allowance equal to the current daily wage of agricultural labour; this added about 5-8 per cent to Poor Law expenditures in the year 1812-14.

Nevertheless, such was the rise in prices during the war that the purchasing power of total relief was probably no higher in 1812 than in 1795. With the great break in wheat prices in 1813, relief expenditures were cut back everywhere, more successfully in rural than in industrial districts. The downward trend was short-lived, however. By 1816, the difficulties of conversion to peacetime production made new demands on the Poor Law authorities. In 1817 and 1818, the government found itself obliged to set the unemployed to work on road projects, financed by the sale of public bonds. With the improvement of conditions after 1818, the burden on the poor rates fell everywhere although in real terms the amount of relief given was still rising. The huge harvests of 1819-21 gave an edge to the agricultural counties where relief fell faster than in the industrial districts. Parliament's stern condemnation of the Allowance System in 1818, however, seems to have had some effect: the downward trend in relief spending is more pronounced in the Speenhamland than in the non-Speenhamland counties. The industrial boom of 1822-5 shows up in the stability of poor-relief expenditures in non-agricultural counties; in agriculture, these were not prosperous years. With the crash of 1825, relief spending in non-agricultural counties rose sharply, but thereafter the pattern in the industrial and agricultural areas did not differ significantly. The Poor Law officers in the Speenhamland counties, however, had come to heed the alarm at the rising burden on the rates: although the general trend was upwards from 1823-31, they prevented relief spending from increasing as fast in their parishes as it did in the country as a whole.

A comparison of index numbers cannot reveal differences that are at present at the outset and that persist through time. We have noted that relief per head was consistently higher in the Speenhamland counties than elsewhere. It was also higher in the agricultural counties than in the non-agricultural counties. What we have just demonstrated is that whatever the reason for this pattern in the absolute amount of *per capita* relief, it was not seriously influenced before 1834 either by differences in the administration of the Poor Laws in different counties or by an alleged deterioration of agriculture under the influence of allowances-in-aid-of-wages. There is no evidence whatever of the most popular of all the charges levied at the Old Poor Law: the "snow-ball effect" of outdoor relief to the able-bodied.

This still leaves us without an explanation of the higher absolute burden of the poor rates in certain counties, to which we now turn.

V

Trustworthy statistics for agricultural wages in this period are available on a county basis for the years 1795, 1824, 1833, 1837, and 1850. Wage data for agricultural workers are notoriously difficult to interpret. Not only are they subject to sharp seasonal variations; they are frequently augmented by money payments for task work and by payments in kind in the form of food, drink, fuel, and cheap rents. Although such supplements to cash earnings varied a good deal between counties in the nineteenth century, being higher oddly enough where money payments were higher, rural conservatism makes it plausible to assume that they did not vary radically from decade to decade. It appears that the ratio of total earnings to money wages changed little throughout the century, earnings generally exceeding wages by 15-20 per cent (see Appendix D). Thus, changes in the trend of money wages can be interpreted as reflecting changes in the trend of total earnings.

To test the effect of the Speenhamland policy, I have formed a composite index of the standard weekly money wage of agricultural workers in all counties which practised the Allowance System in 1814 (see Appendix E). The county is admittedly a poor unit over which to take an average of wages: in many counties, wages varied significantly from district to district. For example, the average wage in Middlesex, including as it does London, has little meaning. Still, we must make do with what we have. The comparison reveals the following:

	1795	1824	1833	1837	1850
Speenhamland Counties	100	100	124	106	104
Average for England and Wales	100	108	120	115	108

For Britain as a whole, the general picture is that of a rise from 1795 to about 1812 and a fall from 1813 to a low in 1824, but evidence about these years is very uncertain. Wages rose again in the latter half of the 1820s, varied little in the 1830s, and then moved down again in the 1840s. Given the rise in the price level during the war, agricultural workers were probably not much better off in 1824 than in 1795. But with the cost of living falling as much as 25 per cent between 1825 and 1850, real wages were much higher at the end of the period.

On the face of it, it seems that the Speenhamland policy depressed agricultural wages between 1795 and 1824. Strangely enough, however, in the decade before the passage of the Poor Law Amendment Act, wages in the Speenhamland counties recovered the ground lost during the war and immediate post-war years. We could attribute this result to stricter enforcement of the Poor Laws in the Speenhamland counties after 1824. But, in that case, why the rapid decline in the years 1833-50, after the Act of 1834 had crushed out the Allowance System?

In 1851, Caird drew a line through the middle of England to distinguish the high-wage counties of the north from the low-wage counties of the south. Above the Caird line, the money wages of agricultural workers averaged more than 10s. per week in 1824; below the line, they averaged less, except in Middlesex, Surrey, and Kent. If we hold with Clapham that "the thorough-going adoption of the Speenhamland policy coupled with the working of poor law settlement tended to keep down the standard weekly money wage of agricultural labour", what accounts for the low wages of Wales and the whole of the south-west and west Midlands where the Allowance System was eschewed?[14] Moreover, agricultural wages in the north were not noticeably lower in the East and North Ridings, where wages were subsidised out of the poor rates, than in other northern counties where they were not. And in the northern Midlands, Nottinghamshire, and Leicestershire, both Speenhamland counties, paid wages about the national average. The fact that the Speenhamland counties were generally located below the Caird wage-line should not be submitted as evidence that subsidies depressed wages. On the contrary, the causal relationship seems to run the other way: wages were only subsidised when, for other reasons, they were too low to provide a minimum standard of living.

The picture of sharp wage differentials for equivalent kinds of labour between the north and the south — differentials which exceeded the real cost of transfer from one region to the other — dates back to the eighteenth century and persisted throughout the nineteenth century. In 1824, the range between the northern and southern counties was about 4s.; by the end of the century, it had risen to 5s.[15] Superimposed upon that pattern was another, which reflected the pull of rapidly growing towns upon the immediately surrounding countryside: in the south, the greater was the distance from London, the lower was the wage, and in the north the same thing was true of the Lancashire towns Manchester and Liverpool, and the Yorkshire towns Leeds and Sheffield. The internal migration of workers which accompanied the Industrial Revolution largely took the form of short-distance travel to the nearest factory town. The people who moved into the cotton towns came almost exclusively from Lancashire and Cheshire itself, or from Ireland. Migration into London came from the extra-metropolitan parts of Middlesex and Surrey, and to a lesser extent from the surrounding counties of Kent, Essex, Hertfordshire and Berkshire. Similarly, migration into the Midlands iron towns of Warwickshire came from the county itself or from Staffordshire and Worcestershire to the west.[16] The pull of these towns not only raised wages in the surrounding rural areas by reducing the supply of labour, but also increased the demand for labour by providing a dependable expanding market for agricultural produce. This accounts for the high level of agricultural wages in the north as well as the relatively higher wage levels in farm areas around London. We have already mentioned the fact that wages in Middlesex, Kent and Surrey compared favourably with the north. Precisely for that reason, the parish officers did not resort to the Speenhamland policy in these counties. But even in East Anglia, where wages were supplemented by the Poor Law authorities, proximity to London produced wages higher than those in the south-west where wages were not subsidised. Again, in Sussex, the most notorious Speenhamland county, agricultural wages were higher than in any county in the south except those immediately around London.

We can hardly resist the conclusion that the parish officers only had recourse to the policy of subsidising wages wherever the attraction of urban industry made itself felt too weakly, leaving a pool of surplus manpower and substandard wages.[17]

VI

It was a favourite doctrine of the Poor Law reformers of 1834 that the abolition of outdoor relief to the unemployed would soon dissipate "the false and unreal appearance of surplus labour"; no labour surplus actually existed, they argued, apart from what had been artificially created by the operation of the Old Poor Law. They recommended emigration from the southern counties but only in the transition period from the old scheme to the new.[18] Nevertheless, the Assistant Commissioners found much evidence of structural unemployment in the Speenhamland counties of the south, and their testimony is particularly clear and detailed for the case of Sussex.[19] The natural periodicity of arable farming found in the wheat-growing counties threw workers entirely on the parish rates for three or four winter months. Seasonable unemployment was much less of a problem in the west, where no wheat was grown. This might explain why the Speenhamland policy was not adopted in the western counties.[20] The main wheat-growing area lay east of Cobden's famous line from "Inverness to Southampton", and the bulk of the domestic wheat supply was produced on the stiff clay lands of eight south-eastern counties. There is a striking coincidence, therefore, between the spread of Speenhamland and the production of wheat. Moreover, the wheat-producing counties were also areas of maximum recent enclosure.[21] Although it was mostly waste lands which were enclosed in this period, thus adding to employment opportunities, the enclosure movement increased the concentration on wheat, giving rise to the characteristic problem of winter unemployment.

Furthermore, the practice of boarding young unmarried farm-workers and guaranteeing them a fixed income irrespective of weather, which was still very common in the north, had by this time given way in the south to the day labourer hired at standard rates. Thus, seasonable unemployment became a social problem in southern agricultural counties which had to be dealt with by public action. The solution was the Roundsman System, which took up the slack by letting everyone work at low intensity; to have allowed wages to fall in order to clear the labour market would only have further reduced the productivity of labour via its depressing effect on the caloric value of the workers' diets.

In the nature of the case, it is very difficult to obtain direct evidence of disguised unemployment, and in practice it may be impossible to distinguish visible seasonable unemployment from invisible structural unemployment. Indeed, since the labour surplus is disguised by reducing the required effort of each worker, the situation gives the appearance of a labour deficit at low wage levels. At higher wages, the work done by each man would increase so rapidly that the deficit would be converted into a labour surplus. In other words, substandard wages, which are nevertheless above the level that automatic market forces would produce, are part of the mechanism which disguises a pool of surplus manpower in an underdeveloped country. Disguised unemployment may be said to exist when it is possible to release workers by means of a simple reorganisation of production without significantly affecting output; but history rarely performs that decisive experiment, and so we must fall back on inference.

Apart from direct evidence of seasonal and technological unemployment in English agriculture, we have other reasons to believe that the countryside was overpopulated at this time. By 1834, manufacturing was already effectively concentrated in the large towns of Lancashire, Cheshire, and Yorkshire. Previously, it had been scattered throughout the country districts. The most famous example of the decay of local industry in this era is the migration of the woollen and worsted industry from East Anglia to the West Riding. But all through the south in, say, 1800 one would have found, here and there, malthouses and breweries; iron, paper, snuff, and flour mills; leather, parchment, and printing works; silk-spinning and silk-weaving factories; and various home industries making hose, ribbons, laces, strings, and cotton goods.[22] The gradual disappearance of this source of demand for labour in rural areas is rarely given its proper due in accounting for the increased burden of poor-relief expenditures. To be sure, the decay of rural industries was a very slow process which took place rapidly in the second rather than the first half of the nineteenth century. But in the second half of the century, the rate of emigration from rural districts was commensurate with the decline of employment opportunities in the countryside. It was the relative immobility of rural labour that made the decay of cottage industry a serious problem in the heyday of the Industrial Revolution.

The abolition of outdoor relief to the unemployed in 1834, at least in the agricultural counties of the south, did not by itself solve the problem of structural unemployment in the countryside. Even ten years later, when reliable figures about the number of people on relief first became available, the Speenhamland counties headed the list with 12-15 per cent of the population on relief, whereas the percentage in the non-Speenhamland counties was typically no more than 6-7 per cent.[23] What is more, in the 1891 census all the Speenhamland counties were found to be losing population to London or to the factory towns of the north — the only exception being Warwickshire, containing Birmingham.[24] This fact alone is indicative of rural overpopulation in the first half of the century.

VII

We bring our analysis of the Old Poor Law to a close by briefly considering the remaining items in the traditional bill of indictment: it promoted the growth of population; it lowered rents; it reduced "yeomanry"; and, most general of all, it depressed agricultural output by destroying incentives.

It may be surprising that we have come so far without saying very much about the Malthusian objection to the Old Poor Law. It is simply that not much can be said. It is worth noting, of course, that the rate of population growth was no smaller in Scotland and Ireland, where earned incomes were never supplemented by the Poor Law authorities. Malthus himself added an appendix to the 1826 edition of his *Essay on the Principles of Population* which conceded that the Old Poor Law did not in fact "greatly encourage population".

The residence requirements of the Settlement Act, he argued, gave landlords a motive to pull down cottages on their estates; the scarcity of rural housing kept the Poor Laws from encouraging marriages. Be that as it may, estimates of birth and death rates for this period depend on the baptisms and burials entered in the parish registers and, as has been shown recently, there was a marked increase in the failure to register between 1780 and 1820; moreover the deficiencies in registration were not randomly distributed among the counties.[25] This renders suspect any quantitative statement about effects of the Old Poor Law on population growth.

Nevertheless, it has been argued that the death rate only became an important element in the "population explosion" after 1820, not, as is usually alleged, after 1780. Between 1780 and 1820, it was the rising birth rate which enlarged the size of families, and this was due in part to the Old Poor Law.[26] Most of the Speenhamland counties had fertility ratios above the national average, and Sussex had the highest fertility ratio of any county in 1821. But the northern industrial counties also showed fertility ratios above the national average. After 1821, fertility ratios began to fall in the Speenhamland counties, either because of stricter administration of relief or because of the agricultural revival. But similarly, fertility ratios fell even faster in the north. A fertility *ratio*, however, is not the same thing as the fertility or crude birth *rate*, being defined as the number of children between zero and four years per 1,000 women between the ages of fifteen and forty-nine. High fertility ratios may be produced by a fall in infant mortality, swelling the number of births registered. In the Speenhamland counties, more generous relief may have worked to reduce the number of infant deaths and in this way increased registered births. To be sure, this implies that the Old Poor Law did promote population growth, but via the death rate rather than the birth rate.

It has also been argued that the family-endowment features of Speen-hamland induced farmers to hire married men with children rather than single men as a method of lightening the rate burden, thus discouraging family limitation. This may have been an important consideration in small parishes where farmers knew the private circumstances of each hired hand. But in larger parishes, an expressed preference for married men must have encouraged workers to misrepresent their situation. On the whole, there is no persuasive evidence that, as the saying went at the time, "population was raised by bounties". Even the bastardy laws, which made it possible for unmarried mothers to claim support from a putative father, do not explain the increase in illegitimate births in the Speenhamland counties down to 1834. Illegitimacy was even higher in the northern industrial counties where the laws of bastardy were not stringently enforced. It seems that the Poor Laws, as Rickman said in the preamble to the census of 1821, were "much less conducive to an Increase of Population than they are usually stated to be in Argument".

Next, there is the contention that the Old Poor Law operated to depress rents. This argument depends entirely upon the way in which the poor rates were actually assessed. They were paid in the first instance by farmers and other estate-dwellers, not by landlords. Assessments seem to have been based on the annual value of lands and real estate occupied, but both the Poor Law Commissioners of 1834 and Cannan, the modern historian of local rating in England, were unable to determine the exact principle upon which they were calculated prior to 1835.[27] It is clear that farmers bore the brunt of the rates even in industrial districts, and when rates were rising they may have pressed landlords for a reduction in rents. We recall, however, that the relief bill varies in the same direction as the income of farmers. Hence, it is far from obvious that rents were in fact reduced when the rates rose.

Wild charges about the poor rates "eating up all rents" circulated during and after the Napoleonic wars. The rates were set by the justices of the peace, the wealthy landowners of the county, who paid rates only insofar as they were occupiers of estates. The pressure on rents when rates were rising, if it came at all, came only after a lapse of time, determined by the customary length of tenant leases in the locality. With tenants-at-will, rentals might respond quickly to an upward trend in poor rates, but leases of seven to fourteen years were not uncommon, and these must have been very insensitive to increased overhead costs incurred by tenants. Thus, the link between rising rates and falling rents made itself felt in different degrees in different counties, supposing, of course, that there really was such a link. The problem is further complicated by the fact that a multitude of non-economic considerations governed the relationship between landlord and tenant: landlords with political ambitions were sometimes willing to charge lower rents to favoured tenants. For the Speenhamland county of Warwickshire, the only county in which this subject has been investigated, it proved impossible to discover any connection between land rentals and rateable value as given in the parochial assessments.[28] Nevertheless, it is theoretically plausible that the incidence of the rates fell ultimately upon landlords, but we know so little about the trend in land rentals after 1815 that it must be left an open question.[29]

The idea of the disappearance of the "yeomanry" in this period is dealt with more quickly. Property-owners were not eligible for relief and so, it is argued, the Old Poor Law discriminated against the cottage-proprietor seeking employment, as well as the smallholder who never used hired labour, but had to pay his share of the rates. But if the "yeomanry" or occupying owner can ever be said to have disappeared from the land, it was in the eighteenth and not the nineteenth century that he vanished.[30] There is evidence of some decline in the number of family farms after 1815, but it is impossible to separate the burden of poor rates from the many other difficulties which afflicted smallholders in the years of deflation after Waterloo.

Nor is the alleged decline in the efficiency of agricultural workers under the influence of the Old Poor Law discernible in statistics of production. There are no reliable series of wheat, barley, and oats production in this period, but isolated unofficial estimates all suggest a continued increase in output per acre during the first half of the nineteenth century. Despite the fact that population had doubled in those fifty years, imports of agricultural commodities never formed an important portion of the total supply, and contemporary observers were convinced that productivity in agriculture had risen.[31] In view of the failure of the money wages of agricultural workers to fall as fast as food prices between 1824-50, it is difficult to deny this conviction.

We have come to the end of our journey to find that hardly any of the dire effects ascribed to the Old Poor Law stand up in the light of available empirical knowledge. This is negative proof at best, but even in theory the weight of forces is not all in one direction. We have to remember that a system of local rating provides its own checks to excessive expenditures. The Allowance System, for example, added to the wages paid by farmers with one hand what it took from them in rates with the other; the link between taxpayer and beneficiary was much closer than it is with modern income-support programmes. Just as it is now realised that the Settlement Laws did not invariably work with the harsh and wasteful rigidity so often assumed,[32] so the Speenhamland policy was not always as imprudently administered as has been thought. And just as the extent to which "paupers" were really transported by parish officers cannot be deduced from the statute books, so the actual effects of the Allowance System cannot be inferred from the purple passages of the *Poor Law Report of 1834*.

VIII

The Old Poor Law, with its use of outdoor relief to assist the underpaid and to relieve the unemployed was, in essence, a device for dealing with the problem of surplus labour in the lagging rural sector of a rapidly expanding but still underdeveloped economy. And considering the quality of social administration of the day, it was by no means an unenlightened policy. The Poor Law Commissioners of 1834 thought otherwise and deliberately selected the facts so as to impeach the existing administration on predetermined lines. Not only did they fail to take account in any way of the special problem of structural unemployment in the countryside, but what evidence they did present consisted of little more than picturesque anecdotes of maladministration. Even the elaborate questionnaire which they circulated among the parishes was never analysed or reduced to summary form. No attempt was made to make a census of the poor, and to this day we know more about the nature and composition of the pauper host in 1802 than in 1834. Anyone who has read the *Report of 1834* can testify to the overwhelming cumulative effect of the endless recitals of ills from the mouths of squires, magistrates, overseers, and clergymen. But as evidence of a social malady it has little value, particularly on the ultimate question of the corrupting influence of lavish relief: in what age would it not be possible to collect complaints from the upper classes about the laziness of workers?

Nowhere in the *Report* is there any hint of a quantitative view of the problem. "This ignoring of statistics," as the Webbs remarked "led, in the diagnosis, to disastrous errors in proportion; and made the suggested remedial measures lopsided and seriously imperfect." For example, Nassau William Senior, who wrote "the exposition of the evils of the old system" in the *Report*, surmised that "the able-bodied paupers and their families now amount to a million". Instead, the Webbs calculated that about 100,000 people were relieved indoors and 900,000 outdoors in 1834, of which perhaps 100,000 or at most 300,000 if we count all their dependants, were able-bodied workers.[33] In subsequent years, the Commissioners were to discover to their grief that the bulk of relief recipients were, indeed, not the able-bodied, but rather the helpless and dependent sick, aged, and infirm.[34] No wonder, the "harsh but salutary Act" fell short, at nearly every point, of effecting a sweeping reform. Gradually, so gradually as to be almost imperceptible to contemporaries, the "principles of 1834" were undermined in practice by the administration of successive governments, while competing public services increasingly took over the functions of the Poor Law.[35] The virtual abandonment of the Malthusian theory of population under the influence of the downward trend in births, the growing recognition of urban destitution caused by involuntary unemployment, the concern over sweated trades, all these contributed to "the breaking-up of the Poor Law". Nevertheless, the *Report of 1834* remained a force against which all changes had to make their way, and the public was still told by the Poor Law authorities that any abrogation of the "principles of 1834" would give a spur to population and thus bring wages down. As late as 1893, Alfred Marshall remarked to the Royal Commission on the Aged Poor: "It seems that whenever I read Poor Law literature of today I am taken back to the beginning of the century; everything that is said about economics has the flavour of that old time."

APPENDIX A:
Poor Relief per Head, by Counties

Speenhamland Counties	1802		1812		1821		1831	
	s.	*d.*	*s.*	*d.*	*s.*	*d.*	*s.*	*d.*
Sussex	22	7	33	1	23	8	19	4
Bucks.	16	1	22	9	19	1	18	7
Wilts.	13	11	24	5	15	8	16	9
Beds.	11	9	17	6	16	6	16	11
Berks.	15	1	27	1	17	0	15	9
Hunts.	12	2	16	9	16	0	15	3
Suffolk	11	5	19	4	18	0	18	4
Norfolk	12	5	20	0	15	7	15	4
Dorset	11	4	17	5	13	3	11	5
Essex	12	1	24	7	20	0	17	2
Cambridge	12	1	17	0	14	9	13	8
Oxford	16	2	24	10	19	1	16	11
Northants.	14	5	19	11	19	2	16	10
Leicester	12	4	14	8	16	6	11	7
Warwicks.	11	3	13	4	12	0	9	7
Devon	7	3	11	5	10	8	9	0
Notts.	6	4	10	10	9	5	6	6
York. E R.	7	6	23	6	13	0	11	11
York, N.R.	6	5	8	4	9	6	8	9
Average	12	3	18	8	16	4	13	8

Non-Speenhamland Counties	1802		1812		1821		1831	
	s.	*d.*	*s.*	*d.*	*s.*	*d.*	*s.*	*d.*
Kent	13	6	17	1	18	5	14	5
Hants.	12	2	18	4	14	11	13	10
Surrey	10	0	13	6	13	11	10	11
Herts.	11	5	13	10	15	1	13	2
Worcester.	10	3	11	11	10	1	7	6
Rutland	10	1	13	8	12	3	9	1
Hereford.	10	5	17	9	14	0	11	4
Lincoln	9	2	10	10	12	3	11	0
Somerset	8	11	12	3	9	11	8	10
Gloucester	8	8	11	7	9	10	8	8
York, W.R.	6	6	9	11	8	2	5	7
Stafford.	6	11	8	6	8	10	6	6
Chester	6	11	10	0	8	4	6	3
Cornwall	5	10	9	5	9	1	6	8
Derby	6	9	10	2	9	1	6	8
Durham	6	6	9	11	10	1	6	10
Salop.	7	11	11	5	10	4	8	2
Northumberland	6	8	7	11	7	11	6	3
Cumberland	4	9	6	9	7	4	5	6
Westmorland	6	8	9	9	11	0	9	8
Lancaster	4	5	7	5	5	6	4	5

Middlesex	8	7	10	7	11	10	10	1
Monmouth	8	0	9	1	7	9	5	5
Wales	5	7	7	7	7	2	7	2
Average	8	4	11	4	10	2	8	7

Select Towns

Manchester	4	7	9	8	3	9	—
Birmingham	6	2	9	6	7	11	—
Bristol	5	7	6	5	9	8	—
Liverpool	6	6	6	5	6	2	—

Sources. The counties are listed in each category roughly in order of average relief per head. The figures are obtained by dividing the "annual expenditures for the poor" reported for each county by the county population as given by the census returns. Up to 1849, Poor Law returns were reported annually for the year that ends at Lady Day (March 25). Hence, figures for, say, 1803, are here regarded as referring to 1802, and so forth. The available official returns up to 1830 are conveniently found in Marshall, *Digest of All the Accounts*, (London, 1833), pp. 36-7. The figures for the towns are also derived from Marshall, *ibid.*, p. 41. The returns for the year 1831-3 are given in Parl. Papers 1835 (444), p. xlvii. The figures for county populations are derived from the decennial censuses of 1801, 1811, and 1831, as given by J. R. McCulloch, *Descriptive and Statistical Account of the British Empire*, (London, 3rd. ed., 1854), II, p. 400.

Andrew Ure in his *Philosophy of Manufacturers* (1835), p. 477, gives figures for poor relief per head in what he calls "factory counties" for 1801, 1811, 1821, and 1831, based, as he says, on the official returns. Since poor-relief expenditures were not returned for the years 1801 and 1811, he probably applied a method similar to my own, dividing decennial census data on population into figures on relief spending for the years 1802 and 1812. His series generally agree with mine, except that they are all unaccountably lower for 1821.

APPENDIX B:
Total Poor-relief Expenditures in England and Wales

Years	Total £000s	Index	Average Price of Wheat per Quarter s. d.	Index of Relief in Wheat	Relief in Speenhamland Counties £000s	Index	Relief in Other Counties £000s	Index
1802	4,078	100	69 10	100	1,782	100	2,296	100
1812	6,676	164	126 6	90	2,975	170	3,701	161
1813	6,295	154	109 9	98	2,672	145	3,623	160
1814	5,419	133	74 4	125	2,223	125	3,196	139
1815	5,725	140	65 7	149	2,279	130	3,447	150
1816	6,918	169	78 6	151	2,971	170	3,947	171
1817	7,890	193	96 11	139	3,374	190	4,516	197
1818	7,532	184	86 3	148	3,174	180	4,358	190
1819	7,330	180	74 6	168	3,069	172	4,261	185
1820	6,958	171	67 10	176	2,894	163	4,064	176
1821	6,359	156	56 1	194	2,673	150	3,686	160
1822	5,773	142	44 7	223	2,549	143	3,224	140
1823	5,734	141	53 4	185	2,473	139	3,261	142
1823	5,734	141	53 4	185	2,473	139	3,261	142
1824	5,787	142	63 11	155	2,498	140	3,289	143
1825	5,929	145	68 6	148	2,579	145	3,350	146
1826	6,441	158	58 8	188	2,704	151	3,738	162
1827	6,298	154	58 6	184	2,616	147	3,716	162
1828	6,332	155	60 5	179	2,683	150	3,649	160
1829	6,829	167	66 3	170	2,937	165	3,892	169
1829	6,829	167	66 3	170	2,937	165	3,892	169
1830	6,799	167	64 3	182	2,905	163	3,894	169
1831	7,037	173	66 4	182	2,997	170	4,040	176
1832	6,791	167	58 8	199	2,903	163	3,888	170
1833	6,317	155	52 11	204	2,596	146	3,721	169

Source. Average monthly gazette prices per quarter of wheat are given by Gayer, Rostow, Schwartz, *Fluctuations, Microfilm Supplement,* pp. 650-l, (see note 13 below). Since the poor-relief figures run from March 25 of one year to March 25 of the next, I have averaged annual wheat prices on the same basis.

APPENDIX C:

*Poor-relief Expenditures in Agricultural and Non-agricultural Counties
in England and Wales*

Years	Agricultural (£000s)	Index	Non-agricultural (£000s)	Index
1802	1,672	100	2,405	100
1812	2,822	169	3,835	160
1813	2,563	152	3,731	155
1814	2,137	128	3,281	137
1815	2,286	136	3,438	143
1816	2,839	170	4,072	170
1817	3,227	193	4,644	193
1818	3,028	181	4,489	187
1819	2,891	171	4,440	185
1820	2,748	164	4,211	175
1821	2,568	153	3,791	158
1822	2,370	140	3,402	142
1823	2,409	144	3,328	140
1824	2,443	146	3,344	140
1825	2,492	149	3,437	140
1826	2,582	153	3,859	161
1827	2,514	150	3,784	158
1828	2,594	154	3,739	155
1829	2,787	167	4,042	170
1830	2,789	167	4,010	170
1831	2,892	173	4,145	173
1832	2,766	166	4,025	170
1833	2,586	153	3,732	155
1834	2,295	140	2,232	136
1840	1,772	106	3,114	130
1850	1,723	103	3,239	134

Source. Gayer, Rostow, and Schwartz used decennial census figures on occupational distribution, by counties, to divide the counties into the two classes: *ibid.* p. 1678. Such counties as Devon, Kent, Somerset, Hampshire, Salop, and the East Riding were borderline cases and the decision had to be made on the basis of a qualitative judgement. Twenty-six counties and the West Riding were designated non-agricultural; the remaining fifteen counties, including East and North Riding, were designated agricultural counties. For a terse description of the character of economic activity in each of the counties in this period, see McCulloch, *Descriptive and Statistical Account*, I, pp. 142-225.

APPENDIX D:*Weekly Money Wages of Agricultural Workers, by Counties*

Counties	1795 s. d.	1824 s. d.	1833 s. d.	1837 s. d.	1850 s. d.
Middlesex	8 0	11 3	13 0	11 6	11 0
Surrey	10 6	10 8	12 0	10 6	9 6
Kent	10 6	11 9	13 1	12 0	11 6
Sussex	10 0	9 6	12 1	10 7	10 6
Hants.	9 0	8 6	10 2	9 6	9 0
Berks.	9 0	8 9	10 5	9 0	7 6
South-Eastern Average	9 6	10 1	11 10	10 6	9 10
Index number	*100*	*107*	*126*	*111*	*104*
Oxford	8 6	8 1	10 1	8 6	9 0
Herts.	8 0	9 0	11 0	9 6	9 0
Bucks.	8 0	8 3	10 2	9 6	8 6
Northants.	7 0	8 0	10 3	9 0	9 0
Hunts.	8 6	7 6	10 5	9 6	8 6
Beds.	7 6	8 6	10 0	9 6	9 0
Cambridge.	8 2	9 0	10 6	9 6	7 6
South Midlands Average	8 0	8 4	10 4	9 3	8 8
Index number	*100*	*105*	*129*	*114*	*109*
Essex	9 0	9 4	10 3	10 4	8 0
Suffolk	10 6	8 3	9 11	10 4	7 0
Norfolk	9 0	9 2	10 9	10 4	8 6
Eastern Average	9 6	8 11	10 4	10 4	7 10
Index number	*100*	*94*	*109*	*109*	*83*
Wilts.	8 4	7 6	9 1	8 0	7 3
Dorset	8 0	6 11	8 2	7 6	7 6
Devon	7 0	7 6	9 0	8 0	8 6
Cornwall	8 6	8 3	8 11	8 9	8 8
Somerset	7 3	8 2	8 6	8 8	8 7
South-Western Average	7 10	7 8	8 9	8 2	8 1
Index number	*100*	*99*	*112*	*104*	*103*
Gloucester	7 0	9 3	9 6	9 0	7 0
Hereford.	8 0	7 0	8 1	8 0	8 5
Salop.	7 6	8 10	9 2	9 0	7 3
Stafford.	7 6	10 7	11 1	12 0	9 6
Worcester.	8 6	8 2	9 6	9 6	7 8

Warwicks.	7	6	8	10	10	10	10	0	8	6

West Midlands Average	7	8	8	9	9	8	9	7	8	1
Index number	*100*		*115*		*126*		*124*		*107*	

Leicester.	11	0	9	10	11	2	10	0	9	6
Rutland	9	0	—		12	2	—		—	
Lincoln.	10	6	10	2	12	4	12	0	10	0
Notts.	9	0	10	3	12	10	12	0	10	0
Derby.	9	3	10	10	12	0	12	0	11	0

North Midlands Average	9	9	10	3	12	3	11	6	10	1
Index number	*100*		*106*		*127*		*120*		*105*	

Chester	9	0	10	8	9	10	13	0	12	0
Lancashire	13	6	12	5	12	2	12	8	13	6
York, W.R.	11	0	12	5	11	5	12	0	14	0
York, E.R.	11	3	11	8	11	0	12	0	12	0
York, N.R.	10	0	10	3	11	4	12	0	11	0
Durham	9	0	11	6	11	0	12	0	11	0
Northumberland	10	6	11	5	11	5	12	0	13	0
Cumberland	9	0	12	2	10	8	12	0	13	0
Westmorland	10	0	12	0	11	0	12	0	12	0

Northern Average	10	4	11	7	11	1	12	2	12	2
Index number	*100*		*113*		*105*		*118*		*118*	

Monmouth	9	0	10	0	10	8	10	6	19	8
Wales	6	8	8	0	8	2	7	6	6	11

General Average	8	11	9	7	10	8	10	3	9	6
Index number	*100*		*108*		*120*		*115*		*108*	

Sources. The data are drawn from A. L. Bowley, "The Statistics of Wages in the United Kingdom During the Last Hundred Years, Agricultural Wages", *Journal of the Royal Statistical Society* (December 1898). The 1798 figures are derived from Eden and Young; the 1824 figures come from the same committee which circulated the questionnaire on the Allowance System; the 1833 and 1837 figures rest on returns from about 1,000 parishes collected by the Poor Law Commissioners; the 1851 figures are given by Caird. All of these represent the average of summer and winter wages; in those counties where free board or lodging was general, they include such payments in kind. The averages for the districts are simple arithmetic averages because no adequate weights were obtainable. Bowley's index numbers, based on 1892, have been reduced to 1795.

Slightly different figures, based on other authorities, are presented in A. L. Bowley, *Wages in the Nineteenth Century* (1900), Chs. 4-5, but the differences are negligible. These are reprinted in Lord Ernle. *English Farming,* Appendix IX. with comparable data down to 1926, giving an overview of trends throughout the whole of the nineteenth century.

After due reflection, Bowley concluded that index numbers found for wages can be adopted for earnings without alteration. See his article "The Statistics of Wages in the United Kingdom During the Last Hundred Years. Earnings and General Averages", *Journal of the Royal Statistical Society* (September 1889), and his *Wages in the Nineteenth Century*, pp. 41-3. For a more sceptical view see O. R. McGregor, "Introduction, Pt. 2: After 1815", to Lord Ernle, *English Farming*, pp. cxix-cxxi.

APPENDIX E:

Index of Weekly Earnings of Agricultural Workers, by Counties
(1795 + 100)

Speenhamland Counties	1824	1833	1837	1850
Sussex	94	121	104	102
Bucks.	105	130	120	105
Wilts.	90	111	95	87
Beds.	113	141	126	120
Berks.	96	114	112	83
Hunts.	88	139	112	100
Suffolk	80	90	99	80
Norfolk	101	120	113	93
Dorset	86	109	94	94
Essex	112	123	123	91
Cambridge.	110	130	120	110
Oxford.	96	121	103	107
Northants.	114	150	128	128
Leicester.	87	108	87	85
Warwicks.	120	145	132	115
Devon	108	130	111	123
Notts.	115	141	133	110
York, E.R.	122	122	125	125
York, N.R.	103	112	120	109
Average	100	124	106	104
Kent	112	126	115	109
Hants.	85	104	92	90
Surrey	101	117	100	90
Herts.	113	142	120	113
Worcester.	96	120	111	90
Rutland	—	140	—	—
Hereford.	88	111	112	105
Lincoln.	99	138	115	96
Somerset	112	121	120	119
Gloucester	133	140	115	100
York, W.R.	107	111	101	124
Stafford.	143	151	159	125
Chester	118	108	145	133
Cornwall	97	106	103	102
Derby.	116	124	130	120
Durham	144	148	150	138
Salop.	96	130	118	92
Northumberland	108	107	113	106

Cumberland	135	130	145	156
Westmorland	122	108	122	122
Lancaster	99	98	98	106
Middlesex	124	165	173	123
Monmouth	111	116	116	108
Wales	120	122	112	105
Average for England and Wales	108	120	115	108

NOTES

1. Alfred Marshall, testifying in 1893 before the Royal Commission on the Aged Poor, deplored the persistence of Malthusian thinking among laymen and illustrated the evolution of professional economic opinion in the nineteenth century in these words: "Suppose you could conceive a Mad Emperor of China to give to every English working man a half-a-crown for nothing: according to the current notions, as far as I have been able to ascertain them, that would lower wages, because it would enable people to work for less. I think that nine economists out of ten at the beginning of the century would have said that that would lower wages. Well, of course, it might increase population and that might bring down wages; but unless it did increase population, the effect according to the modern school would be to raise wages because the increased wealth of the working classes would lead to better living, more vigorous and better educated people with greater earning power, and so wages would rise. That is the centre of the difference." *Official Papers* (London, 1926), p. 249.

2. For theoretical analysis of the phenomenon of disguised unemployment, see H. Leibenstein, "The Theory of Underemployment in Backward Economies", *Journal of Political Economy*, 65 (April 1957); and P. Wonnacott, "Disguised and Overt Unemployment in Underdeveloped Economies", *Quarterly Journal of Economics*, 76 (May 1962).

3. *Parl. Papers* 1803-1804 (175), xiii. The returns of the census are also found in J. Marshall, *A Digest of All the Accounts* (London 1833), pp. 33, 38.

4. *Ibid.*, 34.

5. S. and B. Webb, *English Poor Law History: Part I: The Old Poor Law* (London, 1927), pp. 181, 185, 188-9, 400-1.

6. J. Clapham, *The Economic History of Modern Britain. The Railway Age* (2nd edn., Cambridge, 1939), pp. 123-5. The Webbs dismissed this piece of evidence in a footnote in *English Poor Law History: Part II: The Last Hundred Years* London, 1929), I, p. 61 n.

7. *Ibid.*, p. 182.

8. See *ibid.*, pp. 170-3.

9. See *ibid.*, pp. 182-3; J.L. and B. Hammond, *The Village Labourer* (4th edn., London, 1927). E.M. Hampson, *The Treatment of Poverty in Cambridgeshire, 1579-1834* (Cambridge, 1934), pp. 195-6.

10. See S.E. Finer, *The Life and Times of Sir Edwin Chadwick* (London, 1952).

11. There are no official figures available for total relief expenditures in the years 1785-1801 and 1803-11.

12. T.Tooke, *History of Prices* (London, 1857), VI, App. 6.
13. See A. D. Gayer, W. A. Rostow, A. J. Schwartz, *Economic Fluctuations in the British Economy, 1790-1850* (Oxford, 1953), II, pp. 563-4, 793, 854; R.C.O. Matthews, *A Study in Trade-Cycle History* (Cambridge, 1954), Ch. 4.
14. Clapham, *The Railway Age, op. cit.* p. 125. He cited a few Speenhamland counties which show a fall of wages between 1795 and 1824, but does not mention Buckinghamshire, Bedfordshire, Norfolk, Essex, Cambridge, Northamptonshire, Warwick, and Devon — all Speenhamland counties — where wages were higher in 1824 than in 1795.
15. See C.S. Orwin, B.I. Felton, "A Century of Wages and Earnings in Agriculture," *Journal of the Royal Agricultural Society*, 92 (1931).
16. See A. Redford, *Labour Migration in England, 1800-1850* (Manchester, 1926), Ch. 11, and Appendices.
17. Another explanation suggests itself. The *Report of 1834* presented some evidence to show that small parishes, measured in terms of population per acre, granted more relief per head than large parishes, the reason being that the intimate personal connections between magistrates and farm hands in small parishes invited prodigality. If this were so, the high rates of relief per head in southern rural counties might be due to the fact that most of the 1,000 parishes under 50 inhabitants and most of the 6,000 under 300 inhabitants were located in southern agricultural districts. To test this hypothesis, we would have to examine the size distribution of parishes among counties, a question which cannot be entered into here; but see my "The Poor Law Report reexamined", (Chapter 2 of this volume) Appendix.
18. In the years 1835-7, they arranged for the migration of about 5,000 workers to the northern factory districts. In the same period, some 6,500 Poor Law emigrants went overseas, and in both cases about half the migrants came from the East Anglian counties of Norfolk and Suffolk. Redford, *Labour Migration*, p. 94.
19. For a review of the evidence, see N. Gash, "Rural Unemployment, 1815-1834", *Econ. Hist. Rev* 6, No. 1 (October 1935). The records of the Emigration Inquiry of 1826-7 supply additional evidence of redundant labour in the southern rural counties: See Clapham, *The Railway Age, op. cit.,* pp. 64-5.
20. G.C. Russell, M. Compton, "Agricultural Adjustments after the Napoleonic Wars", *Economic History* (February 1939), show that it was the grain-growing areas which were hit hardest in the post-war years.
21. Clapham, *The Railway Age, op. cit.* pp. 19-22, 124, 467.
22. See Lord Ernle, *English Farming, Past and Present* (6th edn., London, 1961), pp. 308-12.
23. The official returns for the year 1844 are found in J.R. McCulloch, *A Descriptive and Statistical Account of the British Empire* (London, 1854), II, p. 670.
24. Redford, *Labour Migration*, Appendix 1, Map A.
25. J.T. Krause, "Changes in English Fertility and Mortality, 1781-1850". *Economic History Review.*, 2nd series, 9 (August 1958).
26. *Ibid.*, and T.H. Marshall, "The Population Problem During the Industrial Revolution: A Note on the Present State of the Controversy". *Economic History* (1929), reprinted in *Essays in Economic History*, ed. E.M. Carus-Wilson (London, 1954), I.
27. E. Cannan, *The History of Local Rates in England* (4th edn., London, 1927), p. 80.
28. A.W. Ashby, *One Hundred Years of Poor Law Administration in a Warwick-*

shire Village, Oxford Studies in Social and Legal History, ed. p. Vinogradoff (Oxford, 1912), III, pp. 57-8.

29. For the available evidence, see Gayer, *et al.*, *Economic Fluctuations*, pp. 927-9.
30. Clapham, *The Railway Age, op. cit.*, pp. 98-105, 430-2. E. Davies, "The Small Landowners, 1780-1832, in The Light of the Land Tax Assessments," *Economic History Review* (1927) reprinted in *Essays in Economic History* ed. E.M. Carus-Wilson (London, 1954), I; J.D. Chambers, "Enclosure and the Small Landowner", *Economic History Review* 10, No. 2 (November 1940); J.D. Chambers, "Enclosure and Labor Supply in the Industrial Revolution," *Economic History Review* 2nd series, 5, No. 3 (1953).
31. See M. Blaug, *Ricardian Economics. An Historical Study* (New Haven, Conn., 1958), pp. 183-4
32. See D. Marshall, "The Old Poor Law, 1662-1795," *Economic History Review* (1937) reprinted in *Essays in Economic History*, ed. E.M. Carus-Wilson (London, 1954), I.
33. Webbs, *English Poor Law History*, Part 1, p. 88 n.
34. This fact was carefully, and perhaps intentionally, hidden from the public. Throughout the remainder of the century, the Poor Law authorities displayed an incredible reluctance to supply any quantitative information about the body of people relieved, other than the ratio of outdoor to indoor relief recipients. Since some children and old people received outdoor relief, while a proportion of the able-bodied did enter the workhouse, we have no way of knowing just how many of the able-bodied received unemployment compensation; the "able-bodied" were not even defined by the Act of 1834 for purposes of administration. See M. Dessauer, "Unemployment Records, 1848-1859," *Economic History Review* 9, No. 1 (February 1940).
35. See H.L. Beales, "The New Poor Law," *History* (1931) reprinted in *Essays in Economic History*, ed. E.M. Carus-Wilson (London, 1962), III.

2   The Poor Law Report Re-Examined

In an earlier article, I pleaded for a reappraisal of the Old Poor Law.[1] Despite what all the books say, the evidence that we have does not suggest that the English Poor Law as it operated before its amendment in 1834 reduced the efficiency of agricultural workers, promoted population growth, lowered wages, depressed rents, destroyed yeomanry, and compounded the burden on ratepayers. Beyond this purely negative argument, I tried to show that the Old Poor Law was essentially a device for dealing with the problems of structural unemployment and substandard wages in the lagging rural sector of a rapidly growing but still underdeveloped economy. It constituted, so to speak, "a welfare state in miniature," combining elements of wage-escalation, family allowances, unemployment compensation, and public works, all of which were administered and financed on a local level. Far from having an inhibitory effect, it probably contributed to economic expansion. At any rate, from the economic point of view, things were much the same after 1834 as before. The Poor Laws Amendment Act of 1834 marked a revolution in British social administration, but it left the structure of relief policy substantially unchanged.

In the earlier article, I criticised the Commissioners who prepared the famous *Poor Law Report of 1834* for the manner in which they marshalled the evidence against the existing system, noting that the elaborate questionnaire which they circulated among the parishes was never analysed or reduced to summary form. But I accepted the general picture which they presented of the Old Poor Law, in particular the practice of giving outdoor relief to employed workers in the form of supplements to earned wages, the amount of the supplement being proportionate to the ruling price of bread. It was this practice, described at the time as the Allowance System and more recently as the Speenhamland System, that drew most of the fire directed against the Old Poor Law. The Commissioners claimed not only that the Allowance System was "prevalent" in the south of England, but that it was in process of "extending itself over the North of England"; nor was it confined only to the countryside.[2] The circular which they submitted to a sample of parishes in every county contained a question on the matter of making allowances-in-aid-of-wages, and no one doubted that the Commissioners rested their claim of the extent of the practice on the answers returned. In the preamble to the *Report*, the

Commissioners explained why they had not summarised the results of the inquiry:

By January, 1833 ... we had received returns to our circulated queries so numerous, that it became a question of how they should be disposed of. The number and the variety of the persons by whom they were furnished, made us to consider them the most valuable part of our evidence. But the same causes made their bulk so great as to be a serious objection to their publication in full. It appeared that this objection might be diminished, if an abstract could be made containing their substance in fewer words, and we directed such an abstract to be prepared. On making the attempt, however, it appeared that not much could be saved in length without incurring the risk of occasional suppression or misrepresentation. Another plan would have been to make a selection, and leave out altogether those returns which appeared to us of no value. A very considerable portion, perhaps not less than one half, are of this description; their omission would have materially diminished the expense of copying and printing, and the remainder would have been more easily consulted and referred to when unencumbered by useless matter. But on a question of such importance as Poor Law Amendment, we were unwilling to incur the responsibility of selection. We annex, therefore, in Appendix (B), all the returns which we have received.[3]

What this meant was that anyone who wanted to challenge their interpretation of the facts would have to wade through nine folio volumes running to almost 5,000 pages. None of the numerous contemporary opponents of the New Poor Law had the stomach for such an undertaking. Since that day, these volumes have continued to gather dust, for no historian has ever reported on them. Even the Webbs hardly referred to them in their mammoth volumes on the Poor Laws.

The tabulation of the answers presents serious problems, because the questions were poorly framed and the respondents were given licence to answer as they pleased: often the replies were ambiguous or irrelevant; sometimes the questions were not answered at all. The tabulating scheme adopted below is not irreproachable, but it appears to be suitable for assessing the relief policy that actually existed in 1834. The results of the tabulation are rather surprising. The practice of making allowance payments for children, at least after the third or fourth child, was widespread. *But the Speenhamland System as such had generally disappeared by 1832, even in the south.* From the answers given, it appears that many parishes did at one time make allowances-in-aid-of-wages connected in some way to the cost of living. The Speenhamland System had its greatest vogue during the Napoleonic wars, but the severe strictures of the committee reports on the Poor Laws of 1817 and 1818 and the Select Committee on Labourers' Wages of 1824 would seem to have persuaded most of the Poor Law vestries to do away with it.[4] We shall probably never know just when Speenhamland was given up. "We directed our Assistant Commissioners," the Commissioners wrote, "to enquire in every parish in which they found the relief of the able-bodied existing, at what period, and from what causes, it was supposed to have arisen." What a pity similarly explicit instructions were not given to inquire when or why the Speenhamland policy of subsidising wages was abandoned!

There is evidence that Senior and Chadwick, who drew up the questionnaire, were aware of the virtual disappearance of the Speenhamland System and framed the questions so that the answers could be interpreted to convey the misleading impression that wages were regularly subsidised. This is how the relevant question ran: "Q.24. Have you any, and how many, able-bodied labourers in the employment of individuals receiving allowance or regular relief from your parish on their own account, or on that of their families: and if on account of their families, at what number of children does it begin?" This was followed by Question 25 which asked: "Is relief or allowance given according to any and what scale?" It is clear that Question 24 mixed up two very different things: the first part of the question referred to outdoor relief to able-bodied workers in employment, whether married or not; the second part of the question was addressed to the question of children allowance payments. Allowances for children had been an integral feature of the Poor Laws since the eighteenth century and possibly as early as the seventeenth century. The argument against them in 1834 was Malthusian in character, and it was not a strong argument because the allowances were generally paid for a third, fourth, or fifth child, and its amount was related in each parish to the local employment opportunities for children. To be sure, almost everyone was convinced at the time that allowances for children encouraged population growth but, if so, it was not a new phenomenon. What really agitated public opinion was the Speenhamland policy of adding to the earned wages of the able-bodied in order to stabilise their real income at what was considered to be a minimum-of-existence level. This practice did not exist before 1795, and it was this which was widely believed to be destroying work incentives in the countryside. Question 24 was so worded as to confuse family allowances with wage subsidies in the effort to persuade the public that the Poor Laws were still suffering from the same maladministration to which attention had been drawn by earlier Parliamentary committees. In the *Report* itself, the Commissioners pointed out that "the word *allowance* is sometimes used as comprehending all parochial relief afforded to those who are employed by individuals at the average wages of the district. But sometimes this term is confined to the relief which a person so employed obtains on account of his children, any relief which he may obtain on his own account being termed 'Payment of Wages out of Rates.' *In the following Report we shall use the word 'allowance' in its former or more comprehensive sense*."[5] In other words, the purple language on the Allowance System in the *Report* of 1834 which has been quoted by generations of historians as an indictment of the practice of subsidising wages is, in fact, an attack on all welfare payments made to families whose breadwinner is currently employed. Perhaps allowance payments for children are "a bounty on indolence and vice," but that is not what most of us believed when we read of the disastrous effects of the Old Poor Law!

If Senior and Chadwick had wanted to avoid this misunderstanding, they could have done so with very little trouble. Despite their expressed reluctance to abstract the circulated query, the official edition of the *Poor Law Report of 1834* did contain a supplement which extracted a portion of the replies, namely the answers to nine questions for the first seven counties of England, taken alphabetically: Bedfordshire, Berkshire, Buckinghamshire, Cambridgeshire, Cheshire, Cornwall, and Cumberland.[6] The counties selected were deemed to be a fairly random sample of English counties, in terms of geographic, occupational, and economic characteristics: "We believe, in short, that a fairer average of the whole country cannot be taken." The first thing to note is that the first four of these seven are what we earlier called Speenhamland counties, that is, counties which the 1824 committee found to be making use of the principle of supplementing earned wages; all four are south-eastern rural counties. The last three are a mixture of non-Speenhamland counties: a south-western rural county, a northern industrial county, and a northern rural county. The Commissioners summed up the answers to Question 24: of the 92 reporting parishes in the first four (Speenhamland) counties, allowances-in-aid-of-wages to the able-bodied or their families are given in 70 parishes and refused in 22, whereas in the last three (non-Speenhamland) counties, allowances are given in 28 and refused in 52.[7] The fact that poor relief per head averaged 14s. 9d. in the second group was then left to tell its own story. The Commissioners neglected to point out, however, that even in the four Speenhamland counties only 11 out of the 92 reporting parishes admitted that they supplemented wages judged to be deficient; out of the 70 parishes that answered "yes" to Question 24, 59 went on to say that they made payments only to workers with children, usually beginning with the fourth child, for the purpose of relieving the applicant of part of the expense of house rent. The significant fact that the policy of subsidising wages as such was found to exist in only about 10 per cent of the rural parishes was simply glossed over both in the supplement and in the *Report* itself.

To clarify the problem, I have separated the replies to Question 24 between those expressly admitting to supplementing earned wages and those making payments to large families in money or in kind. Due to the confusing question, however, it is sometimes difficult to decide how to interpret the answer. What is one to say when one reads in reply to Question 24 from a parish in Bedfordshire: "Allowance often made out of the Poor Book when the number of children exceeds three. Sometimes idle able-bodied men are let at a low rate of wages to the farmers, and the deficiency paid out of the Poor Book"; or, from a parish in Berkshire: "No relief is given to the Labourer in increase of wages, but relief is given in case of sickness, where there is a large family, and frequently some linen"; or, from two parishes in Warwickshire: "No; but sometimes a pair of shoes, a round frock, or pair of sheets; seldom, unless two or three children"; "No allowance is made except they are in distress, and then according to circumstances." These are of course selected troublesome examples, and most replies state clearly: "No work done for Individuals is paid for by the Parish. Allowance to all Families, beginning at the third Child, at 1*s.* 6*d.* per week." Still, one in twenty answers is equivocal in one way or the other and in such cases a judgment had to be made, sometimes on the basis of other answers to the circular. In addition, it is possible that many parishes simply would not admit to subsidising wages for fear of implying that wages were below minimum standards in their district. In short, the tabulated replies cannot claim to be of statistical value; all that can be claimed is that they are more meaningful than nine volumes of untabulated replies or than the method of selecting quotations from the circular that was used in drawing up the *Report of 1834*.

The following is an explanation of the table on pages 42 and 43. From the "Instructions from the Central Board to the Assistant Commissioners," it appears that the country was divided into twenty-six districts, each Assistant Commissioner being assigned to one district to visit as many parishes as he could manage in the allotted time. The "Rural Queries" were sent out by each Assistant Commissioner in the middle of August 1832, and most of them were returned by January 1833, some four months later.[8] Replies were returned for over 10 per cent of the 15,000 parishes in England and Wales, containing about 20 per cent of the population; but it is impossible to know how many parishes were actually visited by the Assistant Commissioners.

For purposes of making comparisons with previous data furnished in the earlier article, I have divided the counties once again into two groups. Speenhamland and non-Speenhamland, listing them in order of their *per capita* poor-relief expenditures in 1831. The twelve counties of Wales are treated as a separate county. The total number of parishes in a county and the total number of parishes replying to the questionnaire were given in the reports submitted by the Assistant Commissioners. So was the total population of the county, as well as the population of the reporting parishes. Columns 2 and 3, considered together, convey some notion of the representativeness of the reporting parishes.

We do not know, of course, on what basis the reporting parishes were selected, and we certainly cannot assume that they constituted anything like a random sample of the total number of parishes. Initially, one questionnaire was sent out to rural parishes. After a trial run, the wording of the questions was slightly altered and a few new questions were added. At some point, a "Town Query" was added to the "Rural Query" with yet another set of questions. In the following table, the answers to the "Town Query" are separately enumerated. Unfortunately, it proved impossible to determine the population of every town, so that the figures for county populations include the population of towns in the county. Column 6 gives the percentage of reporting parishes that testified to the existence of disguised unemployment in their district. It is the outcome of a comparison between the replies to Question 4: "Number of labourers sufficient for the proper cultivation of land?" and Question 5 "Number of agricultural labourers?" When the numerical answer to Question 5 exceeded the numbers reported under Question 4, or when a non-numerical answer to either question left no doubt as to the answer, the parish was counted as one in which there was disguised unemployment, defined as a situation in which the number of workers employed on the land is greater than the number actually required to produce the current product.

Columns 7 and 8 have already been explained. Under Column 9, referring to Question 25: "Is relief given according to any and what scale?" only those parishes which stated that they scaled relief according to the price of bread or according to the prices of foodstuffs in general were counted as answering affirmatively. Many parishes misunderstood the question and answered: "1s. 6d. per head for every child above four if the wages amount to 10s. per week"; or "Our scale of relief is 1s. 9d. per head per week for all children above three in the family." Answers of this type are covered under Column 8, rather than Column 9. Columns 10 and 11 have reference to the methods of sharing the unemployed among rate-payers. With the Roundsman System, the parish ordered every occupier of property in the district to employ relief applicants at a wage fixed by the parish, the employer being repaid all that he advanced beyond a certain sum. This was the Speenhamland System pure and simple, which disguised unemployment by encouraging farmers to use more labour than they needed. Under the Labour Rate, the ratepayers agreed among themselves to employ and pay a certain share of the available labour in the district, the share being proportionate to the rates paid in each case. Those who did not employ their full complement were forced to pay an additional rate. Since the occupiers of property were also the only ratepayers, the two systems differed little, except that in the latter case an additional arbitrary element was introduced because the rates were not assessed simply on the basis of the market value of the property. Column 12 contains the answers to Question 29: "Are married men better paid than single men?" Many parishes did not need to make payments to large families because farmers

Table 1

Speenham-land Counties	Total No. of Rural Parishes (1)	Percentage of Rural Parishes Reporting (2)	Total County Population in 1831 (in 000's) (3)	Percentage of Population Reporting (4)	Poor Relief per Head in 1831 (s. d.) (5)	Percentage of Reporting Parishes ...							
						With Disguised Unemployment (6)	Giving Allowances in-Aid-of-Wages (7)	Giving Children Allowances (8)	Using Bread Scale (9)	Using Roundsman System (10)	Using Labour Rate (11)	Paying More to Married Men (12)	With Declining Productivity of Labour (13)
Sussex	313	27	275	69	19.4	64	6	82	22	4	14	25	65
Bucks.	230	16	148	23	18.7	69	17	71	9	11	17	46	51
Suffolk	525	10	299	20	18.4	72	10	74	34	0	14	40	34
Essex	413	12	321	31	17.2	64	8	66	44	0	12	8	48
Oxford.	298	10	154	42	16.11	62	10	72	28	14	28	48	41
Beds.	141	12	96	12	16.11	44	6	19	19	6	44	50	50
Northants.	343	5	181	9	16.10	67	11	67	17	22	33	50	44
Wilts.	374	8	243	20	16.9	55	35	72	55	14	14	14	59
Berks.	222	16	147	27	15.9	70	3	73	63	13	27	50	53
Norfolk	753	6	394	10	15.4	61	17	49	34	9	12	42	54
Hunts.	107	13	54	18	15.3	62	8	54	54	0	15	54	31
Cambs.	169	25	145	34	13.8	65	7	51	37	5	23	33	54
York, E.R.	365	3	206	5	11.11	70	30	60	0	20	0	0	20
Leicester.	339	5	199	12	11.7	56	17	33	0	11	0	17	39
Dorset	305	5	161	7	11.5	19	13	44	38	0	13	13	63
Warwicks.	255	15	340	26	9.7	50	11	60	13	24	13	8	18
Devon	475	5	500	6	9.0	50	8	67	0	4	17	0	33
York, N.R.	537	2	193	5	8.9	42	17	42	0	25	8	8	33
Notts.	269	10	228	27	6.6	43	4	4	0	11	29	4	18
Total Group	6,432	9	4,263	21	13.8	60	11	61	27	8	17	27	46

Non-Speenhamland Counties	1	2	3	4	5	6	7	8	9	10	11	12	13
Kent	421	13	484	25	14.5	53	21	49	2	2	12	21	32
Hants.	342	16	318	31	13.10	68	12	74	40	0	9	32	54
Herts.	147	13	145	23	13.2	67	6	17	6	17	11	17	16
Hereford.	274	7	112	13	11.4	23	0	42	0	0	11	5	47
Lincoln.	727	3	321	6	11.0	45	5	20	0	5	10	10	30
Surrey	146	18	491	12	10.11	48	0	55	10	3	0	14	76
Middx.	80	1	1,373	0.6	10.1	100	0	0	0	0	0	0	67
Westmorl.	116	17	56	5	9.8	38	0	24	0	0	25	0	14
Rutland	56	7	19	5	9.1	50	0	0	0	50	8	8	0
Somerset	493	5	409	16	8.10	40	16	64	24	4	21	14	28
Gloucester.	425	7	391	18	8.8	32	18	46	32	4	5	0	71
Salop.	275	7	225	23	8.2	41	0	9	0	14	11	0	32
Worcester.	241	8	214	49	7.6	47	21	32	0	16	11	4	37
Wales	1,182	4	815	16	7.2	18	16	33	0	2	11	11	16
Durham	297	13	257	49	6.10	47	3	5	0	11	20	20	8
Cornwall	212	15	304	19	6.8	57	3	30	0	27	14	14	30
Derby.	331	2	240	0	6.8	57	14	29	0	29	14	7	43
Stafford.	345	4	415	13	6.6	71	6	14	0	29	14	6	14
Chester	500	3	338	2	6.3	50	0	6	0	5	19	0	19
Northumb.	524	4	181	13	6.3	7	6	10	3	5	15	6	5
York. W.R.	666	9	987	36	5.7	52	0	21	0	3	3	0	16
Cumberl.	294	16	172	26	5.6	23	3	6	0	0	4	9	2
Monmouth	157	6	99	13	5.5	0	0	0	0	0	22	0	22
Lancaster	444	4	1,352	4	4.5	11	0	16	0	5	5	5	26
Total Group	5,104	13	9,720	15	8.7	45	7	31	7	6	10	10	30
Parishes in Towns	3,999	9	3,348.0 (in towns)	—	8.4	—	31 (Q.30)	7 (Q.30)	2	—	—	—	—

in the district already paid more to married men than to single men. A parish that answered "Yes" to both Column 12 and Column 8 would be admitting that wages in the district were below the minimum necessary to raise a family. Lastly, Column 13 gives the result of asking Question 37: "Is the industry of the labourers in your neighbourhood supposed to be increasing or diminishing?"

The first thing that strikes us about the results is that all the familiar features of the Old Poor Law are found more often in the Speenhamland counties than in the rest of the country. Next, the striking difference appears, not in the policy of supplementing wages, but in the payment of allowances to large families. Only 11 per cent of the Speenhamland counties and 7 per cent of the non-Speenhamland counties paid allowances-in-aid-of-wages. The worst culprits in the Speenhamland group were not Sussex, Bedfordshire, and Buckinghamshire, as one might expect, but Wiltshire and the East Riding of Yorkshire. In the non-Speenhamland group, Kent and Worcester were almost as bad. A surprisingly large percentage of the town parishes practised the Speenhamland policy; but it ought to be pointed out that of the 113 town parishes that answered "Yes" to Question 30 (Column 7), 47 were in London. Allowances for children were certainly in common use: two out of three Speenhamland counties and one out of three non-Speenhamland counties made such payments.[9] One out of four Speenhamland counties related family allowances to the cost of living, but in the non-Speenhamland group it was only significant in Hampshire, Gloucestershire, and Somersetshire. The Roundsman System and the Labour Rate were rarely found anywhere — a finding that will surprise readers of the *Report of 1834*. Other methods of relieving the unemployed — as, for example, by setting them to work on public roads — were unfortunately not adequately enumerated in the answers to the queries. Only one in ten non-Speenhamland counties paid more to married men than to single men, but one in four Speenhamland counties did so; and the practice of paying more to men with children seemed everywhere to be associated with the policy of family allowances.

Lastly, there is the finding that about half of the parishes in both groups of counties reported the existence of disguised unemployment. This fact was very much played down in the *Report*, which denied that there was any excess labour in the countryside: the "appearance" of an excess was merely the result of the declining productivity of labour in consequence of lavish relief.

The counties are listed in each group in the order of relief spending per head in 1831. This immediately raises the question whether any of the columns 6 to 13 show a similar trend, in which case we may be a little wiser about the causes of variations in relief expenditures. Applying a non-parametric ranking test for trend, a test which assumes nothing about the mathematical properties of the trend line or about the character of the population distribution, it turns out that the only columns which show a significant tendency to decline along with *per capita* poor relief are Columns 8 and 9. It seems that family allowances, particularly when scaled in accordance with the prices of foodstuffs, were largely responsible for variations in the relief expenditures per head between counties. We may notice in passing that no discernible relationship emerged between the percentage of parishes supplementing wages of married men (Columns 7 and 8) and the percentage reporting that "the industry" of workers was diminishing (Column 13). This is in direct contradiction to the claim of the *Report of 1834*:

One of the questions circulated by us in the rural districts was, whether the labourers in the respondent's neighbourhood were supposed to be better or worse workmen than formerly? If the answers to this question had been uniformly unfavourable, they might have been ascribed to the general tendency to depreciate what is present; but it will be found, on referring to our Appendix, that the replies vary according to the poor-law administration of the district. Where it is good, the replies are, "much the same," "never were better . . ." But when we come within the influence of the allowance and the scale, the replies are "they are much degenerated . . . they work unwillingly and wastefully."[10]

That is not to say that answers to Question 37 (Column 13) should be taken too seriously. After all, the overseers and vestrymen making the replies were economic amateurs and their answers in this case depended almost wholly on their social outlook and personal experiences. Just as often as not, they held both that productivity was improving due to better health and nutrition and that it was deteriorating because of the increase of beershops.

At this point, we may probe further by regrouping the counties in the manner of the earlier article. First, there is the well-established division between the high-wage counties of the north and the low-wage counties of the south.[11] Secondly, there is the distinction between agricultural counties and industrial counties. According to the definition of the first occupational census of 1811, an "agricultural county" is one where the majority of families derive their income from agricultural pursuits. There were fifteen such counties in 1831, and of these Herefordshire, Hertfordshire, Lincolnshire, and Rutland were not Speenhamland counties. Defining an "industrial county" as one where the majority of families derive their income from non-agricultural pursuits, there were twenty-two counties of this type in England and Wales in 1831 and none of these were Speenhamland counties. That leaves seventeen "mixed counties," where the proportion of families dependent on agriculture for their livelihood was above the national average for 1831, but in which non-agricultural occupations nevertheless loomed important. This "mixed" group includes six Speenhamland counties: Devonshire, Leicestershire, Northamptonshire, Nottinghamshire, and the East and North Riding of Yorkshire.[12] In other words, whereas no harm is done if we think of the Speenhamland counties as "agricultural," it would be misleading to label the non-Speenhamland counties purely and simply "industrial."

Regrouping the counties accordingly, we reach the following results:

Table 2

Groups of Countries	6	7	8	9	10	11	12	13
Speenhamland	60	11	61	27	10	17	27	46
Non-Speenhamland	45	7	31	7	9	10	10	30
Northern	42	7	15	0	13	10	6	19
Southern	52	10	49	21	8	16	22	42
Agricultural	56	11	57	30	11	20	31	44
Mixed	45	9	35	7	11	12	8	31
Industrial	47	7	28	6	9	9	8	33
National Average	50	9	38	14	10	14	16	37

As we might expect, it is only southern agricultural counties that score above the national average on every count. It is startling to note once again how widespread was the feeling, fancied or real, that there was much disguised unemployment. Rural parishes in industrial counties reported almost as much of it as parishes in agricultural counties. Furthermore, wage subsidies to employed workers were not much more frequent in the south than in the north, but family allowances in conjunction with a bread-scale were certainly more prevalent in southern agricultural counties. The Roundsman System had totally disappeared in the north, but some industrial counties south of the line from the Severn to the Wash still indulged in it. Similarly, the Labour Rate was somewhat more frequently encountered in southern agricultural districts, and so was the practice of paying more to married men. Finally, the Commissioners might have drawn some comfort from the fact that, taking groups of counties at a time, the extent to which the productivity of labour was said to be declining does correspond to the number of parishes in each group resorting to the relief policies they so much deplored. But as we noted earlier, this relationship is not found between counties within the groups.

At the end of our examination of the questionnaire we come back to the conclusion reached in the earlier article: the relatively higher level of relief per head in the so-called Speenhamland counties was due, not to the "snowball effect" of the Old Poor Law, but to the chronic unemployment and substandard wages typical of areas specialising in the production of wheat and lacking alternative opportunities in industry. The relatively heavier burden of the rates in these districts was the result of the policy of giving allowances to families with children. In most cases, the allowance was so modest that it came within the cardinal rule the Commissioners laid down for the New Poor Law: "his [the relief applicant's] situation shall not be made really or apparently so eligible as the situation of the independent labourer of the lowest class." There is no doubt that children allowances were given only where wages were below the national average: a very high negative correlation is found between agricultural wages in each county collected by Bowley from other questions in the Rural Query,[13] and the percentage of parishes providing family allowance ($r = 0.86$ at the 5 per cent level of significance).

Correlation is one thing and causality is another. The *Report of 1834* would have us believe that the causal chain ran from outdoor relief to low wages. On the weight of the evidence, however, it is more reasonable to think that low wages were the cause and outdoor relief to large families the effect. It is true, of course, that low wages are the result of low productivity and that low productivity may be produced by low wages. But this is not to say that supplements to low wages necessarily bring about a decline in productivity and therefore a fall in wages, which is what the Commissioners were arguing. When wages are below the biological minimum, the usual economic relationship between productivity and wages is reversed: the effort of workers now depends on their wages instead of wages depending on their efforts. Under these circumstances, a supplement to wages raises the consumption and hence the energy and productivity of the work force and thereby justifies an increase in wages. It represents one of those exceptional cases in economic life where we seem to get something for nothing. We have seen direct evidence that wages of agricultural workers in England and Wales between 1795 and 1834 were generally below subsistence standards.[14] Furthermore, the very existence of a pool of chronically unemployed labour in the English countryside under the Old Poor Law creates the presumption that wages were inadequate to meet minimum caloric requirements: when wages are sufficient to permit each man to supply a maximum effort per unit of time, automatic market forces will tend to eliminate unemployment by driving down wage rates. In short, British agriculture in 1834 was a classic case of underemployment in backward economies.

Where the *Poor Law Report* went wrong was in its assessment of the causes of agricultural unemployment; its recommendations might have been appropriate at a later date, but they were hopelessly inappropriate to the conditions that prevailed in 1834. The evidence they collected in the town and rural queries should have taught the Commissioners that they had misinterpreted the consequences of the Old Poor Law. But their minds were made up, and where they did not ignore the findings, they twisted them to suit their preconceived opinions. The *Report of 1834* is not only a "wildly unhistorical document," as Tawney once said, but also a wildly unstatistical one.

APPENDIX
THE SIZE OF PARISHES

When I concluded in the earlier article that the higher levels of relief per head in the Speenhamland counties were due to an excess supply of labour coupled with the lack of alternative employment possibilities, I conceded at one point that another and much simpler explanation might account for the facts: "The *Report of 1834* presented some evidence to show that small parishes, measured in terms of population per acre, granted more relief per head than large parishes, the reason being that the intimate personal connections between overseers and farm hands in small parishes invited prodigality. If this were so, the high rates of relief per head in southern rural counties might be due to the fact that most of the 1,000 parishes under fifty inhabitants and most of the 6,000 parishes under three hundred inhabitants were located in southern agricultural districts. To test this hypothesis, we would have to examine the size distribution of parishes among counties, a question which cannot be entered into here."

I avoided testing this hypothesis at the time for fear of cluttering an already complicated argument. This proved to be a tactical error, because a number of my readers seized upon this concession as hinting at what they took to be the true explanation of the heavy relief burden in certain counties. The purpose of this appendix is to close this loophole in my thesis.

The relevant evidence is to be found in Supplement No. 2 of the *Report of 1834*, which gives the population per parish and township in every county in the census year 1831 for fifteen uneven class-intervals. To test the hypothesis, I have aggregated the counties under various headings and reduced the class-intervals to thirteen. I had hoped initially to supplement this information by data on the acreage per parish, but it proved impossible to obtain this material for all parishes. In what follows, therefore, the size of a parish is measured by the number of residents and not by the population density per acre.

There were 15,535 parishes in England and Wales, having a population in 1831 of almost 14 million. The mean population per parish was 898, but the median parish contained 368 residents. With the median so far below

Appendix Table 1

Population per Parish	England and Wales	Speen- hamland Counties	Non- Speen- hamland Counties	Agri- cultural	Mixed Counties	Industrial Counties
Under 50	737	292	445	214	279	244
50-100	1,170	416	754	393	476	301
100-300	4,774	1,848	2,926	1,762	2,080	932
300-500	3,121	1,295	1,826	1,349	1,226	546
500-800	2,232	870	1,362	987	689	556
800-1,000	816	293	513	333	245	228
1-2,000	1,543	489	1,054	584	418	441
2-3,000	437	109	328	128	158	151
3-4,000	209	63	146	60	73	76
4-5,000	133	26	107	42	39	52
5-10,000	245	29	216	26	75	144
10-50,000	118	9	109	7	10	101
Over 50,000	10	1	9	0	0	10
Total parishes	15,535	5,748	9,787	5,983	5,740	3,812
Total population (in thousands)	13,952	3,558	10,394	3,691	4,043	6,318
Arithmetic mean population per parish	898	632	1,060	534	704	1,683
Median population per parish	368	348	384	394	306	428

the mean, it is apparent that the distribution was sharply skewed to the right: a few counties, namely, Lancashire, Middlesex, Surrey, Warwickshire, and the West Riding of Yorkshire contained most of the large urban parishes with populations of 10,000 or more. About 36 per cent of all parishes were located in the seventeen Speenhamland counties, having an average of 632 inhabitants per parish. The remaining parishes in the thirty-seven non-Speenhamland counties had an average population of 1,060, due to the presence of 116 giant urban parishes.

If we are to explain the higher levels of relief per head in certain counties by the small size of the average parish in these counties, the divergence in size from the national average ought to be striking. But the median parish in the Speenhamland counties is only a little below the median for the country as a whole, and if "typical" means modal or more frequently found than any other size, the typical parish in all counties contained one hundred to three hundred people. Even if we select the nine notorious Speenhamland counties (see map on p. 9), it turns out that 50 per cent of the parishes in these counties had no more than 368 residents, a median exactly equal to the national median. And Sussex — that favourite example of the critics of the Old Poor Law, being the county with the highest *per capita* relief burden in England — had a mean population per parish of 847 and a median parish size of 320, neither figure being significantly different from that of England as a whole. It seems, therefore, that we ought to reject the hypothesis that the prevalence of small parishes in what we have called the Speenhamland counties made for a high relief bill. Since the original hypothesis is itself somewhat vague — how small must a parish be for a magistrate to know a relief recipient by name and circumstance? — we shall have to be satisfied with this impressionistic conclusion.

NOTES

1. See Chapter 1. A version of this chapter was read at a Symposium on Victorian Affairs, held under the joint sponsorship of the American Council of Learned Societies and of Indiana University, at that University, in March 1962. The stimulating discussion that followed the reading of the paper led me to pursue my argument in the present article. I wish to thank all the participants of the Symposium for their suggestions and, particularly, R. G. Cowherd, for his helpful comments in private correspondence.
2. *Report of the Poor Law Commission, 1834* (9), XXVII, pp. 11, 25, 35, 44.
3. *Ibid.*, p. 2.
4. See Chapter 1, p. 11.
5. *Poor Law Report*, p. 12 (my italics).
6. *Ibid.*, Supplement No. 1, pp. 207-15. I was not aware of the existence of this supplement when I wrote the earlier article. I had been using one of the many reprints of the *Report of 1834*, all of which unexplainably omitted this supplement.
7. *Ibid.*, p. 212.
8. *Ibid.*, p. 2.
9. It turns out, however, that only 0.2 per cent of the parishes in England and Wales made payments for the first two children, and even in those cases there were usually other children in the family under ten years of age.
10. *Poor Law Report*, p. 68.
11. See Chapter 1, p. 17.
12. For a convenient list of the three groups of counties, see P. Deane and W. A. Cole, *British Economic Growth, 1688-1915* (Cambridge, 1962), p. 103.
13. See Chapter 1, Appendix E.
14. *Ibid.*, pp. 11-13.

3 The Productivity of Capital in the Lancashire Cotton Industry during the Nineteenth Century

The growth of the Lancashire cotton industry has supplied generations of historians with illustrative material to depict labour-saving technical change. Capital-saving innovations, it is said, were hardly very important until the close of the nineteenth century. Whatever the facts for the modern period, technical improvements in the heyday of the cotton industry surely raised not only capital per man but also capital per unit of output. In the absence of reliable statistics on the capital stock this can only be surmised, but this view is not on that account any less widely held.

Shall we ever be able to verify such beliefs? We have few enough overall estimates of capital formation in Great Britain prior to 1865 and even those for the latter half of the century are not broken down into individual sectors other than residential housing, railways and utilities.[2]

For manufacturing there are in fact no data to indicate the rate of growth of the capital stock in any particular industry. The cotton industry, however, proves to be a singular exception to this generalisation: here we have a number of contemporary estimates by informed observers for six benchmark years between 1834 and 1886. Moreover, owing to the provisions of the Factory Act of 1833, increases in capacity in this industry can be gauged by the returns of spindles, looms, and motive-power installed. The annual value of output of the industry can be computed with a fair degree of accuracy for purposes of comparison to the trends in capital and labour. With the aid of the capital and labour coefficients it may be possible to go beyond the purely descriptive treatment of technical change which characterises so much of the literature on the history of the cotton manufacture. Although no industry has been so frequently investigated and written about as the cotton industry, surprisingly little is known about productivity changes in spinning and weaving.

I

According to the 1841 census classification, the cotton industry included all persons employed in the preparation and spinning of raw cotton into

51

yarn and the weaving of yarn into cloth: in 1834 this would have meant some 200,000 factory operatives in England, another 35,000 in Scotland and Ireland, and approximately 200,000 hand-loom weavers. But the early historians of the industry, such as Edward Baines and Andrew Ure, would have included an additional 237,000 persons employed in bleaching, dyeing, calico-printing and the manufacture of lace and hosiery. Other writers were wont to add cotton warehousemen, cotton textile engineers, yarn agents, cloth merchants, and even cotton brokers and dealers.

For my purpose the narrow product-classification of the 1841 census is to be preferred. Quantitive information about the finishing branch of the industry is hard to come by; the finishing of cloth was carried on quite separately from the manufacturing process and was not brought under legislative control until the 1860s. As much is true of lacemaking and hosiery where the bulk of output was still being produced by outworkers or in small workshops as late as 1870. Furthermore, not all hosiery and lace products were made of cotton; in the 1830s they were more often made of silk and wool.[3] The merchanting section, on the other hand, is clearly outside my purview. Hence, for practical reasons, I follow present custom in defining the Lancashire cotton industry as bounded at one end by the Liverpool cotton exchange and at the other end by the Manchester market for unbleached cloth, sold "in the grey". But insofar as imperfect statistics allow we shall have occasion to allude to the cotton industry as a whole, inclusive of the finishing section.

In summary form, the findings are as follows:

Table 1

	1834	1856	1860	1871	1886
Total capital — £m.	22	45.5	57	87	83
Fixed capital — £m.	15	31	35	57	58
Ten year moving average of net output — £m.	11	18	17	28	28
Total capital (constant prices)	22	43	56	85	109
Fixed capital (constant prices)	15	30	34	56	76
Man-hours — m. hrs. p.a.	1570	1254	1432	1404	1586
Ten year moving average of real output — £m.	11	31	24	42	58
Total capital/net output	2.0	2.5	3.3	3.1	3.0
Fixed capital/net output	1.4	1.7	2.1	2.0	2.1
Capital/output (constant prices)	2.0	1.4	2.3	2.0	1.9
Fixed capital/output (constant prices)	1.4	0.9	1.4	1.3	1.3
Man-hours/real output	143	40	34	33	27
Real capital/man-hours	0.014	0.03	0.04	0.06	0.06

Expressed in current prices, capital invested per unit of (net) output shows a marked rise up to 1860, followed by a gentle decline down to 1886.

The ratio of fixed capital to (net) output likewise ceases to rise in the years after 1860. It is evident that the period 1860-86 was marked by significant economies in the use of working capital. But so long as capital and output are measured in current prices there is no way of distinguishing between a fall in the capital-output ratio caused by pecuniary rather than technical economies, by forces external to rather than internal to the industry. Lower equipment prices owing to improvements in the machine goods industry, or, say, lower freight charges and reductions in delivery time produced by technological progress in transportation, will release capital in cotton just as effectively as factor-saving innovations in spinning and weaving. For this reason I have made an attempt to deflate both capital and output. And when both numerator and denominator are measured in constant prices, no rise whatever in the ratio of capital to output is revealed over the whole period: apparently, the price of yarn and grey cloth fell faster than that of machinery and building materials. This finding is particularly striking in view of the fact that the rate of growth of physical output slackened in the 1870s, with the onset of "the great depression".

The cotton industry as a whole exhibits very much the same tendency manifested in the spinning and weaving section. Estimates of the capital invested in the three main branches of the finishing trade are available for some years. The results for the industry, defined in the inclusive sense, are given here for comparison to spinning and weaving.

Table 2

	1834	1845	1856	1860	1886
Total capital — £m.	34	47	75.5	87	108
Ten years m.a. of net output — £m.	29	31	39	35	62
Total capital/net output	1.2	1.5	1.9	2.5	1.7
Capital/output (constant prices)	1.2	1.2	1.1	1.5	1.1

In the earlier period (1834-60) the course of technical change seems to conform to the labour-saving bias popularly attributed to nineteenth-century development. Not only did the working capital-output ratio rise but labour inputs per unit of output fell violently, reflecting the steady contraction and eventual disappearance of the hand-loom weaving trade. But as the average productivity of capital began to rise after 1860, the productivity of labour grew less rapidly, so that the capital per man-hour increased but slightly. Without venturing upon any recondite classification of innovations, we may conclude that the data indicates that capital-saving improvements were prevalent in the decades following the "cotton famine".[4] Indeed, if we could assume that the underlying production functions show diminishing returns to scale we might have concluded that capital-saving innovations predominated throughout the fifty-year period. For such production functions, capital accumulation necessarily raises capital per unit of output; technical change which is biased towards labour-saving improvements cannot offset the upward tendency of the capital-output ratio in constant prices. But we have seen that, on the contrary, the ratio exhibits remarkable stability over the period under consideration. Without pressing this point it is clear that, whatever the nature of the underlying production functions, the slant of technical change *after* 1860 was largely capital-saving. The upward trend in labour's share of net output after 1860 supports this inference.[5] It is interesting to note that the aggregate capital coefficient of the British economy as a whole also declined from 3.7 in the 1870s to 3.3 in the 1890s.[6]

II

The materials and methods of estimation are described in the appendices — but some general remarks about the character of the data is in order before proceeding to discuss their implications.

1. The figures for fixed capital are based upon estimates, sometimes by several independent observers, of the average current value per spindle and per loom of separate spinning and weaving mills; they include the value of land-rights, buildings, machinery, steam engine, and shafting. This ignores the possibility that the capital value per machine in combining spinning and weaving concerns, accounting for about one out of every three or four cotton mills, may have been quite different from those of specialised mills. The problem is aggravated by the fact that the practice of combining yarn and cloth production in one factory grew rapidly between 1825 and 1856 and then declined in relative importance.[7] It is, however, impossible to assess the importance of this deficiency in the data.

2. The figures for working capital must be treated with more caution than the corresponding figures for fixed capital. The standard method of estimating the stock of working capital was to apply an average turnover rate to the flow of annual outlays on wages and raw cotton. Estimates of the turnover rate are difficult to verify. Apparently, the level of raw cotton stocks, not only in the hands of spinners and dealers but also in the ports, was responsible for the prevailing impression that working capital turned over two or three times a year.[8] In a few cases, it was possible to check estimates of fixed plus working capital by applying capital-labour ratios obtained from surveys of particular districts or from small samples of mills. Some available estimates had to be discarded as not subject to any independent verification.

3. All the capital estimates, with the possible exception of the 1871

figures, value buildings and equipment at current prices, net of depreciation. Depreciation quotas seem to have varied little over the period under consideration. Detailed cost statements for individual mills in the 1830s and in the 1880s show a standard charge of 7.5 per cent for replacement of machinery and 2.5 per cent for maintenance of buildings and steam engines.[9] This seems hard to believe but accounting practices are notoriously slow to alter. (Of course, the effect of falling prices through 1815-52 and 1874-86 was to raise the real value of depreciation allowances.) At any rate, if depreciation equalled replacement, capital can be assumed to have grown at the same rate in gross as in net terms. The ratio of gross capital to gross product, however, does not reveal the two-phase movement of the capital to net output ratio: it rose continuously over the half-century under review; fixed capital per unit of gross product, on the other hand, increased only up to 1871. This is due to the fact that total output at first grew faster and then fell behind net output.

The differential rates of growth of gross and net output were due, not to alterations in techniques of production, but to swings in the gap between the prices of raw cotton and finished cloth under the pressure of changing demand and supply conditions abroad. The capital to gross output ratio, measured in constant prices, once again shows a slight decline throughout the period under review.

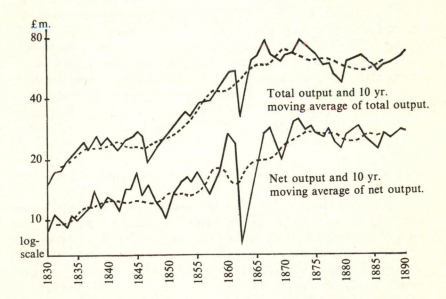

Total output and 10 yr. moving average of total output.

Net output and 10 yr. moving average of net output.

4. Ideally, the benchmark years for which we have capital estimates should occupy the same position in the trade cycle so as not to distort the

calculation of the long-term trend. On balance, it would seem that the benchmark estimates are sufficiently comparable in cyclical position, taking into account the long-lived character of fixtures and implements.

1834 — about midway between trough and peak
1845 — cyclical peak
1856 — about midway between trough and peak
1860 — cyclical peak
1871 — about midway between trough and peak
1886 — slightly past cyclical trough

5. Continuous series for textile machine prices are not available prior to 1885. Hence, capital was deflated by means of a subsitute index of the price level of capital goods. Prior to 1870, it was necessary to resort to an index of wholesale prices.[10] I do not think that this produces a serious bias in the results. Broadly speaking, an index of capital goods prices will vary in the same proportion as an index of prices in general if technical change in the economy as a whole is neutral. For an overall labour-saving slant in technical progress implies that cost-reductions are concentrated in the finishing stages of production; hence, the prices of consumer goods fall faster than machine prices. The reverse is true when technical change is largely capital-saving. By identifying machine prices with wholesale prices I have in fact assumed that productivity rose equally in all sectors of the economy, an absurd assumption to be sure but the most plausible under the circumstances. To argue that the machine goods industry always led the race for technical advances is to make the strong assumption of an overall capital-saving bias in technical change, since *all* cost-reductions in the making of machines release capital involved in the use of machines. If, on the other hand, we assumed that technical change was predominantly labour-saving over the whole of the fifty years 1834-86 we would have to suppose that machine prices lagged behind in the sharp fall of the general price level after 1873. In that case we would reach a still lower real capital-output ratio for the end of our period that is shown above. The same conclusion holds if we accept the argument that any index of machine prices should be given an upward trend to take account of the improved quality of equipment.

6. Real output is estimated as follows: first, the weight of yarn produced is derived by deducting the loss of weight in spinning — the unsaleable short fibres removed by the carding engines — from official statistics of retained imports of raw cotton adjusted for changes in total stocks. An allowance is made for the fact that the proportion of "waste" was permanently reduced in the 1860s due to the improved quality of imported cotton and the more careful preparation of fibre. The weight of piece goods produced is then derived by deducting the weight of yarn exports from the volume of yarn produced. The resulting series for yarn consumed in the

weaving branch of the industry is equated to the weight of grey cloth manufactured, although in fact the weight of yarn was somewhat increased in the weaving process by the application of sizing to reduce friction in the power-looms. In addition, an indeterminate amount of yarn was absorbed by the cotton thread, hosiery and lace trades. There is some tenatative evidence to suggest a secular increase in the relative importance of these consumers of cotton yarn, at least up to the late 1870s.[11] To that extent, the rate of growth of output of grey cloth was less, and the trend in the real capital-output ratio was greater, than is indicated above.

7. The money value of output is obtained by multiplying the volume of cloth produced by the average price of grey cloth quoted on the Manchester market, to which is added the value of yarn exports as declared by British shippers. Net output is derived by deducting the value of raw cotton consumed. Cotton was of course only one of the raw materials used up, albeit the most important. Oil, leather, flour, tallow, and coal were others; in addition, there were fixed expenses for depreciation, interest on borrowed capital, rents, local rates, taxes and insurance. Unfortunately, there are no aggregate figures for these expenditures in any year during the nineteenth century. Thus, the figures for net output presented here are in excess of the true value added. But whether the upward trend in net value added was greater or lesser than that of net output so-called we cannot say.

8. The output of finished piece goods, as distinct from grey cloth, consists of the known value of piece goods exports and the estimated value of the home trade. The pounds' weight of goods retained for the home market is obtained by deducting the volume of goods exported, as recorded in the trade accounts, from the volume of grey cloth produced. There are no reliable price-series for finished goods other than the average declared value of exports. According to common opinion at the time, cotton piece goods sold at home were of better quality and hence dearer than goods shipped abroad. It was often held that the average price of home traded fabrics was about a third above that of exported goods. I have followed contemporary practice in estimating the value of the home trade accordingly. Some observers thought that there had been a secular increase in the magnitude of this price-differential.[12] This would produce an even sharper fall in the capital-output ratio for the industry as a whole between 1860 and 1886 than is shown above.

9. Net output is estimated once again by deducting cotton consumption from gross output. The movements in the two net output series — that of grey cloth and that of finished piece goods — is remarkably similar both in cyclical turning points and in secular rates of growth. Still, there is every reason to believe that such improvements as the introduction of aniline dyes and the complete replacement of block-printing by cylinder printing must in time have reduced the finishing-margins. In the absence of reliable

evidence on the cost of finishing such tendencies are ignored in our net output series. But we err on the side of scepticism: cost-reducing improvements in finishing would lead to a rate of growth of value added in excess of the rate of growth of net output so-called. This would mean that the "true" capital-output ratio for the industry as a whole fell even more than our figures suggest.

III

The trends in capital, labour and output are compared below with the increase of capacity as revealed by the Factory Returns, all expressed in percentage changes from the base 1834.

The break in the upward trend of the capital-output ratio which occurred in the 1860s suggests a qualitative change in the technical structure of the cotton industry. The obvious factor at work was the successful mechanisation of weaving, almost half a century after the introduction of the first practical power-loom. Frequent breakage of yarn from mechanical handling made the early power-looms expensive to operate and unsuitable for anything but the coarsest fabrics. It was not until the 1820s that steam-weaving began to threaten the hand industry. In 1834 there were still twice as many hand-looms as power-looms but thereafter the hand-loom trade fell off rapidly; by 1860, the stock of hand-looms numbered only 7,000. No startling improvements seem to have taken place in mechanical weaving during this period: the increased capacity of the power-looms was barely sufficient to make up for the decline in the volume of hand-woven cloth.

At the same time, spinning capacity was rising very much faster than spindleage, reflecting substantial improvements in technique. Spinning had been a factory industry since 1800. Nevertheless, partly hand-operated mules and jennies were still required for the spinning of finer yarn. It was the introduction of the self-acting mule, power-driven in every movement, which seems to be responsible for the rapid increase of productivity in the spinning section. Patented in 1792 it had not been sufficiently perfected to make it practical before 1825 or thereabouts. At first it had been adapted to medium counts. Further refinements in the 1860s made it suitable for virtually all counts.

Differences in the tempo of productivity advances in the spinning and in the weaving section show up in the trend of product-prices. Between 1830 and 1860 the price of plain piece goods exports declined at almost the same rate as that of yarn exports, suggesting that weaving costs remained relatively constant. Output data for yarn and cloth, after 1860, once again show a rising trend in production per spindle without a corresponding increase in the production of cloth per loom.[14]

Table 3

	1834	1839	1845	1850	1856	1860	1861	1867	1870	1871	1874	1878	1886
Total capital	100	—	—	—	205	257	—	—	—	392	—	—	374
Fixed capital	100	—	—	—	210	236	—	—	—	373	—	2	371
Gross output	100	119	119	133	190	224	238	305	338	333	319	305	305
Net output	100	109	127	136	164	155	190	245	255	255	255	255	212
Wages bill	100	100	—	91	117	—	144	144	170	—	201	198	—
Real capital	100	—	—	—	194	252	—	—	—	386	—	—	491
Real fixed capital	100	—	—	—	200	230	—	—	—	386	—	—	513
Man-hours	100	90	01	85	80	—	91	80	90	—	95	96	100
Real output	100	121	210	202	315	399	422	380	426	484	500	445	569
Factories	100	158	—	167	181	—	250	221	215	—	230	232	228
Spindles	100	—	162	194	260	—	281	317	349	—	388	409	410
Power-looms	100	—	250	250	299	—	400	379	441	—	465	515	561
Hand-looms	100	67	30	21	12	0.04	—	—	—	—	—	—	—
Horse-power[13]	100	146	—	201	237	—	100	69	105	—	—	—	—

Table 4

	Yarn produced per spindle (lbs)	Cloth produced per loom (lbs)
1867	28	1950
1870	30	1880
1874	32	2110
1878	29	1810
1885	32	1850
1890	38	2130

The early period 1834-60 saw the introduction of a series of labour-saving innovations. There were conspicuous advances in the mechanical handling and preparation of raw cotton. In yarn manufacture, the self-acting mule eliminated the need for a highly skilled spinner who used to work one pair of the old hand mules, assisted by two or three children. The strong bargaining power of the adult spinners seems to have provided the chief stimulus for the introduction of the automatic mule.[15] One of its attendant benefits, however, was a greater evenness and strength of yarn, thereby reducing the time lost by breakage. As a result, the traverse of the mule was lengthened, the number of spindles in a single frame was raised and one man was made to work four instead of two carriages by "double-decking".[16] In weaving the same forces were at work. A hand-loom weaver could tent only one loom. When power-looms were first enumerated by the Factory Inspector in 1835, two looms per weaver was the usual number; by 1860 it had risen to 2.5-3; and by 1887 most weavers were tenting four looms.[17] This does not fully indicate the increased productivity of labour in the making of intricate designs — using the Jacquard device, a hand-loom weaver would have needed as many as three assistants.

The separate trends in labour-productivity in spinning and weaving cannot be determined statistically, owing to the failure of the Factory Inspectors to distinguish spinners from weavers in combined concerns. But if Ellison's estimates of the distribution of the cotton labour force between the two sectors is accepted, the figures for output per man-hour reveal a continuous rise, although at a diminishing rate, despite a 20 per cent reduction in hours worked.[18]

In contrast to the appearance of dramatic labour-saving devices, there were no inventions in the period that were themselves particularly capital-saving, barring ring-spinning which was not widely introduced in England until the 1890s. But the mechanisation of spinning and weaving required a smaller outlay of capital than might have been expected at first: for instance it was soon found that a hand-mule could be converted to a self-

Table 5

Three Year Averages	Spinners (000's)	Yarn produced (m. lbs) per man-hour of spinning	Weavers by hand and by power (000's)	Goods produced (m. lbs) per man-hour of weaving
1830	140	0.4	275	0.2
1845	190	0.8	210	0.7
1860	248	1.2	203	1.1
1881	240	1.9	246	1.5
1892	220	2.3	310	1.4

actor merely by replacement of the headstock, costing about one-fifth of the price of a new mule.[19] In addition, capital was being released continuouslyby the greater intensity of utilisation of the new equipment and by piecemeal improvements in their details of construction and accuracy of adjustment. In spinning more spindles were mounted on each carriage at little extra expense and their speed of working was steadily increased. At the time when Baines and Ure published their histories, 350-400 spindles per mule was the common number; both knew of some modern mills in which the mules already carried as many as 1,000 spindles. By the 1850s, 500 had become the average number; this rose to 750-900 by 1875, and in 1876 the upper limit of fifty years' earlier had become the norm. From 1839 to 1862 the number of revolutions per minute of mule spindles rose 20 per cent. No similar figures are available for the later years but there is no doubt that the same process made itself felt.[20] These developments rested in turn upon improvements in the carding and scutching engines, which cleaned the cotton, and the other preparing frames, such as the slubbers and rovers.[21] For instance, the adoption of "differential motion" for the slubbing and roving frames around 1850 markedly reduced the liability to breakage of yarn when subjected to high-speed spinning.

With yarn becoming more uniform in twist and wound more evenly on the cops, it became possible to raise speeds of working in weaving. The number of picks per minute — the standard measure of the number of throws of the shuttle — increased from about 100 in 1834 to 130 in 1850, to 175 in 1873, reaching 200 in 1885. The development of inventions like the automatic temple and weft-stop motion, which made their way slowly over the years, seem to have contributed towards the quickened pace of weaving.[22] "There are power-looms made today", wrote one observer in 1887, "which run more than double the speed of the power-looms fifty years ago, and ten times the speed of the hand-loom".[23]

It is true that greater speeds required the application of additional steam-power. But this was usually obtainable gratis from the increased pressure at which the old Watt engines were operated. Sometimes the addition of a boiler was sufficient to raise the work-duty of an engine by 50 per cent. At the same time, the extraction of more power from engines of a given bulk was accompanied by savings in fuel costs: coal consumption for a ten-hour day fell from 72 lbs. per horse-power in 1835 to 52 lbs. per horse-power in 1887.[24]

G. H. Wood, writing in 1910, concluded that the speeding-up of machinery in the cotton industry had proceeded at a compound rate of one per cent from 1833 on. At this rate it would take about 70 years to double the speed of operations. Everything else remaining the same, this alone would have cut in half the amount of working capital which had to be carried for a given output. The working capital-output ratio actually rose between 1834 and 1860, despite the reductions in inventories of yarn and the saving in time which must have accompanied the replacement of hand-loom weaving in scattered homes by power-weaving in factories. But from 1860 to 1886 the increased speeds at which mules and looms were run released capital tied up in goods-in-process: the working capital-net output ratio fell from 1.3 in 1860 to 0.8 in 1886. Faster ocean and railway carriage contributed to this result. Unfortunately, no separate statistics on the proportion of cotton stocks in the hands of manufacturers are available after 1852. But the trend in total cotton stocks held in England, measured in weeks of consumption at the current annual rate, was strongly down-ward after 1865.[25]

With respect to fixed capital, the years 1825-60 may be regarded as the installation period of the self-acting mule and the power-loom. The process of assimilating these innovations was capital-using because they accelerated the rate of replacement of equipment through obsolescence and created expectations of windfall profit. The years 1860-86 may then be viewed as the operation-period of the installed equipment, cutting costs per unit of output. This distinction, made long ago by Oskar Lange, oversimplifies matters but is nevertheless a useful way of contrasting the two phases in the movement of the fixed capital-output ratio over the years under review.

IV

It is easier to describe what happened than to explain why it happened. One of the essential links is missing: we know next to nothing about variations in the rate of return on capital invested. The best we can do is to piece together some bits of information suggesting the relevant forces at work.

The wage rates of factory workers, which had been falling since the beginning of the century, stabilised in the 1830s and 1840s. Except for an upward bulge in 1845, they did not begin to rise until 1850, after which they moved upwards along an almost constant trend-line. The wage rates of hand-loom weavers tended downward of course, falling permanently below those of factory workers in 1816. If 1834 = 100, Wood's index of the weighted average of weekly wages of spinners and weavers stood at 140 in 1861 and 185 in 1886.[26] It is piece rates, not time rates, however, which provide the motivation for labour-saving innovations. Labour costs per unit of output fell steadily until 1860. Thereafter, hourly wage rates seem to have risen faster than (net) output per man-hour, as shown by the secular increase in labour's share of output. But as the price of yarn and of piece goods fell faster than the price of imported cotton, labour costs as a proportion of all costs probably fell. Hence, the impetus towards labour-saving improvements diminished. And indeed, even in spinning, the period 1860-86 did not witness the same dramatic increases in labour-productivity that had marked the earlier years.

It is worth noting that the tendency to replace dear adult labour by cheap juvenile labour resisted the efforts of factory reformers until the last decades of the nineteenth century. Skilled workers in the cotton industry were almost always adult males; semi-skilled work was done by women and boys 13-18 years old; the unskilled tasks were performed by children under 13. In the eighteenth century, Hargreaves' jenny and Crompton's mule had substituted skilled for unskilled labour.[27] The increased use of Arkwright's water-frame, and its successor the throstle-frame, in the nineteenth century reversed the process, and the coming of the automatic mule increased the demand for female labour at the expense of children and adult males. Once the agitation over the Ten Hours' Bill had died down, child labour once again grew faster than adult labour and this trend continued until 1874.

These variations seem to have taken place within limits set by technological requirements. The striking constancy of the female labour-force — even when girls aged 13-18 are eliminated — and the small range of variation in the proportions of adult male labour suggests that the distribution of skills was largely governed by the technical characteristics of equipment rather than by relative wages. The evidence is inconclusive because the influence of wage-differentials for labour of different skills may have made itself felt in the choice of goods manufactured: the finer yarns and fabrics required more skilled handling.

While wage rates were rising in the later years there is no reliable evidence to show that the profit rate was falling. It is true that the margin between the price of raw cotton and the price of cotton manufactures fell continuously through the whole of the nineteenth century — this accounts

Table 6

Percentage of each class of workers employed in cotton mills[28]

	1834	1839	1847	1850	1856	1861	1867	1870	1874	1878	1885	1890	1895
Children under 13	13.3	4.7	5.8	4.6	6.5	8.8	10.4	9.6	14.0	12.8	9.9	9.1	5.8
Males 13-18	12.5	16.6	11.8	11.2	10.3	9.1	8.6	8.5	8.0	7.2	7.9	8.2	7.9
Females over 13	47.9	53.8	55.3	55.5	55.8	55.7	55.0	55.9	53.9	54.7	55.8	55.8	55.7
Males over 18	26.4	24.9	24.9	28.7	27.4	26.4	26.0	26.0	24.1	25.3	26.4	26.9	27.6

for the different rates of growth of gross and net output of grey cloth. But the downward trend in the general price level, while much less than the downtrend in cotton prices, may have reduced overhead charges. There were complaints about a declining rate of profit per unit of turnover but little is heard about the rate of profit on capital. Still, the price of raw cotton governed the price of output. All available indices show a high correlation in the movements of the prices of raw cotton and of yarn and piece goods.[29] The squeeze in the margin, therefore, stimulated the search for cost-reducing innovations and the rising capital-output ratio up to 1860, implying a higher share of amortisation and interest charges in total cost, invited capital-saving rather than labour-saving changes. If this sounds like *post hoc ergo propter hoc* it is all the available facts will permit us to say.

One may take some comfort from the fact that all explanations of factor-saving improvements in terms of rational optimising behaviour come to grief upon the imponderable element of the state of demand for a product of given quality. Some innovations, such as the comber, patented in 1851, facilitated the spinning of fine yarn with inferior raw material previously unusable. It is impossible to explain its introduction merely by pointing to changes in factor-rewards. And again, the slow adoption of certain cost-reducing innovations must be attributed to their poor efficiency for the finer yarns and fabrics. A notorious example is the failure of ring-spinning to gain a foothold in Lancashire until the last decade of the century, although ring-spinning for warp yarn was already an established practice in the United States by the 1850s. The ring frame was a simpler machine requiring less skill to operate, its output per spindle was twice that of the mule spindle, it saved floor space and could be driven at higher speeds without extra vibration, thus lengthening the life of the plant, and it spun a stronger yarn. But the mule frame produced a softer and finer quality yarn from a given grade of cotton and, in view of the existing pattern of demand for British cotton goods, the introduction of ring-spinning had to wait upon further technical improvements.[30]

V

The relative constancy of the real capital-real output ratio of the cotton industry in the years 1834-86 should occasion no surprise. Still less surprising is the fall in the capital-output ratio, measured in current prices, between 1860 and 1886. The industry reaped external economies, both pecuniary and technological, through localisation in the Lancashire district. Chief amongst these were the economies of vertical disintegration: the textile machinery industry, which was hardly in existence in 1800, grew rapidly in the second and third quarters of the nineteenth century. As Joseph Nasmith, the famous consulting engineer, declared in 1890:

A spinning mill of 40,000 spindles, which in 1835 would be looked upon as a large one, cost, at that time, from 24 to 26 shillings per spindle to erect, including the building and accessories. At the present time, mills are built to contain as many as 110,000 spindles and these are filled ready for work at a cost not exceeding 21 shillings per spindle . . . . Considering the great increase in the productive power of the machinery the fact that it is so much less expensive to work, and that each machine is of much greater capacity, the figures given show that the tendency towards diminished cost is owing very largely to the efforts of machine makers.[31]

In 1833, manufacturers testifying before a Parliamentary Committee concurred in the view that it would cost no more, perhaps even less, to put up a cotton mill in 1833 than at the time of Waterloo.[32] Henry Holdsworth, inventor and spinner, summed up majority opinion:

Q.5262: Has the price of machinery fallen? — I think the price of machinery is reduced, or rather the nominal price per spindle is reduced considerably, and the workmanship of it has increased at least 50 per cent, so that it is not as good a trade for machine makers as it was.
Q.5263: Supposing a manufacturer were to spin a certain number of pounds weight of cotton in a year, in 1815, and to spin the same number of the same quality at the present time, what would be the difference in the expense of establishing all the machinery for the manufacture in 1815, as compared to the present time?
I think it would not be greater; at present we are spinning 20 per cent more upon the same number of spindles than in 1815, and at the same time the present mode of spinning required 15 per cent more machinery in order to effect that improvement in quality which enables us to do that extra quantity.
Q.5264: Then, upon the average, you think that, as far as the cost of machinery goes, there is no considerable saving to the manufacturer? — Comparing the sum that a factory will cost now with what it cost in 1815 to do the same work, I would say that the expense of the mill is as much now as it was then.

May we conclude that fixed capital requirements per unit of output were constant between 1815 and 1833? This should warn against the easy assumption that capital-using innovations dominated technical change in the heyday of the Industrial Revolution. After all, a good many of the crucial inventions of the age on balance released rather than absorbed capital: from the smelting of iron with coal, Cort's puddling and rolling process, Watt's vacuum engine, and chlorine bleaching in the eighteenth century, to Neilson's hot blast and Woolf's compound engine in the nineteenth, not to speak of the canal era and the coming of railroads with their effect in reducing the prices of coal, timber and iron. It may be true that an industrial economy uses not only more capital per man but more capital per unit of output than a pre-industrial economy. The question is whether, for Great Britain, the line should be drawn in 1780, in 1800, in

1815, or in 1851. The history of the cotton industry suggests an earlier date than has hitherto been thought reasonable.

NOTES

1. This paper was prepared during the tenure of a Guggenheim Fellowship. Some of the material was gathered under a grant-in-aid from the Social Science Research Council. Mr. D. E. Chapman assisted with the calculations.
2. For the first half of the century see R. Giffen, *The Growth of Capital* (Oxford 1889), Ch. 5; A. D. Gayer, *et al, The Growth and Fluctuation of the British Economy 1790-1850* (Oxford, 1952), Microfilm Supplement, pp. 1574-81. For the second half of the century see E. H. Phelps-Brown, S. J. Handfield-Jones, "The Climacteric of the 1890s," *Oxford Economic Papers* (October 1952).
3. J. Clapham, *An Economic History of Modern Britain* (Cambridge, 1950), II, pp. 32-3, 85-7, and see Appendix B2.
4. I follow Harrod in classifying technical improvements as labour-saving, capital-saving, or neutral according to whether they raise, lower, or leave unchanged the ratio of capital to output. This despite the fact the capital/output ratio is influenced not only by the factor-saving slant of innovations, but also by the composition of output and by investment designed to expand the capacity of existing plant and equipment.
5. See Appendix C.
6. E. H. Phelps-Brown, E. H. Weber, "Accumulation, Productivity and Distribution in the British Economy, 1870-1938," *Economic Journal* (June 1953), p. 266.
7. J. Jewkes, "The Localisation of the Cotton Industry," *Economic History* January 1930); A. J. Taylor, "Concentration and Specialisation in the Lancashire Cotton Industry 1825-50", *Economic History Review*, 2nd series 1 (1949), Nos. 2 and 3.
8. Through 1834-52 we have statistics on mill-stocks but none at all on stocks in the ports (see J. A. Mann, *The Cotton Trade of Great Britain* (Manchester, 1860)). After 1860 we have data on port stocks but none on mill-stocks. It seems that as much as 80 per cent of total stocks were normally held in Liverpool. This makes the level of total stocks a poor index of the working capital required by spinners and weavers.
9. H. Ashworth, "Statistics of the Present Depression of Trade at Bolton", Journal of the Royal Statistical Society (April 1842); T. Ellison, *The Cotton Trade of Great Britain* (Manchester, 1886), pp. 46, 338 (subsequently referred to as Ellison); G. v. Schulze-Gaevernitz, *The Cotton Trade in England and on the Continent* (Manchester, 1895), p. 158.
10. See Appendix A, i.
11. See Appendix B, 2.
12. See Appendix B, 10.
13. Horse-power series after 1861 are not comparable to those for previous years. See Appendix C, 5.
14. Spinning spindles were first distinguished from doubling spindles in the Returns of 1867; prior to that year yarn output per spindle cannot be precisely determined. (Ministry of Labour estimates give practically the same figures

cited above: see G. T. Jones, *Increasing Returns* (London, 1933), p. 114.) It must be remembered that, despite the growth of combined spinning and weaving mills, spinning was also carried on as a final stage of production; owing to the large export trade in yarn, spinning plants were not always balanced by corresponding weaving plants within the country.

15. S. J. Chapman, *The Lancashire Cotton Industry* (Manchester, 1904), pp. 69-70; A. Ure, *The Cotton Manufacturers of Great Britain* (London 1861), II, pp. 152-8 (subsequently referred to as Ure); G. H. Wood, *The History of Wages in the Cotton Trade* (London, 1910), p. 27 (subsequently referred to as Wood).

16. *Reports of the Inspectors of Factories* (London, 1842) XXII, pp. 26-8.

17. S. Andrews, *Fifty Years of the Cotton Trade* (Oldham, 1887), p. 2; Schulze-Gaevernitz, *op. cit.* p. 108; Wood, pp. 30-1, 79-80.

18. Ellison, pp. 68-9; F. Merttens, "The Hours and Cost of Labour in the Cotton Industry at Home and Broad," *Manchester Statistical Society* (1893-4). The fact that power-weavers increased faster than spinners between 1860 and 1892 is only partly attributable to more pronounced labour-saving changes in yarn manufacture. Owing to the decline of the yarn export trade in the later years, the demand for cloth rose faster than the demand for yarn.

19. J. Montgomery, *The Theory and Practice of Cotton Spinning* (Glasgow, 1833), pp. 78-80; Ure, II, 155-6; *Rep. Insp. Fact* (1842) XXII, p. 26.

20. E. Baines, *History of the Cotton Manufacture* (Manchester, 1835), p. 202 subsequently referred to as Baines); Ure, II, p. 154; Wood, pp. 140-1; *Reports of the Inspectors of Factories* (1874) XIII, p. 62; Schulze-Gaevernitz, *op cit.* pp. 88-90.

21. The evidence cannot be set down briefly, but compare the detailed technological descriptions of current machinery in Ure's book, published in 1836, with E. Leigh, *The Science of Modern Cotton-Spinning* (Manchester, 1873) and J. Nasmith, *Modern Cotton-Spinning Machinery* (Manchester, 1890).

22. Ellison, pp. 37, 142; Wood, pp. 142, 161.

23. Andrews, *op. cit.* p. 6.

24. See Appendix C, 5; Ure, I, pp. 309-12; Andrews, *op. cit.* p. 7.

25. See Ellison, Table 1.

26. Wood, pp. 127-8.

27. Chapman, *op. cit.* pp. 53-60.

28. *Ibid.* p. 12.

29. T. S. Ashton, "Some Statistics of the Industrial Revolution," *Manchester School* (May 1948); Gayer, *op. cit.* II, pp. 838-9; A. H. Imlagh, "The Terms of Trade of the United Kingdom, 1789-1913," *Journal of Economic History* (November 1950), pp. 188-90; Jones, *op. cit.* p. 116; R. C. O. Matthews, *A Study in Trade Cycle History* (Oxford, 1954), pp. 129-30.

30. Chapman, *op. cit.* p. 70; Clapham, *op. cit.* III, p. 176; R. E. Naumburg, "Two American Textile Pioneers," *The Newcomen Society Transactions*, VI (1925-6).

31. J. Nasmith, *op. cit.* p. 7.

32. Parl. Papers *Manufactures, Commerce and Shipping, Sel. Cttee* (1833), VI, QQ. 476, 1896, 2438, 9059-72, 11008-14.

APPENDIX A — CAPITAL

a) Estimates prior to 1834

The year 1812 saw the first estimate of capital invested in the cotton industry.[1] In a petition to Parliament from "the merchants, cotton spinners and manufacturers of Manchester" it was stated that "ten millions sterling fixed capital was invested in cotton mills and machinery." Several prominent spinners personally endorsed this figure.[2]

No estimates appeared between 1812 and 1832, the year that Samuel Greg testified before the Children's Employment Commission. With five mills and 2,000 employees, spinning 1.5 per cent of the yard produced and goods woven in the United Kingdom, Greg and Co. held first rank among the cotton firms of the day. The five mills, Greg argued convincingly, were sufficiently representative to form a basis for generalisations about the industry. Having put the labour force in cotton mills in England and Wales at 160,000, he applied the capital-labour ratio obtained in the five plants (93.75), reaching a total figure of £15m., i.e. fixed capital = £10m. and working capital = £5m. Since the cotton-work force in Scotland and Ireland was then approximately 36,000, the same method yields £18.4m. for the capital stock of the industry in the United Kingdom, £12.25m. of which was sunk in machinery and buildings. Two other spinners, testifying before the same committee, estimated fixed capital at £12.35m.[3]

b) 1834

McCulloch's estimate for 1834 is as follows:[4]

	£m.
Capital to purchase raw materials	4
Capital to pay wages	10
Capital vested in equipment, buildings and stock	20
	34

McCulloch put the total expenditure on raw cotton for the year at £8m. and the total wage bill at £20m. By supposing that circulating capital turns over twice a year, he reached the first two figures cited above. No explanation is given for the estimate of fixed capital.

Cotton consumption in 1834 amounted to £11.5m., not £8m. The wage bill in spinning and weaving alone was £9.5m.; Baines's figure for the wage bill of the whole cotton industry is £16.6m., not £20m.[5] McCulloch had estimated the output of the cotton industry at £34m. Probably, the figure for fixed capital was reached by deducting £14m. for circulating capital from £34m. For the belief that the ratio of capital to total sales was close to unity in the cotton industry was widely shared at the time. This conviction was based partly upon data for the American cotton industry, later confirmed by the American census of manufacturing in 1839 — but it was supported by British experience as well.[6] The five plants of Greg and Co., for example, show an average capital-sales ratio of 1.07.

Baines accepted McCulloch's estimate of total capital after some discussion of its reliability.[7] According to Burn's *Commercial Glance*, an oft-quoted annual circular compiled by a Manchester commission merchant, the current capital value of a typical cotton mill spinning medium counts in 1832 was 17s.6d. per spindle. The estimated number of spindles in 1834 was 12,000,000. Hence, fixed capital in spinning alone was £10.5m. We may add that power-looms are known to have cost about £21-25 each in 1836;[8] there were over 100,000 of such looms in 1834. Fixed capital in spinning and weaving mills, therefore, amounted to at least £12.6m. Baines quoted "a highly respectable and intelligent cotton-spinner," who estimated that the capital-labour ratio in combined spinning and weaving firms was approximately 100. This gives a figure of £23.7m. for total capital in the manufacturing branch of the industry. Capital in bobbin-net lace and hosiery was put at £3m. (fixed capital=£1m. and working capital=£2m.) by W. Felkin, who had just completed a private survey of the two trades.[9] Capital in bleaching, dyeing, and printing, although unknown, might reasonably be put at £8.9m. On the whole, Baines was satisfied that McCulloch's figure of £34m. was more or less correct.

I have separated spinning and weaving from the rest of the industry by applying the capital-labour ratio of 93.75 obtained from the plant of Greg and Co. This yields of conservative estimate since capital-intensity must have risen through 1832-4, a period of extensive building of cotton mills.

	£m.
Fixed capital in spinning and weaving	14.8
Circulating capital	7.4
Fixed capital in bleaching, dyeing, printing, hosiery and lace-making	5.4
Circulating capital	6.4
	34.0

c) 1835-8

The figure of £3.75m. is sometimes cited as the amount of investment in the cotton industry between 1835 and 1838.[10] Actually, this is the amount which Ure predicted would be spent on cotton mills and machinery from 1835 to 1837. A questionnaire circulated in 1835 asking cotton manufacturers to estimate planned additions to steam-power up to 1838 produced the figure of 7,507 h.p. (in fact, the power installed July 1835 - January 1835 was 13,226 h.p.[11]). In Ure's opinion "the outlay in buildings and machinery necessary to bring this horse-power into operation may be safely estimated at £500 per horse-power"; hence, he concluded that £3,753,000 would be invested in the industry over the next two years.[12] He did not explain how he had arrived at £500 as the amount of capital required per h.p. But since installed h.p. in 1834 was 41,056, the ratio 500:1 was obviously derived from McCulloch's estimate of £20m. for fixed capital in the cotton industry — this ignores the fact that the spinning and weaving section accounted for only £15m. The *Circular to Bankers*, however, surmised that "the additional machinery brought into play (since January, 1835), for the manufacture of cotton, in England and Scotland ... is equal to ¼ of all that was at that period in action."[13] If we take this statement seriously it does imply a fixed capital stock of £15m. in 1834.

It is worth noting that h.p. figures were at no time an accurate index of additional investment in the industry. The increased speeds at which mules and looms were run meant that more power was required unaccompanied by a proportionate increase of equipment. Thomas Ashton, a leading spinner of the day, testified to the reduction in fixed capital per unit of h.p. of "new establishments" from £500 in 1835 to £400 in 1842. He attributed this to "altered cost of the mills and machinery, and the application of more power to the same number of spindles or looms."[14]

d) 1845

McCulloch's estimate for 1945 was as follows:[15]

	£m.
Capital for purchase of raw materials	4
Capital for payment of wages	8
Capital in equipment, buildings and stock	35
	47

McCulloch estimated gross output in 1845 at £36m.; apparently he had abandoned the notion of a capital/gross output ratio of unity. The figure for fixed capital is not improbable, and that is about all one can say of it. Thomas Ashton put the average capital cost of spinning mills in 1841 at 24-25s. per spindle.[16] At this valuation, fixed capital in spinning in 1845 amounted to £21m. The price of some 250,000 power-looms would add at least another £5m. When we include the finishing branch, hosiery and lace, the figure of £35m. does not seem unreasonable. McCulloch calculated that £10m. was spent on raw cotton; 542,000 spinners, weavers and bleachers earned £13m., to which he added £4m. for the wages of 80,000 engineers. Assuming an annual turnover rate of approximately 2, circulating capital required was £12m.

e) 1856

Alderman Baynes's estimate for 1856 formed the basis of several later efforts:[17]

	£m.
Spinning mills: 28m. spindles costing 24s. new, now valued at 17s. 6d. per spindle	25
Weaving sheds: 300,000 looms, costing £24 new, now valued at £20 per loom	6
Floating capital	14.5
	45.5

The numbers of spindles and looms are derived from the factory returns of 1856. The wage bill in that year was £11m.; cotton consumption equalled £22m.; circulating capital is assumed to turn over about two and one half times a year. To this estimate by Baynes, Mann added £30m. for capital in the finishing trades and £9.5m. for the floating capital of importers and shipowners; the source for these figures is not supplied.[18]

f) 1860-2

Chadwick revised Baynes's estimate in 1860:[19]

	£m.
Spinning mills: 28m. spindles at 18s. per spindle	25.2
Weaving sheds: 300,000 looms at £24 per loom	7.2
Floating capital	20.0
	52.4

The increase in the valuation per loom since 1856 is explained by the unprecedented boom in power-weaving which took place in the late 1850s: between 1856 and 1861 the number of spindles rose 7 per cent but power-looms increased 33 per cent. The significant increase in working capital over the 1856 figure is likewise plausible in the light of the sharp rise in cotton stocks through 1859-60. The cost of cotton used up in 1860 was £28m.; the wage bill was approximately £13m.

Chadwick's estimate pertains to England and Wales, not the United Kingdom. The figures for numbers of spindles and looms are his own; the returns of 1861 show that looms were underestimated. I have recalculated the figures to apply to the United Kingdom. Spindles and looms are estimated by linear interpolation of the returns of 1856 and 1861. Working capital is raised by the proportion of the industry carried on in Scotland as measured by spindles, looms, and employment.[20]

	£m.
Spinning mills: 29m. spindles at 18s. per spindle	26.1
Weaving sheds: 378,000 looms at £24 per loom	9.1
Floating capital	21.4
	56.6

g) 1871

The Factory Inspectors put the value of buildings and machinery in 1871 at £57m. and floating capital at £30m.[21] The figure for fixed capital seems to have been reached as follows:

	£m.
38,120,000 spindles at 24s.	45.7
446,176 looms at £24	10.7
	56.4

The returns for 1870 give the number of spindles as 37,719,000; the increase in spindles from 1870-1 was 400,000.[22] There were 440,676 looms in 1870; by linear interpolation of the two adjacent returns of 1870 and 1874, their number rose 5,500 in 1870-1. The valuation per spindle, however, seems to be too high. Platt and Bros., a leading manufacturer of cotton textile machinery, estimated the cost of a modern mill for spinning 32's in 1866 at 18s. per spindle.[23] Machine prices probably rose somewhat in the late 1860s but this hardly accounts for the discrepancy. In all probability, the estimate values equipment at original cost, not at current prices.

h) 1886

Ellison's estimate for 1886 was as follows:[24]

	£m.
Spinning mills: 47m. spindles costing 24s. new, now valued at 20s. per spindle	47
Weaving sheds: 550,000 looms costing £24 new, now valued at £20 per loom	11
Floating capital	25
Capital in printing, bleaching and dyeing	18
Capital in cotton lace and hosiery	7
	108

The number of spindles in 1885, according to the official count, was 44.3m. 1886 was a bad year in the trade and the number of spindles fell between 1885 and 1886.[25] I have not adjusted Ellison's figure, however, because the factory returns did not count spindles standing idle; there was a 13 weeks cotton strike in the Oldham District in 1885. The number of looms in 1885 was 561,000, and their number fell to 550,000 in 1886.

The capital value per spindle of 20s. is verified by Ellison for 71 joint-stock companies in the Oldham District. A year later an independent survey of the 90 incorporated mills in the Oldham district, representing about one-quarter of the whole spinning trade, confirmed this figure. Again, the Superintendent Inspector of Factories estimated that the cost of erecting a mill in 1885 was about 21s. per spindle, "being 20 per cent lower than it was 10 years ago."[26]

The value of cotton consumption in 1886 was £33m.; the wage bill for spinning and weaving was £20m. We notice that once again working capital is thought to turn over a little more than twice a year.

For the first time we have a fairly detailed estimate for the capital of printworks, although it is for the year 1889. The figure is £5m.[27]

An estimate slightly higher than that of Ellison's for the year 1885 was furnished by the Manchester Chamber of Commerce to a Royal Commission.[28]

	£m.
Spinning mills: 48m. spindles at 21s. per spindle	50.4
Weaving sheds: 565 looms at £23 per loom	13
Floating capital	25
Capital in bleaching, printing and dyeing	18.7
Capital in cotton lace and hosiery	7
	114.1

The outstanding disagreement is about the value per loom. There is no material to guide our choice of the two estimates. I have preferred Ellison's as being, on the whole, the more authoritative source: his books and his *Annual Review of the Cotton Trade* (1870-1911) repeatedly demonstrate his careful handling of data.

The capital estimates given above yield the following ratios of fixed to working capital in spinning and weaving.

i) Ratio of fixed to working capital

1834	1856	1860	1871	1886
2	2.1	1.6	1.9	2.3

It is curious that most trade opinion in the 1830s put the ratio as high as 4 or 5.[29] Manufacturers, testifying in protest against factory legislation, insisted upon the preponderance of fixed costs in their outlays, making short-time working unprofitable. They translated a high ratio of fixed to variable costs into a high ratio of fixed to working capital, although the two are of course quite different things: heavy overhead charges in current operating periods are compatible with a "low" ratio of fixed to working capital if working capital turns over "slowly".

Price deflator

Cotton machine prices were not published until 1885. There are some figures for machine prices in the literature but these are not adequate to construct an index. For the period 1870-86 the best available alternative is an index for the price level of capital goods constructed by Phelps Brown and Handfield-Jones.[30] It is made up of Jones's index of building costs in London, Sauerbeck's index of raw materials' prices, Schlote's index of the prices of finished export goods and an index of the average declared value of iron and steel exports. Of these only the prices of finished export goods are available back to 1834. Even the prices of pig iron, coal, bricks and timber, which might have been used to gain an impression of fluctuations, are not continuously available over the period 1834-70. Under the circumstances I have fallen back on the Jevons-Sauerbeck index of wholesale prices on the assumption that the prices of capital goods varied in the same way as the level of wholesale prices.[31] I have spliced the Jevons-Sauerbeck index with the Phelps Brown index in 1870. For the relevant years, the index numbers are as follows:

$$
\begin{aligned}
1834 &= 100 \\
1845 &= 95 \\
1856 &= 105 \\
1860 &= 102 \\
1871 &= 102 \\
1886 &= 76.5
\end{aligned}
$$

	1.	2.	3.	4.	5.	6.	7.	8.	9.	10.	11.	12.	13.
27	176	131	22.0	19	14	—	—	65	17	34	29	—	—
28	184	143	21.4	16	10	—	—	77	19	36	30	—	—
29	195	134	19.2	15	10	—	—	61	14	31	26	—	—
1830	221	156	17.1	16	8	—	—	75	17	37	30	—	—
31	234	170	19.6	18	11	—	—	93	20	37	30	—	—
32	247	170	18.9	18	10	19	10	86	16	33	25	37	28
33	256	185	19.6	20	9	20	10	94	18	36	25	38	28
34	270	194	20.6	22	11	21	11	93	17	38	27	39	29
35	284	201	22.3	24	10	22	11	99	20	42	28	40	29
36	309	221	21.9	26	11	23	12	105	21	45	30	41	29
37	326	223	17.1	23	12	24	12	126	22	43	32	41	29
38	371	256	18.5	28	15	24	12	130	21	46	33	42	29
39	340	234	19.0	25	12	25	12	100	16	41	28	42	30
1840	409	291	16.0	27	14	25	13	147	22	47	34	43	31
41	390	267	16.0	25	13	26	14	130	19	43	31	44	32
43	461	321	13.7	26	15	25	14	153	19	42	31	43	31
44	484	346	13.7	27	15	25	14	155	19	45	34	43	31
45	539	404	13.1	29	18	25	14	205	25	51	40	43	31
46	547	385	11.7	27	14	25	14	190	22	48	35	43	30
47	369	249	12.1	19	16	26	14	77	10	33	20	43	30
48	514	379	10.5	23	13	27	14	179	19	41	31	45	32
49	561	412	11.5	26	12	28	14	168	17	44	30	47	33
1850	523	392	13.2	28	10	28	15	144	16	44	26	48	33
51	587	443	12.6	30	14	29	15	161	17	47	31	48	33
52	662	517	12.1	33	16	30	15	239	25	55	38	50	33
53	677	530	12.8	35	17	32	15	239	26	59	41	52	35
54	691	544	11.9	34	16	34	15	235	24	55	37	54	35
55	746	581	12.8	38	18	37	16	227	22	57	37	57	36
56	793	612	11.8	38	16	40	18	241	25	63	41	61	39
57	735	558	13.6	40	14	42	19	197	21	60	34	64	41

Year													
58	38	63	35	61	18	182	18	42	17	43	13.1	606	806
59	36	62	44	72	24	227	17	44	22	50	14.0	595	887
1860	35	64	52	80	28	261	17	47	28	56	14.4	768	965
61	34	67	52	83	36	350	17	50	26	57	14.0	818	996
62	36	71	11	38	2	12	19	54	6	33	20.1	314	407
63	39	75	12	55	8	76	20	58	10	53	27.7	388	462
64	40	79	28	76	21	115	21	60	16	65	30.6	435	510
65	41	81	29	78	21	201	21	61	20	69	24.6	569	672
66	42	84	61	111	36	220	21	62	29	79	22.8	690	829
67	44	87	61	101	31	223	21	64	30	70	17.9	740	909
68	50	93	54	95	27	218	24	68	24	65	15.7	761	932
69	55	100	48	92	25	192	26	70	20	64	16.6	716	883
1870	60	103	64	107	35	290	27	71	26	69	15.7	826	1010
71	63	105	71	109	36	318	28	70	32	70	14.0	942	1134
72	63	104	65	110	30	248	29	69	32	77	15.9	894	1105
73	64	104	72	117	39	322	29	68	29	74	14.6	958	1171
74	64	103	68	109	34	313	29	67	30	71	14.1	971	1190
75	64	102	66	104	32	293	28	66	28	66	13.5	943	1157
1876	65	101	64	99	31	297	28	65	27	62	12.3	967	1198
77	64	100	63	95	25	239	28	65	29	62	12.6	940	1163
78	64	100	56	86	20	202	28	64	24	54	11.3	863	1106
79	64	99	54	82	18	194	28	63	23	51	10.6	874	1103
1880	63	96	65	101	25	264	27	62	28	64	11.6	1084	1290
81	62	96	64	101	22	234	27	61	29	67	11.7	1106	1353
82	61	96	70	108	32	349	27	61	30	68	11.5	1143	1374
83	61	98	66	105	29	323	26	61	26	65	10.7	1151	1408
84	61	98	62	100	27	318	27	62	25	63	10.6	1124	1387
85	62	98	53	86	19	237	27	63	23	56	10.2	1035	1273
86	62		60	92	23	279		64	28	60	10.0	1164	1410
87	—	—	60	94	23	282	—	—	27	61	10.2	1177	1420
88	—	—	59	95	23	285	—	—	28	64	10.4	1205	1452
89	—	—	59	94	24	293	—	—	31	66	10.8	1206	1449
1890	—	—	65	105	31	373	—	—	30	70	10.8	1308	1559

Notes

1. An earlier estimate, made in 1788, must be rejected as guesswork. Cf. P. Colquhoun, *An Important Crisis in the Calico Manufacture Explained* (London, 1788); Baines, pp. 216-9; Ure, I, p. 298; see also M'Connel and Co., *A Century of Fine Cotton-Spinning* (Manchester, 2d. edn. 1913), p. 30.
2. Quoted in G. French, *Life and Times of Samuel Crompton* (Manchester, 1860), p. 285.
3. Parl. Papers *Employment of Children. R. Comm. First Rep.* (1833) XX, D2, pp. 36-8, 95
4. J. R. McCulloch, *Commercial Dictionary* (London, 1834), p. 443.
5. Baines, p. 412. McCulloch later pared down his employment figure, *op. cit.* (1852 edn.), p. 457.
6. Parl. Papers *S.C. on Manufactures* (1833) VI, QQ. 2293-60, 2683, 5440; *Economist* (1844) p. 1357.
7. Baines, pp. 414-5.
8. Parl. Papers *Hand-Loom Weavers. Ass. Comm.* (1840) XXIV, p. 435.
9. Quoted in Baines, pp. 342-5.
10. From *Circular to Bankers*, cited in L. H. Jenks, *The Migration of British Capital in 1875* (London, 1927), p. 362; Matthews, *op. cit.* p. 135.
11. Parl. Papers *Population of Stockport. Asst. Poor Law Comm.* (1842) XXXV, pp. 53-4.
12. Ure, I, pp. 413-4.
13. *Circular to Bankers* (August 4, 1837) p. 33.
14. Parl. Papers *Population of Stockport, Poor Law Comm.* (1842) XXXV, p. 114.
15. McCulloch, *op. cit.* (1852 edn.), p. 457.
16. Parl. Papers *Exportation of Machinery* (1841) VII, p. 25.
17. A. Baynes, *The Cotton Trade. Two Lectures* (London, 1857). I have omitted a mysterious item of £10 m. for "cash in hands of bankers".
18. Mann, *op. cit.* p. 93.
19. D. Chadwick, "On the Rate of Wages in the Manufacturing District of Lancashire, 1839-59," *Journal of the Royal Statistical Society* (March 1860).
20. An estimate of £59 m. for 1861, based upon Chadwick's calculations, but made without benefit of the 1861 returns, is given by P. L. Simmonds in his supplement to Ure, II, p. 393.
21. *Reports of the Inspectors of Factories* (1874) XIII, p. 118.
22. A. K. Cairncross, *Home and Foreign Investment, 1870-1913* (Cambridge, 1953), p. 167.
23. Andrews, *op. cit.* p. 6.
24. Ellison, p. 70.
25. Cairncross, *op. cit.* p. 167.
26. Ellison, pp. 39, 46, 139; Andrews, *op. cit.* p. 7; *Reports of the Inspectors of Factories* (1884-5) XV, p. 93.
27. G. Turnbull, *A History of the Calico-Printing Industry* (Altrincham, 1951), p. 115.
28. Parl. Papers *Depression of Trade and Industry. R. Comm. First Rep.* 1886, XXI, App. A, Pt. I, p. 427.
29. Parl. Papers *Royal Comm. on Employment of Children. First Rep.* (1833) XX, D1, p. 69; Parl. Papers *Hand-Loom Weavers. Royal Comm. Rep.* (1841) X,

p.32; H. Ashworth, *op. cit.*; N.W. Senior, *Letters on the Factory Act* (London, 1834), pp.3-4.
30. *Oxford Economic Papers* (October 1952), p.305.
31. W.T. Layton, G. Crowther, *Introduction to the Study of Prices* (3d edn. Oxford, 1938), p.237.

APPENDIX B—OUTPUT

1. Yarn produced

Derived by deducting loss of weight in spinning from raw cotton entered for consumption, i.e. net imports of raw cotton adjusted for changes in mill-stocks and stocks in the ports.[1] 1828 to 1861 waste is reckoned at 11 per cent of cotton consumed; through the years 1862-5 it is reckoned at 10, 9, 8, and 7 per cent respectively; after 1865 it is taken at 6 per cent.

The underlying series for cotton consumption raises certain difficulties which have been discussed by others.[2] The practice of estimating yarn production by deducting 6 per cent for unsaleable waste from raw cotton consumed, was first used by Ellison in his *Annual Review of the Cotton Trade* (1870-1911). The first Census of Production in 1907 confirmed his procedure.[3] J.W.F. Rowe, therefore, used the same percentage of deduction for his output series down to 1923, G.T. Jones then applied it back to 1845, and W.G. Hoffman in turn carried it back to the eighteenth century on the grounds that "some random checks" had verified the procedure for the whole of the nineteenth century.[4] But, in fact, authorities writing in the 1830s agree in estimating waste at 10-11 per cent of cotton entered for consumption.[5] Subsequently, the improved "ginning" of cotton in the country of origin as well as refinements in the design of carding machines reduced the initial weight lost in spinning. In addition, it became increasingly the practice to work up some of the wasted short fibres into very coarse yarns or to mix them with wool for special uses. Thus, Ellison notes that the amount of unsaleable waste fell in the 1860s from 11 to 6-7 per cent of cotton consumed.[6] To avoid underestimating the rate of growth of real output I have followed Ellison and have assumed that the reduction in waste was accomplished during the cotton famine (1862-5) when the unusually high price of raw cotton encouraged stringent economy measures. After 1865 my series is identical to that of Jones. A contemporary series for yarn production through 1814-76 by Thomas Bazley has been rejected because it assumes a constant proportion of waste over the whole period and seems to make idiosyncratic allowances for changes in stocks.[7]

2. Yarn consumed or cloth produced

Yarn produced (1) - net exports of yarn = yarn consumed. Yarn exports
are derived from Board of Trade returns as given by Ellison. There are very
slight discrepancies between the Board of Trade series and the Trade and
Navigation Accounts series as given by Robson.[8]

Some yarn was diverted in the form of sewing cotton, hosiery and
bobbin-net lace. In 1834 less than 2 per cent of cotton consumed was
absorbed by the hosiery trade. Cotton lacemaking was even less important
and cotton thread manufacture was in its infancy. All three trades,
however, expanded rapidly later in the century. This is apparent from the
fraction of spindles used to double the yarn for manufacture of thread,
hose and embroidered goods which rose from 6 per cent of all spindles in
1867 to just under 10 per cent in 1885. Although the cotton hosiery trade
for one declined rapidly after 1875,[9] we are left with the general impression
that the identification of yarn consumption with cloth production somewhat overestimates the actual rate of growth of the output of cloths.

3. Price of grey cloth

From 1845 to 1890 the average annual price per lb. of a composite bundle
of six representative grey cloths based upon the weekly returns from the
Manchester market is recorded in the *Economist*. The prices in shillings
were summed for each year and divided by the indicated total pound
weight. These are the same quotations used by Jones to construct his index
of the price of grey cloth.[10] From 1827 to 1845 the price has been estimated
on the basis of a series for a particular type of grey cloth, on the assumption
that its movements are indicative of changes in the average price of all grey
cloths.[11] The cloth in question (27 in. 72 Reed Printers) is one of the six
cloths reported in the *Economist* and its price after 1845 does behave
similarly to that of the bundle as a whole. The price of 72 Reed Printers in
1845 was 12.3d per lb; the price of the bundle of six cloths was 13.1d per lb;
the two series have been spliced in 1845 by multiplying the first by 1.065.

4. Gross output

(Yarn consumed (2) x the price of grey cloth (3) + the declared value of
yarn exports = gross output.

5. Net output

Gross output (4) - value of raw cotton consumed = net output. The cost of
cotton used up is calculated by multiplying Holt's series for raw cotton
consumption by the average price, inclusive of insurance and freight, of
raw cotton imported. The average declared value per lb. (c.i.f.) of raw
cotton imports is available from 1854 on;[12] prior to 1854 it can be

estimated from knowledge of the proportions of various kinds of cotton imported and their prices, after making a reasonable allowance for insurance and freight. Imlah's index of the price of East Indian and American cotton, with due allowance for the changing proportions of the supplies taken, was used as a check. Through 1836-60 my estimates agree with a contemporary series.[13]

6. Ten years' moving average of gross output

7. Ten years' moving average of net output

8. Home trade (all cotton)

Cloth produced (2) — lbs of piece goods exports = lbs. of goods for the home trade. Up to 1920 only the linear yardage of piece goods exported (divided into the categories white or plain and dyed or printed) was recorded in the trade accounts. Figures in yds were subsequently converted to 3 lb equivalent at 1 lb = 5.47 yds, a ratio which pertained from 1870 to 1910.[14] It should be noted that the cloth is stretched in the course of each finishing process; to reckon the same linear yardage for cloth, whether unfinished, bleached, dyed or printed, is to understate the amount of grey cloth exported. This would not matter if the proportions of finished and unfinished cloths in total exports did not vary over time. Probably they did vary but since grey cloth was not distinguished from bleached cloth in the trade accounts we can say nothing about it.

9. Value of the home trade (all cotton)

Weight of goods retained for the home trade (8) x ⅘ of the average declared value of cotton goods exports = value of the home trade. The average declared value of piece goods exports in pence per yd is available from 1814 on;[15] these have been converted to pence per lb. according to the lb-yd ratio given above. I have followed Mann and Ellison in estimating the value of the home trade upon the assumption that goods sold at home were 33 per cent dearer than goods sold abroad.[16]

10. Gross output (all cotton)

The value of the home trade (9) + the declared value of piece goods exports = gross output of the cotton industry as a whole. The declared value of piece goods exports is given in the trade returns.[17] My figures for gross output are virtually identical to Mann's estimates, continued by Ellison. There are divergences prior to 1845 due to the fact that Mann uses his own series for cotton consumption.

If Ellison is to be believed the rate of growth of total output was actually greater than that indicated by Mann's series. Although Ellison extended

Mann's estimates in his *Annual Review*, he based his own estimates of output in his book on the cotton industry upon a gradually increasing price-differential between home and foreign markets. He assumed that home-consumed goods were 14 per cent dearer than goods exported in 1830, 38 per cent dearer in 1845, 70 per cent dearer in 1860, and twice as dear from 1871 to 1885.[18]

I have found no evidence, however, that bears directly upon Ellison's conjecture. It is sometimes said that the average count of yarn rose through the nineteenth century. Since the count of yarn relates its weight to its length, the higher the count the greater the value of yarn in proportion to its weight. Contemporary opinion on the matter, however, is conflicting and the evidence is too scrappy to support any generalisations.[19]

Nevertheless, despite significant differences in the price assumptions, my estimates of gross output do not differ much from Ellison's, owing to the fact that he used, for some unknown reason, a lower lb.-yard ratio than is indicated above to estimate the weight of goods exported.[20]

An additional check upon our estimates is provided by the calculations submitted to a Royal Commission in 1886 by the Manchester Chamber of Commerce.[21] It makes no allowance whatever for loss of weight in spinning or for the admittedly higher price of home-consumed goods. Since these considerations are opposite in effect upon the value of output there is once again a close agreement with my estimates (with the exception of the period 1875-80 where the Manchester Chamber of Commerce reckons cotton consumption at 20 per cent below the figure given in Holt's *Circular*).

R. C. O. Matthews, using a different method of estimation — a method that could not be applied to more than a decade or two — has recently computed the value of output of the cotton industry between 1825 and 1842.[22] His figures are generally about 10 per cent below mine.

11. Net output (all cotton)

Gross output (10) - value of raw cotton consumed = net output.

12. Ten years' moving average of gross output.

13. Ten years' moving average of net output.

Notes

1. G. Holt's *Annual Circular* as given in Ellison, Table I.
2. See Gayer, *op. cit.* microfilm supplement, pp. 884-5.
3. Parl. Papers *Census of Production. Final Report* (1907) Cd 6320, p. 288.
4. J. W. F. Rowe, *The Physical Volume of Production* (London and Cambridge,

1924); Jones, *op. cit.*; W.G. Hoffman, *British Industry, 1700-1950* (Manchester, 1956), pp. 225-6.

5. Baines, p. 367; Montgomery, *op. cit.* p. 33.
6. Ellison, pp. 58, 307.
7. "Cotton Manufactures," *Encyclopaedia Britannica* (London, 8th edn. 1854; 9th edn. 1877), VI.
8. R. Robson, *The Cotton Industry in Britain* (Manchester, 1957), Table I.
9. F.A. Wells, *The British Hosiery Trade* (London, 1935), p. 133.
10. Jones, *op. cit.* pp. 101-2.
11. A. Neild, "An Account of the Prices of Printing Cloth and Upland Raw Cotton, from 1812 to 1860," *Journal Royal Statistical Society* (December 1861).
12. Parl. Papers *Report on Wholesale and Retail Prices* (1903), LXVIII, p. 45.
13. Mann, *op. cit.* p. 91.
14. Robson, *op. cit.* Table I.
15. Parl. Papers (1903) LXVIII, p. 48.
16. For 1836-60, Mann, *op. cit.* p. 104; for 1863-85, Ellison's *Annual Review* (Manchester, 1872) p. 8; (1885) p. 3.
17. Robson, *op. cit.* Table I.
18. Ellison, pp. 59, 308.
19. Andrews, *op. cit.* p. 7; Ellison, p. 69. The problem is complicated by cyclical swings in the average count produced; mills were set up to produce a range of at least 10 counts so as to permit adjustment to changing cotton prices. See *Economist* (1849) p. 1328.
20. Ellison, pp. 58-9.
21. Parl. Papers *Royal Comm. on Depression of Trade, First Report* (1886) XXI, Appendix A, p. 104.
22. Matthews, *op. cit.* p. 151.

APPENDIX C — MISCELLANEOUS DATA

Unless stated otherwise, the source of the statistics are the Factory Returns: P.P. 1836, XLV; 1839, XLII; 1842, XXII; 1843, LVI; 1846, XX; 1847, XLVI; 1849, LIV; 1850, XLII; 1857, (Sess. I), XIV; *Miscellaneous Statistics*, 1857-8, LVII; 1862, LV; 1867, LXIV; 1868-9, LXII; 1871, LXII; 1875, LXXI; 1878-9, LXV; 1884-5, LXXI; 1890, LXVII.

The area to which the data refers is the United Kingdom. But, in fact, the industry was already highly concentrated in Lancashire and two or three other northern counties by 1830 and the Scottish industry steadily contracted through the nineteenth century. The cotton industry in Ireland was never large enough to matter.

The exact date at which the factory returns are drawn up is never made explicit by the Inspectors. For example, the returns for 1885 were submitted to the printer on March 6, 1885. Were the figures collected in the winter of 1884 or in the opening months of 1885? I have followed Page[1] in

	1	2 (000's)	3 (000's)	4 (000's)	5	6 (000's)	7 (000,000's)	8 (£m)	9 %
1834	1154	10,800	100	200	41,056	237	(850) 1570	(5.8) 9.5	95
1839	1819	—	—	135	59,805	259	(929) 1413	(7.3) 9.5	70
1845	—	17,500	250	60	—	340	(1220) 1435	—	—
1850	1932	20,977	250	43	82,555	331	(1188) 1342	(7.9) 8.6	72
1851	—	—	—	—	—	—	—		—
1856	2210	28,010	299	23	97,132	379	(1182) 1254	(10.6) 11.0	70
1861	2887	30,387	400	7	294,130	452	(1410) 1432	(13.6) 13.7	69
1867	2549	34,215	379	—	201,062	401	1251	13.7	50
1870	2483	37,719	441	—	308,870	450	1404	16.1	61
1871	—	—	—	—	—	—	—	—	—
1874	2655	41,882	465	—	—	480	1498	19.1	66
1878	2674	44,207	515	—	—	483	1507	18.8	74
1881	—	—	—	—	—	—	—		—
1885	2635	44,348	561	—	—	504	1586	20.1	79

the choice of relevant years, usually the year preceding the publication of the returns.

1. Factories

The 1834 figure was obtained from the Factory Inspectors by Baines. Baines regards it as complete, unlike the corresponding figure for horse-power.[2] This is confirmed by the fact that the returns for 1835 give 1262 working mills and another 42 mills standing idle. Prior to 1850, both idle and working mills were enumerated; thereafter only mills at work were recorded. All figures given here are for working mills. No total figures are available for 1845 since one of the Inspectors failed to return for his district.

A "factory" is designated in the factory returns as a separate building, irrespective of whether the building housed several distinct firms or was owned entirely by a multi-plant firm. In the 1830s, the numbers of mills exceeded the number of firms by 10-20 per cent.[3]

2. Spindles

Spindles were not enumerated officially until 1850. Usually, only working spindles were recorded; but in 1874 the figure given refers explicitly to spindles "running and standing." From 1867 on spinning and doubling spindles were reported separately. Since the figures for 1850 to 1861 include doubling spindles,[4] the figures after 1861 given here represent spinning and doubling spindles.

The 1834 figure is based upon Ure's estimate of 25 lbs of yarn for the annual output per spindle in 1835 and my estimate of yarn production in 1834. Baines estimates that there were 9,333,000 spindles in 1832 on the basis of Burn's figure of 26.6 lbs of yarn per spindle. Burn's figure seems excessive inasmuch as spindle capacity was 28 lbs in 1867. Kennedy of M'Connel & Kennedy put it at 21.6 lbs p.a. in 1830. Ellison's estimate for 1845 is 26.8 lbs.

The figure for 1845 was supplied by Messrs. du Fay & Co, a firm of Liverpool cotton brokers.[5]

3. Power-looms

Baines estimated the number of power-looms in 1834 on the basis of a questionnaire sent to 300 mills by a Manchester accountant. The official returns for 1835 give 109,319 power-looms in operation. The estimate for 1845 is Ellison's. The 1870 figure includes 35,554 looms "standing but not working."[6]

4. Hand-looms

There are no official statistics for hand-looms. Their number in 1883 was estimated by several manufacturers. The figures for the other years are Wood's linear interpolations, using Ellison estimates for 1845 and 1860.[7]

5. Horsepower

Incomplete returns were obtained by the Inspectors in 1834. Baines added to this an estimate for the horsepower of the English mills for which no returns were obtained. Clapham cites Baines's total figure but incorrectly adds 15 per cent to an already corrected figure for Lancashire and Cheshire and a complete return for Scotland.[8]

Steam and water-power were enumerated separately. Water-power accounted for about 33 per cent of the total in 1834 but for less than 3 per cent in 1870.

The figures for motive-power, particularly those for years prior to 1861, must be used with great caution. For example, the enormous increase between 1856 and 1861 is illusory, being the consequence of a change in measurement from nominal to indicated h.p. Nominal h.p. was calculated by a formula devised by Watt based upon the given mean effective pressure and piston speed of a low pressure condensing engine. In the 1840s pressures were systematically increased by the addition of new boilers to the same engine; frequently, cotton engines of the Watt type were converted to compounding by "M'Naughting": the addition of a high-pressure cylinder at the other end of the beam. Piston speeds were likewise advanced. According to Inspector Horner, the combined effects of these improvements by the 1850s was to increase the real h.p. of existing engines by 25 per cent over the nominal h.p. returned. This was partly outweighed, he thought, by the fact that not all the enumerated power was actually employed at any time.[9] At any rate there is no doubt that the Watt formula had then become obsolete and the change in 1861 to measuring indicated h.p. was long overdue. Unfortunately, there seems to be no reliable method for splicing figures of nominal and indicated h.p. Rankine in his famous *Manual of the Steam-Engine* (1859) asserted that 1 N.H.P. = 3.3 I.H.P. but seven years later he gave the ratio as 1:6[10]. Neither formula makes sense of the later figures in view of other information. The factory returns ceased to count installed motive-power after 1870.

6. Number of persons employed in cotton factories

The factory returns for 1834 are incomplete. Baines corrected the official figure of 220,825 to make up for the total number for the United Kingdom. The figure for the boom year of 1845 is given by Ellison.[11] The Inspectors returned 316,327 in February 1847, a year of severe depression in the industry.

I have ignored census data for employment in "cotton manufacture" because of the treacherous shifts in the classification of occupations in the succeeding censuses between 1851 and 1891.

7. Man-hours of employment
Weekly hours of work of women and children fell from 69 in the 1820s to 60 hours after the Act of 1847, to 56.5 hours after the Act of 1874. The work day of adult males, although not subject to legislative control, was gradually adjusted to the hours prescribed for women and children. It appears that the struggle over the relay system postponed the introduction of the 60 hour week until 1856. Similarly, 56.5 hours did not become the norm until 1879-81.[12] Man-hours of labour inputs were obtained accordingly from the figures for factory employment and hand-loom weavers. The bracketed figures represent factory workers only.

8. Wage bill of spinners and weavers
The average weekly wage of factory operatives and hand-loom weavers is given by Wood on the basis of detailed wage statistics from a large number of sources.[13] The bracketed figures represent the wage bill of factory workers only.

9. Labour's share in net output
Owing to the uncertain date at which employment was enumerated, 3 year averages of net output were used.

Notes

1. *Commerce and Industry* (1919), II.
2. Baines, pp. 384-94.
3. H. D. Fong, *Triumph of the Factory System in England* (Tsientsin, China, 1930), p. 28.
4. *Reports of the Inspectors of Factories* (1863) XVIII, p. 60.
5. Ure, II, 312-5; Baines, pp. 367-8, 353; Ellison, pp. 68-9; Baines, *op. cit.* p. 39.
6. Baines, pp. 235-7; Ellison, pp. 65-6.
7. Baines, pp. 237-9, 382-4; Ellison, pp. 65-6; Wood, pp. 127-8.
8. Baines, pp. 384-94; Clapham, *op. cit.* I, p. 442.
9. *Reports of the Inspectors of Factories* (1852-3) XL, p. 26; (1856) XVIII, pp. 13-4, 24; (1863) XVIII, pp. 60-1.
10. W. J. M. Rankine, *Useful Rules and Tables* (London, 1866), p. 289.
11. Baines, pp. 396-7; Ellison, pp. 65-6. Chapman and Wood ignore the fact that the 1834 returns are incomplete: *op. cit.* p. 12; p. 127.
12. See G. H. Wood, "Factory Legislation," *Journal Royal Statistical Society* (June 1902).
13. Wood, pp. 127-8.

Part II
The History of Economic Thought

4　The Empirical Content of Ricardian Economics

I think it fair to say that Ricardian economics is popularly depicted as having evolved in a state of almost complete factual ignorance. The weight of modern scholarship concurs in regarding the empirical content of Ricardian economics, whatever its character, as irrelevant to an understanding of economic thought in the half-century after Ricardo's death. To be sure, the initial postulates of the Ricardian "vision" are granted to have been influenced by casual observation and a variety of impressions of the contemporary scene.[1] But it is held that to criticise the classical economists for not having checked their theoretical conclusions against empirical data is to expect the thinkers of a previous age to meet the rigorous standards of modern economics, and that after all is a historical fallacy. The paucity of statistical material in the period, it is said, made it impossible to entertain any but an abstract and deductive approach to economic reasoning.[2] In consequence, the disciples as well as the critics of Ricardo appear to have spent their energies in debating the logical imperfections of Ricardo's system and, at best, the descriptive "realism" of its assumptions. In short, classical economics in its Ricardian phase is considered to be a product of theoretical discussion and nothing more.

Schumpeter in his *History of Economic Analysis* expresses himself very differently on this issue: "The opinion — the source of so much pointless controversy — that the economic profession then neglected factual research is utterly unfounded ... the 'classic' period fully maintained the tradition of factual research that, as we know, harks back to the sixteenth century."[3] The sceptical reader may well question this assertion, particularly since Schumpeter does little to substantiate it. The present essay should be regarded as an attempt to explore the implications of Schumpeter's remarks.

My purpose here is to show, first of all, that the body of doctrine which Ricardo bequeathed to his followers rested on a series of definite predictions about the course of economic events which were subject to empirical verification, in the strictest sense of the term. Second, I shall try to show that the statistical data and methods of the time, crude as they may have been, were adequate to test the validity of Ricardian theory; in terms of its predictive accuracy for the class of phenomena which it was intended to explain, and, moreover, that such evidence was within the purview of all the economists of the day. Lastly, I shall argue that few of the classical thinkers were willing to surrender economic propositions on the grounds that they were contradicted by the available evidence; but, I stress, this had nothing to do with lack of empirical information.

Indeed, the divorce between abstract theory and empirical work was never more complete than in the heyday of Ricardian economics. The existence of this dichotomy, for which I have sketched a tentative explanation in the closing section of this chapter, constitutes the central problem in the interpretation of "economics as Jevons found it."

I.   RICARDO'S VIEW OF THE FUTURE

The keystone of Ricardo's system is the proposition that "profits depend on wages, not on nominal, but real wages." Apart from the familiar distinction between (1) *per capita* money wages and (2) *per capita* real wages, Ricardo speaks of (3) natural wages, (4) market wages, and (5) "real wages." It is in the last sense, in which wages are a function of the labour time required to produce wage goods (that is, corn) on the rentless margin of production, that profits are said to depend upon wages.[4] Owing to the growth of population and the resort to ever poorer or less accessible grades of soil, a greater quantity of labour comes to be embodied in each additional unit of agricultural produce; consequently, the value of labour's share of the physical product must rise, independently of the effect on *per capita* wages, and the value of capital's share must fall.[5]

The rising cost of corn via its effect on "real wages" indicates a historical tendency toward declining profits and increasing rents. But, whereas the landlord's real income rises with additions to his money income, the labourer's position fails to improve.[6] So long as capital accumulation continues unabated, money wages tend to rise with the price of corn, leaving real wages unaltered.

Although Ricardo speaks of labour as paid in bushels of corn, he recognises, of course, that labourers will exchange some corn wages for other consumption goods. Real wages tend to rise insofar as the labourer's standard of living depends upon the purchase of manufactured goods which become progressively cheaper with the increasing productivity of labour. Nevertheless, Ricardo states that "there are few commodities which are not more or less affected in their price by the rise of raw produce."[7] Cost reductions in manufacturing, therefore, cannot offset the progressive rise in the cost of producing corn.[8] In addition, the population doctrine of Malthus posited a latent and often actual excess of the supply of labour over the demand for labour, implying a perpetual downward pressure on money wages.[9] Ricardo specifically considers a lag of population behind a rise in money wages due to an upward shift in the standard of living, only to conclude that "in practice it is invariably found that an increase of population follows the amended condition of the labourer ... and it is because the number of people is increased, that wages again fall."[10]

It is clear that the entire analysis rests ultimately on the crucial assumption that money wages are governed by the price of wheaten bread or, at any rate, by the cost of production of wheat.[11] Whatever the doctrinal precedence for such a view, this was nothing more than "the simple belief common among the commercial classes of his time."[12] And, in a sense, this belief was broadly consonant with experience. Throughout the years of the Napoleonic Wars changes in the price of wheat seem to have dominated the "cost-of-living index."[13] Moreover, the notion of a causal relationship between wages and the price of corn drew support from the upward drift of both money wages and wheat prices from 1790 to 1820, with the prices of meats and dairy products keeping pace with the rise in the price of bread.[14] But, whatever the rationale, there is no doubt that Ricardo used "corn" as an omnibus term for wage goods and invariably assumed that the demand for grain was highly inelastic.[15]

The theory required only one additional argument to become a guide to public policy, namely, that the price of wheaten bread within the country was higher with a system of import duties on corn than without one. The ultimate purpose of Ricardo's chain of reasoning was to demonstrate the deleterious effects of agricultural protection. If the Corn Laws were not amended to permit the importation of cheap food, thereby encouraging the transfer of resources to industry, the growth of capital and population would automatically undermine the possibilities of further economic growth. That is to say, the alleged "pessimism" of Ricardo was entirely contingent upon the existence of the Corn Laws.

The notion of an impending stationary state was at most a useful device for frightening his complacent contemporaries. In point of fact, Ricardo did not regard it as imminent.[16] "I contend for free trade in corn," he wrote to Trower, "on the ground that while trade is free, and corn cheap, profits will not fall however great be the accumulation of capital. If you confine yourself to the resources of your own soil, I say, rent will in time absorb the greatest part of that produce which remains after paying wages, and consequently profits will be low."[17]

Ricardo's system is clearly grounded upon the faith that England was capable of becoming "the workshop of the world" and that its future was bound up with the development of industry. For all practical purposes, the limits to economic progress were political and not economic in character. Misunderstanding on this score proved to be the decisive weakness of the

Ricardian school. When free trade was not immediately forthcoming, the Ricardians were faced with the problem of accounting for the rapid economic growth of the 1830s and 1840s. It is true that Ricardo's programme did not call for the immediate or total repeal of agricultural protection; in view of vested interests in "the restrictive system," he suggested a gradual reduction in grain duties over the next decade and a corresponding bounty on exportation to countervail the special taxes with which the landowners were burdened.[18] But in the absence of such measures the Ricardian "engine of analysis" predicted (in the long run) a rising price of corn, a rising share of the national income going to rent-receivers, constant real wages, and a gradual vanishing of investment opportunities in industry.

Needless to say, Ricardo's legislative proposals were not enacted. The return in 1828 to the pre-1815 device of a sliding scale of duties did little to lessen the protection of agriculture, which survived until 1846. Yet the consequences predicted by Ricardo failed to materialise. It was the task of his disciples to resolve this dilemma.

II. THE ECLIPSE OF MALTHUSIAN DOCTRINE

The Ricardian antithesis of wages and profits tied the general rate of profit to the price of wheat and, thereby, to the productivity of labour in agriculture. Consequently, the law of diminishing returns, encompassed in the Malthusian "pressure" of population upon "the means of subsistence," served as the fulcrum of the Ricardian system. If the concept of diminishing returns could be shorn of its short-run implications, the rate of profit could no longer be held to be dependent upon the physical returns of land; not only the Ricardian system but Malthus' doctrine as well would then become untenable. It was, in fact, in the area of population controversy that the contradictions of Ricardian economics first became manifest. The Malthusian theory of population underwent a total eclipse in the 1830s, a phenomenon which has not received the attention it warrants. With the decline of confidence in the principle of population, the Ricardian theory lost much of its logical rigour and became incapable of specifying the strength and direction of movement of the major economic variables with which it was concerned.

The historical rule of diminishing returns in agriculture, confirmed by the events of the war, was converted by Ricardo's followers into what Cannan has called "the pseudo-scientific law of diminishing returns"; though the progress of civilisation postponed the effect, the spectre of diminishing productivity was held to be ever present and operative.[19] The law was never rigorously formulated as an analytical statement about *per capita* returns under static conditions in the instant of a shift of population. Instead it came to be regarded as a law of dynamics, uniquely applicable to agriculture and verified by the extension of cultivation to inferior soils. Proof of the principle of population now took the form of a syllogism: If "capital" or the "fund of subsistence" had a tendency to increase faster than population, conditions would be prosperous. Conditions were not prosperous. Therefore, population had a tendency to increase faster than capital.[20]

It was not admitted, however, that improvements in the standard of living were incompatible with the supposed constancy of the pressure of population on the food supply. Under certain circumstances even Malthus was willing to grant that subsistence actually increased at a greater rate than population, even for centuries at a time. With the addition of the check of "moral restraint" in the second edition of the *Essay on Population*, Malthus provided the theory with a perfect escape clause, which made it impossible to grapple with it successfully. Whenever an increase of population was accompanied by a rise instead of a fall in the level of real wages, the "contradiction" was resolved by crediting the result to the operation of the moral check. This enabled Malthus to propose his law of population as the principal generator of economic progress and, at the same time, as the perennial barrier to social improvement.

Furthermore, Malthus had never clearly grasped the nature of the "population explosion" in the 1780s. What accounted for the rapid growth of population after 1780 was the spectacular fall in the death rate (particularly in the rate of infant mortality), owing to the development of medical services and sanitation, allied with a revolution in agricultural methods. Malthus was aware of the decline in the crude death rate but underestimated its significance, emphasising instead the birth and marriage rates.[21] But the birth rate, which had been rising throughout the eighteenth century, actually began to fall after 1790, first imperceptibly and then sharply in the 1820s.[22] The marriage rate, on the other hand, showed no definite secular trend for the whole period. It tended to decline from 1800 to 1817 and to rise until 1824, and then it declined for the next two decades. The fall in the marriage rate was counteracted to some extent by a rise in the fertility of marriage due to a downward shift in the age distribution of the population and a lower average age of marriage. Nevertheless, the birth rate did not increase until after the 1840s, and the death rate reached a minimum point in 1815, after which it rose again until 1830.[23]

These statistical trends did not go long unrecognised. As early as 1830, John Barton denied that the rising number of births was responsible for the increase in population.[24] Three years after the death of Malthus, Mc-Culloch produced his *Statistical Account of the British Empire* (1837) in which he supported Barton's thesis with a wealth of statistics [25] and noted that the decennial census of 1831 revealed a significant decline in the rate of population growth. [26]

Moreover, by the 1830s, not only did most economists realise that the growth of population was the net effect of two separate rates, but the inverse relationship between living standards and births was singled out as the major element in Britain's new demographic balance. The discussion went through two clearly discernible stages. First came the notion that the spread of birth-control techniques might enable families to limit their size with little violence to natural instincts. Only later was there recognition of some of the causes which made people desire to have smaller families.

Malthus himself placed all his hopes on the inculcation of prudent forethought as "the only effectual mode of improving the conditions of the poor." His plea for moral restraint, however, was as utopian in its own way as Godwin's claim that the progress of the human mind would bring about universal benevolence. Both required an entire change in human conduct but provided no means for bringing such a transformation about. Nevertheless, Malthus' didactic admonitions to the working class to practise forbearance, while they had nothing in common for him with the defence of birth control, paved the way for the advent of neo-Malthusian ideas. The argument that the birth rate could be limited by voluntary decision to postpone marriage was subtly transformed by hinting at the existence of "expedients" that might accomplish the same result without ascetic restraint. Francis Place and James and John Stuart Mill all employed this device to lighten the darker tints of the principle of population.

The publication of correspondence between Malthus and Nassau Senior in 1829 marked the first break with the doctrine by a leading economist. [27] Despite Senior's emphasis on the verbal ambiguities of Malthus' writings, it is clear that his criticism had an empirical basis. "I should still say," he wrote, "that, in the absence of a disturbing cause, food has a tendency to increase faster, because, in fact, *it has generally done so*, and because I consider the desire of bettering our condition as natural a wish as the desire for marriage." [28] Malthus, however, was not to be conflicted, and the discussion broke down over the social implications of the Malthusian theory.

Senior had submitted the theory of population to the historical test and found it wanting. But he had not questioned the rule of diminishing returns in agriculture, and, so long as its validity went unchallenged, the so-called arithmetical ratio had a certain presumption in its favour. In 1831 Richard Jones attempted to undermine this assumption by emphasising the consequences of continuous improvements in cultivation and the phenomenon of returns to scale in industry. [29] A sceptical tone began to dominate the debates at the Political Economy Club; in 1831 the discussion turned once again to "the merits of Ricardo," and now some of the members were ready to question Ricardo's acceptance of Malthus' population theory.[30]

A few weeks prior to the publication of the Malthus-Senior correspondence, Robert Torrens published a new edition of the *Essay on the External Corn Trade* in which he declared: "There is no tendency in population to increase faster than capital, and thus to degrade wages."[31] Afterward he claimed credit for being the first to refute the Malthusian doctrine.[32] For a moment Malthus' *Essay* was overshadowed by the furious discussion provoked by Sadler's *Law of Population* (1830), which substituted a biological principle of declining fertility for the Malthusian check of moral restraint.[33] Macaulay gave the work notoriety by a derisive attack in the *Edinburgh Review* (July 1830), while the *Quarterly Review* featured an analysis of the controversy by George Poulett Scrope which condemned Malthus and Sadler alike and criticised Senior for his frequent concessions to Malthus' arguments.[34] Richard Whately rose to Senior's defence with another verbal clarification.[35] Two years later Scrope published *Principles of Political Economy*, which had as one of its primary objects the refutation of the Malthusian theory of population.[36]

Malthus' remaining disciples only brought the doctrine into further disrepute. In a work entitled *Political Economy, in Connexion with the Moral State of Society* (1832) Thomas Chalmers propounded the Malthusian programme with a fervour that bordered on monomania. McCulloch reviewed the book in the pages of the *Edinburgh Review* and objected strenuously to Chalmers' conclusion that the growth of population and the necessary recourse to inferior soil had steadily reduced the English standard of living over the last fifty years.[37] Citing the annual increases in meat and grain consumption, the fall in the death rate and the mounting funds of savings banks, whose depositors consisted largely of wage-earners, McCulloch observed: "Though wages have declined since the peace, they have not declined to anything like the extent to which prices have declined; and ... the condition of the labourers has been decidedly improved."[38] In the second edition of his *Principles* (1830) McCulloch did not hesitate to chide Malthus for having "overlooked and undervalued the influence of the principles which countervailed the tendency to increase of population."

The opponents of Ricardo were not adverse to pressing this kind of argument to its logical conclusion. William Whewell, who accepted Richard Jones as a guide in economic matters, expressed himself unequivocally before the Cambridge Philosophical Society:

Ricardo ... neglected altogether the effects of an increase in the powers of agriculture, which, in England, has been a change at least as important and as marked, as the increase in population. This being the case, it is evident that the whole of his assumption as to the nature of the economical progress of this country, and the views of the distribution of wealth arising from this assumption, must fall to the ground.[39]

After the passage of the Poor Law Amendment Act of 1834 and the early efforts of Edwin Chadwick and others to improve medical and sanitary conditions, the Malthusian bogy was all but vanquished and ceased to carry conviction. Senior's view of the doctrine now prevailed without opposition at the Political Economy Club,[40] and the Malthusian faith in the check of moral restraint was virtually abandoned. Malthus himself had shown that a reduction in the birth rate could not affect wages until after a lapse of sixteen to eighteen years.[41] Obviously, it was pointed out, no wage-earner would ever be actuated by such remote consequences.[42] Furthermore, the level of wages might conceivably be raised by concerted effort but not by individuals acting in isolation. "Universal distress fails to suggest any motive for individual restraint," declared William Lloyd, Professor of Political Economy at the University of Oxford.[43] Hortatory appeals to the working class, it came to be realised, had little effect on the supply of labour, and more could be accomplished by direct improvements in the standard of living; habit and custom would convert the new amenities into conventional necessities, and a taste for these additional comforts would provide the wage-earner with an effective motive for family limitation.

In his *Wages and Combinations* (1834) Torrens tried to elaborate on the notion that the size of the family tended to decline with the increase of *per capita* wealth. His argument illustrates the prevailing departure from classic Malthusian theory. In countries where an abundance of fertile soil remains to be cultivated, he reasoned, a large family is an economic asset; but in densely populated areas, such as England, the unmarried worker finds himself at a financial advantage compared with the married worker. Therefore, he wrote,

as a country approaches the limits of her agricultural resources (and food prices mount), marriages become less frequent; and the *power* to increase and multiply . . . is checked and controlled by the prevailing efficacy of these causes to such an extent, that the tendency in every civilised community is . . . for capital to increase faster than population.[44]

After 1834 no writer of economics expounded the Malthusian theory without taking note of the empirical evidence that contradicted it. When Herman Merivale, Senior's successor to the Chair of Political Economy at Oxford, defended the Malthusian thesis in 1837, he expressed himself in the following words:

The doctrine of population is, in Political Economy, what that of original sin is in theology — offensive to philosophical pride, and irksome to sanguine temperament; and hence the endless attempts which are made to contradict or to evade it. It is humiliating to feel that society must rely on the slow process of moral restraint as the only corrective of a necessary evil ... We prefer to be told ... that machinery and science, and facilities of communication, are outstripping the rapid march of numbers, and rendering our sage apprehensions wholly imaginary. *The extraordinary advance of England in these respects, in the course of the last few years, has no doubt had an effect in lessening the practical belief in economical doctrines.* [45]

In John Stuart Mill's *Principles* (1848) the Malthusian theory of population became, once again, the key to the Ricardian theory of distribution. In his effort to restore Malthus' arguments Mill indeed affected something of a counter-revolution. The population controversy of the 1830s, however, left its marks on his view of the question. Nowhere did Mill invoke the plea of self-restraint in the manner of Malthus; he recognised that family limitation tends to follow in the wake of rising living standards and saw the need for positive state action to change the habits of the labouring classes. [46] Although Mill never committed himself explicitly on the matter in later life, there is little doubt that he continued to entertain a belief in the restraint of population by birth control. [47] In the *Principles* he joined the demand for full equality of women with the hope of voluntary family limitation and spoke diffidently of the possibility of continence in marriage. [48] Having defended the Malthusian theory of population as analytically "correct," he was forced to concede that the census reports did not uphold the theory: "Subsistence and employment in England has never increased more rapidly than in the last forty years but every census since 1821 showed a smaller proportional increase of population than that of the period preceding." [49] When he came to deal with "probable futurity of the labouring classes" in the closing section of the *Principles*, he went so far as to support the Senior-Whately viewpoint:

It appears to me impossible but that the increase of intelligence, of education, and of love of independence among the working classes, must be attended with a corresponding growth of the good sense which manifests itself in provident habits of conduct, and the population, therefore, will bear a gradually diminishing ratio to capital and employment. [50]

III. THE USE OF QUANTITATIVE DATA

As yet I have shown little more than that the classical economists read the census returns. The principle of population was not "constantly in operation," real wages were rising despite the Corn Laws and despite diminishing returns, and the investment horizon seemed unlimited. Anything that we would call statistical reasoning, however, was still lacking.

By the third decade of the nineteenth century the mathematical theory of probability, including the normal law of error, was already widely disseminated among European astronomers and physicists. In England, De Morgan's classic article on probability appeared in the *Encyclopedia Metropolitana* in 1836, while Ellis delivered a paper on the method of least squares before the Cambridge Philosophical Society in 1844. But, so far as social phenomena were concerned, the new statistical methods were applied solely to legal testimony, mortality tables, and the computation of annuities.[51] The work of Quetelet, with its use of the normal curve to describe sociological trends, did not come until the 1850s; and the idea of correlation was not developed until the last quarter of the century.

In economics the concept of a price index (pioneered by Joseph Lowe and George Scrope) marked the only technical advance.[52] Descriptive statistics, however, received official recognition as a separate branch of inquiry as early as 1832 with the addition of a statistical department to the Board of Trade. Within a year the British Association for the Advancement of Science formed a statistical section, and in the same year a statistical society was founded in Manchester and in London (later the Royal Statistical Society). Richard Jones and Charles Babbage were instrumental in launching the London Society's *Quarterly Journal*, and by 1835 the "Index of Fellows" included Chadwick, Malthus, McCulloch, Merivale, Scrope, Senior, Tooke, and Torrens.[53]

The function of the new society, as announced in its prospectus, was to "procure, arrange and publish facts to illustrate the conditions and prospects of society"; nevertheless, the members were cautioned to observe the distinction between statistics and economics:

The Science of Statistics differs from Political Economy, because, although it has the same end in view, it does not discuss causes, nor reason upon probable effects; it seeks only to collect, arrange, and compare, that class of facts which alone can form the basis of correct conclusions with respect to social and political government.[54]

Very shortly, however, one member expressed the view that "the study of Statistics will, ere long, rescue Political Economy from all the uncertainty in which is is now enveloped",[55] and in 1843 James Lawson, then Professor of Political Economy at the University of Dublin, declared before the Statistical Section of the British Association that "statistics affords at once the materials and the test of political economy ... but the latter points out the proper objects of statistical inquiry, and draws conclusions from their results."[56]

Indeed, the tabulation and interpretation of the growing body of data gathered by various state departments and Royal Commissions soon provided "the materials and the test of political economy." George Porter's *Progress of the Nation*, the first serious attempt at a statistical manual of the British economy, succeeded in framing a simple factual argument to invalidate the rule of diminishing returns in agriculture. From 1801 to 1831 the population of the United Kingdom had increased by nine million; yet "where the people are deprived of any considerable proportion of their accustomed supply of food, it is highly improbable that their number should increase." Since grain imports had never risen above the average annual figure of 500,000 quarters of wheat (only exceeding one million quarters in five separate years of deficient harvest), it followed that "a most important extension of agriculture must have taken place within the Kingdom." [57] Moreover, while the number of families in Great Britain rose by 34 per cent between 1811 and 1831, the number of families employed in agriculture increased by only 7 per cent. "It is impossible . . . to arrive at any other conclusion," Porter wrote, "than that a larger amount of produce has of late been continually drawn from a given portion of ground than was obtained in general at the beginning of the century"; although cultivation has been extended, "the produce of equal surfaces of ploughed land has increased in a still greater ratio." [58]

Much of this, of course, was still inspired guesswork; the available data on the yield of different classes of arable soil were too scanty to allow for any definite conclusions about the productivity of agriculture. [59] Porter himself despaired eventually at the lack of adequate statistical material; in an address before the Statistical Section of the British Association in 1839 he voiced the complaint that "to this day the public is without any authoritative document from which to know even the quantity of land under cultivation in any county of England." He went on to say that almost no information existed regarding "the proportion required for reproduction" and blamed the landed interests for obstructing statistical inquiries on the ground that the publication of the facts might damage their claim to protection. [60]

McCulloch's *Statistical Account of the British Empire*, however, followed Porter's argument in every detail. [61] In 1846 McCulloch was prepared to commit himself even more explicitly. Difficult as it was to distinguish "pure rent" and "gross rent", he nevertheless ventured to assert that "estimating the whole rental of Great Britain at *forty-five* millions, if we set apart *twenty* millions as real rent, and regard the remaining *twenty-five* millions as interest on account of buildings, fences, drains, roads, and other improvements of the soil, we shall certainly be within the mark." [62] Although gross rents had risen by 30 per cent from 1815 to 1845, McCulloch noted, [63] rents on the whole were "moderate in England", because of "a disinclination on the part of many landlords to raise rent, and a wish not to remove tenants, and to keep their estates always under-rented." [64]

Three years later the analysis of rent in the third edition of McCulloch's

Principles gave no hint that the law of diminishing returns, the exclusive dependence of rent on differences in the quality of soils, and the tendency of "pure rents" to rise with the progress of wealth and population, all fundamental tenets of the Ricardian system, had been contradicted by data which the author himself had gathered. It never seems to have occurred to McCulloch to re-examine his theoretical views in the light of statistical findings.

Even the opponents of Ricardo reveal the same basic pattern. Despite Senior's attack on the Malthusian population theory and his emphasis on the economies of large-scale production, he admitted "the connection between rent, population and distribution as elucidated by Ricardo to be formally correct."[65] Restrictions on the importation of agricultural produce, he argued, constitute restrictions on the exportation of manufactured articles; by limiting the scale of production, the Corn Laws diminish the efficiency of industry and make it necessary to raise additional food on domestic soil at rising cost.[66] Since workers consume chiefly "raw or slightly-manufactured produce," the advantages of economies of scale in industry are of no avail: the net effect is always "a constant tendency towards an increase of capital and population; and towards a fall in the rate of profit."[67] But during the last century "the total amount of the annual agricultural produce of Great Britain has more than doubled ... it is highly improbable that the amount of labour annually employed in agriculture has also doubled."[68] Nevertheless, recognition of this fact did not cause Senior to doubt that the physical limits to cost reductions in agriculture were irrepressible in the long run.

John Stuart Mill, of course, gave credence to the familiar contention that the decreasing productivity of agriculture would eventually result in a weakening of investment incentives and a rising share of the national income going to the landlord class. Mill first defined the rule of diminishing returns as a self-evident axiom, then qualified it by listing a number of dynamic checks or counteracting factors, but in the end maintained it as "the most important proposition in political economy."[69] Although he did not wish to go to the length of asserting an inherent law of increasing returns in industry, he recognised that "manufactured articles tend, as society advances, to fall in money price."[70] Indeed, he did not stop there but denied the operation of the law of diminishing returns over the whole period since 1825:

There are times when a strong impulse sets in towards agricultural improvement. Such an impulse has shown itself in Great Britain during the last fifteen or twenty years. In England and Scotland agricultural skill has of late increased considerably faster than population, insomuch that food and other agricultural produce, notwithstanding the increase of people, can be grown at less cost than they were thirty years ago.[71]

The leading economists of the period all preserved this curious separation between theory and fact. The major debatable issues in Ricardian economics hinged upon the race between the variables of technical progress and diminishing returns in agriculture. On this score, both the disciples and the critics of Ricardo contradicted the facts, which they all acknowledged, with hypothetical comparisons of the increase of population and the increase of food. We need not look far for an explanation of this phenomenon. Statistical data which showed rising yields per acre in agriculture, a declining rate of population growth, a continuous increase in domestic capital formation, and a rising level of real wages weakened the case for free trade. In fact, when we look at the attitudes of the classical economists toward free trade, not as an abstract policy proposal, but as an issue to be fought for with allies like Richard Cobden and John Bright, we obtain a vital clue to the virtual isolation of economic theory from empirical work.

IV. THE ECONOMIC EFFECTS OF THE CORN LAWS

The campaign of the Anti-Corn Law League in the 1840s revolved largely about the effects of the Corn Laws on prices and the income of productive factors — in short, about the predictive accuracy of the Ricardian theory. Spokesmen of industry and almost all writers on free trade had insisted for more than a half-century that repeal would lower the price of bread, reduce money wages, and raise profits. Certainly Ricardo, James Mill, and McCulloch had argued that cheap corn involved low money wages and dear corn high money wages. In this sense, the Ricardians were generally exponents of what German critics have labelled the *Paralleltheorie*.[72]

By 1840 the downward trend of wheat prices over the preceding decades, the growth of industry, and the gradual shift of consumption patterns away from landusing products gave rise to the *Konträrtheorie*, the doctrine that a low price of food did not imply a low rate of money wages and might well be accompanied by an increase of money wages through the stimulus given to foreign trade. In fact, the demand for industrial labour had always been a disturbing factor in the alleged relationship between wheat prices and wages.[73] But contemporary writers were reluctant to admit this, and the available data on wages proved inconclusive.[74] The debate was invariably confused by the failure to draw a distinction between aggregate and per unit wages and between money and real wages; the literature of the league carefully preserved the umbrella term "wages" in order to appeal to all shades of opinion.

By the 1840s, however, the *Paralleltheorie* had become the thesis of the protectionists and the league's cry was now "Cheap bread, dear labour;

dear bread, cheap labour." Cobden's very first speech in Parliament took up "the fallacy of wages ... which is at the bottom of all opposition to the repeal of the Corn-laws." "The rate of wages," he announced, "has no more connection with the price of food than with the moon's changes."[75] In the very same speech he estimated that 50 per cent of wages were on the average spent on food and that the Corn Laws had raised the price of bread by 40 per cent and, hence, had taxed wages by 20 per cent.[76] He left it to his audience to resolve the contradiction.

Cobden repeatedly disavowed any interest in free trade merely because it would reduce the price of corn. What was wanted, he would say, was a uniform international price of wheat, regardless of its consequences for domestic prices. Nevertheless, his earlier public addresses are filled with implicit references to the Ricardian notion that the Corn Laws maintained the price of home-grown produce above the competitive level; consequently, repeal would reduce the cost of labour (money wages) and permit Britain to compete on the international market.[77] Eventually he learned to place the subject on a broader footing. Free trade, he argued, would bring expanded markets; wages would rise as profit margins improved, and, so far from injuring agriculture, repeal would benefit it by stimulating the demand for wheat.

In his anxiety to secure the widest support for his cause, however, Cobden fell between two stools. He declared without hesitation that rents had doubled since 1793 and had risen steadily since 1828.[78] Without this consequence, it was clear that the attack on the personal motives of landlords lacked any foundation. But on the eve of repeal Cobden, deserting his Ricardian tenets, declared that the abolition of the Corn Laws would not diminish rents;[79] three years later he denied that he had ever dwelt upon a reduction of rents or a shifting of resources from land to manufacturing as a consequence of free trade.[80]

The ambiguous stand of the league on the relationship between the price of corn and the rate of wages, an ambiguity which it had largely inherited from Ricardo's school, soon exposed it to attack. Protectionist writers had no difficulty in culling a long list of contradictory statements from *The Anti-Corn Law Circular* and from Cobden's public speeches, which they employed to damage the claims of the free-traders.[81] But professional economists remained aloof from the discussion. Torrens alone divorced himself explicitly from the viewpoint of the Manchester School, but on special grounds of his own.[82] For the most part, the economists now agreed that the rate of wages did not vary with the price of food and that repeal would not necessarily produce a fall in monetary wages.[83] John Stuart Mill noted that temporary fluctuations in the price of provisions probably affect wages in the opposite direction; but in the long run "wages do adapt themselves to the price of food, though after the interval of almost a generation."[84] "I cannot, therefore, agree," Mill declared, "in the importance so often attached to the repeal of the corn laws, considered merely as a labourer's question, or to any of the schemes, of which some one or other is at all times in vogue, for making the labourers *a very little better off*."[85] In its day this statement could have been read only as a sharp disavowal of the vulgar propaganda of the Anti-Corn Law League. But it is more than that; it is an attempt to salvage Ricardo's *Paralleltheorie*.

Mill was aware that the Corn Laws had not succeeded in maintaining the price of corn at wartime levels, much less in raising it.[86] In the attempt to square this fact with the deductions of Ricardian theory, he closed the door against any possibility of disproof on empirical grounds:

The difference between a country without corn laws, and a country which has long had corn laws, is not so much that the last has a high price or a larger rental, but that it has the same price and the same rental with a smaller aggregate capital and a small population. The imposition of corn laws raises rents, but retards that progress of accumulation which would in no long period have raised them fully as much. The repeal of corn laws tends to lower rents, but it unchains a force which in a progressive state of capital and population restores and even increases the former amount.[87]

This statement has to be compared to another in which Mill suggests that a time series of wheat prices, deflated by an appropriate index and adjusted for seasonal variations, would provide a rough measure of the relative strength of the forces making for diminishing returns and increasing returns in the process of capital formation.[88] Needless to say, he did not carry out the investigation; it would merely have proved what he already knew.

If the precise effect of free trade on the British price of wheat could have been clearly established in 1850 or thereabouts, Fawcett and Cairnes might never have written. But the discovery of gold in California and Australia in 1849-50 soon exerted an independent influence on the level of prices and radically altered Britain's terms of trade. In other respects, however, the course of events in the thirty years following repeal was such as to support the viewpoint of the Manchester School. A larger quantity of grain was imported in the decade after 1846 than in all the thirty-one years between Waterloo and repeal, yet there was no ruinous drop in wheat prices or in acreage under cultivation. In fact, the period between repeal and the 1870s was the golden age of British farming.[89] Moreover, the rise in corn imports did serve to stimulate the export of British manufactures; a considerable part of the increased foreign supply after 1846 was derived from the Levant, and by 1855 this area constituted the major foreign outlet for Manchester cotton goods. Judged by the results, the hopes of Cobden and Bright had been broadly vindicated.

There remains the question: Did the Corn Laws have a material influence on prices, and, if so, what was the magnitude of the effect? Unfortunately, this issue cannot be settled even with modern statistical methods. The difficulty of estimating the repercussions of the Corn Law of 1815 is that of measuring the indirect effect of a nonexistent tax.[90] Under the fixed-price provisions of the act, foreign grain entered freely or was shut out altogether. Consequently, between 1817 and 1824 no revenue was derived from import duties on grain, and bread went literally untaxed.[91] Even under the sliding scale of 1828 corn was not imported until the price rose above a certain level, and the volume of imports, as well as the level of import duties, fluctuated violently from month to month.[92] During some years the failure of Continental harvests prevented the shipment of grain to England; free trade would not have lowered the price of grain in those years. As a matter of fact, years of scarcity in European grain areas almost always coincided with poor harvests in England and Ireland. Evidence collected in the 1820s indicates that the available foreign supply was normally limited to meeting a one-tenth deficiency of the British harvest. If this is so, as it seems to be for the period up to the 1840s, the Corn Laws must have had little effect on the level of corn prices.

The fact that the price of wheat in the post-war period showed a discernible declining trend and never again approached the famine levels of 1816-20 is not in itself decisive. Jevons showed subsequently that the price of corn never fell as low, from 1815 to 1850, as the average price of forty basic commodities and that the price of wheat considered separately did so only once, namely, in 1835.[93] On the other hand, both fell below the base-year price (1782) in 1822 and 1850, but neither fell as much as the average of the entire forty commodities combined. Hence Jevons' calculations suggest that the secular decline in the price of agricultural produce during the period was not so great as that of prices in general. This is to say that agricultural prices were preserved at relatively higher levels.[94] But it would be difficult to say whether this "price scissor" was due to the superior productivity of industry and resulting cost reductions on manufactured articles or to the existing scheme of protection for agriculture.

V. CAIRNES'S ATTACK ON STATISTICS

In the years that followed the publication of Mill's *Principles*, the science of statistics gained ever wider currency, but its pertinence for economic theory was still obscure. The rise in *per capita* income, despite the Malthusian theory of population, and the failure of wheat prices to reflect the alleged tendency toward diminishing returns were now credited to the "disturbing influence" of free trade.[95] That the same facts had been in evidence when the population of England was largely restricted to its own soil for food supplies was conveniently ignored.

The blatant discrepancy between theory and observation, however, provided the motive for Cairnes's significant attack on statistics. "The discussions of Political Economy have been constantly assuming more of a statistical character," he complained in 1857; "results are now appealed to instead of principles; the rules of arithmetic are superseding the canons of inductive reasoning; till the true course of investigation has been well-nigh forgotten." [96] Cairnes conceded that "on the whole, as nations advance in civilization, the proportion between population and subsistence generally alters in favour of subsistence — a proposition which, I think, can scarcely pretend to the dignity of a 'law' even in the loosest sense of the word." [97] Economic laws for Cairnes are principles deduced from "human nature and external facts," not "from the statistics of society, or from the crude generalizations of history." [98] Of course, he granted that the hypothetical conclusions of the science ought to be checked against positive results; if "the correspondence was not complete," the economist "would have to consider how far the discrepancy admitted of being explained by reference to the presence of known disturbing causes." [99]

This was a far cry, however, from the assertion that economic laws could be upset by empirical evidence. One of the "external facts" which were thus contravened was the law of diminishing returns based upon the physical character of the soil. Here Cairnes resorted to proof by *reductio ad absurdum* and declared:

The attempt to meet the doctrine in question by statistical data implies . . . a total misconception, both of the fact which is asserted, and of the kind of *proof* which an economic doctrine requires. The doctrine contains, not an historical generalisation to be tested by documentary evidence, but a statement as to an existing physical fact, which if seriously questioned, can only be conclusively determined by actual experiment upon the existing soil. [100]

No one, however, denied the doctrine as a "physical fact"; what was in question was the specific predictions drawn from it. Cairnes recognised as much when he observed that were the law of diminishing returns to be invalidated "the science of Political Economy, as it at present exists, would be as completely revolutionized as if human nature itself were altered." [101]

Cairnes's writings serve to indicate the methodological predilections of classical economics which barred the way to quantitative verification. The classical economists were agreed (with the possible exception of Richard Jones) that economics was a deductive science based on simple premises derived from experience and conscious introspection. Methodological disputes took the form of disagreement over the relative significance and sufficiency of the underlying assumptions on which the whole deductive

structure was built.[102] Whether the structure itself was empirically meaningful was a question which was never squarely considered.

To be sure, all the classical writers gave lip service to the Baconian
method of "direct induction." John Stuart Mill pointed out in his classic
essay on methodology,

> we cannot too carefully endeavour to verify our theory, by comparing ... the
> results which it would have led us to predict, with the most trustworthy accounts we
> can obtain of those which have been actually realized ... The discrepancy between
> our anticipations and the actual fact is often the only circumstance which would
> have drawn our attention to some important disturbing cause which we had
> overlooked.[103]

The reference to a "disturbing cause" contains the whole of classical
teachings on the problem of testing the predictive success of economic
hypotheses.

VI. WHY DID THE RICARDIAN SYSTEM SURVIVE?

Methodological preconceptions were by no means the only factor responsible for preserving the Ricardian system in the face of uncomfortable
statistical evidence. It was one thing to reject the Malthusian population
theory but quite another to deny its corollary, a perfectly elastic supply
curve of labour in the long run. If the rate of population growth was not a
positive and unique function of earnings, no level of wages could be said to
represent an equilibrium level. To assert this was to invite the working class
to obtain an ever larger share of the national income through the bargaining process. An alternative answer was to assume a permanent reservoir of
unemployed labour which exerted a downward pressure on wages by
providing increasing competition for employment. Marx chose this explanation when he rejected Malthus' law of population. But the concept of
involuntary unemployment was foreign to classical political economy.
Within the framework of the prevailing identification of "population" with
"labour force" it was impossible to postulate a horizontal long-run supply
curve of labour without recourse, implicitly or explicitly, to Malthus'
principle.

Consequently, the opponents of Malthus were left with no wage at all or
were forced to reintroduce the doctrine in the course of their analysis.
Senior, for example, never related his discussion of population to the
question of wages;[104] other critics of Malthus, such as Read, Scrope, and
Torrens, likewise failed utterly to supply an alternative theory of wages.[105]
On the other hand, it was John Stuart Mill's recognition of the logical
interdependence of Ricardo's theories that led him to defend the Malthusian principle of population, even while denying its practical implications.

Once it was discarded, he realised, Ricardo's whole theory of distribution would cease to carry conviction. Ricardo's system was eminently suited to Mill's political programme of land reform and income redistribution, and in the final analysis, he was less interested in the "principles of political economy" than in "their applications to social philosophy."

Moreover, in an era of industrial expansion, based upon the invincible comparative advantage of British manufacturing, but impeded by high import duties on corn and the importance of wheaten bread in the workers' budget, a macro-economic theory had all the advantages of what Keynes called "a complex of suitabilities in the doctrine to the environment into which it was projected." On this level of analysis, Ricardo had no competitors. Although Senior's theory of value and capital, for example, derives from sources almost diametrically opposed to Ricardo, his theory of income distribution conforms to the pattern of the Ricardian school. What matter if he gave a superior explanation of the specific economic problems of the day, his writings bore the same conclusions as Ricardo's? To be sure, the deductions of Ricardo had been upset by "disturbing causes", but, so long as the Corn Laws remained in force, their general relevance to the contemporary scene was undeniable. Ricardian economics addressed itself to the major policy questions and provided a rationale for a definite course of action. Indeed, the Ricardian emphasis on distribution and long-run economic growth so permeated economic thinking in the period that even those who revolted against it accepted its major tenets, such as the link between rising costs in agriculture and the rate of capital accumulation and the notion of free trade as a bulwark against the stationary state.[106]

Ricardo's system has been aptly described as "magnificent dynamics",[107] its aim was to analyse the development of the economy over decades and even centuries. As such, it was difficult to expose on factual grounds in that less-than-long-run period which Ricardo calls "the progressive state." Like so many other dynamic systems, Ricardo's model is indeterminate with respect to its major variables and is capable of supporting a variety of interpretations. The analogy that suggests itself is that of Marx's "law of the increasing misery of the proletariat," which was not called into question until some three decades after the publication of the first volume of *Capital*. In the absence of an alternative structure of equal scope and practical import, yielding superior predictions for as wide a range of phenomena, the classical economists were bound to retain the Ricardian system in its broad outlines. Its survival, despite the existence and knowledge of adverse factual evidence, should serve to remind us of the subtle ambiguity that is implied whenever we speak of macroeconomic doctrine as confirmed or refuted by "experience."

NOTES

1. See, e.g., C.F. Dunbar, "Ricardo's Use of Facts," in *Economic Essays* (New York, 1914), and Edwin Cannan, *History of the Theories of Production and Distribution* (3rd edn., London, 1953), esp. pp. 116-32.
2. This "justification" is implicit in virtually every history of economic doctrines. For an explicit statement of this view see W.C. Mitchell's *Lecture Notes on Types of Economic Theory* (New York, 1949), pp. 160-1.
3. J.A. Schumpeter, *History of Economic Analysis* (New York, 1954), pp. 519-20.
4. See David Ricardo, *Works*, ed. P. Sraffa (Cambridge, 1951), I, pp. 27, 50, 102, 115, 119, 289, 411.
5. For a more detailed analysis of the argument see G.J. Stigler, "The Ricardian Theory of Value and Distribution," *Journal of Political Economy*, 60 (June 1952), pp. 203-4.
6. Ricardo, *op. cit.*, I, pp. 102-3, 112, 125.
7. *Ibid.* I, p. 117. I ignore the problem of reconciling this assertion with the usual Ricardian assumption of constant returns to scale in industry.
8. Ricardo went so far as to assert that the rate of profit was entirely independent of the productivity of labour in industry (*ibid.*, pp. 132-3).
9. *Ibid.*, I, p. 101.
10. *Ibid.*, I, p. 207.
11. See *ibid.*, I, pp. 117-48, 161-6, 215-22, 305-6.
12. Cannan, *op. cit.*, p. 129. Years later, Richard Cobden observed: "In reading the debates upon the passing of the first stringent Corn-law of 1814 I am struck to find that all parties who took part in that discussion were agreed upon one point, — it was that the price of food regulated the price of wages. That principle was laid down, not by one side of the House, but by men of no mean eminence on each side, and of course of opposite opinions in other respects" (*Speeches on Questions of Public Policy*, ed. J. Bright and J.E.T. Rogers [London, 1878], I, pp. 16-17).
13. See A.D. Gayer, *et al., The Growth and Fluctuations of the British Economy, 1790-1850* (Oxford, 1953), I, pp. 499-500, II, p. 817 ff. Institutional factors, such as the Speenhamland System, may have been responsible for the dominating influence of wheat prices.
14. Élie Halévy, *England in 1815* (London, 1949), pp. 2456.
15. Ricardo, *op. cit.*, I, pp. 190-1.
16. *Ibid.*, I, p. 265.
17. *Ibid.*, VIII, p. 208.
18. *Ibid.*, I, pp. 266-7.
19. See, e.g., James Mill, *Elements of Political Economy* (London, 1822), p. 41.
20. *Ibid.*, pp. 29-30.
21. See T.R. Malthus, *An Essay on the Principle of Population* (6th edn., 1826; London, 1890), pp. 222-30, 292-3, 466-70, 549-50.
22. G.T. Griffith, *Population Problems during the Age of Malthus* (Cambridge, 1926), p. 44.
23 T.H. Marshall, "The Population Problem during the Industrial Revolution," *Economic History*, supplement to the *Economic Journal*, (January, 1929).
24. *An Inquiry into the Progressive Depreciation of Agricultural Labour* (London, 1820), pp. 40-3.

25. J. R. McCulloch, *A Statistical Account of the British Empire* (London, 1837), I, pp. 417-18; see also G. R. Porter, *The Progress of the Nation* (London, 1836), I, p. 25. It is extraordinary how frequently it is assumed that the classical economists were ignorant of these facts. In a recent biography of John Stuart Mill, for example, it is asserted that the increase in population between 1801 and 1831 "was normally taken as evidence of an increasing birth-rate. In fact it was so taken until 1926, when G. Talbot Griffith showed that the birth-rate was declining steadily during the period, the increase in population being due to a marked reduction in the death-rate" (M. St. J. Packe, *The Life of John Stuart Mill* [London, 1954], p. 56 n.).

26. The average annual percentage rates of growth of population by decades for the period 1800-1850 are as follows: 1801-11, 1.3; 1811-21, 1.7; 1821-31, 1.5; 1831-41, 1.2; 1841-51, 1.2.

27. N. W. Senior, *Two Lectures on Population: To Which is Added a Correspondence between the Author and the Rev. T. R. Malthus* (London, 1829). The correspondence is reprinted in G. F. McCleary, *The Malthusian Population Theory* (London, 1953).

28. Senior, *op. cit.*, pp. 114-15. (My italics.)

29. *Essay on the Distribution of Wealth* (London, 1831), pp. 217-44, 248-55.

30. *Proceedings of the Political Economy Club, 1820-1821*, VI, London, (1921), p. 225.

31. *An Essay on the External Corn Trade* (5th edn.; London, 1829), p. 473.

32. Robert Torrens, *Letters on Commercial Policy* (London, 1833), pp. 43-4.

33. See K. Smith, *The Malthusian Controversy* (London, 1951), pp. 190-7.

34. *Quarterly Review*, (April 1831), pp. 97-145.

35. *Introductory Lectures on Political Economy* (2d edn.; London, Dublin, 1832), pp. 249-50.

36. George P. Scrope, *Principles of Political Economy* (London, 1833), pp. 257-92.

37. Cannan contended that Chalmers was the first writer of eminence to question the historical validity of the law of diminishing returns (*op. cit.*, pp. 135-6). Chalmers did argue that the deterioriation of living standards was not a necessary consequence of the extension of cultivation; but throughout his writings he spoke of "a limit to the augmentation of our physical resources," because of which "there must, especially in old countries, be a pressure and discomfort throughout every community" (*Selected Works of Dr. Chalmers*, ed. W. Hanna [Edinburgh, 1856] IX, pp. 334-43.

38. *Edinburgh Review*, (October 1832), p. 62. For the same view about the rise of real wages between 1815 and 1830 see *Proceedings of the Political Economy Club*, VI, pp. 234-35; *Quarterly Journal of the Statistical Society of London*, (August, 1850), pp. 210-14. This general assertion has been confirmed by the researches of Clapham, Bowley, and Wood. See also T. S. Ashton, "The Standard of Life of the Workers in England, 1790-1830," in *Capitalism and the Historians*, ed. F. A. Hayek (Chicago, 1954).

39. "Mathematical Exposition of Some of the Leading Doctrines of Mr. Ricardo's 'Principles,'" *Transactions of the Cambridge Philosophical Society*, IV, Part I (1833), pp. 178-9.

40. *Proceedings of the Political Economy Club*, VI, pp. 265-6. The "new" view on population crept into the seventh edition of Mrs. Marcet's *Popular Conversations on Political Economy* (London, 1839), p. 136.

41. T. R. Malthus, *Principles of Political-Economy* (London, 1820), p. 307.

Ricardo had expressed the same idea in his *Principles* without, however, stipulating the duration of the lag.

42. See the *Edinburgh Review* (May 1828), pp.316-17; S. Read, *Political Economy* (Edinburgh, 1829), pp. 162-6; *Proceedings of the Political Economy Club*, VI, p.252; Porter, *op. cit.*, I, p.33. Francis Place and John Barton had voiced this argument in the early 1820s, and the plea of moral restraint had long been a favourite butt of the Owenites.

43. W.F. Lloyd, *Two Lectures on the Checks to Population* (Oxford, 1833), p.22.

44. *On Wages and Combinations* (London, 1834), pp.30-1. Torrens' argument would be unimpeachable if he had spoken of a decline in natality rather than in marriages.

45. *Edinburgh Review*, (October 1837), pp.94-5. (My italics.)

46. J.S. Mill, *Principles of Political Economy*, ed., W.J. Ashley (London, 1909), pp.352-3.

47. See N.E. Himes, "J.S. Mill's Attitude towards neo-Malthusianism," *Economic History*, supplement to the *Economic Journal* (January 1929).

48. J.S. Mill, *op. cit.*, pp.375, 378-9.

49. *Ibid.*, (5th edn.; 1862), p.161. The same statement, but for the phrase "in the last forty years," appears in the first edition.

50. *Ibid.*, p.759. Earlier in the book, however, he attacks "several writers" who belabour the different meanings of the term "tendency," asserting that in fact population has slackened its rate of increase relative to subsistence. Mill insisted that any tendency for the pressure of population to diminish has been "extremely faint" (*ibid.*, pp.337-60). The reference is obviously to the Senior-Whately view of population, which had received renewed support from the new Drummond Professor of Political Economy at Oxford (see T. Twiss, *Certain Tests of a Thriving Population* [London, 1845], pp.27-8; *View of the Progress of Political Economy* [London, 1847], p.222).

51. See H.M. Walker, *Studies in the History of Statistical Method* (Baltimore, 1929), Ch. 2.

52. See T.S. Adams, "Index Numbers and the Standard of Value," *Journal of Political Economy*, 10 (December 1901), pp.1-31, for a history of the theory of index numbers before Jevons.

53. *Annals of the Royal Statistical Society* (London, 1934), pp.7 ff.

54. *Quarterly Journal of the Statistical Society of London* (May 1838), pp. 1-3.

55. *Quarterly Journal of the Statistical Society of London* (September 1838), p.317.

56. *Quarterly Journal of the Statistical Society of London* (December 1843), p.322.

57. Porter, *op. cit.*, I, p.145.

58. *Ibid.*, p.148.

59. Official agricultural statistics in England begin only in 1866. There are isolated official and unofficial estimates of the yield as well as of the acreage of the three main British cereals for the first half of the century which strongly suggest a sharply rising output of wheat and barley per acre for the years 1800-60 (see L. Drescher, "The Development of Agricultural Production in Great Britain and Ireland from the Early Nineteenth Century," *Manchester School*, May 1955).

60. *Quarterly Journal of the Statistical Society of London* (October 1830) pp. 291-6.
61. *Op. cit.*, I, pp. 551-2.
62. *Ibid.* (3rd edn.), p. 561.
63. Porter also found that "revenue drawn in the form of rent, from the ownership of land, has been at least doubled in every part of Great Britain since 1790" (*op. cit.*, I, p. 164). Recent research has shown that the sharp rise in rental values which characterised the period 1800-20 was not sustained in the years that followed; contrary to the prevailing contemporary impression, there was no clear trend in the rental series from 1820 to 1839 and only a slight increase in the 1840s (Gayer *et al.*, *op. cit.*, II, p. 927).
64. *Op. cit.*, pp. 557-8.
65. M. Bowley, *Nassau Senior and Classical Economics* (New York, 1949), p. 174.
66. N. W. Senior, *Outline of the Science of Political Economy* (1836) (New York, 1949), p. 178.
67. *Ibid.*, p. 193; see also pp. 81-3.
68. *Ibid.*, p. 86.
69. *Op. cit.*, p. 177.
70. *Ibid.*, p. 703; see also pp. 185-6, 444-5.
71. *Ibid.*, p. 704. The "fifteen or twenty years" of the first edition was replaced in the sixth edition (1865) by "twenty or twenty-five years" and in the seventh edition (1871) by "twenty or thirty years."
72. See K. Diehl, *Sozialwissenschaftliche Erläuterungen zu David Ricardos Grundgesetzen* (3rd edn.; Leipzig, 1921), pp. 86-145.
73. See Gayer *et al.*, *op. cit.*, II, pp. 925-5.
74. See Diehl *op. cit.*, pp. 105-23, for some representative opinions in the 1820s and 1830s on the relation between corn prices and wages.
75. Cobden, *op. cit.*, I, pp. 6-7.
76. *Ibid.*, pp. 3-4.
77. In all his writings I have been able to discover only one statement that indicates an understanding of the "high-wage economy" theory (*ibid.*, p. 19). There were times, particularly in years of good harvests and a falling price of corn, as in 1842, 1843, and 1844, when the league announced that repeal would be followed by a rise in wheat prices. But Cobden claimed in 1849 that real wages had risen 15 per cent owing to the repeal of the Corn Laws (*ibid.*, pp. 399, 437-8).
78. *Ibid.*, pp. 53-4; see also pp. 154, 192, 402.
79. *Ibid.*, p. 382.
80. *Ibid.*, p. 402.
81. See G. Barnes, *A History of the English Corn Laws from 1660-1846* (Boston, 1930), pp. 255-7.
82. Torrens believed that the unilateral repeal of protection, without guaranteed reciprocal action on the part of other countries, would prove a disastrous policy (*The Budget* [London, 1843], pp. 418-9).
83. See, in particular, W. T. Thornton, *Over-Population and Its Remedy* (London, 1846), p. 305; J. A. Lawson, *Five Lectures on Political Economy* (London, 1844), p. 8 n; N. W. Senior, *Industrial Efficiency and Social Economy*, ed. S. L. Levy (London, 1929), II, pp. 256-7.
84. *Op. cit.*, p. 347.
85. *Ibid.*, p. 348. (My italics.)

86. *Ibid.* (4th edn., 1857), p. 193.

87. *IBid.*, pp. 849-50.

88. *Ibid.*, p. 704.

89. See J. H. Clapham, *Economic History of Modern Britain: Free Trade and Steel, 1850-1886* (New York, 1932), pp. 2-9.

90. See C. R. Fay, *The Corn Laws and Social England* (London, 1932), pp. 109ff.

91. Barnes, *op. cit.*, p. 301.

92. Undoubtedly, the sliding scale of duties accentuated the amplitude of price fluctuations. On this point see R. C. O. Matthews, *A Study in Trade-Cycle History* (Cambridge, 1954), pp. 35-6.

93. W. S. Jevons, "The Variations in Prices and the Value of the Currency since 1782," *Journal of the Statistical Society of London* (June 1865). Reprinted in his *Investigations in Currency and Finance* (London, 1909), pp. 112-42. For a summary of Jevons' findings see Barnes, *op. cit.*, pp. 205-8.

94. This was also Marshall's opinion (see Alfred Marshall, *Industry and Trade* [4th edn.; London, 1923] pp. 754-7.

95. H. Fawcett, *Manual of Political Economy* (2d edn.; London, 1865), pp. 91-3, 146-8; *The Economic Position of the British Labourer* (London, 1865), pp. 137, 147-8.

95. J. E. Cairnes, *The Character and Logical Method of Political Economy* (London, 1857), pp. 5-6.

97. *Ibid.*, p. 172.

98. *Ibid.*, p. 173.

99. *Ibid.*, p. 80.

100. *Ibid.*, p. 35 n.

101. *Ibid.*, p. 36.

102. See Bowley, *op. cit.*, pp. 33-9.

103. J. S. Mill, *Essays on Some Unsettled Questions of Political Economy* (1844) (London, 1948), p. 154.

104. See Bowley, *op. cit.*, pp. 173-6.

105. The exception to this statement is Longfield, whose *Lectures on Political Economy* (Dublin, 1834) develop a marginal productivity theory of wages which allow him to shed all the trappings of the wages-fund doctrine or the population theory of wages. Longfield's book met with some success in Ireland but attracted no attention in England, either from the press or from other writers on political economy.

107. When Ricardo's system is defined in terms of the labour theory of value or the wages-profits maxim, its vital influence is by definition limited to a few disciples. Professor Robbins has recently registered his protest against this restricted conception of Ricardian economics ("Schumpeter's *History of Economic Analysis*," *Quarterly Journal of Economics*, February, 1955, pp. 10-11).

107. W. J. Baumol, *Economic Dynamics* (New York, 1951), p. 6.

5 Ricardo and the Problem of Public Policy

1. INTRODUCTION

Leo Rogin once wrote an unique history of economic thought, entitled *The Meaning and Validity of Economic Theory* (1956), which argued that all economic theories are invariably designed for the sole purpose of justifying a particular set of policy recommendations, and that their validity can only be judged in terms of the solution which they offer for some practical economic problem. Taken at face value, Rogin's thesis is untenable: some of the most famous economic theories have no policy implications whatsoever and many others have ambiguous implications for policy action. Nevertheless, there is little doubt that the desire to improve the economic system has always been a principal motive for the study of economics and that the genesis of many economic theories can be traced to an initial preference for some particular policy proposal. Certainly, one of the great differences between the social and the natural sciences is that social scientists are rarely content simply to explain the workings of society in order to satisfy a purely idle curiosity. Of course, natural scientists hope likewise to employ science wherever possible to transform nature but some of the most powerful theories of natural science, such as celestial mechanics, were clearly not devised to serve a practical purpose. At any rate, physical scientists typically ask the question whether their understanding of Mother Nature is true or false, not whether Mother Nature is good or bad, whereas social scientists cannot ultimately avoid asking both sets of questions. Social science attempts to explain states of the world but it is also driven to evaluate them if only because they are man-made. Thus, there is an inherent connection between economic theories and economic policies, which is not simply the product of the practical zeal of certain individual economists.

We can trace the concern with policy questions right back to the very origins of economic science and, indeed, sixteenth-, seventeenth-, and eighteenth-century economics was obsessed with matters of economic policy to the virtual exclusion of the analytical development of economic theory. Even in the nineteenth century, however, problems of what to do about the economy were always near to the surface of economic theorising. I think it is fair to say that writings on economic policy, not just in the nineteenth but also in the twentieth century up to and perhaps including the present time, have always suffered from four central weaknesses. The first of these is what might be called "the benevolent-despot view" of government, namely, that only ignorance can account for the failure of governments to adopt economic policies with demonstrably favourable consequences; economics is the science that studies the allocation of scarce means among given but competing ends and it is up to governments to will the ends; whether governments actually implement economic advice is a question that lies outside economics. This attitude to government as a *deus ex machina* that perfectly reflects the wishes of the citizenry has only recently begun to break down under the impact of public choice theory, Niskanen's economics of bureaucracy, and Stigler's economics of regulation, but throughout the long history of economic thought it has held sway virtually without challenge.

The second weakness of traditional writings on economic policy is the time-honoured device of appealing to the long-run consequences of economic changes, while neglecting the short-run effects over clock-time periods in which governments actually hold office. A third weakness is the tendency to take refuge in conclusions which spell out the direction of an economic change but say nothing about the amount of that change. Orthodox economic theory is strong, as we know, in what Samuelson called "the qualitative calculus", specifying the algebraic sign of the change in some endogenous variable that results from a change in one or more of the exogenous variables, but it is weak in "the quantitative calculus", specifying the precise magnitude of that change. But if we want to control the economy, it may not be enough to know that, say, a decline in interest rates will bring about a rise in private investment; what we need to know is by how much to lower the rate of interest in order to stimulate investment. Thus, many of the policy recommendations of economists based, as they so frequently are, on comparative static reasoning are beside the point for government action.

Finally, there is a fourth weakness, which is intimately associated with the other three, namely, a tendency to ignore the distributional effects of economic policies. Once again, orthodox theory is powerful in demonstrating that there is a considerable agenda of feasible economic changes which constitute what are nowadays called "potential Pareto improvements", that is, changes which are capable of making at least one economic agent better off without making any other agent worse off. To implement such changes, however, involves a value judgment about the distribution of the extra benefit and, besides, most economic policies are only capable of making some agents better off by making others worse off, thus forcing us to make a value judgment about gainers and losers. Increasingly we have learned to make such distributional judgments explicit rather than implicit and to analyse them critically without of course dissolving them.[1] Throughout the history of economic thought, however, they were simply ignored or else consigned to a limbo of purely personal expressions of preference for one or another social group.

All these four weaknesses in the analysis of questions of economic policy are beautifully illustrated by the works of David Ricardo. Ricardo must be our prime exhibit, not only because he is one of the greatest economists that ever lived, but because he is the single, best example of an economist whose theories were directly aimed at the solution of the outstanding policy question of his times, the protection of agriculture. If Rogin's thesis makes any sense at all, it makes sense for the case of Ricardo and perhaps only for that of Ricardo. Ricardo's system originated in a contemporary concern about the high price of corn and focused all its analytical cutting power on the economic repercussion of the famous Corn Laws. It is not exaggeration to say that Ricardo's overriding interest in developing his economic theories was to persuade Parliament to repeal the laws that prohibited the importation of cheap corn.

2.   THE BENEVOLENT-DESPOT VIEW OF GOVERNMENT

Ricardo's theoretical system was designed to prove one fundamental proposition: that the rate of profit depends on real wages, which in turn depend on the real cost of growing wheat. Owing to the action of diminishing returns in agriculture, the real cost of growing wheat at home must rise as population grows. It follows that unless wheat can be obtained abroad where land is plentiful, the rate of profit will eventually decline and, hence, capital will sooner or later cease to be accumulated. The Corn Laws, which shut out cheap grains from foreign sources except in periods of famine prices, thus produced a "hot-house effect" which exaggerated the natural resource scarcities that would eventually throttle the growth process. Britain had many economic problems but to abolish the Corn Laws was clearly the first item on the agenda of economic policy.

The next item, however, was to abolish the Poor Laws, which relieved the old, the sick, and the disabled in poor houses but also supplemented the substandard wages of agricultural workers by means of outdoor relief, as well as paying farmers to employ workers currently unemployed. The Poor Laws, Ricardo had learned from Malthus, encouraged population growth and thus acted, not to raise real wages, but to lower them. Abolition of the Poor Laws would thus tend, like the repeal of the Corn Laws, to stave off the stationary state of zero growth.

Third on the list of desirable actions was a once-and-for-all capital levy to pay off the public debt which had been accumulating as a result of the failure to finance the Napoleonic wars by taxation. Ricardo did not entertain the facile argument that the national debt, being an internal debt, simply represents an intergenerational transfer of resources. He believed that the burden of the debt is not shifted forward because the future burden of interest payments is immediately capitalised in current incomes and therefore becomes a burden as soon as the debt is created (here is an early version of the concept of rational expectations). Nevertheless, he preferred tax finance to debt creation as a method for meeting the cost of wars apparently because a public debt is said to encourage the flight of capital, because deficit financing "crowds out" private investment, and because capital consumption by governments is inherently unproductive.[2] In other words, what is nowadays called "the Ricardo equivalence theorem" between taxation and borrowing to finance public expenditure is yet another misnomer associated with the name of Ricardo. Be that as it may, the idea of a capital levy to pay off the debt was not a fundamental deduction of the Ricardian system but simply an implication of his particular views on the wasteful nature of public expenditure.

Finally, there was his equally radical proposal to nationalise the note-issue functions of the Bank of England. Ricardo was convinced that the Bank had overissued coins and notes during the Napoleonic wars and that its eagerness to extend loans, and not an adverse balance of payments due to government overseas spending and heavy corn imports, had been the cause of the wartime inflation. The Bank had avoided acknowledging its responsibility as a central bank, while pretending that it was no more than *primus inter pares*, passively serving the banking community. Ricardo seems to have doubted that any private bank like the Bank of England could ever pursue a clearly defined monetary policy in the national interest, and therefore advocated a plan for note issue by a National Board subject to Parliamentary scrutiny.[3]

I have said nothing yet about the eminently practical question of taxation to which one-third of Ricardo's *Principles of Political Economy* is devoted. But Ricardo's analysis of taxation is very little connected with the actual taxes prevailing in his time — for example, he does not so much as mention the controversial income tax which prevailed all through the Napoleonic wars — and consists largely of intellectual exercises in which the analytical apparatus he had previously developed is applied to some leading types of taxes to assess their incidence.[4] No Chancellor of the Exchequer could ever have implemented Ricardo's tax proposals because in a real sense he made no practical proposals to alter existing taxes or to introduce new ones.

Faced with his leading policy recommendations — to repeal the Corn

Laws, to abolish the Poor Laws, to raise a levy on capital wealth, and to nationalise the issue function of the Bank of England — one might have expected him to consider the probability that any of these would be adopted by the government of his day. Parliament, he knew perfectly well, was dominated by the landed interests and on monetary questions there was a vocal group from the City of London which usually took charge of banking legislation. On the question of the Poor Laws, he was largely on the side of "the establishment", but on all the other questions he held what were regarded at the time as "radical" views. He was at least consistent in recognising that his views stood little chance of being accepted unless Parliament was reformed, and he therefore favoured an extension of the franchise, an annual session of Parliament, and the secret ballot.

He was also a profound believer in the inviolable rights of private property, not in terms of natural law doctrine, but because he regarded the absolute security of property as something that was indispensable to social stability. Hence, he believed that undesirable legislation which had benefited certain groups at the expense of others ought not to be abolished peremptorily. He constantly reverted to the doctrine that the Corn Laws should be gradually scaled down over a ten-year period, coupled with a small bounty on exportation in years of bumper crops, so as to cushion the blow of the real losses that landlords would suffer from the withdrawal of agricultural protection. Similarly, he did not countenance the sudden and peremptory abandonment of "outdoor relief" to all able-bodied paupers but instead favoured Malthus' solution of refusing assistance to those born after a certain date in the immediate future, accompanied by an educational programme directed at the poor to encourage them not to marry until they could support a family. Such ideas were not cynical concessions to an unsympathetic Parliament but sprang from a deep-seated conviction that all property rights deserve consideration. Nevertheless, what is lacking in Ricardo is any carefully spelled out programme for implementing policies that threatened contemporary "interests". The argument that new policies should be gradually introduced in a piecemeal fashion is as far as he ever went in the art of practical policy-making.

3. THE FOCUS ON THE LONG RUN

The Ricardian system gave rise to a number of definite predictions — a rising price of corn, a rising rental share of national income, a constant level of real wages, and a falling rate of profit on capital — and, given the absence of a freely imported corn, these were all positive predictions, not hypothetical ones, because Ricardo boldly denied that countervailing forces could annul them except "for a time". Thus, agriculture was held to be subject to historically diminishing returns despite the occurrence of land-saving technical progress; Ricardo even went so far as to argue that landlords had no private incentive to introduce technical improvements in food production. Similarly, Ricardo recognised that workers would increasingly switch over to manufactured goods rather than agricultural products, in which case the rising costs of growing food would not necessarily raise money wages and depress profits. Likewise, workers might also begin to practise "moral restraint", allowing capital to accumulate faster than the rate at which population grew. But all these were merely realistic concessions: Ricardo had no theory to explain either technical progress, or changes in the composition of the average worker's consumption basket, or the disposition of families to control their size. The point is that he never seriously contemplated that the various temporary checks of which he was aware would in fact counteract the basic forces at work over the foreseeable future. Under pressure, he committed himself to a "short run" of about twenty-five years to exemplify the long-run effects of the causes he postulated,[5] which is not to say, however, that he would ever have advocated waiting for twenty-five years to see if his theories were true. They were true by the nature of their assumptions and time would necessarily prove them right.

Schumpeter labelled Ricardo's habit of specifying comparative static relationships between a strictly limited number of endogenous and exogenous variables, while bundling absolutely everything else into a *ceteris paribus* clause whose precise content is never specified, "the Ricardian Vice".[6] But the true Ricardian Vice is, surely, that of treating the short run as merely postponing the long run because all possible disequilibrium departures from the long-run growth path must necessarily lead the economy back to that path? Worse than that is the fact that the Ricardian system mixes comparative statics and comparative dynamics within one and the same framework, making it difficult to decide where the short run leaves off and the long run begins. Thus, the Ricardian model may for some purposes be interpreted as a half-way house to a steady-state growth model in which a long-term steady state has been achieved in the labour market via population growth, while at the same time the capital accumulation process is still characterised by disequilibrium adjustments which will only achieve stationariness at some future time.

At first glance, this interpretation, due to Pasinetti,[7] resolves many difficulties in interpreting Ricardo's writings. On the other hand, it fails to account for many passages, particularly in Chapter 5 of the *Principles* dealing with wages, in which Ricardo declares that population is growing because the short-run "market price" of labour in fact exceeds its long-run "natural price". John Hicks and Samuel Hollander therefore reject the Pasinetti interpretation and treat the Ricardian system as if it were as much preoccupied with short-run disequilibrium adjustments in both labour and capital markets as with long-run stationary-state solutions.[8] In a still more radical revision of Pasinetti, Carlo Casarosa rejects the notion that short-run adjustments in Ricardo are tending towards two independent steady-state solutions in labour and capital markets respectively; he argues that Ricardo's principal reasoning is in terms of a dynamic "moving equilibrium" (in the sense of Frisch) in which the rate of growth of population is kept equal to the rate of growth of capital; in short, the wages-population mechanism in Ricardo interacts in a definite way with an investment-profits mechanism.[9]

All these commentators are concerned to express Ricardo's frequently reiterated dictum that "profits" vary inversely with "wages" and the equally reiterated proposition that the rate of profit only falls "in the last instance" because of diminishing returns to agriculture. Pasinetti, however, is unable to account for those passages in which Ricardo more or less clearly says that real wages, expressed in terms of a basket of physical commodities, can fall alongside the falling rate of profit well before the economy has reached the stationary state. The great merit of the "new" view on Ricardo is that it can neatly accommodate those remarks of Ricardo which the "old" view had to treat as *obiter dicta*.

At the same time, even the "new" view has difficulty in making sense of passages in which Ricardo declares unambiguously that the rate of profit depends only on the cost of producing wage goods, and on nothing else; such passages are easy to interpret, however, if we stick with the Pasinetti version of Ricardo. Thus, we are driven to conclude that Ricardo operated with two models, a Pasinetti-type, comparative static model — "strong case" 1 — and a Casarosa-type, dynamic equilibrium model — "strong case" 2 — adopting one or the other as circumstances warranted.

It is not possible, therefore, to square everything that Ricardo said with any totally consistent formulation of the entire Ricardian system. The famous question of whether Ricardo held a subsistence theory of wages is a perfect example of the point at issue. In the tax chapters of the *Principles*, in which Ricardo argues that a tax on wages is always passed on to profits via the wages-population mechanism, there is simply no question that real wages are conceived as fixed at a subsistence level. But in Chapter 5 "On Wages", wages are treated as a variable and are permitted to stand above the "natural price" of labour for long periods of time. I say "long periods of time" but actually Ricardo used phrases such as "a considerable interval", "in no long time", "at the end of a very few years", etcetera, which allowed him to have his cake and to eat it too.[10]

4.   THE QUALITATIVE CALCULUS

Ricardo had no difficulty in arguing that the Poor Laws encouraged population growth, which tended to depress both money and real wages. But in order to amend or to abolish the Poor Laws, such qualitative arguments are insufficient: what is needed is knowledge of the quantitative effects first on the growth of population and secondly on the rate of wages. Ricardo seems to have believed that the practice of giving "outdoor relief" to able-bodied workers had reduced wages to the minimum subsistence requirements of single men, with parish allowances making up the difference between the subsistence needs of single men and that of married men and their families. If so, it was clear that the Poor Laws acted to encourage early marriages and larger families. But since Ricardo defined the "natural price" of labour as a family wage of a couple with two children, it is impossible to swallow this argument about the Poor Laws if it really is true that the "market price" of labour not only can exceed the "natural price" for long periods of time but actually did exceed it at the time he was writing. Even so, there was the further question of what would happen if outdoor relief were stopped for all those born at some early date in the future? This would presumably have discouraged early marriages and large families but for a generation to come the numbers receiving outdoor relief would still have exceeded those deprived of outdoor relief and, indeed, the echo effects of the Old Poor Law would have continued to make themselves felt for as much as fifty years. Unless we are going to argue that farmers paid married workers enough to maintain a family as a matter of social convention — which violates the principle of competitive wage determination — money wages would only have risen slowly as population declined; the rise in money wages, however, would in turn act to encourage the further growth of population. The interaction of all these effects is so complex that, even if we believe as Ricardo did in a wages-population mechanism, it is impossible to stipulate the actual time path of wages and population over the foreseeable future. But that is virtually to say that the Ricardian "qualitative calculus" provided little if no guidance to a government in choosing between total abolition of the Poor Laws and drastic reform of its system of administration.

Ricardo had a hard-line attitude towards the Poor Laws: he not only favoured their abolition but also approved of harsh administration of the Poor Laws so as to mitigate their worst effects on the economy. Unfortunately, as he confessed to a friend, he was woefully ignorant of the practical details of the subject.[11] Thus, he failed to discuss the question whether the outdoor-relief features of the Poor Laws (which supplemented wages in relation to the price of bread and the size of workers' families) encouraged farmers to hire married rather than single men and even to pay them more than single men in order to lighten their own rate burden, in which case the Poor Laws would have acted to encourage population growth even in the absence of substantial outdoor relief. Nor did he distinguish between the separate effects of outdoor relief on the age of marriage, the birth rate, and the infant mortality rate, which is to say that he never clearly analysed the mechanism by which the Poor Laws were supposed to stimulate population growth.

On balance, both he and Malthus emphasised variations in the marriage rate as the principal control mechanism for population, while almost certainly misconceiving the true situation. Malthus himself added an appendix to the 1826 edition of his *Essay on the Principles of Population*, which conceded that the Poor Laws, being harshly administered, did not in fact "greatly encourage population": they caused landlords, he thought, to pull down cottages so as to minimise property assessable under the poor rates and this tended to cause agricultural workers to marry late rather than early.

In point of fact, however, the age of marriage varied little throughout the period in question. Moreover, outdoor relief to able-bodied workers was practised in only 18 out of the 43 counties in England and Wales; it provided extremely modest supplements to wages and in any case began only with the third child in the family; and it was steadily reduced as time passed because of continuous complaints about the rising relief bill. It is doubtful, therefore, that the Poor Laws, taken as a whole, could have had much effect on population growth.[12] However, my point is not that both Malthus and Ricardo paid little attention to the administrative niceties of the system they were attacking but rather that comparative static reasoning of the purely qualitative type is rarely of much practical use in tackling complex policy problems. The Poor Laws tried to guarantee workers a minimum real income by tying wages to the cost of living; they provided unemployment compensation of a sort together with a scheme to promote private employment; and they coupled both of these to a system of family allowances. They constituted, so to speak, a welfare state in miniature, administered and financed on a local level. As such, a real analysis of the Poor Laws called for something more powerful than the Malthusian theory of population with its simple-minded belief in the direct connection between wage rates and family size.

5. DISTRIBUTIONAL EFFECTS

Marx was full of admiration for Ricardo because Ricardo, he asserted, was the last bourgeois economist to give overriding priority to the growth of total output as the touchstone of all economic questions. But Marx was less than fair to Ricardo who was in fact cognisant of the distributional aspects of economic growth. Thus, he had conceded that however gradual was the repeal of the Corn Laws, landlords would suffer losses in consequence of falling rents. But the loss of landlords from free trade, Ricardo observed, would be more than offset by the welfare gains of other classes.[13] To express it in modern language, what he was asserting was that the gains of free trade were large enough to allow capitalists and workers to bribe landlords to agree to the repeal of the Corn Laws, while still being better off themselves under free trade than under protection. Of course, this proposition lacked any warrant in his theoretical system because he was unable to specify by how much the Corn Laws raised rents, much less to quantify either the welfare losses of landlords or the welfare gains of the rest of the community. It was a purely arbitrary interpersonal comparison of utility, which was typical not just of the economics of his times but also of the economics of the next hundred years. Ricardo deserves credit for at least recognising the problem of compensation payments for losses suffered in consequence of public policy measures but he did nothing to resolve the problem, which remains to this day the Achilles Heel of the economist giving advice to governments.

6. ANOTHER INTERPRETATION?

This completes the case against Ricardo as the paragon of policy-oriented economics. Nothing I have said is new and all of it can be found somewhere in the great commentaries on Ricardo. However, the whole of it is vigorously denied by Samuel Hollander in his recent book, *The Economics of David Ricardo*. Hollander argues a number of themes: Ricardo's theoretical system did not originate in a concern over the Corn Laws but in a purely technical criticism of Adam Smith's theories; Ricardo did not attack the Corn Laws because they reduced the rate of profit but because they led to exaggerated price fluctuations and thus reduced economic efficiency; Ricardo did not seriously contemplate the prospect of a stationary state even with the continuation of the Corn Laws, and, besides, he never pretended to make any specific predictions about the actual course of events; finally, Ricardo only had a "predilection" for long-run analysis and was actually preoccupied with short-run questions relating both to theory and policy, including "the appropriate *timing* of proposed reforms".[14] This is only a small sample of the many fantastic arguments of this work, which are almost always diametrically opposed to what absolutely everybody else has said on Ricardo.

I will forgo the pleasure of arguing against Hollander point by point because there is little to add to Denis O'Brien's devastating critique of Hollander.[15] Hollander's method of interpretation is based on what appear to be four cardinal principles: the first is to deny that Ricardo held a consistent model about the determination of the rate of profit, the rate of wages, population growth, or, for that matter, anything else; the second is always to read Ricardo's qualifications of a particular proposition as his main argument, and the defence of the proposition itself as just another qualification; the third is to give absolutely equal weight to statements made in public and in private, so that a letter or a Parliamentary speech is made to appear as significant as a paragraph in the *Principles*; and the fourth is to assume that Ricardo was always right and that it only requires a little ingenuity to supply the missing link in any of his arguments, after which we may suppose that Ricardo would really have said this himself if only he had taken the time to think it out. Thus, according to Hollander, Ricardo was one of the inventors of the concept of price-elasticity of demand and it cannot be ruled out that he had something like a completely general marginal productivity theory of distribution at the back of his mind.[16]

This method of discerning Ricardo's meaning by what O'Brien aptly calls "negative flights of imagination" reaches almost ludicrous heights in the pages in which Hollander struggles in vain to exonerate Ricardo's analysis of the Poor Laws:

Ricardo throughout had in mind the *contemporary system of allowances*, and the undesirable consequences flowing therefrom — excess population growth and low market wages — when insisting upon abolition of poor relief: he objected to palliatives which did not come to grips with these two issues. It cannot, therefore, be excluded that in the event of some *alternative* form of relief for the able-bodied, without these defects, he might have been prepared to reconsider the issue.[17]

Yes, he might have but also he might not have ...! Similarly, the mind boggles when we read in Hollander that "the case made [by Ricardo] against agricultural protection was not based upon the secular downward trend in the rate of return on capital"; "Ricardo did not intend to draw from the model the implication of a general running down of the growth potential, *at least within a time horizon of much interest to policy-makers*".[18] Notice the phrase "growth *potential*": if Ricardo's model did not imply the running down of the growth potential of the economy, what was the model about?

7. CONCLUSIONS

The great fascination of Ricardo's system is its peculiar combination of an unusually high level of abstraction with an equally unusual emphasis on the immediately practical deductions that can be drawn from the analytical model. In short, Ricardo has always served economists with a paradigm example of how one can join rigour and relevance within one and the same framework. Nevertheless, when one carefully examines his policy proposals, they turn out to be vaguely formulated and hedged about with extensive qualifications: they lack precision, they lack any judgments of quantitative magnitudes, they conflate the distinction between clock-time and analytical time, and they fail to confront the political problems of implementation. If this is our leading example of policy-oriented economics, we have nothing to be proud of.

NOTES

1. See M. Blaug, *The Methodology of Economics* (London, 1980), pp. 149-56.
2. For a good account of Ricardo's peculiar views on the public debt, see D. P. O'Brien, *The Classical Economists* (Oxford, 1975), pp. 262-4.
3. That is not to say, however, that he ever recognised the role of a central bank as a lender of last resort in times of a panic: R. S. Sayers, "Ricardo's Views on Monetary Questions", in *Papers in English Monetary History*, eds. T. S. Ashton and R. S. Sayers (Oxford, 1953), p. 92.
4. C. S. Shoup, *Ricardo on Taxation* (New York, 1960), pp. 248-55; also O'Brien, *op. cit.*, pp. 55, 244.
5. N. B. de Marchi, "The Empirical Content and Longevity of Ricardian Economics", *Economica*, (August 1970), pp. 255-6.
6. J. A. Schumpeter, *History of Economic Analysis* (New York, 1954), pp. 472-3.
7. L. L. Pasinetti, *Growth and Income Distribution. Essays in Economic Theory* (London, 1974), Ch. 1.
8. J. R. Hicks and S. Hollander, "Mr. Ricardo and the Moderns", *Quarterly Journal of Economics* (August 1977).
9. C. Casarosa, "The Ricardian theory of Distribution and Economic Growth", *Revista di Politica Economica*, (August-September, 1974) and, in a similar vein, "A New Reformulation of the Ricardian System", *Oxford Economic Papers* (March 1978). G. Caravale and D. Tosato, *Ricardo and the Theory of Value Distribution and Growth* (London, 1980, and earlier in Italian in 1974) had arrived simultaneously but independently at a similar view before either Hicks-Hollander or Casarosa.
10. See W. C. Mitchell, *Types of Economic Theory*, ed. J. Dorfman (New York, 1967) I, pp. 319-25.
11. *The Works and Correspondence of David Ricardo*, ed. P. Sraffa (Cambridge, 1973), XI, p. xv.
12. See Chapters 1 and 2; and J. P. Huzel, "Malthus, the Poor Law, and Population in Early Nineteenth-Century England", *Economic History Review* (December 1969), J. P. Huzel, "The Demographic Impact of the Old Poor Law: More Reflexions on Malthus", *ibid.*, (August 1980).
13. *Works and Correspondence*, I, pp. 270-1.
14. S. Hollander, *The Economics of David Ricardo* (London, 1979), pp. 113-22, 600-2, 604, 639-40, 658.

15. D. P. O'Brien, "Ricardian Economics and the Economics of David Ricardo", Oxford Economic Papers (November 1981); S. Hollander, "Response to Professor O'Brien", *ibid.* (March 1982); D. P. O'Brien, "Ricardian Economics", *ibid.*
16. Hollander, *op.cit.*, pp. 273-9, 670-1.
17. *Ibid.*, p. 723.
18. Hollander, *op.cit.*, pp. 604, 639-40.

6 Welfare Indices in *The Wealth of Nations*

Adam Smith, an old legend has it, tried to formulate a labour theory of value but got horribly confused between the purchasing power of a commodity over labour and the amount of labour embodied in its production. The origins of this legend are to be found in Ricardo's *Principles* but the authorised version is by Marx.[1] As a result, generations of critics have dealt unkindly with Smith as a theorist who identified such totally different things as the labour-price and the labour-cost of a product.

An unprejudiced reading of *The Wealth of Nations* destroys the legend. Adam Smith was well aware of the distinction between the measure and cause of value. He was little concerned with the latter. The traditional problem of value theory — why are relative prices what they are at any moment of time? — received only summary treatment. Rather he was interested in finding some invariant measure of real income. To be sure, the order of topics in *The Wealth of Nations* invited misunderstanding of his purpose. Book I, Chapter 4, "The Origin and Use of Money," closes with a promise to analyse the determination of "relative or exchangeable value of goods." But the next chapter, "The Real and Nominal Prices of Commodities," attempts instead to define an intertemporal standard to evaluate changes in money prices. The determination of relative prices is not discussed until Chapters 6 and 7 where Smith rejects the notion that capital can be reduced to labour expended in the past, ending up with a simple money-costs of production theory. But this conclusion does not affect the labour-yardstick advanced in Chapter 5. All this would have stood out much better if Chapter 5 had followed, not preceded, Chapters 6 and 7.

Most of the difficulties created by the Marxian interpretation of Adam Smith have been cleared up by modern commentators. Smith's discussion of "the measuring rod of labour" is now properly regarded as a stab at subjective welfare economics, involving an effort to surmount the index-numbers problem. Few critics, however, have gone beyond generalities in discussing Smith's standard of welfare. Myint's stimulating analysis is a notable exception.[2] But Myint's analysis is not always free from ambiguity. Other readers may have been left wondering, as I was, exactly why Ricardo or anyone else should have objected to Smith's yardstick. It is to this question that the following note is devoted.

II

Smith employs a labour-standard in two distinct senses: as an index of the rate of capital accumulation and as an index of the magnitude of subjective income. The spearhead of his argument is to show that in a developing economy the two indices come to the same thing. And so they should, but not upon Smith's assumptions.

The first idea is, relatively speaking, plain sailing. The notion is that capital accumulation involves a definite trend in the money value of the national product expressed in wage units (the going money wage rate of unskilled labour). In Book II, Chapter 3 of *The Wealth of Nations* "productive labour" is defined as activity producing storable items of wealth, particularly wage-goods, which can put "more labour in motion" in the next cycle of production. That is to say, measuring all value in current wage units, productive labour produces physical output whose value exceeds the value of labour embodied in it.[3] This is, of course, nothing but a cumbrous way of stating that such labour normally produces a value-surplus above its cost of maintenance and replacement.[4] Now, if "net revenue" is always promptly reinvested and if the supply of labour is perfectly elastic, an upward trend in the number of wage units commanded by total output is guaranteed (p.54).[5] Capital and labour are combined in fixed proportions (p.421). Hence, the volume of employment will increase *pari passu* with the increase of capital. With real wages constant, the growth of output must result in a positive trend of the labour-index.

A growing labour force, Smith was wont to say, is a "decisive mark" of increasing real income (p.70). But, on the other hand, so is a "liberal reward of labour" (p.73). The latter, however, creates a dilemma: when real wages are rising, a positive rate of investment does not necessarily imply an increase in the purchasing power of total output over wage units. Indeed, if real wages rise as fast as the average productivity of labour, the labour-standard will show no change through time. We return to this difficulty in a moment.

Consider now the second proposition, the index of subjective income. In the chapter on "Real and Nominal Prices" Smith takes a leaf from the pages of Locke's *Second Treatise on Civil Government*, by posing the question of how to measure real income in the context of a "rude and original state of society". For all practical purposes, this is a single-factor world in which the personal labour embodied in products coincides with the labour these products can purchase. A man is "rich or poor" according to the value of his own labour services or his purchasing power over other men's labour, for the two are identical. With the rise of property income this coincidence is broken. Now real income varies solely with the ability to command other men's *products*. But as labour is irksome, everyone strives to save himself "toil and trouble" and to impose it upon others (p. 30). In one sense, what is purchased with products is still the "toil and trouble" of others. And so, an increase of real income means not merely more purchasing power over goods, but more purchasing power over labour. What is true of individual income is true of aggregate income: the wealth (read: income) of a nation is measured by the number of wage units commanded by the whole product.

This seems to be the gist of Smith's reasoning. Capital accumulation by producing a positive change in the labour-index, means an increase in subjective welfare. A standard of measurement, however, must itself be invariable to accurately reflect changes in the things being measured. On the face of it, the wage unit fails to meet this condition: it varies with every change in the price of wage-goods and in the demand and supply of labour. But supposing for the moment that money and real wages do remain the same. In what sense would this provide an invariant standard of subjective welfare? Clearly, in the sense that we could then assume that the average disutility of labour per unit of effort is the same for all individuals at all times: "Equal quantities of labour, at all times and places, may be said to be of equal [esteem] value to the labourer" (p. 33).[6]

This is surely a heroic assumption. A constant outlay of subjective sacrifice per man-hour implies unit elasticity of supply of effort, or unit elasticity of demand for income in terms of effort. This is a poor assumption for an analysis concerned with welfare appraisals in the long run: a falling effort-price of income in a growing economy is itself a major element in the improvement of welfare.

Fortunately, the validity of this assumption can be tested by its consequences. The effort-price of income must be expressed in terms of an operational standard of measurement. The first difficulty is that of selecting a representative money wage unit. In the chapter on relative wages (Book I, Chapter 10) Smith had shown that, despite differences in the hourly wage rates of different occupations, perfect competition does tend to equalise monetary returns to units of disutility of labour; the market does reduce the various types of labour to a common standard. Therefore, in principle, a representative money wage unit can be constructed.[7] The second difficulty is that of selecting a stable value-coefficient to express real wages. Smith argues that for calendar periods of moderate length a nominal wage unit in terms of silver will prove satisfactory owing to the relative stability in the value of silver "from year to year" and even "for a half a century or a century together" (p. 35). However, for longer periods a corn-wage unit would be more suitable: the price of corn fluctuates sharply in the short run and rarely in the same direction, or with the same amplitude, as money wages (pp. 36, 74, 75, 83, 85), but "from century to century" corn prices are remarkably stable" (pp. 36-7, 477, 482). The reason for this is that cost-reducing improvements in agriculture are "more or less counterbalanced" by the rising price of cattle, "the principal instruments of agriculture" (pp. 187, 219-24, 240). And since corn is "the basic subsistence of the people," the money price of corn governs money wages in the long run: "from century to century, corn is a better measure than silver, because from century to century, equal quantities of corn will command the same quantity of labour more nearly than equal quantities of silver" (pp. 37, 187, 476).[8] The argument is complete: the wage unit in real terms and in money terms, i.e., the wages of common labour measured in corn, is invariant through time and reflects an invariant disutility of labour.

Smith did not doubt that "at all times and places, that is cheap which costs little labour to acquire." And so, as output per man-hour rises, the "real prices" of goods should fall relative to corn, meaning they will command less labour. Likewise, the number of wage units commanded by the total product year after year should tend downward. This is reasonable enough since the labour commanded by commodities is the reciprocal of labour's purchasing power over real income. However, this line of reasoning is in direct contradiction to Smith's positive index of subjective welfare. The contradiction is due to the fact that the positive index assumes constant real wages and constant returns to technological progress. Actually, Smith believed that an increase of population would raise output per man by extending the scope of the division of labour; and this tendency alone implies that every addition to output will command less additional wage units. Or, as Ricardo would say, an increase in welfare may mean an increase in "riches" or a fall in "value." An increase of riches is what we would now call "capital widening," an increase in output without a change in the capital and labour coefficients. Whereas a fall in value denotes a rise in the average productivity of labour, or, in Smith's language, a fall in the amount of labour commanded per unit of output.

Ricardo dismissed riches *per se* as irrelevant to economic welfare. This is a defensible position. But both Smith and Ricardo do agree essentially in treating "value" as an inverse index of the average productivity of labour and therefore of economic welfare. Ricardo regards welfare as a matter of minimising human effort per unit of output while Smith regards it as a matter of maximising labour's *potential* purchasing power over real income. But Smith's standard, just because it is tied more explicitly to subjective income, rests upon a greater number of dubious assumptions. If, for example, real wages vary through time, the entire argument breaks down. Commodities may command less labour simply because money wages have risen or because prices of wage-goods have fallen. The resulting effect upon investment, and hence upon the trend of wage units commanded by total output, will be very different in the two cases. This difficulty disappears only if both real and money wages tend to remain constant in the long run. This is the source of Ricardo's disagreement with Smith. In Ricardo's system, capital accumulation spells a rising price of corn; real wages remain unaltered but money wages rise with corn prices; this is what causes rents to rise and profits to fall.

"Dr. Smith's error throughout his whole work," Ricardo declared, "lies in supposing that the value of corn is constant."[9] It would have been a simple matter to have shown that Smith's belief in the stability of corn prices "from century to century" is irrelevant to the analyses of such policy measures as the Corn Law of 1815 — Ricardo's purpose was, after all less ambitious than Smith's. This Ricardo failed to do. By assuming that Smith was concerned with Ricardian questions, he filled his *Principles* with a series of misguided attacks on Smith's standard.[10] It would take a monograph to unravel Ricardo's criticisms; Malthus' prolix but perverse defence of Smith's measures would provide some entertaining chapters. But we have done with it here.

III

Properly understood, there is nothing wrong with Smith's labour-standard. It is simply that Smith applied it indiscriminately. Actually, as has been pointed out, modern methods of making international comparisons of economic welfare per head are nothing but applications of Smithian welfare economics. For instance, Soviet living standards may be compared with American living standards by asking how many hours of work, rewarded at the going rate, would be required to buy specific articles at current prices in each of the two countries. This procedure assumes, among other things, that the disutility of labour in the U.S.S.R. is the same as in the U.S.A. Or, real earnings may be compared in terms of a given basket of wage goods valued at constant dollar prices (Colin Clark's International Units), which involves similar assumptions. No one will deny that these methods ought to be supplemented by comparisons of the productivity of labour and of capital — and of personal income distribution, an aspect of welfare which the classical economists completely neglected — before secure pronouncements can be made about economic welfare. As soon as this is understood, the controversy between Ricardo and Smith on the proper "standard of value" takes on the character of so many battles in intellectual history: a conflict between two poorly expounded half-truths.

NOTES

1. *Works of David Ricardo*, ed. P. Sraffa and M. H. Dobb (Cambridge, 1951), I, p. 14; K. Marx, *Theories of Surplus Value*, trans. G. A. Bonner and E. Burns (London, 1951), pp. 108-16. But see the incisive comment by J. S. Mill, *Principles of Political Economy*, ed. W. J. Ashley, (London, 1909), p. 568.
2. See M. Bowley, *Nassau Senior and Classical Economics* (New York, 1949) pp. 67-71; J. A. Schumpeter, *History of Economic Analysis* (New York, 1954), pp. 180-8; H. M. Robertson and W. L. Taylor, "Adam Smith's Approach to the Theory of Value," *Economic Journal* (June 1957); H. Myint, *Theories of Welfare Economics* (Cambridge, Mass., 1948), Chapter 2.
3. Only physical output is considered because services, being non-durable, are incapable of being accumulated. With the important exception of the transmission of knowledge, this is true enough but what difference it makes is another matter.
4. A similar argument is used in Book II, Chapter 5 to show that equal quantities of capital with equal rates of turnover "put in motion" more labour in agriculture than in manufacturing because in agriculture the value of the product is sufficient to pay rent in addition to wages and profits. This is obviously wrong if rent is an intramarginal return, as Ricardo was quick to see (*Works*, I, pp. 76-9). But elsewhere Ricardo contradicts himself, unwittingly adopting Smith's standpoint (ibid., pp. 350, 429).
5. All subsequent references are to the Cannan edition of *The Wealth of Nations* (New York, 1937).
6. Once this is granted, it can be said that when labour temporarily receives more wage-goods "it is their [esteem] value which varies, not that of the labour which purchases them" (p. 33). This remark, which has puzzled so many commentators, is perfectly logical in its context.
7. One could object here and argue that the relevant question is whether the wage structure is rigid through time.
8. The whole of the famous "Digression concerning the Variations of the Value of Silver during the Course of the Four last Centuries" is devoted to justifying the notion of the long-run constancy of corn-wages. But it is difficult to know whether this is anything but a simplifying assumption. At one place Smith remarks upon the lack of time series data on money wages in contrast to the regularly recorded series of corn prices. This fact alone, he suggests, forces us to resort to corn prices "not as always exactly in the same proportion as the current prices of labour, but as being the nearest approximation which can commonly be had to that proportion" (p. 38).
9. *Works of David Ricardo*, I, p. 374.
10. Ricardo's favourite method is to construct a numerical example to show that Smith's measuring rod cannot distinguish between "a rise in the value of labour" and "a fall in the value of things ... on which wages are expended." A single illustration will suffice to indicate the character of the critique.

(*Ibid.*, pp. 19-20; see also pp. 103-4, 306.) Suppose that labour is paid in corn and consumes ½ bushel of corn per week, trading the rest for other goods. Now corn falls in price. Labour receives more corn but yet can buy less of other goods which have not varied in price (despite changes in relative prices, the composition of the market basket remains the same).

Wages in corn	Corn prices per bu.	Money wages	Expend. on corn	Expend. on other goods
1 bu.	80s.	80s.	40s.	40s.
1¼ bu.	40s.	50s.	20s.	30s.

In this case, Ricardo alleges, Smith would have to say that labour has risen in value because "his standard is corn, and the labourer receives more corn for a week's labour," whereas he should have said that the value of labour has fallen because labour's real wages have decreased. Obviously, the criticism is unfair. Ricardo ignores the fact that Smith's standard is meant to be employed for long-run comparisons, and a huge long run at that. Naturally if the price elasticity of demand for corn is zero and the cross-elasticities of demand for all consumption goods are also zero, a fall in corn prices associated with a fall in money wages may leave the labourer worse off. But what of the repercussions of the fall in real wages? Population growth will slacken, Smith might have replied, the demand for corn will fall off, corn prices will rise, followed by money wages, etc.

7 The Classical Economists and the Factory Acts: A Re-Examination

I

British historians of the Industrial Revolution are unanimously of the opinion that early factory reform was achieved in the face of strong hostility from the economic experts of the day. It does not matter whom we consult: Toynbee, Trevelyan, the Hammonds, Cunningham, Clapham; the classical economists are always depicted as unalterably opposed to the Factory Acts.[1] But if we turn to the historians of economic thought a very different interpretation emerges. Marshall, for instance, asserts that the classical economists "supported the factory acts, in spite of the strenuous opposition of some politicians and employers who claimed to speak in their name"; he cites McCulloch and Tooke as examples in point.[2] In his *History of Economic Analysis*, Schumpeter flatly declares that "Most 'classic' economists supported factory legislation, McCulloch especially."[3] K.O. Walker, in an article which examines the question in some detail, concludes that "the direct influence of the political economists on labour legislation was negligible" and that "any influence that was exerted tended to favor, rather than oppose, the passage of the Factory Acts."[4] Lionel Robbins' study of *The Theory of Economic Policy in English Classical Political Economy* deals briefly with this issue; he suggests that the classical authors generally favoured regulation of child labour while disapproving of legislation for adults.[5]

How can we account for such widely divergent interpretations of what is, after all, a matter of record? One answer is that the evidence which has so far been considered is highly selective.[6] Moreover, little attention has been paid to the successive phases of the factory reform controversy: generalisations have been advanced on the basis of writings published at different times and under distinctly different circumstances.

The fact of the matter is that the attitude of the classical writers was conditioned at each stage of the debate by the degree of regulation that had already been achieved. Many a factory bill, whose introduction had been bitterly opposed, met with approval once it became law. Although the

135

classical economists supported the *principle* of granting protection to children, they were aware that the unavoidable consequence was a shorter working day for adult operatives; rather than countenance that they preferred to dispense with the benefits of regulated child labour. Thus, we are faced on the one hand with differences of opinion among the classical economists as to the desirability of further restrictions on the employment of children, and on the other hand with a general tendency towards rearguard action designed to prevent the effective regulation of adult labour.

For this reason the question whether the classical economists did or did not favour the Factory Acts cannot be answered. This much, however, is a matter of pure academic interest. The real significance of the discussion lies in the opportunity which it affords to study the quality of classical policy-pronouncements. Were their opinions based upon economic consider-ations, such as the effects of shorter-hours on employment and real wages, or solely upon fundamental value judgments embodied in the tenets of laissez faire? In the concluding section of this chapter I shall attempt to evaluate the merits of the classical economists' position in the light of their own analytical apparatus and the relevant factual knowledge available to them.[7]

II

The history of factory legislation in England begins with Peel's Bill of 1819. An earlier Act of 1802, regulating the labour of parish apprentices, was an extension of the Poor Laws, not a factory act; no new power of the state was at issue. Peel's bill, however, did raise the question of state interference in private industry; it reduced the working day of children under sixteen to twelve hours and prohibited altogether the employment of children under nine years of age. The Act applied only to the cotton factories and inadequate inspection provisions made it largely inoperative. Neverthe-less, there was opposition to the bill, particularly from the House of Lords, in the form of an appeal to "that great principle of Political Economy, that labour ought to be left free." The proponents of Peel's bill, on the other hand, defended the measure on the grounds that children were not "free agents."[8] Economists took little interest in the debate; Malthus alone gave public support to the measure.[9]

Additional restrictions on child labour in the cotton factories in 1825 and 1831 improved but little upon the Act of 1819. But with the publication of Oastler's letters on "Yorkshire Slavery" and the appearance of Sadler's Committee Report (1833) the movement for factory reform began to assume a more radical tone. Lord Ashley's motion of a Ten Hours bill, applicable to all persons under the age of sixteen, led to the appointment of Commission to collect further evidence. The Commissioners — Thomas Tooke, Edwin Chadwick, and Southwood Smith — proposed several amendments to Ashley's bill to prevent interference with the free employment of adults.[10] The final version, known as Althorp's Act, limited the working day of persons between thirteen and eighteen to twelve hours a day and of those between nine and thirteen to nine hours a day.[11]

After the passage of Althorp's Act it was necessary to employ children in part-time relays since the work of the adult spinners and weavers depended, for technical reasons, upon the labour of their young assistants. The Factory Inspectors devised a variety of schemes for co-ordinating the work day of different categories of labour but none of the plans proved completely successful. The relay system soon became one of the major devices for evading legislative control. The leaders of the Ten Hours party were quick to point out that it was impossible to separate the adult from the child for purposes of legislative control; in short, they did not attempt to disguise their ulterior aim of limiting the hours of adult labour by means of placing restrictions upon the hours of children. Classical political economy, however, sanctioned a limit on the employment of children below "the age of consent" so long as this could be achieved without encroaching upon the working hours of adults. Consequently, economists arraigned themselves against the Ten Hours movement as its ultimate purpose became increasingly evident.[12]

The years between the Acts of 1833 and 1844 mark the first phase of the debate; at this point there was still great variety in the attitudes of individual economists. It was only in the 1840s that something like a uniform position began to emerge. Nevertheless, all the leading arguments in the controversy make their appearance at this stage of the discussion.

The first to commit himself, even before the passage of Althorp's Act, was John Stuart Mill. Writing in a popular weekly in 1832, he expressed a desire to see "a law established *interdicting* altogether the employment of children under fourteen, and *females of any age*, in manufactories".[13] He anticipated objections to such a law drawn from the "non-interference philosophy" and admitted that he, too, was a partisan of this principle "up to a certain point." He drew attention, however, to a significant exception:

The case in which it would be to the advantage of everybody, if everybody were to act in a certain manner, but in which it is not in the interest of an individual to adopt the rule for the guidance of his own conduct, unless he has some assurance that others will do so too. There are a thousand such cases; and when they arise, who is to afford the security that is wanted, except the legislature?

The case of child and female labour is a typical example, he went on to say; here private and public benefit must diverge unless a universal compact can be secured. This argument could have been applied with the same force to the labour of adult males but Mill failed to carry it through.[14]

Robert Torrens supported Ashley's Ten Hours bill when it came up for debate in Parliament, but with an important qualification. Since the Corn Laws had raised the cost of food and thus depressed real wages, the working class was entitled to shorter hours without a reduction in money wages. Still, the tariff on agricultural produce should be lowered so as to "create a margin on which your short time might safely stand."[15] In a work published shortly before the passage of Althorp's Act, he declared:

The evidence presented by the Royal Commission of 1832 makes it imperative on Parliament to interpose, to shorten the hours of labour, and to save the infant labourer from the cruel oppression of excessive toil. But while humanity cries aloud for such intervention, and while it must be promptly and freely granted, the truth should at the same time be declared, that a Bill for regulating the hours of labour, though framed by a consummate wisdom, cannot reach the root of the disease.[16]

The "root of the disease," of course, is the Corn Laws.

George Poulett Scrope took a similar view in his *Principles of Political Economy*: the Factory Bill is "a measure which in a healthy state of society would be a needless interference, though in the existing circumstances of the country, it seems to us highly desirable."[17] *The Westminster Review* (under the proprietorship of Colonel Perronet Thompson, an ardent Benthamite and free-trader), varied the argument; it condemned Althorp's Act as a "restrictive blunder" and depicted the Ten Hours movement as "the stalking-horse to cover and protect — the Corn Laws and West Indian Slavery."[18] Within a decade this became the standard reply of the Anti-Corn Law League to the factory reform movement.[19] The Corn Laws were made the scapegoat of distress in the factory districts, and cheap bread was hailed as the nostrum to remedy all ills.

While the Factory Act of 1833 was still under discussion, Lord Ashley solicited McCulloch's views on the question. McCulloch had spoken approvingly of factory legislation in 1827, adding the warning, however, that "no farther interference ought, in any account, to be either attempted or tolerated."[20] Now he wrote to Ashley: to contend that children have the power to judge for themselves on such matters."[22] McCulloch's modern reputation as a friend of factory reform is largely based upon this private communication, penned under the stimulus of the shocking disclosures of Sadler's committee report. It is to be noted, however, that the argument goes no further than the admission that children are not "free agents," a notion that was rapidly becoming a commonplace.

Indeed, in the pages of the *Edinburgh Review* McCulloch continued to deprecate the case for legislative control. In 1835 he devoted a major article to Ure's *Philosophy of Manufactures*, a crass apology for the factory system.[22] "That abuses have existed in some factories is certain," McCulloch admitted, "but these have been rare instances; and speaking generally, factory work-people, including non-adults, are as healthy and contented as any class of the community obliged to earn their bread in the sweat of their brow." He saw no reason to object to the exclusion of children under thirteen years of age from factory employment provided that they were properly looked after at home. But in view of parental attitudes among the lower classes, it was likely, he argued, that children turned out of factories would become delinquent paupers. The factory system, he observed, did imbue children with disciplined habits and allowed them to extend material assistance to their parents. Nevertheless, "the Legislature did right in prohibiting altogether the employment of children in mills under nine years of age." Lest these words give comfort to factory reformers, McCulloch hastened to add that the limitation of hours was "a matter of great nicety and difficulty"; on the whole, he concluded, the less the textile trade is "tampered with" the better.[23] Senior's *Letters on the Factory Act* (1837) is too well known to require discussion. Its importance lies in the fact that it carried the debate out of the realm of such general considerations as the proper "age of consent," the character of parental supervision, or the priority of free trade over factory legislation. Senior accepted Althorp's Act as it stood but argued that, given the cost structure of the typical textile mill, further reductions in hours would wipe out the margin of profit.[24] Senior's thesis proved to be a serviceable argument against the extension of regulation and in the next round of discussions which took place in 1844 several members of Parliament succumbed to its logic.[25] Senior's fellow economists, however, did not take it very seriously: *Letters on the Factory Acts* is hardly mentioned, much less analysed, in the economic literature of the day. The records of the Political Economy Club clearly suggest that Senior's argument was not accepted by his colleagues: They objected to his unrealistic estimate of capital investment upon which his conclusions were grounded.[26] But one of Senior's basic assumptions, that output would fall proportionately with the reduction of hours, was not challenged and became an essential feature of the classical analysis of factory legislation.

III

A new Factory Act was passed in 1844 which lowered the working hours of children to six and one-half hours and that of "young persons" (boys below eighteen and girls below twenty-one) to twelve hours. This Act proved to be a stepping-stone to the Ten Hours bill of 1847 which finally secured a fifty-eight hours' week for "young persons" and for women of all ages. The passage of both measures was accompanied by an intense discussion that marked the high point of three decades of debate. Economic arguments became more concrete and were now clearly divorced from the precept of non-interference. However, there were no dramatic conversions to the Ten Hours camp.[27] At the Political Economy Club in 1844, Edwin Chadwick put up this question for debate: "Is legislative interference between the Master and the Adult labourer, to regulate the hours of work, expedient?" The diary of one of the participants reveals that Charles Buller, the radical philosopher, was the only member to vote in favour of such interference.[28] Chadwick, Senior, Torrens and Tooke answered the question in the negative. McCulloch admitted much of Buller's reasoning but thought the matter could be settled in general terms. The views of John Stuart Mill at this point are not clear; but in an article on "The Claims of Labour" for the *Edinburgh Review* (1845) he referred to the Ten Hours bill as falling into the category of "quack schemes of reform."

The prevailing economic argument against the Ten Hours bill is set forth in Torrens' *Letter to Lord Ashley* (1844), a curiously neglected work.[29] Torrens begins his discussion with a strong condemnation of the principle of "leaving things to their course." The concept of "free agents," however, is not mentioned at all. His analysis is largely concerned with "the delusion" of the operatives that "upon the passing of a Ten Hour Bill, they would receive the wages of twelve hours for the work of ten." Torrens lays it down as an incontrovertible fact that "the rate of profit in this country is already approaching the minimum at which no margin remains for an advance of wages"; "capital to an enormous amount already emigrates from our shores."

Torrens' conclusion is that the Ten Hours bill would check production and diminish wages: "Enact your Ten Hours Bill and one of two events must inevitably ensue: — the manufactures of England will be transferred to foreign lands, or else the operatives must submit to a reduction of wages to the extent of 25 per cent."[30]

There is no mention in Torrens' pamphlet of the possible productivity effects of a shorter working day. Yet this had long been a favourite argument of the factory reformers. Robert Owen testified in 1818 before Peel's committee that a reduction from fourteen to twelve hours a day in his factory at New Lanark had actually resulted in an increase of output.[31] Speaking in the House of Commons in 1844, Lord Ashley recalled Owen's testimony by ways of an attack on Senior's "last hour" theory. Reviewing the successive Factory Acts since 1819, he pointed out: "you had no diminution of produce, no fall in wages, no rise in prices, no closing of markets, no irresistible rivalry from foreign competition, although you reduced your hours of working from 16, 14, 13, to 12 hours a day."[32] The implication is that productivity per man-hour had risen with each reduction in the length of the working day.

Ashley's argument is loose, of course: dynamic factors unrelated to shorter hours might account for the facts. The same argument, however, more carefully stated, appears in a popular treatise of the 1840s, William Thornton's *Over Population and Its Remedy*. Thornton reviewed the whole question in the light of the imminent repeal of protection. If "the daily labour of British operatives were shortened," he thought it "very possible that their wages would fall." But once the Corn Laws were abolished, lower food prices might leave real wages constant, or even raise them, despite the fall in money wages owing to a Ten Hour bill. Moreover,

It is not quite certain that a diminution of produce would result from shortening the duration of labour. Persons who are not obliged to work so long may work harder than before, and may get through the same quantity of work in a short time as formerly occupied them for a longer period ... If so, the limitation of labour to ten hours daily would not in any circumstances reduce wages, and at all events the reduction might be either prevented or neutralised by the establishment of free trade in food.[33]

Unhappily, Thornton's analysis made no impression on his contemporaries. McCulloch, for example, continued to discuss the regulation of hours along traditional lines. "We should be inclined to think," he wrote in 1846, "that the existing regulations respecting factory labour in this country are about as reasonable and judicious as they can be made." Then he went on to praise Torrens' *Letter to Ashley* as "the best tract in opposition to the ten-hours project."[34] In the fourth edition of his *Principles* (1849) he added a few pages on the Factory Acts, lauding the Act of 1844 as consistent with "claims of humanity" and "the interest of manufacturers" but roundly condemning the bill of 1847 because it tended to restrict the hours of adults. At this point he turned to a new argument. The conditions of the working class, he declared, rest ultimately upon the size of the wages fund relative to population; the real issue, therefore, is not whether eight, ten, or twelve hours constitutes the "proper" length of a working day.

If ... the longer be introduced by the customs of the country, in preference to a shorter period, it is a proof that there is, if not an excess, at all events an extremely copious supply of labour; and that the labourers are, in consequence, obliged to submit to the drudgery of lengthened service ... it is difficult to perceive how the hours of work ... should be lessened by a legislative enactment without at the same time, and by the same act, reducing wages.[35]

John Stuart Mill touched briefly on the economic objections against the Factory Acts in his *Principles* (1848). Whether a reduction of hours without a cut in wages would inevitably displace labour was, he said, "in every particular instance a question of fact, not of principle." For the most part his analysis of factory legislation dealt with the propriety of government intervention along the lines laid down in his earlier article of 1832.[36] If a nine-hour day were proved to be in the interest of the working class, Mill reasoned, state action would be required "not to overrule the judgment of individuals respecting their own interest, but to give effect to that judgment." He concluded: "I am not expressing any opinion in favour of such an enactment ... but it serves to exemplify the manner in which classes of persons may need the assistance of law, to give effect to their deliberate collective opinion of their own interest." He condemned the Acts of 1844 and 1847, however, on the grounds that they excluded working women from factories, although women were "free agents" as much as men.

IV

The Ten Hours bill of 1847 had failed to abolish the system of employing children in part-time shifts, consequently, it was possible to keep adult male operatives at the bench for fifteen hours a day without violating the letter of the Act of 1847. Renewed agitation at last secured the "normal working day" for women and children in 1853: hours of legal employment and meal times were specified in greater details so that it became difficult to employ relays. The scope of the Ten Hours bill was extended in the 1860s, although industries other than textile were not covered until the Consolidating Act of 1878. The minimum age of child labour was now raised to ten, the employment of women was further restricted, and sanitary inspection and safety regulations were improved. None of this legislation, except the details of sanitation, was applicable to adult males but their weekly hours, of course, were almost everywhere scaled down to sixty or less.

Meanwhile, fragmentary statistical data on the effect of the Act of 1847 had been gathered by the Factory Inspectors. The initial consequences were partly obscured by a severe trade depression. Wages in textiles fell, but much less than the 16 per cent reduction in hours or the 10 per cent reduction in piece rates. After the revival of prosperity in the 1850s, Horner and Tooke declared that the Ten Hours bill had not depressed either earnings or output owing to an increase in the intensity of labour.[38]

There is no indication that economists shared the belief that shorter hours had paid for themselves through a rise in output per man. New editions of Mill's *Principles* in the 1850s and 1860s reveal no alterations with respect to the topic under discussion. Cairnes' writings contain no explicit discussion of the Factory Acts. Fawcett, however, delivered a lecture on the question in 1872 in the midst of a new campaign for a nine-hours' day. At the outset he expounded the familiar theme of the free agent:

It certainly appears to me that it is quite as desirable to pass a law limiting the number of hours which a child is permitted to work, as it would be undesirable to impose similar restrictions upon men and women. If grown-up persons overwork they do it of their own free will.

Moreover, he had no patience with Mill's "hypothetical argument" in favour of state intervention. This is "the old story," Fawcett complained, which requires us to believe in the collective wisdom and infallible judgment of the legislature. He proceeded to examine the notion that a diminution of hours could increase the efficiency of labour and thus leave output unaffected. He admitted that there was some factual evidence which might be adduced on behalf of this argument. Still, he insisted that generally entrepreneurs could be trusted to maximise profits and, thereby, to achieve an optimum length of the work day from the viewpoint of maximising output per man-hour.[39]

The success of the Nine Hours movement, Fawcett warned, would open the way to a campaign in favour of eight hours, and so forth. Already England "can scarcely hold her own in some trades in which she once had an almost undisputed supremacy." When the Nine Hours Law came up for debate in Parliament Fawcett spoke against it on the grounds that "this House has no right to interfere with the labour of adults" or to place the employment of women on a different footing from the employment of men.[40]

Although Jevons is not a classical economist, his treatment of the Factory Acts contains some instructive differences as well as similarities to the classical analysis. Jevons denied, first of all, that the question can be decided once and for all on "some supposed principle of liberty." The same principle, if it existed, would apply to adult women whose hours were already regulated. Moreover, a mass of "paternal legislation," such as the Truck Acts, the Coal Mines Act, and a series of bills relating to merchant shipping and the fencing of machinery, had long ago been sanctioned for the protection of adult men. On the face of it, he saw no reason to prohibit state action in the matter "if it could be clearly shown that the existing customs are injurious to health and there is no other probable remedy."[41]

At the same time, Jevons' analysis is quite innocent of the type of consideration introduced by Thornton.[42] Jevons believed it to be "an economic fallacy" to suppose that shorter hours could give rise to any counterbalancing advantage other than the workmen's enjoyment of more leisure.[43] Then, ignoring Mill's contention that private interests were fundamentally interdependent, he concluded:

When we observe too, that trades unions are already constantly wrangling with employers for a reduction of hours, while individual workmen are generally ready to work overtime for a moderate inducement, we shall be led to think that there is no ground whatever for legal limitation of adult male labour in the present day.

V

The classical analysis of the Factory Acts consisted of two quite separate strands of thought. On the one hand, factory legislation was criticised in terms of the doctrine of "freedom of contract" between enlightened economic agents. On the other hand, it was held that something like a Ten Hours bill would spell the ruin of British industry if unaccompanied by a drastic fall in money wages. We will examine each argument in turn.

Insofar as the problem was treated as a matter of enlightened individualism, the attitude of the classical economists was unambiguous: where self-interest was plainly unenlightened, as in the case of children, they recommended intervention by the state, differing only about the proper age of consent and the scope of parents' right of supervision. Nevertheless, in practice this meant that they acquiesced in just so much legislation as had already been achieved; at each stage of the debate they warned against further measures. Invariably, notions about the age at which a worker becomes a "free agent" changed in the wake of legislation, at each turn approving a *fait accompli*.

McCulloch's treatment of the question is typical in this respect. One would hardly describe him as a supporter of the Factory Acts. Senior is another telling example. In his *Letters on the Factory Acts* he agreed that no child of eleven should be employed as much as twelve hours a day; this implied acceptance of Althorp's Act which defined thirteen as the age at which "the period of childhood, properly so called, ceases." In 1841 he thought that the "age of consent" ought to be raised from thirteen to fourteen; in 1847 he urged that it be set at sixteen, that is two years below the age of consent stipulated in the Ten Hours bill. Similarly, he now assented to a six and one-half hour day for children, as called for in the Act of 1844. But he never changed his mind about the undesirability of regulating adult labour.[44]

Apart from being wise too often after the event, the classical economists never faced the question whether it was, in fact, possible to protect women and children without interfering with the employment of adult males. Strictly speaking, economists are not concerned with administrative feasibility. Still, the total neglect of the difficulties created by the relay system rendered most of the classical prescriptions for legislation void of practical significance. In addition, the notion of "free agents" was in itself extremely vague. The whole case against the Factory Acts based on this concept falls to the ground once we consider Mill's argument that the ability of adult operatives to recognise their own self-interests does not prevent them collectively from working longer hours than each alone might have found desirable. Although Mill presented this argument in one of the most widely read treatises of the period, he never for one moment succeeded in deflecting the debate from the well-worn theory of free agents. This is all the more surprising since this doctrine is repeatedly attacked in the reports of the Factory Inspectors.[45]

In the case of Mill and Fawcett the problem of factory reform was complicated by the issue of feminism. They feared that the Ten Hours bill would encourage the substitution of unprotected adult males for protected female workers.[46] Since the emancipation of women was held to be dependent upon unlimited access to factory employment, they thought it necessary to condemn the Factory Acts insofar as these involved restrictions upon the hours of women workers.

All things considered, the Ten Hours camp was not far wrong in regarding "political economy" with its slogan of "free agents" as a major obstacle to factory reform. This is even more true when we consider the arguments based directly upon economic theory. It cannot be doubted that the Ten Hours movement would have met with much less hostility if economists had insisted from the outset, as did John Stuart Mill in 1848, that the wage and employment effects of shorter hours were "in every particular instance a question of fact, not of principle." To be sure, economic theory added very little in the way of theoretical analysis to popular thinking about the Factory Acts. The level of formal analysis barely rose above the commonplace: no effort was made to distinguish the short-run and long-run effects of a change in hours, without which a distinction any analysis was bound to be naïve. In this sense, it is true to say that "had there been no classical economic theory, the arguments would have been essentially the same."[47] Nevertheless, the assumption of a constant productivity of labour irrespective of the length of the working day had been challenged by at least one economist, William Thornton. On the face of it, there is nothing in classical theory which would have prevented a consideration of this factor; once introduced there is little left of Torrens' *Letter to Lord Ashley*, "the best tract in opposition to the ten-hours project."

McCulloch's use of the wages fund doctrine to show that it is fruitless to restrict hours by legislative enactment is simply wrong. He failed to realise that at bottom, and apart from humanitarian motives, the leaders of the Ten Hours movement were trying to restrict the supply of labour in order to maintain the rates of wages in periods of severe unemployment. It is no accident that all the Factory Acts in the first half of the nineteenth century were passed after vigorous working-class agitation "at, or close to, a low point in cyclical fluctuations."[48] At such times employers were more inclined to accept restrictive legislation, but that is not the point. Only under depressed conditions can workers hope to gain instantly by an elimination of child and female labour; in a boom the immediate effect would be a reduction in real income per family. Needless to say, the wages fund doctrine is quite adequate to show why a reduction in the labour supply does tend to reduce wages. At the same time, it must be said that the doctrine is really inappropriate to a discussion of the Factory Acts: it assumes that the size of the labour force is a constant proportion of the total population, thus ignoring variations in the child and female participation rate.

In a class by itself is Fawcett's contention that pecuniary motives alone bring about the adoption of a work day that optimises output per man-hour. This argument is open to the objection that it assumes perfect foresight. Contrariwise, Thornton's thesis amounts to a denial of perfect knowledge on the part of the entrepreneur. We should say today that entrepreneurs may have little incentive to reduce hours since the immediate effect, if wages are kept constant, is to increase costs and decrease output; whereas, a simultaneous reduction in wages under these circumstances is bound to affect efficiency adversely. Thus, employers may fail to maximise output per man-hour owing to an excessive emphasis on profit maximisation in the short run.[49] Be that as it may, Fawcett's line of reasoning clearly shows where the classical economists' treatment of hours legislation is deficient: they had no theory of the firm.[50]

There is a simple moral in all this: for some purposes a theory of economic growth is not enough.

NOTES

1. For a recent example see R. G. Cowherd, *The Humanitarians and the Ten Hour Movement in England* (Boston, Mass., 1956). pp. 5-6, 9-10.
2. A. Marshall, *Principles of Economics (London, 8th edn, 1926), pp. 47, 763n.* See also Marshall's *Industry and Trade* (London, 1923), pp. 763-65.
3. (New York, 1954), p. 402.
4. K. O. Walker, "The Classical Economists and the Factory Acts," *Journal of Economic History*, 1 (November 1941), p. 170. See also L. R. Sorenson, "Some Classical Economists, Laissez Faire, and the Factory Acts," *ibid.*, 12 (Summer 1952), which reaches similar conclusions. Sorenson documents the assertion made above about the opinions of economic historians.
5. (London, 1952), pp. 101-3.
6. This is particularly true of Walker's analysis which deals only with the literature up to 1833.
7. The presentation of the argument has gained in clarity through the criticisms of Mr. M. Leiserson.
8. W. Smart, *Economic Annals of the Nineteenth Century* (London, 1910), I, 688, 702-3; Walker, *loc. cit.*, p. 175.
9. T. R. Malthus, *Essay on Population* (5th edn.; London, 1817), p. 282. Only

some dozen tracts appeared on Peel's bill in contrast to the flood of pamphlets that accompanied the legislation of the 1830s and 1840s. See J. B. Williams, *A Guide to the Printed Materials for English Social and Economic History, 1750-1850* (New York, 1926), II, pp. 192-4.

10. See M. W. Thomas, *The Early Factory Legislation* (London, 1948), pp. 55-6.
11. In addition, night work was abolished for those under eighteen, and the scope of regulation was extended to all textile factories, with the exception of lace and silk mills. Furthermore, employment for children was made conditional upon attendance at school for two hours a day and machinery of inspection was provided to supervise the enforcement of the Act.
12. As one of the advocates of shorter hours put it bitterly:
    "They could not refuse to protect children, but they are 'political economists'; and though, as men, they could no longer screw up their minds and hearts so far as to sacrifice any more limbs and lives of infants, the science would not suffer them to invade the 'freedom of industry' by involving the adults in that protection which they were obliged to give the child. It is this absurd attempt to separate the adult from the child in its labour, that has rendered every Act that has ever been passed to give protection to children almost void." C. Wing, *Evils of the Factory System Exposed* (London, 1836), p. 17, quoted by Thomas *op. cit.*, p. 89.
13. "Employment of Children in Manufactories," *The Examiner*, (January 29, 1832), p. 67. The article appeared anonymously; for evidence of Mill's authorship, see *Bibliography of the Published Writings of J. S. Mill*, ed. N. MacMinn, *et al.* (Evanston, Illinois, 1945).
14. In his *Principles* (1848), however, Mill pursued the argument to its logical conclusion. See *infra*.
15. *Hansard's Parliamentary Debates*, 3rd series, XV, pp. 414-15. See also Sorenson, *loc. cit.*, pp. 253-4.
16. *Letters on Commercial Policy* (London, 1833), p. 73.
17. (London, 1833), p. 51; also pp. 241, 358
18. *Westminster Review*, (April 1833), pp. 380-1. See also G. L. Nesbitt, *Benthamite Reviewing* (New York, 1934), pp. 147-8.
19. See A. E. Bland, *et al., English Economic History: Select Documents* (London, 1919), pp. 611-12; J. Morley, *The Life of Richard Cobden* (London, 1910), pp. 166-70.
20. *Edinburgh Review* (June 1827), p. 35.
21. Quoted by Robbins, *op. cit.*, pp. 101-2. See also G. Ramsay, *An Essay on the Distribution of Wealth* (Edinburgh, 1836), pp. 102-3, for the same argument.
22. On the basis of personal experience, Ure testified that child labour in factories "seemed to resemble a sport": children, working twelve hours a day, spent nine hours in idle contemplation and "sometimes dedicated these intervals to the perusal of books."
23. *Edinburgh Review* (July 1835), pp. 464-7.
24. Contrary to popular belief, fostered by Marx's attack, Senior did not advance a general theory that profits are produced in the "last hour." Even on his own assumptions, Senior's calculations actually show no more than that a shortening of the working day by one hour would cause profits to fall from 10 to 8 per cent, given a constant output per man-hour. See K. Wicksell, *Lectures on Political Economy* (New York, 1934), I, pp. 194-5.
25. See A. E. Bland, *et al., op. cit.*, pp. 605-66.
26. See Walker, *loc. cit.*, pp. 171-2.

27. There is some evidence that Dr. Thomas Chalmers, a leading Scottish divine and author of several economic treatises, was finally won over by the Ten Hours campaign in 1847. If so, Chalmers was a singular exception. See C. Driver, *Tory Radical. The Life of Richard Oastler* (New York, 1946), pp. 476-9.

28. *Proceedings of the Political Economy Club, 1821-1920* (London, 1921), VI, pp. 287-8.

29. Sorenson *(loc. cit.)* contends that Torrens was definitely sympathetic to factory legislation. The evidence for this comes from Torrens' Parliamentary speeches in the 1830s while *Letter to Lord Ashley*, the most important of Torrens' writings on the Factory Acts, is not considered.

30. *A Letter to Lord Ashley* (London, 1844), pp. 64-5, 71-3. Torrens' argument was reproduced in the popular journals: see the article on "Protection of Labour," *The Economist* (April 6, 1844). Typically, however, *The Economist* based its case on laissez faire (see S. Gordon, "The London *Economist* and the High Tide of Laissez Faire," *Journal of Political Economy*, 63 (December 1955), pp. 478, 483).

31. See B. L. Hutchins and A. Harrison, *A History of Factory Legislation* (London, 1911), pp. 19-23.

32. *The Ten Hours Factory Bill. The Speech of Lord Ashley, M. P. in the House of Commons on Friday, May 10, 1844* (London, 1844), pp. 15-16.

33. (London, 1846), p. 399.

34. *The Literature of Political Economy* (London, 1846); London Reprints No. 5 (1938), pp. 294-6.

35. *Principles of Political Economy* (London, 4th edn., 1849), pp. 427-30. See also McCulloch's *Treatise on the Circumstances Which Determine the Rate of Wages* (London, 1851), pp. 93-7, and *Treatises and Essays* (Edinburgh, 1859), pp. 453-4.

36. Mill's argument here is nothing but an early example of Pigou's famous distinction between private and social costs, as W. J. Baumol pointed out: *Welfare Economics and The Theory of the State* (Cambridge, Mass., 1952), pp. 15-16, 150-2.

37. J. S. Mill, *Principles of Political-Economy*, Ashley edn., pp. 964-5, 959. Senior took the same view on female labour: *Industrial Efficiency and Social Economy*, ed. S. L. Levy (London, 1929), II, pp. 307-8.

38. See G. H. Wood, "Factory Legislation, considered with reference to the Wages, etc., of the Operatives Protected thereby," *Journal of the Royal Statistical Society*, 65 (June 1902), p. 297.

39. H. Fawcett, *Essays and Lectures on Social and Political Subjects* (London, 1872), pp. 36, 113-15, 120.

40. H. Fawcett, *Speeches on Current Political Questions* (London, 1873), p. 122 ff.

41. W. S. Jevons, *The State in Relation to Labour* (London, 1882), p. 65.

42. Thornton's argument was finally "rediscovered" by Marshall (*Principles*, pp. 695-6).

43. See Jevons, *The Theory of Political Economy* (2nd edn.; London, 1879), pp. 63-4, and *Methods of Social Reform and Other Papers* (London, 1883), p. 109.

44. Sorenson, *loc. cit.*, pp. 260-1. Walker's observation *(loc. cit.)* that "reputable and orthodox economists like Colonel Robert Torrens, Joseph Hume, Thomas Tooke, Edwin Chadwick, and Leonard Horner, were all favorable to factory legislation as long as it was limited to children" completely begs the question.

Not only were some of these "economists" never regarded, by themselves or others, as spokesmen of economic science, but all public figures after 1820 or thereabouts approved of factory legislation limited to children below some age or other.

45. See the citations by K. Marx, *Capital* (New York, 1939), p. 288.

46. Their fears seem to have been unfounded. Available data covering the period 1835-70 reveal a steady tendency to replace protected children with similarly protected adults and young persons; women above thirteen comprised from 50-56 per cent of the labour force throughout the period. See Wood, *loc. cit.*, pp. 310-11.

47. Walker, *loc. cit.*, p. 177.

48. W. W. Rostow, *British Economy of the Nineteenth Century* (Oxford, 1948), p. 118.

49. See J. R. Hicks, *The Theory of Wages* (London, 1932), pp. 104-10. Even on the assumption of perfect foresight, this is a clear case of private costs diverging from social costs. There is no reason why the classical economists could not have considered this possibility; the distinction between private and social costs is implicit in Adam Smith's discussion of public works.

50. Since Jevons likewise had no theory of the firm he was unable to improve upon classical analysis in this respect.

8 The Economics of Education in English Classical Political Economy: A Re-Examination

There is a small but growing literature on the role of education in the doctrines of the English classical economists, most of which is unfortunately contradictory if not downright misleading.[1] Among its shortcomings is a failure to emphasise the fact that Adam Smith's important ideas on the economics of education were largely ignored by his followers and that the very topic itself was neglected until John Stuart Mill took it up again in the 1840s, only to repudiate most of Smith's analysis. In addition, the literature is prone to ancestor worship: it seems forever to be crediting early nineteenth-century authors with a modern grasp of the subject and, in particular, with the insights of what has been described as "the human investment revolution in economic thought", namely, Schultz-Becker-Denison and all that. I shall argue, however, that classical political economy made virtually no contribution to the theory of human capital; indeed, in some respects it undermined its foundations. Lastly, the secondary literature is marred by a tendency to lose sight of the dates at which various classical writers made their educational pronouncements, almost as if the precise historical context had no bearing whatever on the views that they expressed. And yet it is only by paying attention to dates that we come to realise that the classical economists gradually adjusted their ideas on education in the wake of legislative changes; instead of having an influence on policy, policy had an influence on them. I have now said enough, I hope, to justify a re-examination of classical writings on the economic aspects and consequences of education.[2]

1 ADAM SMITH AND THE REMUNERATION OF UNIVERSITY TEACHERS

When the National Board for Prices and Incomes (PIB) delivered its first report on the pay of British university teachers in 1968, it found that the salary structure was biased towards research: "all the evidence we have received shows that promotion tends to be awarded for research as measured by publication."[3] To counter this bias, the PIB proposed a system of discretionary payments to those members of staff who taught either more or better than the average, where "better" was judged at least in part by students responding to "a carefully drafted questionnaire".[4] Although the use of student assessments is a familiar feature of American higher education, the PIB proposal was greeted in Britain with jeers about "gearing salaries to popularity polls" and soon came to be rejected first by the universities and then by the government. The participants in this acrimonious controversy, virtually all of whom rejected the notion of relating salaries in any way to student opinions, divided neatly into a minority who flatly denied that the quality of teaching could be objectively assessed and a majority who asserted that it was already being assessed informally by heads of department as an essential element in deciding on promotions.[5]

It must be conceded that there is in fact very little firm evidence that "publish or perish" is the basic principle of promotion in British universities. On the other hand, casual empirical observation confirms the PIB view and one would have thought that the burden of proof is on those who deny the research bias. In any case, as soon as it is argued that the quality of teaching is actually taken into account in making promotions, it remains only to decide how to assess that quality as objectively as possible. In that case, encouraging students to express their views can only aid assessment, serving in addition as an expression of faith in their essentially sound judgment. It goes without saying, of course, that a really comprehensive judgment of teacher effectiveness would combine student assessments with tests of student learning and with assessments by colleagues.[6]

None of the contenders in this debate cited Adam Smith, although he had indeed addressed himself at some length to precisely the same problem: how should we reward teachers so as to best induce them to perform their tasks with maximum efficiency? In the fear that any summary of his argument would meet with incredulity, we cite his own words:

In some universities the salary makes but a part, and frequently but a small part, of the emoluments of the teacher, of which the greater part arises from the honoraries or fees of his pupils ... In other universities the teacher is prohibited from receiving any honorary or fee from his pupils, and his salary constitutes the whole of the revenue which he derives from his office. His interest is, in this case set as directly in opposition to his duty as it is possible to set it. It is the interest of every man to live as much at his ease as he can; and if his emoluments are to be precisely the same, whether he does, or does not perform some very laborious duty, it is certainly his interest, at least as interest is vulgarly understood, either to neglect it altogether, or, if he is subject to some authority which will not suffer him to do this, to perform it in as careless and slovenly a manner as the authority will permit. If he is naturally active and a lover of labour, it is his interest to employ that activity in any way, from which he can derive some advantage, rather than in the performance of his duty, from which he can derive none.

If the authority to which he is subject resides in the body corporate, the college, or university, of which he himself is a member, and in which the greater part of the other members are, like himself, persons who either are, or ought to be teachers; they are likely to make a common cause, to be all very indulgent to one another, and every man to consent that his neighbour may neglect his duty provided he himself is allowed to neglect his own. In the university of Oxford, the greater part of the public professors have, for these many years, given up altogether even the pretence of teaching.[7]

Clearly, this is the PIB model: although universities are not profit-making institutions, nevertheless the behaviour of university teachers as utility-maximisers gathered together in a kind of syndicalist club to pursue common ends is broadly predictable.[8] So is the behaviour of students, which Adam Smith described with a generosity rarely encountered these days among university dons:

The discipline of colleges and universities is in general contrived not for the benefit of the students, but for the interest, or more properly speaking for the ease of the masters. Its object is, in all cases, to maintain the authority of the master, and whether he neglects or performs his duty, to oblige the students in all cases to behave to him as if he performed it with the greatest diligence and ability ... Where the masters, however, really perform their duty, there are no examples, I believe, that the greater part of the students ever neglect theirs. No discipline is ever requisite to force attendance upon lectures which are really worth the attending, as is well known wherever any such lectures are given.... Such is the generosity of the greater part of young men, that, so far from being disposed to neglect or despise the instructions of their master, provided he shows some serious intention of being of use to them, they are generally inclined to pardon a great deal of incorrectness in the performance of his duty, and sometimes even to conceal from the public a good deal of gross negligence.[9]

II ADAM SMITH AND THE ORGANISATION OF EDUCATION

What distinguishes Adam Smith's views on economic development from later nineteenth-century and even twentieth-century efforts is the emphasis that he placed on the organisation of economic institutions that harness the self-interests of individuals to the interests of society as a whole. He never lost sight of the fact that the remuneration of individuals working in public institutions, insulated as they are from ordinary market pressures, raises special difficulties. "Public services", he pronounced, "are never better performed than when their reward comes only in consequence of their being performed, and is proportioned to the diligence employed in performing them" (*WN*, Book V, Ch. 1, p. 20). He goes on to argue, however, that to define and measure "diligence" in a strictly quantitative sense in such fields as law, education, and the Church may create more problems than it solves; the principles that govern pay in these areas can only be guidelines of a qualitative nature. Virtually the whole of the first chapter of Book V, "Of the Expenses of the Sovereign or Commonwealth", is taken up with the question of devising techniques for rewarding lawyers, clerks, judges, clergymen, and teachers which will force them to advance social interests even as they pursue their own interests.[10]

We have already considered Adam Smith's views on university teaching and particularly university teaching in England. The situation in the English independent schools was much better than in the universities, he believed, because "the reward of the schoolmaster in most cases depends principally, in some cases almost entirely, upon the fees or honoraries of his scholars" (*WN* Book V, Ch. 2, p. 17). On balance, however, he favoured the Scottish system: the cost of school buildings in rural parishes was met by a tax on the local heritors and tenants (in towns these costs were financed out of municipal funds); the teachers received a small fixed stipend from the same source, supplemented by private fees which frequently varied with the range of the subject they offered to teach. "In Scotland", he noted, "the establishment of such parish schools has taught almost the whole common people to read and a very great proportion of them to write and account. In England the establishment of charity schools has had an effect of the same kind, though not so universally" (*WN*, Book V, Ch. 2, p. 55). Some suggestions for curriculum changes in those schools, to include geometry and mechanic,[11] and a proposal for a system of occupational licensing completed his recommendations for educational reform.[12]

Adam Smith's marked preference for private over public education is evident throughout Book V. Nor is there a hint of the argument that education can only be competently judged after it has been received and not before, which was to become so popular in the last half of the nineteenth century. On the contrary: "Those parts of education, it is to be observed, for the teaching of which there are no public institutions, are generally the best taught .... The three most essential parts of literary education, to read, write, and account, it still continues to be more common to acquire in private than in public schools" (*WN* Book V, Ch. 2, p. 16). Nevertheless, the effects of occupational specialisation are such as to deprive "the labouring poor" of their "intellectual, social, and martial virtues", or, in the language of today, to "alienate" workers.[13] For that reason, state aid to education is justified and perhaps so is compulsory attendance:

For a very small expence the public can facilitate, can encourage, and can impose upon almost the whole body of the people, the necessity of acquiring those most essential parts of education ["to read, write, and account"]. The public can facilitate this acquisition by establishing in every parish or district a little school, where children may be taught for a reward so moderate, that even a common labourer may afford it; the master being partly, but not wholly paid by the public; because, if he was wholly, or even principally paid by it, he would soon learn to neglect his business. (*WN* Book V, Ch. 2, pp. 54-5)

Driving the argument home, Adam Smith summed up by advancing an entirely new reason for state aid to education derived from an unformulated theory of "social control":

Though the state was to derive no advantage from the instruction of the inferior ranks of people, it would still deserve its attention that they should not be altogether uninstructed. The state, however, derives no inconsiderable advantage from their instruction. The more they are instructed, the less liable they are to the delusions of enthusiasm and superstition, which, among ignorant nations, frequently occasion the most dreadful disorders. An instructed and intelligent people besides, are always more decent and orderly than an ignorant and stupid one. They feel themselves, each individually more respectable, and more likely to obtain the respect of their lawful superiors, and they are therefore more disposed to respect those superiors. They are more disposed to examine, and more capable of seeing through, the interested complaints of faction and sedition, and they are, upon that account, less apt to be misled into any wanton or unnecessary opposition to the measures of government. In free countries, where the safety of government depends very much upon the favourable judgment which the people may form of its conduct, it must surely be of the highest importance that they should not be disposed to judge rashly or capriciously concerning it. (*WN* Book V, Ch. 2, p. 61).

The thoughts contained in this passage made a lasting impression on the members of the classical school. The rest of Smith's views on education — the role of fee-paying as an incentive device for teachers; the harmful effects of educational endowments on schools and universities; the stress on a more practical syllabus in elementary schools; the plea for a system of occupational licensing of manual trades — were soon forgotten and even the issues raised by them simply dropped out of English classical political economy.

Likewise, the brief hint at the concept of human capital in the famous chapter on relative wages in Book I, while reproduced in almost identical words in every classical text, was never developed in any substantial way by any of Smith's disciples.

When an expensive machine is erected, the extraordinary work to be performed by it before it is worn out, it must be expected, will replace the capital laid out upon it, with at least the ordinary profits. A man educated at the expence of much labour and time to any of those employments which require extraordinary dexterity and skill, may be compared to one of those expensive machines. The work which he learns to perform, it must be expected, over and above the usual wages of common labour, will replace to him the whole expence of his education, with at least the ordinary profits of an equally valuable capital.

The difference between the wages of skilled labour and those of common labour, is founded upon this principle.[14]

In modern language, this passage says that monetary rewards in any occupation must in equilibrium suffice to indemnify individuals for the costs of any education and training they have acquired. As such, it amounts not to a finished piece of analysis but rather to an invitation to examine the problem of skills differentials from a new angle. Fruitful theorising only begins when it is recognised that such dissimilar phenomena as formal schooling, on-the-job training, the consumption of medical care, geographical migration, and the general process of job search are all essentially similar ways of investing in oneself by incurring present costs for the sake of future benefits. In some circumstances, these purely personal investments in human beings also become social investments in the quality of the labour force. A necessary but not sufficient condition for this coincidence between private and social returns is the existence of perfectly competitive labour markets. In this sense, the analysis of wage differentials, which of course constituted an essential element of classical economies, remains incomplete without an investigation of the economic value of education. But the classical economists, as we shall see, simply failed to explore the implications of a human capital view of labour supply. Adam Smith made a start; John Stuart Mill carried it a little further; and Marshall certainly began to do justice to the theme of human capital formation. Nevertheless, these three authors between them did no more than to open the door to Becker's *Human Capital* (1964), which actually constructed the foundations of the subject for the first time.

III MALTHUS AND McCULLOCH ON STATE EDUCATION

It has been aptly observed that "the economics of education in English classical economics could be presented as a discussion of material in the works of Adam Smith and John Stuart Mill".[15] To be sure, Malthus, James Mill, Chalmers, McCulloch, Jones, Chadwick, Senior, Cairnes, and Fawcett, to mention only English members of the classical school, each had something to say about education. In almost every case, however, what they said consisted either of *obiter dicta* or of general but impractical pronouncements in favour of a "national" system of education. The absence of the name of Ricardo from the list is itself revealing: the leading economist of the day never addressed himself directly to any educational question. Likewise, Torrens hardly ever mentioned education. In another context, Bentham's vast educational treatise, *Chrestomathia*, would warrant discussion and Malthus and Senior, in particular, deserve our attention if only because the former was the most widely read economist of the nineteenth century and because the latter took a leading part in several Royal Commissions which dealt with educational problems. Nevertheless, practically nothing new was added and a great deal was lost in the seventy years that separate the publication of *The Wealth of Nations* from the appearance of Mill's *Principles*. In those years, Parliament launched its first tentative efforts to subsidise the education of the poor, private schooling grew by leaps and bounds to a point where most children were attending school many weeks of the year, most working-class adults having by then achieved rudimentary literacy with or without the benefit of schooling, while all the time the debate on the Religious Question — Church schools or lay schools — raged on without being resolved.[16] It is not too much to say that one can read all the great names in English classical economics without learning anything about these questions. Clearly it is not only in the twentieth century that economists have neglected the economic aspects and economic consequences of education.

The standard treatment of educational issues by early nineteenth-century economists was firmly established by Malthus in the second edition of the *Essay on Population* (1803). His remarks are characterised by an exaggerated regard for the achievements of the Scottish parochial system, a fervent but vague plea for the adoption of something like it in England, in opposition to the Tory view that popular instructions endangered the security of property,[17] and a pronounced emphasis on the tendency of education to promote self-reliance with hardly a mention of the formation of productive skills. Where Malthus goes beyond Adam Smith is in suggesting that the curriculum of elementary schools should include political economy, and particularly "the real state of the lower classes of society, as affected by the principle of population". This too was a point which was echoed by virtually every classical economist who ever mentioned education.[18]

Charity day schools, Sunday schools, Dame schools, and factory schools (the latter dating from the Health and Morals of Apprentices Act of 1802) all saw a rapid growth in the first few decades of the nineteenth century and even in Scotland, as we shall see, private schooling had long ago caught up and surpassed the statutory school provision. Nevertheless, Malthus mentioned only Sunday schools and these pages were left unrevised between the second edition of 1803 and the sixth and last edition of 1826. "It is surely a great national disgrace", he wrote, "that the education of the lower classes of people in England should be left merely to a few Sunday schools, supported by a subscription from individuals, who can give the course of instruction in them any kind of bias which they please. And even the improvement of Sunday schools (for objectionable as they are in some points of view, and imperfect in all, I cannot but consider them as an improvement) is of very late date." [19] He concluded his comments by pronouncing: "no government can approach to perfection that does not provide for the instruction of the people. The benefits derived from education are among those which may be enjoyed without restriction of numbers; and as it is in the power of government to confer these benefits, it is undoubtedly their duty to do so" (*ibid.* p. 441).

Malthus' failure to make any reference to the Religious Question, at least in the sixth edition, is somewhat surprising. The British and Foreign School Society was launched in 1814 to encourage local efforts in establishing schools that would provide non-denominational religious teaching. This came hard on the heels of the formation of the National Society for Promoting the Education of the Poor in the Principles of the Established Church Throughout England and Wales, and by the 1820s every educational issue was fought out in terms of the two rival organisations. [20] Malthus' recommendation of a public system of elementary education, without any indication of how the problem of religious teaching was to be resolved, must have meant little to his readers.

In the last chapter of the *Essay on Population*, significantly entitled "Our Rational Expectations Respecting the Future Improvement of Society", Malthus returns to the question of education. He touches briefly on what we would now describe as one of the external effects of schooling, namely, its tendency to promote a climate of opinion conducive to family limitation, and adds: "The practical good effects of education have long been experienced in Scotland ... education appears to have a considerable effect in the prevention of crimes, and the promotion of industry, morality, and regular conduct." [21]

The contrast between law-abiding Scotland and unruly England became one of the clichés of the period, as much with the Scottish as with the English members of the classical school. It appears in some of the early essays of James Mill, [22] although not in the more famous article on education for the Supplement to the fifth edition of the *Encyclopaedia Britannica*, and it is one of McCulloch's recurrent themes. McCulloch, however, was more realistic about the law-and-order argument for education than either Adam Smith or Malthus. He always took the view that factory employment would make workers less deferential and compliant but he accepted this consequence as part of the price of economic growth. After endorsing "a really useful system of public education", which would join reading and writing to the teaching of religion, morality and political economy, with the object of persuading the poor that "they are really the arbiters of their own fortune", he added the comment that "we are not of the number of those who expect that any system of education will ever ensure tranquillity in periods of distress, or that it will obviate the vicissitudes and disorders inherent in the manufacturing system".[23]

Once again one is struck by the failure to explain what particular system of public education is being advocated. Nevertheless, it is clear from other references that McCulloch's model is that of the parochial system of Scotland: "there cannot be the shadow of a doubt that were government to interfere so far as to cause a public school to be established in every parish in England, where the fees should be moderate, and where really useful instruction should be communicated to the scholars, its interference would be in the highest degree beneficial."[24] Elsewhere, he endorsed all that Adam Smith had said on the appropriate method of remunerating school teachers.[25]

IV HUMAN CAPITAL AND THE ECONOMIC VALUE OF EDUCATION

McCulloch is frequently singled out among classical economists for his explicit recognition of the concept of human capital, linking the provision of education to economic growth. But as a matter of fact, all that McCulloch did was to go one step further than Adam Smith in defining capital to include not only the "skill, dexterity, and judgement" of workers, but also workers themselves as measured by the accumulated costs of rearing them.[26] No doubt, this was perfectly consistent with the general logic of classical wage theory, which treated the supply of labour as being perfectly elastic at the going wage rate. But the point is that McCulloch made no analytical use of the idea. He never committed himself to anything as clear-cut as Chadwick's assertion in 1862 that educated workers are at least 20 and perhaps 25 per cent more productive than uneducated workers[27] — and nor did any of the other classical economists.

The question whether to categorise either human beings themselves or the acquired skills of human beings as fixed capital has actually very little economic significance *per se*. As we know, Marshall rejected Fisher's idea of counting the skills of the labour force as part of the capital stock of an economy but that did not prevent him from exploring Adam Smith's suggestion that an investment motive makes itself felt in the demand for education.[28] Contrariwise, many classical economists defined capital to include human skills and even described the earnings differentials between skilled and unskilled labour as "profit on capital" and yet drew no inferences from such statements with respect to either the private demand for education or the effects of subsidising elementary education.

McCulloch is a case in point but an even better one is Senior. Senior was of course insistent on the notion that the time-consuming acquisition of a special skill requires "abstinence", which must earn the going rate of return in the economy on physical capital. Nevertheless, he denied that the personal motive of "a gentleman's son" in acquiring education was primarily that of investment in future earning power.[29] Similarly, in his unpublished lectures of 1847-52, while asserting that "good elementary schools" will pay for themselves via improvements "in diligence, in skill, in economy, in health", he declined to include knowledge and skills in the definition of "capital" (*Industrial Efficiency*, II, pp. 328-9; I, p. 170); indeed, he went out of his way to deny that the most powerful influences of schools lie in the domain of either cognitive or manual skills.

The word "education" may be defined, he observed, as the sum of

the influences which one person intentionally exercises over another by precept or by example .... These influences are of two kinds: first, the imparting knowledge, which may be called *teaching*; secondly, the creation of habits, which may be called *training* .... As between teaching and training, there can be no doubt that training is by far the more important .... Training, therefore, or the formation of habits, rather than teaching, or the imparting of knowledge, is the great business of society. (*op. cit.,* II, pp. 329-31).

This passage, asserting unambiguously that the economic value of schooling is much more a matter of effective behaviour than of cognitive knowledge, undoubtedly expresses the more or less implicitly held belief of all the classical economists. What was critical, they seemed to be saying, was to disseminate among workers the behavioural traits appropriate to an industrialised society. Indeed, the "left" and the "right" in this period, if we can use such words, were entirely united on the principal effect of education: Tory extremists were convinced that elementary schooling would cause the poor to question the necessity of their poverty and therefore opposed the spread of education, while liberal Whigs were equally convinced that education would "tame" the poor and therefore favoured its extension. What is striking in all this is the failure to take any explicit account of the role of education in the formation of so-called "vocational skills".

John Stuart Mill's treatment of education is an even more striking example of the failure to develop the main implications of the human capital concept. In his discussion of "the degree of productiveness of productive agents", he lays great stress on "the economical value of the general diffusion of intelligence among the people" and draws an unflattering comparison between Continental and English workers: "If an English labourer is anything but a hewer of wood and a drawer of water, he is indebted for it to education, which in his case is almost always self-education."[30] This sounds indeed as if Mill saw a vital connection between education and economic growth, but when he came later in the book to make his case for government intervention in education, he made no reference of any kind to the economic value of education. The emphasis in the famous 1845 essay on "The Claims of Labour" and in the chapter "On the Probable Futurity of the Labouring Classes" in the *Principles* is altogether on character-formation and self-improvement.[31]

Similarly, after denying that the expenses of rearing children are motivated by investment considerations, Mill concedes that the costs of acquiring "technical or industrial education" are incurred for "the sake of the greater or more valuable thereby attained, and in order that a remuneration equivalent or more than equivalent, may be reaped by the learner" (*Principles*, p. 40). This is a clear statement of the fundamental axiom of the theory of human capital but it is as far as Mill went, probably because he had come to doubt the significance of the Smithian principle that the labour market tends to equalise the net advantages of different occupations. Believing as he did that professional men constitute a non-competing group with manual workers, he drew attention to the fact that clerks earn more than bricklayers in violation of Smith's theory: "The higher rate of his [the clerk's] remuneration ... must be partly ascribed to monopoly" (*op. cit.*, pp. 392-3). But he did agree that the diffusion of education was beginning to erode these monopoly rents, which is easier to square with Smith's theory than with his own:

Until lately [writing in 1848], all employments which required even the humble education of reading and writing, could be recruited only from a select class, the majority having had no opportunity of acquiring those attainments .... Since reading and writing have been brought within the reach of the multitude, the monopoly price of the lower grade of educated employment has greatly fallen, the competition for them having increased in an almost incredible degree. (*Ibid.*, p. 392)

In short, throughout this period the theory of human capital remained more or less in the embryonic form in which it appears in *The Wealth of Nations*, a suggestion of a theory rather than a theory properly so-called. Senior denied it outright and even McCulloch and John Stuart Mill only glanced at it in passing.

V COMPULSION AND TUITION FEES

In analysing classical views on matters of educational policy, it is essential to distinguish opinions expressed before 1833 from those expressed after that date. 1833 constitutes a natural dividing line as marking the year in which Edwin Chadwick and Southwood Smith introduced the "Prussian" principle of compulsory education under cover of a Factory Act, albeit for a strictly limited category of children, and in which Parliament was persuaded for the first time to make an annual grant to approved schools. The Factory Act of 1833 prohibited the employment of children under the age of 13 in textile mills unless they produced a certificate of their attendance in a school in the previous week; it said nothing about how the schooling in question was to be provided or how it was to be paid for; certainly there was no intention to make it free except on the basis of charity to the very poorest children. This point deserves some emphasis. When Charles Roebuck earlier in the same year had laid the educational programme of the Philosophical Radicals before the Reformed Parliament, he shocked the House by demanding compulsory education for all children between the ages of 6 and 14. But even he emphasised the importance of retaining school fees for all but the poorest.[32] Of course, outside the Radical camp literally nobody entertained the idea of elementary education that was both compulsory and free.

Some reformers, however, seem to have soon moved beyond the position adopted by Roebuck. At any rate, the *Report on the Hand-Loom Weavers in 1841* contained the following remarkable statement:

The merit … of the education clauses in the Factory Act is, not what they have done, but what they have acknowledged. It is obvious, at first sight, that the legislature, which fines a parent for sending a child to work at a power loom without having sent it the day before to school cannot consistently exempt from the same obligation the parent who sends his child to … any employment beyond his own doors. And we think that, on reflection, everyone must feel that the mere accident of the child's being employed in the house of a stranger, or in that of his own parent, and to go a step further, of his being or not being employed at all, does not affect the parent's obligation, or the duty of the state to enforce it. It is equally obvious that, if the state be found to require the parent to educate his child, it is bound to see that he has the means of doing so. The voluntary system, therefore, … a system which has been repudiated in principle will not be permitted to continue in practice.[33]

The report was largely written by Senior, one of the four Commissioners, and the language in this paragraph is unmistakably that of Senior. It defines a position from which, as we shall see, he was later somewhat to retreat. The passage just cited is, to my knowledge, unique in the period in publicly recommending something close to the twentieth-century remedy of compulsory elementary education for all, provided by the state without fees of any kind.[34] Nevertheless, it is noteworthy that even this statement does not go quite so far as to recommend abolition of all fees as a matter of principle.

To demonstrate that it is nevertheless unrepresentative of advanced opinion in the day, let us consider John Stuart Mill's application of the "Non-Interference Principle" to education. For the first time since Adam Smith, we meet here with an entirely original contribution to the classical theory of educational policy. Furthermore, having first advanced his ideas in the *Principles* in 1848, Mill went on to develop them further in the essay *On Liberty* (1859) and returned to them once again ten years later in an essay on "Endowments".

The new contribution is the notion that the commodity "education" represents a clear-out case of market failures on the grounds that its production is inherently plagued by problems of consumer ignorance. In a nutshell: "The uncultivated cannot be competent judges of cultivation" (*Principles*, p. 953). The modern phrase "market failure" is used advisedly as Mill's words leave no doubt of his meaning: "It will continually happen, on the voluntary system, that, the end not being desired, the means will not be provided at all, or that, persons requiring improvement having an imperfect or altogether erroneous conception of what they want, the supply called forth by the demand of the market will be anything but what is really required" (*ibid*). It is perhaps misleading to label this argument as being one of consumer ignorance. Here ignorance in making choices can be remedied, in principle at any rate, by the provision of information, but the assertion that the opinions of uneducated people about education are necessarily worthless is really a proposition about the effects of education on the formation of tastes and hence on the ultimate foundation of choice. At first glance, this proposition appears to be a value judgment but on further examination it is seen to be an empirical generalisation for which there is indeed a good deal of evidence.[35] At any rate, education seems to be a commodity the demand for which "grows by what it feeds on".

Nevertheless, Mill's thesis is liable to self-contradiction when combined, as he wished to combine it, with a belief in the desirability of enfranchising the lower classes. If the uneducated are incompetent judges of education, why are they regarded as competent judges of Parliamentary representatives that vote funds for education? To be sure, people may be unwilling to indulge "the irrational passion for rational calculation", preferring to delegate certain difficult choices to Parliamentary representatives, but it takes an argument of some kind to make the case. Without directly facing the difficulty inherent in his position, Mill nevertheless recognised the logical necessity of claiming a quasi-paternalistic role for government:

any well-intentioned and tolerably civilised government may think, without presumption, that it does or ought to possess a degree of cultivation above the average of the community which it rules, and it should therefore be capable of offering better education and better instruction to the people, than the greater number of them would spontaneously demand. Education, therefore, is one of those things which it is admissible in principle that a government should provide for the people. (*Ibid.*)

He now moves on to "elementary education" in particular, by which phrase he and other nineteenth-century authors always meant, not first-stage education for children, but rather education for the poor as a social class, whether children or adults. What he advocated was compulsory instruction either at school or at home, while relegating the role of the state to the provision of financial assistance to permit all parents to comply with this requirement: "It is therefore an allowable exercise of the powers of government to impose on parents the legal obligation of giving elementary instruction to children. This, however, cannot fairly be done, without taking measures to insure that such instruction shall be always accessible to them either gratuitously or at a trifling expense" (*ibid.* p.954). It is significant that at this point he found it necessary to confront the contemporary belief in the positive virtues of fee-paying: "This is not one of the cases in which the tender of help perpetuates the state of things which renders help necessary." Holding that the poor could not be expected to defray the full cost of elementary education, he concluded:

The education provided in this country on the voluntary principle has of late been so much discussed, that it is needless in this place to criticise it minutely, and I shall merely express my conviction that even in quantity it is [in 1848], and is likely to remain, altogether insufficient, while in quality, though with some slight tendency to improvement, it is never good except by some rare accident, and generally so bad as to be little more than nominal. I hold it the duty of the government to supply the defect, by giving pecuniary support to elementary schools, such as to render them accessible to all the children of the poor, either freely, or for a payment too inconsiderable to be sensibly felt ... the remainder of the cost to be defrayed, as in Scotland, by a local rate. (*Ibid.* pp.955-6)

Having said this much, he qualified it immediately by attacking the idea of a state monopoly of education:

Though a government ... may, and in many cases ought to, establish schools and colleges, it must neither compel, nor bribe any person to come to them; nor ought the power of individuals to set up rural establishments to depend in any degree upon its authorization. It would be justified in requiring from all the people that they shall possess instruction in certain things, but not in prescribing them how or from whom they shall obtain it. (*Ibid.*)

Mill wrote as if the principle of state subsidies to elementary education was yet to be established. But, of course, Treasury grants to voluntary schools amounted in 1849 to £125,000, having risen sixfold from the date of their inception in 1833. The argument by 1848 was not so much over the very principle of state assistance but rather over the religious character of aided schools. By 1851, when the *Census of Education* produced the first reliable figures for the nation as a whole, the Church of England provided 90 per cent of all elementary school places in the country; in rural areas, its monopoly was almost complete. In consequence, Church schools had been receiving the lion's share of government grants to elementary education,[36] and this is perhaps the reason that Mill, firmly opposed as a Radical Utilitarian to the Established Church, took a poor view of the growth of voluntary schooling. This is, of course, a pure speculation. But consider what it would have meant to have endorsed the voluntary system. That would be to imply that there was nothing wrong with the powerful grip which the Anglican Church had by then secured over the school system. Surely, this must have been too much to swallow for the son of James Mill and the pupil of Bentham?

According to Mill then the duties of the state are to set minimum educational standards; thereafter, private schools operating their own subsidised fee system, in competition with state schools waiving the fee payment for poor children, can be relied on to provide education. But how is such a scheme to be enforced? Mill does not tell us in the *Principles*: he makes no reference to the central education inspectorate, which had been created by 1848 as an essential element in the Whig programme of state-aided elementary education, and he says nothing about how the income of parents is to be discovered for purposes of remitting fees. In the last chapter of the essay *On Liberty*, however, he becomes slightly more explicit.

The treatment of education in the essay begins with a clear assertion of the central doctrine: "Is it not almost a self-evident axiom, that the State should require and compel the education, up to a certain standard, of every human being who is born its citizen?"[37] This "self-evident axiom" seemed to Mill both to resolve the vexed Religious Question and to avoid the dangers of the Leviathan state.

Were the duty of enforcing universal education once admitted there would be an end to the difficulties about what the State should teach, and how it should teach, which now convert the subject into a mere battlefield for sects and parties .... If the government would make up its mind to require for every child a good education, it might save itself the trouble of providing one. It might leave the parents to obtain the education where and how they pleased, and content itself with helping to pay the school fees of the poorer classes of children, and defraying the entire school expenses of those who have no one else to pay for them. The objections which are urged with reason against State education do not apply to the enforcement of education by the State, but to the State's taking upon itself to direct that education; which is a totally different thing. That the whole or any large part of the education of the people should be in State hands, I go as far as anyone in deprecating .... A general State education is a mere contrivance for moulding people to be exactly like one another .... An education established and controlled by the State should only exist, if it exists at all, as one among many competing experiments, carried on for the purpose of example and stimulus, to keep the others up to a certain standard of excellence.[38]

The scheme he proposed runs as follows: children are to be tested at an early age in the ability to read; failure to pass the examination subjects the parents to a fine and, thereafter, to compulsory schooling at their own expense; these examinations are to be held annually and the range of subjects is to be gradually extended up to some unspecified age; apart from these, all examinations are to be voluntary and designed merely to certify competence in a field. The implied strictures against occupational licensing, by the way, are made to apply explicitly to the teaching profession (*Utilitarianism*, p. 162).

Mill's final statement on educational questions came in 1869 in an essay on "Endowments", undoubtedly provoked by the publication of the report of the Taunton Schools Inquiry Commission. This paper largely goes over the same ground as the *Principles* and the essay *On Liberty* but it does add some new points. Firstly, Mill took the next step in the steady tendency to deprecate fee-paying by rejecting Adam Smith's view that the quality of teaching must deteriorate if teachers' salaries are unrelated to the number of pupils they succeed in attracting; since teachers serve consumers who are essentially ignorant of the product they are buying. Mill argued, pecuniary incentives will fail to produce desirable results.[39] These remarks had a special contemporary relevance because the Revised Code of 1862 had recently introduced the principle of payments-by-results. Secondly, Mill extended his earlier views on state subsidies to elementary education and now proposed free secondary and university education for those members of the working class who exhibited "capacities ... for the higher departments of intellectual work".[40] No other economist, not even Fawcett,[41] ever went so far.

VI   SENIOR'S LATER VIEWS

To round off our discussion, it remains only to say a few words about Senior's views in later years. There is almost nothing original to report and were they the views of anyone else they would hardly deserve comment. The Newcastle Commission on the State of Popular Education, appointed in 1858 with Senior as one of its members, was split between a minority who opposed subsidisation of fees but approved central grants for the construction and maintenance of school buildings and a majority who insisted on an extension of the annual Parliamentary grant specifically designed to allow fees to be set well below costs. Senior clearly took the majority view. Rejecting a colleague's eloquent statement of free-market principles applied to education, he wrote in a private memorandum: "I agree with Mr. G. Smith in thinking that part of the money paid directly for the child's education ought to be paid by the parent. The payment of school pence promotes regularity of attendance, adds in the parent's mind to the value of what is purchased, and gives a feeling of independence. But a small fee is sufficient for these purposes."[42] He calculated the costs of elementary education at not less than 30*s*. a year and declared: "there is no reason to believe that now, or at any time that can be defined, that sum is or will be obtainable from the parent" (*ibid.*, p. 185).

In 1861 he published a volume of his notes and resolutions submitted to the Commission, entitled *Suggestions on Popular Education*. Once again, he reiterated his belief that the poor could not afford cost-covering fees, this time adding to the expense of tuition fees "the much greater expense of foregoing the child's wages".[43] He now borrowed from Mill the notion that poor parents would neglect the education of their children even if they were not poor and he combined this idea with his own long-standing dislike of working-class organisations. Someone had proposed the introduction of parents into the management of schools; Senior violently rejected this proposal on the grounds that the "lower classes" were not even competent to run their own benefit societies or trade unions: "For fifty years they have been managing their own trades' unions. There is not one which is not based on folly, tyranny and injustice which would disgrace the rudest savages. They sacrifice their wives', their children's, and their own health and strength to the lowest sensuality. The higher the wages the worse seems, in general, to be the condition of the families."[44]

The shrill paternalistic tone of these remarks is consistently maintained in all the notes and resolutions of *Popular Education*. As in the case of John Stuart Mill, there is some reason to believe that Senior shared the increasing tendency of Dissenters to despair of ever competing successfully with Church of England schools. The average parent, he observed, simply would not accept non-denominational education.[45] Detailing the deplorable quality of most private schools, he concluded: "yet to these dens of ignorance and malaria one third of the labouring classes still send their children ... although good and cheap public schools are at their door" (*ibid.*, p. 29). Nevertheless, the earlier principal rejection of the "voluntary system" is missing in this book, although there are many passages which suggest that it is only political expediency which prevented Senior from again recommending possibly free and certainly compulsory schooling for all.

VII CONCLUSION

A brief review of the secondary literature will serve to underline some of the points we have been making about the educational doctrines of the classical economists.

The subject first came into prominence with the publication of Lord Robbins' masterly volume of lectures on the classical theory of economic policy. Robbins devoted a few pages to the question of education, passing quickly from Adam Smith to Malthus to the hand-loom weavers report with a passing glance at McCulloch. Adam Smith, according to Robbins, "urged that the government should provide subsidized, but not quite free, elementary education".[46] I would have thought that a better summary is: Adam Smith urged that local government should provide subsidised, but definitely not free, elementary education. After noting Malthus' endorsement of Adam Smith's views, Robbins quotes the hand-loom weavers report as a "typical illustration of opinion some forty years later". "After which", he remarks, "nothing surely remains to be said" (*ibid*. p.93). Curiously enough, Robbins does not even mention John Stuart Mill's repudiation of the principle of free, compulsory schooling. We must conclude therefore that a great deal more remains to be said — a thought which appears to have struck other commentators.

The next round in the discussion is by Blitz, an essay which first appeared in Spanish in 1961 but which was soon translated and circulated privately.[47] Blitz's treatment is distinguished by a clear grasp of the central element in the classical economists' approach to education: "the early classicists saw little place for mass education as a strictly *economic* investment — except as it might contribute indirectly through effects on population and civic order"; the nineteenth-century literature "seems to show much greater concern over the problem of the discipline of the labour force than over the problem of skill" (*ibid*. p. 37, 46). Before the creation of a national police force and the development of small arms weapons, there was a widespread fear of rioting mobs, inspired by the example of the French Revolution. The classical economists, Blitz points out, did take what was then the enlightened view that the spread of education among the poor would promote rather than endanger political stability. Malthus, a Tory in respect of the Corn Laws, nevertheless played an important role in establishing what might be described as the Whig attitude of the classical economists to popular education.

Unfortunately, Blitz exaggerates the role of Senior and attributes views to him which are in fact due to John Stuart Mill. In a sense it is true to say that Senior of all the classical economists showed "the greatest explicit concern for education" but Senior published nothing on education until

1861. So far as the printed word is concerned, it is clearly John Stuart Mill who is the key figure and Blitz has little to say about him. This brings us to the first chapter in Vaizey's pioneering textbook on the economics of education. His treatment of Adam Smith is excellent, although it is marred by some serious historical inaccuracies, such as the statements that education was compulsory in eighteenth-century Scotland and that all Scottish schoolmasters in 1776 were university graduates.[48] Vaizey emphasises the Malthusian tradition which linked the spread of education to family planning and then cites John Stuart Mill as favouring state provision of and assistance to elementary education, alongside private schooling, possibly but not necessarily financed by compulsory levies (*ibid.*, p. 20-1). But he makes no reference to the passages in Mill's *Principles* which distinguish between minimum educational standards and school attendance as such. Having cited Smith, Ricardo, Malthus, McCulloch, and Marshall, but not Senior, he concludes: "Thus there is a long and honourable tradition from Adam Smith to Alfred Marshall which assigns to publicly supported education a major role not only in promoting social peace and harmony, and self-improvement, but in the process of wealth-creation itself" (*ibid.* p. 23). To label the bits and pieces that can be collected from writers other than Adam Smith, John Stuart Mill and Marshall as "a long and honourable tradition" is, surely, something of an exaggeration. Furthermore, if there was such a tradition, it certainly did not assign a major role to education in the process of wealth creation, although it did assign a definite role to education subordinate to that of law and legislation in "promoting social peace and harmony, and self-improvement".

Two remarkable articles by West in 1964 threw a new light on the view of the classical economists. West is basically concerned to demonstrate that Mill and Senior departed radically from Adam Smith in respect of the applicability of free-market principles to education: whereas Smith held that the market mechanism merely required financial assistance from the state to make it more effective, Mill and Senior denied the relevance of the principle of freedom of choice in the field of education.[49] Although Mill did in the end come down in favour of private schooling, he did not do so because of the classic liberal argument that the experience of making choices in education is itself an education in the art of choice, but rather because he was afraid that the state would abuse its monopoly of education. In short, Mill and Senior moved a long way towards educational paternalism. Nevertheless, West summarises their views in these words:

While the early economists argued for *some* State education, they conceived it in very qualified terms indeed. If we were asked to select the most conspicuous of the main features which distinguished them from current practice, it would probably be their insistence that fees should not be abolished and should always cover a substantial part of the education ... there is indeed nothing in the evidence of their writings to suggest that any one of them would have supported the degree of State predominance in education that is experienced in our own times.[50]

Even this apt summary errs by omission as both Mill and Senior did call for the selective abolition of fees in elementary education, or, more accurately expressed, for a means-tested scale of fees.

Central to West's argument is his contention that the quantity of private schooling in the period was much greater than most modern historians would credit and that even its quality was tolerable given the circumstances of the time. In that connection, the views of Mill and Senior present something of an obstacle since it is perfectly clear that they had a very low opinion of the private schools of their own day. West's attempt to deal with their objections is not, I think, altogether convincing. "The fact was", he writes, "that neither Senior nor Mill liked the type of school that the free market was providing by the middle of the nineteenth century. This was undoubtedly due to their opinion that these schools were inferior to the large scale models which the poor law institutions were dutifully producing to the order of their Benthamite supervisors."[51] This appears to be a reference to workhouse schools conducted in accordance with the precepts of "the monitorial system", in which case it is an elliptical comment as both Mill and Senior envisaged standard-sized state schools outside the jurisdiction of the Poor Law Commissioners; by 1848, the earlier enthusiasm for the economies-of-scale features of the monitorial system had long since waned.[52]

Two years after West's articles there appeared what is undoubtedly the best single, certainly the least misleading, commentary on the theme in question: "The Economics of Education in English Classical Economics" by Miller. His review is topical rather than chronological but he does not disguise the fact that the classical economists were generally not at their best on the topic of education. Here, for the first time, John Stuart Mill commands the centre of the stage and the classical stress on "better men rather than better workers" is continuously kept in mind.[53]

There followed a curious paper by Hollander in which he begins by posing a spurious question and ends by answering it to his own satisfaction.[54] The classical economists generally favoured government intervention in elementary education, Hollander declares, but why did they not extend this principle explicitly to vocational training in specific skills? In view of the fact that John Stuart Mill was worried about monopoly rents in earnings, he might be expected to have advocated government support of vocational training as a device for equalising incomes. That he did not do so must have been due, Hollander argues, to his preoccupation with Malthusian considerations on the labour supply side.

It is not altogether clear what Hollander means by vocational training but it appears that he is thinking of formal vocational training in educational institutions rather than on-the-job training. In that case, it is worth noting that the distinction between general and vocational training is something which would never have occurred to the classical economists. When they wrote on education they were usually thinking of elementary education, and as Hollander himself admits: "starting from an illiterate base it is difficult to distinguish elementary from vocational training since, frequently, the former is a necessary prerequisite of the latter" (*ibid*, p.520). In those instances where they addressed themselves to secondary and higher education, they took it as a matter of course that the state had no obligations in these matters; it is true that John Stuart Mill went so far as to advocate free higher education to bright working-class children, and even government subventions to universities for purposes of encouraging research (*Principles*, pp.976-7), but he is a singular exception in this regard. In any case, whatever the stage of education under consideration, the classical economists paid little attention to the tendency of schools to develop vocationally useful skills. Instead they threw all their weight behind the law-and-order argument for education. It is significant the Hollander is in fact driven to argue that the classical writers recognised, not just the social and political benefits, but also the "specifically economic advantages" of elementary schooling; he even asserts that McCulloch was by no means exceptional in relating education to economic growth (*loc. cit*. p.520). In some sense, therefore, Hollander's article loses all the ground gained by Blitz and Miller.

It remains only to add that Robbins' earlier treatment of the classical theory of economic policy was deepened and extended by Samuels' full-scale study.[55] Parts of this book analyse the classical economist's conception of the role of education as a type of "nondeliberative social control" after which the issue may be said to have been settled.

The last and most recent contribution to the debate begins provocatively enough: it denies that Robbins, Vaizey, West, or Miller have done justice to "the richness, detail and consistency of the Classical analysis" and baldly asserts that "qualitatively they [the classics] said, though often in general and non-technical language, everything that is to be said about the economics of education".[56] The impact of these remarks is somewhat lessened when we learn that the author defines the term "Classical economists" as Keynes did to refer to all pre-Keynesian economists and that much of the article is concerned with the views of Sidgwick, Marshall, Wicksteed, Taussig, Pigou, Dalton, and Cannan. Although the essay is a useful compendium of opinions arranged in chronological order, the treatment of the classical economists as such is not entirely satisfactory and once again does less than justice to the ideas of Mill and Senior.

Let us sum up our "review of the troops". All the classical economists, without a single exception, approved of state assistance to locally provided schools and usually they justified such proposals in terms of the role of education as a more or less deliberate method of "social control"; at least until John Stuart Mill, no definite argument was ever advanced to suggest that education would fail to be optimally provided by a pure market mechanism. However, neither before nor after Mill did any leading classical economist advocate compulsory and completely free elementary, much less secondary, education — the only possible exception is Senior but of course the public was unaware of his role in drafting the hand-loom weavers report — and none of them entertained the idea of confining the teaching force to a state-licensed profession. What is true is that from Mill onwards there was increasing dissatisfaction with the voluntary system and a growing desire to see public schools competing with private schools; how much this has to do with the great Religious Question we can only conjecture.

With respect to the details of educational policy, there was a general tendency to be wise after the event: no clasical economist suggested that the employment of children should be made conditional on prior school attendance until the Factory Act of 1833 had actually established this principle; no one called for the central training and recruitment of teachers until the pupil-teacher system had been invented in the early 1840s; and even the proposal to import the Scottish parochial system into England was left vague and unrelated to the steady growth of the English voluntary system before and after 1833. In short, the classical economists had no impact on the history of education in the century between the publication of *The Wealth of Nations* and Forster's Education Act of 1870, but the history of education certainly made an impact on them.[57]

So much for policy questions. What about theory and, particularly, the theory of human capital? Far from it being true that the classical economists had said "everything that is to be said about the economics of education", I have been arguing that economic analysis of education systems had hardly begun. To be sure, the concept of human capital has a long history going back to the seventeenth century, largely connected with such questions as measuring the costs of wars and evaluating preventive health programmes, all of which has little to do with the demand for education or with the contribution of education to economic growth. Statements to the effect that education pays for itself by making people more productive, which one occasionally encounters in the classical literature, are actually of little import as the same may be said with equal force of sanitation, housing, food, and clothing at low levels of economic development. In fact, until Lyon Playfair wrote his famous letter to the Taunton Commission, attributing Britain's poor performance at the 1862 Paris Exhibition to inferior educational provision in Britain as compared to the Continent,[58] it never occurred to anyone to relate the quantity and quality of schooling directly to a country's economic performance.[59] Where the classical economists did make a contribution is in the area of welfare economics applied to education; and here it is all in John Stuart Mill. But as for human capital and education as investment in human beings, one can pass straight from Adam Smith to Marshall without the slightest loss.

Perhaps this is too severe. Although they rarely entertained the notion that education affects economic growth directly, they did think of the provision of education as a kind of national investment; it is simply that they interpreted this proposition in a way which we would now label "sociological" rather than "economic". Modern economists are sometimes accused of attributing the economic value of education entirely to the effects of cognitive learning in schools. But this does less than justice. It would be more accurate to say that modern economists view schooling as a "black box"; without pretending to know precisely what goes on in classrooms, they nevertheless do know that passing through schools increases the earning power of people. The classical economists did know, or thought they knew, what went on inside the box: schooling effectively altered the behaviour of students, breeding attitudes of punctuality, persistence, concentration, obedience, and at the same time self-reliance; employers recognised this tendency of education to inculcate definite social values and hence were willing to pay educated workers more than uneducated onces, even if what they had learned was of no specific use to employment.[60] It may well be that the classical accent on values and attitudes, rather than on manual or intellectual skills, is closer to the heart of the matter than we like to think, particularly in societies that have not yet become fully industrialized.[61] It would certainly be far-fetched to argue that industrialisation necessarily produces a growing demand for literate and educated workers and that these "manpower requirements" provide the key to the role of education in the Industrial Revolution.[62] There is still something to be learned from reading the classical economists, even if, as in this case, it had to be a reading between the lines.

HISTORICAL APPENDIX

We have so far ignored a hidden presumption in most of the commentaries on our period, namely, that there was little schooling in the heyday of the British Industrial Revolution and that most of it was bad. It has become evident from recent research, however, that literacy rates in early nineteenth-century Britain were astonishingly high, which raises the question of how this could have been achieved without widely diffused schooling. Furthermore, it appears that private schooling, far from stagnating, grew at a phenomenal rate right up to the 1870s, which is precisely why men like Mill and Senior were alarmed about its unsatisfactory quality. The fact is that if we are properly to understand the views of the classical economists, we must begin by putting to one side the standard histories of nineteenth-century education, which seem to have been written largely to prove that education is only adequately provided when the state acccepts its responsibility to furnish compulsory education *gratis*.[63]

We take up first the question of literacy. An article by Sargant, published as early as 1867, first recognised the potentialities of the marriage register as a crude index of literacy rates during the Industrial Revolution.[64] Since then other evidence on birth and death registers, spot surveys of literacy in particular towns and the sale of unstamped working-class newspapers have led to the conclusion that "by 1840, two-thirds to three-quarters of male adult workers were literate (the percentage for women being slightly smaller), with rates in towns regularly above those of rural areas".[65] When we consider that the world mean literacy rate in 1970 is about 60 per cent and that the whole of tropical Africa, the Middle East, and large stretches of Latin America fail to attain even 40 per cent, the statistics cited above for adults in Britain in 1840, and working-class adults at that, are nothing short of extraordinary.

A careful reading of the classical economists would of course have prepared us for the new view on literacy during the Industrial Revolution. We recall that Adam Smith noted in passing that "In Scotland, the establishment of ... parish schools has taught almost the whole common people to read, and a very great proportion of them to write and account. In England the establishment of charity schools has had an effect of the same kind, though not so universally."[66] Similarly, there are sentences in John Stuart Mill that show that he took it for granted that most contemporary workers could read and write: "Since reading and writing have been brought within the reach of the multitude, the monopoly price of the lower grade of educated employments has greatly fallen ...".[67] There are similar hints of high literacy rates among the poor in the writings of James Mill, Bentham, Brougham, and McCulloch.

If schooling was as insufficient in quantity and as poor in quality as most modern historians of education allege, how did so many workers learn to read and write? It is true that it is not uncommon for literacy to run ahead of schooling, and in any country at any stage in its history there are always more literate people than individuals who have gone to school. Nevertheless, the apparently large gap between the literacy rate and the school enrolment rate during the British Industrial Revolution does raise some intriguing questions. Conventional histories of education neatly dispose of the problem by simply ignoring the literacy evidence.[68] But as a matter of fact, it is generally conceded that nearly universal literacy was achieved in Victorian England by 1900 or thereabouts, and it is easy to show that unless literacy rates around the middle of the nineteenth century were about 40 to 50 per cent, 100 per cent literacy rates could not have been achieved in two generations.

The simple truth is that formal education was much less important in the nineteenth century than it is now and much reading and writing was acquired without benefit of formal schooling. Out-of-school education and particularly the adult educational movement is certainly discussed in all the standard educational histories but it is rarely emphasised; moreover, the subject is usually raised in order to show to what lengths people had to go to make up for the inadequacies of state provision.[69] Examples of out-of-school education in the period are, first of all, mutual improvement societies and Dissenting Academies, particularly in northern towns, of which the best known are the Literary and Philosophical Institutes, the Mechanics' Institutes and the Owenite Halls of Science.[70] Secondly, there were the libraries, reading rooms, and working-class newspapers, which flourished despite the stamp duties.[71] Thirdly, freelance lecturers travelled the towns and stimulated self-study among the poor, which in such cases as the Welsh Circulating Schools reached the point of being formally organised;[72] those were the days when, in the words of one economic historian, "the towns, and even the villages, hummed with the energy of the autodidact."[73] All of this amounts to an impressive array of devices and arrangements outside the formal educational system, none of which is given proper credit in promoting the knowledge of reading and writing by most historians of education.

This brings us to part-time formal education, such as Sunday schools and adult evening schools, which figure prominently in all the histories of the period. Less frequently mentioned are the factory schools, which proliferated in the northern textile schools long before the 1833 Act made them mandatory.[74] And, finally, we come to full-time day schools for children, which is where we do face what appears to be an almost unresolvable controversy.

There was actually little controversy until the publication of West's *Education and the State* (1965), inasmuch as most historians of education are agreed that the figures of the Newcastle Commission of 1861 can be dismissed as absurdly optimistic. The Newcastle Commission attempted the first comprehensive survey of school attendance in nineteenth-century England and it concluded that almost every child received some school education during the year, largely in private charity and proprietary schools, and that there were no serious geographical gaps in the physical provision of schools. In brief, West's argument is that the Newcastle Commission gives a much more reliable picture of educational provision around the middle of the century than the hurriedly assembled report of conditions in four selected industrial towns that served Forster as his main evidence in urging the Education bill of 1870.[75] Every piece of statistical evidence, he contends, points to a spectacular spontaneous growth in private voluntary education in the first half of the nineteenth century, and the Act of 1870, far from multiplying schools, largely replaced private schools by state schools. He sums up his case in these words: "in 1869 most people were literate, most children had some schooling, and — what may come as the biggest surprise of all — most parents [working-class included] were paying fees for it."[76]

Since then he has taken the argument a little further by producing the striking finding that the percentage of national income which was spent on full-time education of children of all ages in 1833 actually exceeded that of 1920! What is even more amazing is that the 1833 figure for children below the age of eleven is nearly the same as that for 1965. Furthermore, these calculations, initially carried out on the assumption of a drop-out rate of 20 per cent in 1833, survive the assumption of a 50 per cent drop-out rate.[77]

Replying to West on behalf of traditional historians of education, Hurt largely gives up the argument about numbers, instead asserting that the day schools of the period were nothing more than baby-minding crèches, not educational institutions as we would now understand them.[78] The dispute about quality is as old as the Newcastle Commission itself: the reports of the Inspectors of the Commission held that the standard of teaching in most elementary schools was "excellent, well and fair", while the Assistant Commissioners pronounced an almost wholly unfavourable verdict on the quality of instruction, particularly for the younger children. This debate is unlikely ever to be effectively settled. Contemporary opinion was in each case no more than a judgment based on casual impressions, and the variance in quality between individual schools must have been enormous; it always is at early stages of educational development. Besides, the problem of fairly assessing these judgments now without the hindsight of twentieth-century standards is almost insuperable. Suffice it to say that a fair summary of the evidence about quantity leads to the view that one-half to two-thirds of all children in Britain around the middle of the century attended full-time schooling for about two and possibly three years, few remaining after the age of eleven.[79] Granted that the schooling was probably of very low quality, it nevertheless remains an impressive achievement for what was then an underdeveloped country. Consider, for example, that there are few poor countries today where as many as half the children complete the first six grades of primary school; the average years of schooling in Africa, Asia and Latin America nowadays is not more than two to three years. Perhaps England did not compare favourably with France and Russia in the nineteenth century in terms of formal schooling; informal schooling, however, probably made up the whole of the difference.

It is part and parcel of West's thesis that the growth of education in Scotland in this period under the impact of the Act of 1696 has been widely misunderstood. It is generally acknowledged that the Scottish Lowlands achieved almost universal literacy by 1760 before the "take-off" into the Industrial Revolution, and of course this remarkable feat is usually attributed to the Scottish parochial system. Be that as it may, once the Industrial Revolution started, the shifts of population from rural areas to the towns seem to have relegated the parochial schools to a minor role. At any rate, by 1818 fee-paying private schools enrolled twice as many children as did the parochial schools and, when we add charity day schools and Sunday schools, four times as many children as the parochial system. Furthermore, the government's returns of 1833/4 showed that the proportion of the population receiving schooling was practically the same in the two halves of Britain; thus, if we can assume identical population age structures in Scotland and England, we may conclude that the growth of education in Scotland during the Industrial Revolution was largely unaffected by the statutory provision of the Act of 1696.[80] In short, the fondly held belief of the classical economists that the law-abiding conditions of Scotland could be traced directly to Scotland's superior school provision consequent on the Act of 1696 is now seen to have been nothing less than a total misunderstanding of the actual course of events.

A final word about fees must bring the discussion to an end. We have seen that none of the classical economists advocated free elementary education except for the children of the poor. It is remarkable how the early nineteenth-century presumption that parents in general are perfectly willing to pay directly for education but that some cannot afford to do so is lost sight of in most modern histories of education. To quote only one authority: "Education, universal, compulsory, gratuitous . . . this formula describes the aim in the educational sphere which English Radicals and Liberals strove to attain throughout the nineteenth century."[81] Impelled by recent experience to believe that only compulsion can ever make education universal and that compulsory education logically implies free education, modern historians find the views of the early nineteenth-century writers strangely self-contradictory. If West is to be believed, however, elementary education during the Industrial Revolution was neither compulsory nor free, but it was practically universal. Similarly, Forster in 1870 retained school fees with free tickets for the poor, and most schools only became completely free in 1891; however, elementary education became compulsory in 1881 so that for ten years education was compulsory but not free. Even the organised working class did not begin to demand a free system of secular elementary education until 1847.[82] But middle-class opinion did not come round to 100 per cent publicly financed education until after the Revised Code of 1862 and all through the period under examination fee-paying was widespread, no less among the working classes than among the middle classes: "Working-class parents in Bristol, which had a population of 120,000 [in 1834], were paying over £15,000 a year for their children's education, a sum over half that reluctantly granted by Parliament in 1833 to aid the building of schools throughout England and Wales. This gives a glimpse of the extent to which the working class supported schools out of their own pockets."[83] Were the uncultivated really incompetent to be judges of cultivation, or were they simply too poor to do much judging?

NOTES

1. For references, see Section VII, below.
2. I take this opportunity to thank A. W. Coats, D. P. O'Brien, A. S. Skinner, and D. Winch for their helpful comments on an earlier version of this chapter.
3. N.B.P.I., Report No. 98, *Standing Reference on the Pay of University Teachers in Great Britain,* Cmnd. 3866 (London, 1968), p. 13.
4. *Ibid.* p. 14.
5. The majority view is well expressed by D. C. Corner and A. J. Culyer, the only British economists to have written at length on the P.I.B. Report: "University Teachers and the P.I.B.", *Social and Economic Administration* 3, (1969), pp. 138-9.
6. It is interesting to ask oneself how British university teaching is now evaluated, given the absence of student assessments and the prevailing taboo against attending a colleague's lectures: obviously, it is done, if it is done at all, by talking to students on a casual basis or by inference from a colleague's performance in a staff seminar. Is it conceivable that anyone could oppose the use of supplements to such crude devices? Apparently yes.
7. A. Smith, *The Wealth of Nations*, ed. E. Cannan (London, 1937), Book V, Ch. 1, pp. 6-8. (Hereafter *WN*). Glasgow in 1776 was one of those universities where "the salary makes but . . . a small part of the emoluments of the teacher". Smith's own salary at Glasgow may have been £70 a year with a house, while his fees amounted to about £100. J. Rae, *Life of Adam Smith* (London, 1965), pp. 48-9. Several witnesses testify to Adam Smith's own pedagogic zeal: see E. G. West, *Adam Smith* (Indianapolis, 1969), 112-13.
8. For an attempt to develop the model in a twentieth-century context see A. J. Culyer, "A Utility-Maximising View of Universities", *Scottish Journal of Political Economy*, 17 (November 1970) and R. Layard, R. Jackman, "University Efficiency and University Finance", *Conference Volume of the Association of University Teachers of Economics*, ed. M. Parkin (Manchester, 1972).

9. *WN*, Book V, Ch. 1, p. 15. It is evidence that there is a missing link in the argument. Smith assumes as a matter of course that teachers do not have exclusive control of their own examinations; if they did, the quality of teaching would justify itself, whatever it was. The system of internal and external examiners in Glasgow in the eighteenth century was not unlike that of British universities today. See G. Davie, *The Democratic Intellect. Scotland and her Universities in the Nineteenth Century* (Edinburgh, 1961), pp. 14-25.

10. For a brilliant exegesis of Book V, see N. Rosenberg, "Some Institutional Aspects of *The Wealth of Nations.*" *Journal of Political Economy*, 68 (December 1960).

11. Concern about the social and economic "relevance" of curricula was very common in eighteenth-century Scotland: see D. J. Withrington, "Education and Society in the Eighteenth Century", *Scotland in the Age of Improvement*, eds. T. N. Phillipson and R. Mitchison (London 1970). Book V, Ch. 2, pp. 55-7)

12. *WN*, E. G. West, drawing on a long private letter by Adam Smith, shows that Smith objected to a medical or for that matter a teaching profession confined to university graduates and he implies that Smith rejected the general principle of occupational licensing. "Private versus Public Education. A Classical Economic Dispute", *Journal of Political Economy* (1964), reprinted in *The Classical Economists and Economic Policy*, ed. A. W. Coats (London 1971), pp. 126-8. However, the wording in *The Wealth of Nations* on the licensing of mechanical trades, as distinct from the learned professions, is unambiguously favourable. See also J. Viner, "Guide to John Rae's Life of Adam Smith", in Rae, *Life of Adam Smith, op. cit.*, pp. 10-13.

13. *WN* Book V, Ch. 2, p. 50. With the exception of the invisible-hand paragraph in the second chapter of Book IV, this is perhaps the most frequently cited passage in the whole of *The Wealth of Nations*, and the commentaries on its meaning would fill several library shelves.

14. *WN*, Book I, Ch. 10, pp. 6-7; see also Book II, Ch. 1, p. 17 where the "maintenance" of someone during "his education, study or apprenticeship" is defined as "capital fixed and realized, as it were, in his person".

15. W. L. Miller, "The Economics of Education in English Classical Economics", *Southern Economic Journal* (January 1966), p. 294.

16. See Historical Appendix below.

17. Malthus is known to have advised Whitbread whose Poor Law bill of 1807 sought a national system of education incorporated in the structure of parish relief, appealing for authority chiefly to Scotland.

18. Here at any rate they succeeded in having an impact on events. In 1821, James Mill and Bentham, among others, were instrumental in forming the Society for the Diffusion of Useful Knowledge for the express purpose of producing cheap literature for the poor, including the *Penny Magazine*, full of homely truths about political economy. See R. K. Webb, *British Working Class Reader, 1790-1848*, (London, 1955), pp. 85-92; M. Blaug, *Ricardian Economics*, (New Haven, 1958), pp. 145-6. Then in 1833, Richard Whately published his immensely influential *Easy Lessons on Money Matters for the Use of Young People* and a year later Harriet Martineau took the reading public by storm with her *Illustrations of Political Economy*. See J. M. Goldstrom, "Richard Whately and Political Economy in School Books, 1833-80", *Irish Historical Review*, 15 (September 1966); Blaug, *Ricardian Economics*, Ch. 7; R. K. Webb, *Harriet Martineau* (London, 1960), Ch. 4; and H. Scott Gordon, "The Ideology of Laissez Faire" in Coats, ed. *The Classical Economists and Economic Policy*,

London, *op.cit.*, pp. 189-97. In fact, as J. M. Goldstrom has now shown, *The Social Content of Education 1808-1870. A Study of the Working Class School Reader in England and Ireland* (London, 1972), political economy conquered all the elementary school books in Britain between 1830 and 1860; after that date the vogue for teaching economics to children seems to have passed away as quickly as it came.

19. T. R. Malthus, *An Essay on the Principle of Population* (London, 1878), p. 437 (Book IV, Ch. 9). Sunday schools, first launched in 1879 by Robert Raikes, enrolled by 1803 some 850,000 pupils in 7,000 schools throughout Great Britain.

20. The title of an early pamphlet by James Mill conveys the flavour of the debate: *Schools for All, Not Schools for Churchmen Only* (London, 1812).

21. Malthus, *Essay on Population*, 470, 478 (Book IV, Ch. 13).

22. J. Mill, "Education of the Poor", *Edinburgh Review*, 21 (February 1813).

23. J. R. McCulloch, *Principles of Political Economy* (3rd edn., Edinburgh, 1843), pp. 431-2; a similar, but less explicit statement appears in the 1st edn., 1825, pp. 360-1.

24. *Quarterly Journal of Education* (1831) quoted in D. P. O'Brien, *J. R. McCulloch, A Study in Classical Economics* (London 1970), p. 346. O'Brien's book gives a brief but informative account of McCulloch's views on education (*ibid.* pp. 344-7).

25. See McCulloch's edition of *The Wealth of Nations* (Edinburgh, 1828), p. 589.

26. See B. F. Kiker, *Human Capital: In Retrospect* (Columba, South Carolina, 1968), pp. 30-1.

27. E. Chadwick, "Opening Address of the President of Section F of the British Association of the Advancement of Science", *Journal of the Statistical Society of London*, 25 (March, 1862), p. 519. McCulloch did lay stress on the diffusion of knowledge as a source of economic growth (O'Brien, *J. R. McCulloch*, 280, 346) but it is not clear that he regarded schooling as such as a significant element in the diffusion of knowledge.

28. See my *Introduction of the Economics of Education* (London 1970), pp. 2-6. Kiker, after a comprehensive survey of eighteenth- and nineteenth-century doctrines of human capital, concludes that "the concept of human capital was somewhat prominent in economic thinking until Marshall discarded the notion as 'unrealistic'" (*op. cit.*, p. 112). But this is doubly misleading: the concept was by no means prominent in nineteenth-century economic thought and Marshall only discarded it in his definition of capital; elsewhere in his treatise he came back repeatedly to its economic implications and contributed more to the analysis of the idea than any other economist since Adam Smith.

29. N. W. Senior, *An Outline of the Science of Political Economy* (London, 1836), pp. 205-7. Also N. W. Senior, *Industrial Efficiency and Social Economy*, ed. S. L. Levy (Boston, Mass., 1928) II, pp. 334-5.

30. J. S. Mill, *Principles of Political Economy*, ed. W. J. Ashley (London, 1909), p. 109 (Book I, Ch. 7, §5).

31. The sentence which hails education as "not the principal, but the sole remedy" for poverty in the 1845 essay (*Collected Works of John Stuart Mill. Essays on Economics and Society*, ed. J. M. Robson, (Toronto, 1967) IV, p. 378) is not repeated in the *Principles* where the accent is as much on "spontaneous education" and "newspapers and political tracts" as on "the quantity and quality of school education" (*Principles*, pp. 757-8).

32. J. E. G. de Montmorency, *State Intervention in English Education, A Short*

History from the Earliest Times Down to 1833 (London, 1902), p. 347. The whole of the speech is reprinted in this book, which is incidentally an invaluable primary source for the period before 1833.

33. *Report of the Commissioners for Inquiring into the Condition of the Unemployed on the Hand-Loom Weavers in the United Kingdom*, Parl. Papers (London, 1841), x. p. 122. The report goes on to recommend a school inspectorate, a system of teacher training to be financed from "the national revenue" rather than from local rates, and a Royal Commission to investigate the entire question of educating the poor (*ibid.* p. 123).

34. The passage is discussed by M. Bowley, *Nassau Senior and Classical Economics* (London, 1937), p. 262, but without emphasis on its startling character.

35. I am reminded of the Hollywood argument that commercial film producers make bad films because the public wants bad films, to which some retort: "Make better films and tastes will soon improve". When generalised, this sounds like a reason for ignoring consumer sovereignty in everything, leaving us only to argue over the selection of sovereign taste-makers. But inasmuch as it is a testable proposition about the influence of supply on the formation of tastes, it is far from general: it may be true of films and even of education but on the other hand it may not be.

36. In addition, the Anglican Church's National Society raised £870,000 in 1851 from its own resources, while the secular British Society, together with Wesleyan, Baptist, and Congregational schools, managed to raise only £125,000.

37. J. S. Mill, *Utilitarianism, Liberty and Representative Government* (London, 1910), p. 160.

38. *Ibid.* p. 161. It is curious how few historians of economic thought have drawn attention to these striking sentences. But see E. G. West, "Liberty and Education: John Stuart Mill's Dilemma", *Philosophy*, II (April 1965); and J. M. Robson, *The Improvement of Mankind. The Social and Political Thought of John Stuart Mill* (Toronto, 1900), pp. 209-12. It requires only one addition, the substitution of education vouchers for subsidised fees, to be pure Milton Friedman. See M. Friedman, *Capitalism and Freedom* (Chicago, 1963), pp. 85-108.

39. Mill, *Collected Works*, V p. 624. Mill had denied the full force of Smith's objections to endowed schools even earlier in an essay on "Corporations and Church Property" (1833): *ibid.* IV, p. 214ff.

40. *Ibid.* V, pp. 627-8. But the passage begins with the maxim; "The State does not owe gratuitous education to those who can pay for it. The State owes no more than elementary education to the entire body of those who cannot pay for it."

41. Writing in 1871, Fawcett came out strongly in favour of compulsory elementary education. Nevertheless, he opposed the total abolition of fees although by this time, as he said, "free and compulsory education has come to be the watchword of a party": *Pauperism: Its Causes and Remedies* (London, 1871), pp. 61-6, 123ff.

42. Quoted in S. L. Levy, *Nassau W. Senior 1790-1864* (Newton Abbot 1970), p. 184. Ch. 22 of this book contains a garbled and entirely ahistorical account of Senior's views on education.

43. N. W. Senior, *Suggestions on Popular Education* (London, 1861), pp. 3-5; also pp. 18, 44. An almost identical statement is found in *Industrial Efficiency and Social Economy*, *op. cit.*, II, pp. 334-5. It appears that virtually the whole of Senior's book of 1861 derives from his lecture notes of 1847-52. Bowley,

Nassau Senior, op. cit., p. 268, supplies a succinct precis of the 1861 book and deals elsewhere with Senior's general views on educational questions (*ibid*). pp. 267-9, 330-1).

44. Senior, *Popular Education*, pp. 31-2; an identical statement is found in *Industrial Efficiency*, II, p. 340.

45. Senior, *Popular Education*, pp. 19-20. It is perhaps odd that he should regret this fact. He was the son of a Berkshire clergyman of the Church of England and remained an Anglican throughout his life, although a sceptical one (Levy, *Nassau Senior*, pp. 57-9). I can throw no light on this apparent contradiction but it may be similar to his position on Philosophical Radicalism: he worked with the Benthamites and clearly agreed with most of their social views and yet he never committed himself explicitly to their cause.

46. L. Robbins, *The Theory of Economic Policy in English Classical Political Economy* (London, 1952), p. 90.

47. R. C. Blitz, "Some Classical Economists and Their Views on Education", in UNESCO *Readings in the Economics of Education*, ed. M. J. Bowman *et al.* London, 1968).

48. J. Vaizey, *The Economics of Education* (London 1962), pp. 18, 19, Primary education became compulsory in Scotland in 1891; many eighteenth-century Scottish schoolmasters were university graduates but by no means all. See M. Cruickshank, *History of Teacher Training in Scotland* (Edinburgh, 1970), pp. 16-17.

49. Bowley, (*Nassau Senior*, p. 276) noted long ago that Mill and Senior marked a breach with the preceding generation respecting the question of state intervention. West's contribution was to relate this insight to educational issues.

50. E. G. West, "The Role of Education in Nineteenth-Century Doctrines of Political Economy", *British Journal of Educational Studies*, 12, (May 1964), reprinted in E. G. West, *Education and the State* (2nd. edn., 1970), Ch. 8. See also E. G. West, "Private versus Public Education" in Coats, ed., *The Classical Economists and Economic Policy, op. cit.*

51. West, *British Journal of Educational Studies*, pp. 170-1.

52. In the 2nd edn. of his *Education and The State*, p. xxxiii, West reiterates his belief that Senior was a paternalist who sought to impose "Benthamite and Protestant" schooling on less-than-willing parents. This comment sounds nearer the mark.

53. Miller, *Southern Economic Journal*, pp. 296-300.

54. S. Hollander, "The Role of the State in Vocational Training: The Classical Economists' View", *Southern Economic Journal*, 24 (April 1968).

55. W. J. Samuels, *The Classical Theory of Economic Policy* (Cleveland, Ohio, 1966).

56. P. N. V. Tu, "The Classical Economists and Education", *Kyklos*, 22, fasc. 2 (1969), pp. 691, 716.

57. A similar observation applies to the history of factory legislation: see "The Classical Economists and the Factory Acts — A Re-Examination", *Quarterly Journal of Economics* (1958), reprinted as Chapter 7 of this volume.

58. The letter is reprinted in W. H. Court, *British Economic History, 1870-1914: Commentary and Documents* (London 1965), pp. 168-9.

59 Alas, Mill is once again the exception. See the passage in Mill's *Principles*, p. 109, quoted above.

60. There is a good deal of evidence that employers during the Industrial Revolution were deeply concerned with the problem of "labour commitment"; see

S. Pollard, "Factory Discipline in the Industrial Revolution", *Economic History Review*, 2nd series. 16 (1963), and his *Genesis of Modern Management. A Study of the Industrial Revolution in Great Britain* (London 1965), pp. 181-92; see also N. J. Smelser, *Social Class in the Industrial Revolution. An Application of Theory to the Lancashire Cotton Industry, 1770-1840* (London 1959), pp. 105-7.

61. See my "Correlation Between Earnings and Education: What Does It Signify?" *Higher Education*, 1 (February 1972), for a discussion of alternative theories of the content of the "black box".

62. Most British economic historians have argued that the early stages of the Industrial Revolution generated very little demand for literate workers. This seems to be correct judging at any rate from the contemporary experience of developing countries (Blaug, *Economics of Education*, pp. 252-3). It does not follow, however, that education during the Industrial Revolution was therefore unimportant from an economic standpoint. M. Hartwell, *The Industrial Revolution and Economic Growth* (London, 1971), Ch. 11, attacks leading British economic historians for neglecting the role of education in the Industrial Revolution but his attack is spoiled by a very simple-minded view of the relationship between education and economic growth. For an antidote to Hartwell, see M. D. Shipman, *Education and Modernisation* (London, 1971), Ch. 3; Goldstrom, *Social Content of Education*, Ch. 5, and particularly, M. Sanderson, "Literacy and Social Mobility in the Industrial Revolution in England", *Past and Present* (August 1972), pp. 89-95.

63. Mr. D. J. Davies provided valuable research assistance in combing the literature.

64. W. L. Sargant, "On the Progress of Elementary Education", *Journal of the Statistical Society* (March 1967).

65. Hartwell, *The Industrial Revolution*, p. 238, and the references cited, pp. 236-8.

66. Cited above in the text.

67. Cited above in the text.

68. See e.g. J. W. Adamson, *English Education 1789-1902* (Cambridge, 1930); F. Smith, *A History of English Elementary Education* (London, 1931); C. Birchenough, *History of Elementary Education in England and Wales* (3rd edn., London, 1938); B. Simon, *Studies in the History of Education 1780-1870* (1960); H. C. Barnard, *A History of English Education from 1760* (2nd edn., London 1961); W. G. Armytage, *Four Hundred Years of English Education* (Cambridge, 1964); S. J. Curtis, *History of Education in Great Britain* (6th edn., London 1965); S. J. Curtis and R. Boultwood, *An Introductory History of English Education Since 1800* (4th edn., London 1966); M. Stuart, *The Education of the People. A History of Primary Education in England and Wales in the Nineteenth Century* (London, 1967); and D. Wardle, *English Popular Education 1780-1970* (Cambridge, 1970). None of these books even mentions the word "literacy" in their index. But some of them, such as Simon and Curtis, at least discuss the problem of literacy rates from Tudor to Victorian times (Curtis, *History*, p. 196). A few specialist studies do weave the new evidence in their story but turn it around so as to allow for expressions of dismay that as much as a quarter of the working class was illiterate around 1850. See J. F. C. Harrison, *Learning and Living 1790-1960. A Study in the History of the English Adult Education Movement* (London 1961), p. 42. However, G. Sutherland, *Elementary Education in the Nineteenth Century* London, 1971), makes up for the deficiencies of all the rest.

69. The tone of Adamson's chapter on "The Workman's Self-Education" (*English Education*, Ch. 6) illustrates the point. But see Smith, *English Elementary Education*, pp.36-7; Birchenough, *History*, p.52; and Armytage, *Four Hundred Years*, pp.51-60. Armytage in fact concentrates on informal and part-time formal learning, and refers only incidentally to formal elementary education; nevertheless, his treatment leaves much out of account. But R. D. Altick, *The English Common Reader 1800-1900* (Chicago, 1957), pp.149-66, provides just the right emphasis.

70. See e.g. Harrison, *Learning and Living*, pp.43-57; Simon, *Studies*, pp.235-53.

71. Altick, *Common Reader*, pp.198-293; Webb, *Working Class Reader*, Ch. 1; and particularly P. Hollis, *The Pauper Press. A Study in Working-Class Radicalism of the 1830s* (London, 1970).

72. A. E. Musson and E. Robinson, *Science and Technology in the Industrial Revolution* (London, 1969), is rich in detail on self-education; see in particular their essay, "Training Captains of Industry" on the education of Boulton and Watt. See also Simon, *Studies*, pp.183-93.

73. E. P. Thompson, *The Making of the English Working Class* (London, 1968), p.781. Ch. 16 of this book provides an excellent treatment of working-class literacy in the first half of the nineteenth century.

74. M. Sanderson, "Education and the Factory in Industrial Lancashire, 1780-1840", *Economic History Review*, 2nd series 20 (August 1967); also G. Ward, "The Education of Factory Child Workers, 1833-1850", *Economic History*, *Supplement to the Economic Journal*, 3, (February 1935).

75. West, *Education and the State*, Ch. 10. For a counter-view, see W. P. McCann, "Elementary Education on the Eve of the Education Act", *Journal of Educational Administration and History*, 2 (December 1969).

76. West, *Education and the State*, p.xvii.

77. E. G. West, "Resource Allocation and Growth in Early Nineteenth-Century British Education", *Economic History Review*, 2nd series 23 (1970).

78. J. S. Hurt, "Professor West on Early Nineteenth-Century Education", *Economic History Review*, 2nd series 24 (1971), and E. G. West, "Interpretation of Early Nineteenth-Century Educational Statistics", *ibid*.

79. The evidence for a model period of four years, which goes further than what is endorsed by received opinion, is argued by E. G. West in his *Education and Industrial Revolution* (London, 1975).

80. West, *Education and the State*, pp.73-5; also T. G. Smout, *A History of the Scottish People*, 1560-1830 (London, 1969), pp.452-72.

81. Adamson, *English Education*, p.7. It would be easy to cite other examples.

82. Simon, *Studies*, pp.340-6. "Free education for all children" was one of the ten immediate objectives in the *Communist Manifesto* of 1848.

83. *Ibid*. p.254.

9   Technical Change and Marxian Economics

Marxian economics claims to provide an analysis of "the laws of motion of capitalism". Orthodox economics in recent decades has devoted much attention to explaining the hitherto successful performance of the capitalist system so as to discover what light past trends may shed on future prospects. For the first time in a century of debate between Marxian and orthodox economics the nature of the central issue is not in dispute. In the past, fruitful discussion was impeded by fundamental differences in approach: the two schools of thought were simply interested in different things. This is no longer true, and the recent flurry of articles on Marx suggests that there is still something to be learned from the Marxian theory of economic development. Its persistent emphasis upon technical change as an inherent feature of the process of capital accumulation provides a healthy antidote to the static bias of received doctrine. Even Marx's mistakes are extraordinarily instructive. But the one great merit of the Marxian system — a merit which supplies the rationale of this paper — is that criticism of it leads one to consider all the difficulties which have so far stood in the way of a satisfactory theory of technical change. The central point I wish to make is that Marxian economics, despite its prescient insights into the nature of technological progress, contains no systematic theory of the factor-saving character of technical improvements. It is for this reason, and not because of any logical errors, that it failed correctly to predict the evolution of capitalism.

I

The basic axiom of Marxian economics is the proposition that surplus value (profit plus interest plus rent) is unearned income, in the strict Marshallian sense of the phrase; for Marx, capital has no supply price and property income is purely a function of the private ownership of the means of production. Since the argument proceeds in the context of a perfectly competitive economy, we might think that the individual entrepreneur — whose contribution to total output is too small to influence price — would expand output in the effort to reap more surplus value, until wages are bid up so as to reduce the surplus to zero. What is it that holds wages down? Having abandoned the Malthusian theory of population, Marx could not assume that population growth would preserve wage rates at the subsistence level. Instead, he postulated the existence of "the industrial reserve army" of the unemployed, providing unceasing competition for vacancies. Booms deplete the reserve army and slumps replenish it, but secular growth at full employment levels is conceptually impossible, according to Marx. Unemployment arises initially from inappropriate factor endowments, combined with limited possibilities of factor-substitution; full capacity use of the capital stock is insufficient to absorb the available labour supply. When this ceases to be true at some levels of the capital stock, further accumulation must involve a sufficient flow of labour-saving innovations so as to produce chronic unemployment. Thus, the Marxian conception of mature capitalism is predicated upon a bias towards labour-saving technical change.

It is not difficult to demonstrate that if the underlying production functions show either diminishing or constant returns to scale, a persistent labour-saving slant in technological progress must lead to a rise in capital requirements per unit of output. And, unless the property share of output rises proportionately, this will cause the rate of profit to fall. Marx's law of the falling rate of profit is, in fact, based upon exactly this kind of reasoning.

The argument is in principle very simple. Since most of Marxian economics thrives under a cloud of terminological confusion, the first step in translating Marx is to agree upon a set of definitions. Writing small letters for flows and capital letters for stocks, Marx's 'constant capital' c is defined as the sum of depreciation charges on fixed capital and inputs of raw materials. Adding the wages of production workers v, Marx's "variable capital", we get the flow of outlays k. Dividing the components of k by the appropriate rates of turnover, we get the stock of capital invested K. $K = C + V$, where C stands for the value of the stock of durable equipment and inventories of raw materials and V stands for working capital required to meet weekly pay-rolls. Following Marx, surplus value s is defined on a flow basis as the excess of gross revenue over variable and fixed costs. For the economy as a whole this amounts to the excess of net national product over the wages bill. The rate of surplus value s' is s/v. The rate of profit p', as Marx defined it, is s/k; on a stock basis it is s/K^1.

Marx himself never explicitly defined the so-called "organic composition of capital". What he had in mind, however, is clearly the ratio of embodied labour to current labour or of machine costs to labour costs: C/v^2. When multiplied by the wage rate, and ignoring V as negligibly small, this becomes the amount of capital per man, i.e. K/v. $v/L = K/L$.

At all times Marx shuffled freely between stock and flow definitions without warning the reader. His expression for p' is actually the share of profits in the turnover of capital; it is equal to profits per unit of capital on the assumption that the whole of capital turns over once a year. Marx was aware of variations in the turnover rates of v and c and to that extent he recognised the distinction between stocks and flows.[3] Still, he put no stress upon the point and it soon dropped out of sight in the Marxian literature.

So much for definitions. The rate of profit p' varies inversely with "the organic composition of capital" Q and directly with the ratio of surplus to wages.[4] Taking into account variations in wages per man, p' may be said to vary inversely with the capital/labour ratio and directly with the amount of surplus per man, i.e.

$$p' = \frac{s}{v} \cdot \frac{v}{L} \bigg/ \frac{K}{v} \cdot \frac{v}{L}$$

As far as Marx was concerned this established the law that the rate of return on capital must fall with the increased mechanisation of industry. Having concluded that the wage rate rises little, if at all, in the course of capital accumulation while technical change constantly raises the stock of equipment per worker, he thought it obvious that the organic composition of capital must show a steady upward trend. It is true that this will not lower p' if the rate at which s' is rising exceeds that of Q. And as mechanisation raises the productivity of labour it can hardly fail to raise s'. Marx realised that there was some functional connection between Q and s', but, after satisfying himself that s' could rise only within "certain impassable limits", he assumed it to be constant. He did recognise the influence of autonomous increases in s', which he handled under the label of "absolute and relative surplus value", but these too he dismissed with more justification as having definite physical limits.[5]

The constancy of s' was only a simplifying assumption but, as both Sweezy and Robinson have pointed out, it was a particularly clumsy simplification for the Marxian system. Since wages and profits exhaust total income, a constant s' for the economy as a whole implies constant relative shares. This means that real wages rise as far as the average productivity of labour, i.e.,

$$s' = \frac{s}{v} = \frac{s}{o} \bigg/ \frac{v}{L} \cdot \frac{L}{o}$$

But not only did Marx frequently imply that labour's share would decline but it is the function of "the reserve army" to keep wages at subsistence.

However loosely interpreted, this presumably means that wages do not rise as fast as the average productivity of labour. And so long as this is true, every increase in output per man raises s'. *A fortiori*, if real wages are constant, s' will rise sharply as K/L increases. Thus, the tendency for p' to fall is indeterminate: it all depends on the nature of the explicit function $s' = f(Q)$. Marx's attempt to demonstrate the existence of an upper bound to this function involved him in a horrible confusion between physical-productivity and value-productivity.[6] On his own terms, the only relevant question is whether productivity is likely to increase faster in the wage-goods industries than in other sectors. If so, this will mean a fall in the value of the Marxian measuring rod of labour-hours with the result that p' will tend to rise. The law of the falling rate of profit, therefore, calls for some denial of this effect, be it on logical or on empirical grounds.

It is possible, however, to make out a case for Marx's law on orthodox grounds. Assume that the aggregate production function shows constant return to scale, the obvious assumption for the Marxian two-factor case. By the properties of the function, output rises for every increase in capital per man along the given function but less than proportionate to the increase in capital. As the capital/output ratio rises, the increase in capital will entail a fall in p' even though $s' = f(Q)$.[7] Innovations as such are not enough to upset this conclusion. If technical change does not work to reduce capital per unit of output, p' will nevertheless fall. This is because the capital-absorbing effects of the innovational process govern the degree to which wages rise as capital increases. If wages rose as fast as output per man, relative shares would be unaffected and the rising capital/output ratio alone would lead directly to a fall in p'. In the Marxian system labour's share is alleged to fall through time; therefore, a rising capital/output ratio here does not necessarily imply a falling p'. But this is only to say that the Marxian law of the falling rate of profit is predicted upon a very rapidly rising capital/output ratio, which implies in turn that technical change is heavily slanted towards labour-saving improvements. For the claim that capital per man rises faster than profits per man, or in Marxian terms that Q rises faster than s', is tantamount to claiming that the capital/output ratio rises faster than the property share in output:

$$p' = \frac{s'}{Q} = \frac{s'}{L} \bigg/ \frac{K}{L};$$

dividing through by L/o, we get

$$p' = \frac{s}{o} \bigg/ \frac{K}{o}.$$

The fact that the aggregate capital/output ratio has remained practically unchanged in advanced economies over the last seventy-five years is fatal to the Marxian schema. Together with the observed long-run stability in relative shares, it leads directly to the conclusion that profits per man have risen as fast as capital per man and hence that p' has not declined. In the American case, the rate of return to privately owned physical capital has in fact shown a slight tendency to fall in the twentieth century. But the reason for this is not that technical change has been excessively labour-saving; on the contrary, the evidence suggests a mild capital-saving bias in the American economy over the last four decades.[8]

The facts make it unnecessary to consider the deeper contradictions in Marx's argument. After all, a labour-saving slant in technical change implies that the rise in man-hour productivity is concentrated in the finishing stages of production: all cost-reducing improvements in the capital goods industries are capital-saving for the economy as a whole. Hence, the prices of consumer goods fall faster than machine prices. In terms of the labour theory of value, this means that the value of v declines faster than the value of c or s, so that it is not at all certain that Q or s will increase. The Marxian law of the falling rate of profit, even when accepted on its own grounds, is caught up in a bewildering mesh of opposing forces whose outcome is not deducible from elements supplied by the theory.

II

Given the weaknesses of Marx's argument, it is hardly surprising that his predictions failed to materialise. Even Marxists have now conceded the point. A recent book by an American Marxist for the first time submits the law of the falling rate of profit to a statistical test.[9] Using census data for American manufacturing over the period 1849 to 1939, the author, J. M. Gillman, starts out by accepting Marx's categories on a flow basis. The results are very disquieting: although q showed a fairly strong tendency to rise until the turn of the century, the trend-value through 1919-39 was constant. Since s' rose persistently, the trend in s/k was decidedly upward over the whole of the ninety-year period.

When the ratios are converted to a stock basis, however, the data breaks clearly into two historical phases.[10] Until 1919 capitalism in manufacture behaved very nearly as Marx had predicted: Q rose significantly and s' did not increase sufficiently to prevent p' from falling. Then something went wrong. The organic composition of capital stabilised in the 1920s at levels reached in 1919 and fluctuated counter-cyclically in the 1930s; it fell all through World War II and had risen little by 1950. If the decade of the 1930s is excluded, there is in fact some indication of a secular decline in Q. In addition neither s' nor p' showed any definite trend.[11]

Gillman has nothing to say about the average productivity of capital. But his findings are complemented by studies of the capital/output ratio in American manufacturing: measured in current prices, it rose from 1880 to 1909 and then fell continuously until 1948. When capital and output are estimated in 1929 prices, the peak is reached in 1919. Furthermore, the downtrend since 1919 holds both for the ratio of fixed capital and of working capital to output.[12]

Thus, Marxists and orthodox economists do not disagree about the facts. Not so long ago some Marxists were predicting an even sharper tendency towards labour-saving technical change,[13] but Gillman adduces evidence of the increasing importance of capital-saving innovations.[14] This is where agreement ends, however. Gillman seems to regard capital-saving improvements as novel manifestations of a complex technology which Marx could not have foreseen. Apparently, labour-saving innovations are induced by rising real wages eating into profit margins but capital-saving innovations just happen, for technical reasons, to occur only in late-stage capitalism. Capital-saving innovations play the same role in Gillman's book as trade union pressures in the works of other Marxists: they enter into the analysis as exogenous variables which reconcile the theory with reality.

Ironically enough, Gillman here adopts an attitude which not so long ago was widely shared by most orthodox economists but, as we shall see, not by Marx himself. A brief digression will help to place the matter in perspective. Economic development was traditionally said to involve continuous capital deepening in the sense of increased capital requirements per unit of output; capital-saving innovations were regarded as only becoming important when an economy was already richly endowed with capital. The temptation to draw unwarranted conclusions from the historical increase in capital per man proved irresistible:[15] technical innovations lighten human toil by substituting mechanical power for hand labour; therefore, technological progress as such is necessarily labour-displacing and, in the absence of sufficient capital-widening, will lead to chronic unemployment. The constant preoccupation with the problems of technological unemployment, out of all proportion to its actual importance, testifies to the hold of this line of thought. Implicitly, it will be noticed, technical change was being discussed as if it consisted mainly of inventions in the narrow sense of the term rather than of any change, for whatever reason, in the technical horizon of producers.[16]

With hindsight it is hard to believe that anyone could ever have doubted that capital-saving improvements are as normal a feature of technical change as labour-saving innovations. It is difficult now to appreciate how quickly and how recently economists have changed their minds on this question. In 1937 Joan Robinson declared that:

It appears obvious that the development of human methods of production, from the purely hand-to-mouth technique of the ape, has been mainly in the direction of increasing "round-aboutness", and the discovery of short cuts, such as wireless, are exceptions to the general line of advance.

But in 1956 she concluded:

There is no reason to expect technical progress to be exactly neutral in any one economy, but equally there is no reason to expect a systematic bias one way or the other. Capital-using innovations raise the cost of machines in terms of commodities and give entrepreneurs an extra motive to find ways to cheapen them. Capital-saving innovations tend to produce scarcity of labour in the consumption sector and give entrepreneurs an extra motive to increase productivity. Each type of bias tends to get itself compensated by the other.[17]

Capital-saving innovations fall into two classes, those that save fixed capital and those that save working capital. Apart from cheaper and better machines, any improvement that widens the scope of auxiliary instruments, reduces floor space, or lengthens the physical life of a plant, belongs to the first class of innovations. Economies of working capital, on the other hand, release operating funds by reducing the stock of goods which must be carried for given output. Typically, they take the form of lower freight charges, faster handling of materials, reductions in delivery-time, and fuel savings through recovery and use of waste-products. Put this way it would be surprising indeed if capital-saving innovations had not proved important even in the earlier phases of capitalist development. A good many of the crucial inventions of the Industrial Revolution on balance released rather than absorbed capital: the smelting of iron with coal, Cort's puddling and rolling process, chlorine bleaching, Watt's vacuum engine, Neilson's hot blast, Woolf's compound engine, not to speak of the transport revolution associated with the names of Macadam and Bridgewater.[18] The canal era, or for that matter the replacement of the stagecoach by railroads, certainly drew heavily on capital resources. But its effect in reducing the prices of coal, timber, and iron in which the cost of carriage weighed heavily, was such that it is doubtful whether it raised capital requirements per ton-mile of freight carried.[19]

Capital-saving innovations *may* involve such revolutionary inventions as explosives for mining, radio, telegraphy and aeroplanes, but they need not. Frequently, they consist of minor but not necessarily routine improvements in technique and for that reason they tend to escape recognition. Indeed, awareness of the very existence of capital-saving innovations came late in the history of economic thought. Even the classical economists realised that time-saving improvements raise the rate of profit by increasing the turnover rate of capital funds; when railways were first introduced, their advantages in economising working capital were thoroughly canvassed.[20] But such ideas were not systematised and economies of fixed capital were never seriously contemplated. Sidgwick in 1883 seems to have been the first to hint at the general concept of a capital-saving innovation; Taussig and J. B. Clark made references to it in their writings. But none of them doubted that technical change had been overwhelmingly labour-saving in the past.[21] The growing influence of the Austrian theory of capital around the turn of the century, emphasising as it did capital formation which increases the durability of plant and equipment, further encouraged the belief that capital deepens as it grows.[22]

Marx, on the other hand, was not only aware of capital-saving changes but spoke of them as the product of automatic market forces. "Capitalist production," he writes, "enforces economies in the employment of constant capital" which tend "to check the fall in the rate of profit." "This shows once more," he concluded, "that the same causes which bring about a tendency of the rate of profit to fall, also check the realisation of this tendency."[23] Chapter five of the third volume of *Capital*, written by Engels in the early 1890s, elaborates upon the tendency of certain inventions to shorten the time of production, thus raising profits by saving goods in the pipelines. This contention is richly illustrated with examples drawn from British industry. Engels notes that "the revolution in the means of communication in the last fifty years . . ." has more than doubled or trebled "the productive capacity of the capital engaged in world commerce". These comments, however, were merely suggestive and even as such they were confined to innovations which save working capital; neither Marx nor Engels considered the effects of technological progress concentrated in the capital goods industries. In the final analysis, Marx too remained a victim of the myth of a labour-saving bias in technical change.

III

Technological progress acts to offset diminishing returns to the faster growing factor. When innovational investment is insufficient to offset diminishing returns it is possible that both profits and wage rates decline as capital per man increases. But if technical change is strongly biased it would require a very low level of innovating activity to produce the perverse result of unfavourable trends in both profit and wage rates. Viewed in this light, the Marxian view of capital accumulation seems almost deliberately paradoxical. Marx draws no distinction between movements along production functions and shifts in the production functions themselves: capital cannot be invested without altering the state of the arts. Hence, there is no question in the Marxian system of insufficient offsets to diminishing returns. At the same time, Marx assumed that innovations would be heavily slanted in the labour-saving direction. Yet, he concluded that capital accumulation will depress the rate of profit without necessarily raising real wages per man. The mechanism that is supposed to produce this result is entirely independent of any third factor receiving an increasing residual. It is solely due to what Marx liked to call "the passion for accumulation". An excessive rate of capital formation lowers the profit rate while the innovations embodied in the increments of capital hold down wage rates by being largely labour-saving.

The Marxian situation is theoretically possible.[24] Events have not turned out that way, but is there any reason to think they could have done so? If a given rate of accumulation depresses the yield of capital (say, by hastening the rate of obsolescence or driving down the prices of finished goods), what prevents the system from settling down to a slower rate of growth? After all, if capitalists accumulate wealth for reasons of prestige and status irrespective of the rate of profit, so long as it is positive, and this is what Marx implies, a rate of accumulation so rapid as to depress the rate of return must defeat itself.[25] Putting this aside, it is still true that if capital is incessantly being invested in labour-saving improvements, the capital/ output ratio must rise. This means a higher share of depreciation and interest charges in total costs with consequent pressures to affect economies in the use of capital. Likewise, "the passion for accumulation" should lead to a chronic excess demand for capital; consequent difficulties in obtaining finance, expressing itself in an upward sloping supply curve of funds available to the firm, should be enough to induce capital-saving innovations. No matter how we look at it, the investment-demand function must be of a very peculiar shape to sustain the Marxian case.

Under perfect competition innovations as such cannot *for long* lower both profit and wage rates. Any sharp trend in factor-returns will generate a stabilising shift in technical change. This is not to imply that innovations can be said to have a unique effect upon rates of return to productive agents: without knowledge of the underlying production functions nothing specific can be inferred.[26] Nevertheless, if technical progress is plentiful and yet produces a fall in the rate of return to capital it does suggest that the factor-saving slant of innovations is out of line with relative factor scarcities. In an economy in which capital is the scarcer factor, a persistent bias towards labour-saving improvements must erode the profits which each individual producer expects to reap from an improvement; this is the case Marx had in mind. When labour is the scarcer factor, as in advanced western economies, a bias towards capital-saving improvements likewise works to reduce the yield of capital. The reason that technical change has not exhibited either bias to any marked degree is that the long-term pattern of innovations is the outcome of successive adjustments to differential rates of growth in the factor supplies as reflected in relative prices. Producers in a perfectly competitive market face infinitely elastic supply curves in factor markets; hence, the perfectly competitive market seems to provide no signal to induce the "appropriate" factor-saving innovation. But the factor-supply curves do shift through time and there is nothing in the static theory of the competitive firm which leads us to deny that firms will learn to adapt themselves to a persistent trend in the shifting of factor-supply curves. Producers simply become conditioned by experience to avoid disappointment by choosing improvements which save the relatively scarcer factor. This process of adjustment damps down sharp cumulative changes in factor returns and thus works to stabilise the relative shares.[27]

It is not necessary to assume that factor-prices have a *conscious* redirecting effect on firms: the familiar "realistic" objections to marginal productivity theory are irrelevant in this context. The argument rests essentially on competitive survival, regardless of the nature of individual motivation and foresight.[28] Firms adopting, say, capital-using devices in the light of falling wage rates and rising interest charges will not prove viable. The successor innovator will be saving capital and absorbing labour and the economist looking on will find the system as a whole adapting technical change to relative factor scarcities.

This response mechanism is not likely to operate very smoothly, as the existence of business cycles will testify. At the crude aggregative level adopted here, objections crowd in from every direction. Technical constraints may not permit enough substitution of other factors for labour to prevent a rise in total labour costs as wages rise; when labour costs bulk larger in total costs than do capital charges, the effect of a change in wages is not symmetrical with the effect of a change in the rate of interest. Moreover, scarcity of capital is not adequately reflected by the rate of interest owing to the practice of capital rationing.

In addition, indivisibility of capital in some industries may cause capacity to be installed far ahead of the market. Such industries may be impervious, for relatively long periods of time, to changes in wages and interest rates. Capital-saving improvements are often the result of external economies generated by the growth of social overhead facilities. Since external economies are not reflected in the price system, improvements so originated form an important exception to the theory of market-induced innovations. Then too, it has been tacitly assumed up to this point that all innovations are cost-reducing. What of product-replacing or demand-creating innovations for which there is no basis of comparison with previous cost-outlays? These are certainly as significant nowadays as process-improvements but little can as yet be said about them. Variations in the level of inventive efforts raise further questions but we need go no further to make the point. Nevertheless, these reservations do not destroy the notion that the innovational process as a whole is the outcome of responses to market pressures: rational optimising behaviour precludes the possibility of any pronounced bias in technical change over long periods of time.

IV

The idea of an adjustment-mechanism governing the innovational process goes back to Marx. But Marxian economics provides only a truncated theory of factor-saving innovations. Changes in factor-prices are said to affect the choice of new techniques but capital-saving innovations are not treated on the same footing as labour-saving innovations. Yet Marx recognised that a falling rate of profit will induce entrepreneurs to economise upon fixed and working capital. The failure to consider the consequences of such tendencies is the fatal weakness of the Marxian theory of capital accumulation. It results in a theory of economic growth in which investment prospects dry up not because there have been too few labour-saving improvements but because there have been too many. This conclusion is hard to justify in any competitive economy and has certainly proved to be irrelevant to the experiences of developed capitalist countries. Marx erred in not envisaging the possibility that labour might become the relative scarcer factor. It is only fair to say that this was in fact a common error of all nineteenth-century economic thought. It matters more for Marx, however, because he alone claimed to predict the historical evolution of capitalism.

NOTES

1. The expression $\bar{s}/K$ is still not the rate of profit as conventionally understood; this is given by $\bar{s}/K$, where $\bar{s}$ stands for non-labour income minus administrative overhead, sales and advertising expenses, rents and indirect business taxes. Marx himself includes administrative and sales expenditures in the numerator of the expression s/v but excludes salaried personnel from the denominator.
2. Some commentators interpret him to mean the capital/output ratio which seems far-fetched or the ratio c/K which varies through time in much the same way as c/v.
3. See *Capital* (Chicago, 1909), II, Ch. 16; III, Ch. 4.
4. Marx writes the gross profit rate as $s/(c + v)$, which is identically equal to

$s'/(q + 1)$, where $q = c/v$. Strictly speaking, this should be amended to $p' = s'/Q$ where $Q = q.t$, t being a weighted average of the durabilities of c and v.

5. For references to Marx's writings on this point, see H. D. Dickinson, "The Falling Rate of Profit in Marxian Economics", *Review of Economic Studies* (February 1957), p. 123 n.

6. *Capital*, III, p. 290.

7. This rather obvious point is proved indirectly in Dickinson's paper, *loc. cit.* By itself it provides no support for Marx's law since Marx denies that capital can increase without technical change. Dickinson's defence of Marx's argument, however, abstracts from innovations.

8. For a discussion of the evidence, see W. Fellner, *Trends and Cycles in Economic Activity* (New York, 1956), pp. 246-57.

9. J. M. Gillman, *The Falling Rate of Profit* (London, 1957).

10. In the absence of data on the rate of turnover of raw materials before 1922, and neglecting V as too small to matter, K is calculated on fixed capital only, i.e. the value of plant and equipment estimated at their reproduction cost in current prices net of depreciation.

11. Since production workers declined as a fraction of the total labour force in manufacturing, Gillman infers that the rate of net profit $\bar{s}/K$ did fall very slightly over the years 1910-50 (*Ibid.*, p. 98). But in fact the regression line estimated by the method of least squares shows no trend component whatever on the 5 per cent level of significance. The same negative results are shown by Mann's non-parametric ranking test for trend which makes no assumption about the mathematical properties of the trend line or about the character of the population distribution.

12. D. Creamer, *Capital and Output Trends in Manufacturing Industry* (New York, 1954). The fall in the capital/output ratio since 1919 is all the more remarkable if it were true, as Marxists allege, that late-stage capitalism reveals a chronic tendency towards under-utilisation of capacity. As the denominator is usually measured, a fall in the utilisation of capacity should, everything else being the same, increase the capital/output ratio.

13. P. M. Sweezy, *The Theory of Capitalist Development* (New York, 1942), p. 276.

14. *Op. cit.*, pp. 74-9.

15. This ignores the fact that changes in the capital to labour ratio over time reflect not merely technical change or even factor-substitution without technical change, but also autonomous changes in the supply of savings and in the growth of population.

16. See e.g. J. R. Hicks, *The Theory of Wages* (London, 1932), pp. 123-5, and the comments by G. F. Bloom, "A Note on Hicks' Theory of Invention", *American Economic Review* (March 1946); for a recent version of Hicks' argument, see K. W. Rothschild, *The Theory of Wages* (New York, 1954), pp. 117-19.

17. J. Robinson, *Essays in the Theory of Employment* (London, 1937), p. 135; *The Accumulation of Capital* (London, 1956), p. 170.

18. For the most part, the economic history of the period has been written with other questions in mind. But see the works of T. S. Ashton, *The Industrial Revolution* (London, 1948), pp. 91-2; *An Economic History of England: The Eighteenth Century* (London, 1955), pp. 90, 100, 108-13. No historian has done more to attract attention to the importance of capital-saving improvements in the eighteenth century.

19. W.T.Jackmann, *The Development of Transportation in Modern England* Cambridge, 1916), I, pp.404-51; II, pp.724-9.
20. *Ibid.*, II, pp.490, 543-4.
21. For page references to the neoclassical authors see A.Gourvitch, *A Survey of Economic Theory on Technological Change and Employment* (Philadelphia, 1940), pp.93-5.
22. Böhm-Bawerk maintained that while some inventions do reduce roundaboutness, the capital so released tends to be applied to lengthening the period of production elsewhere. Only if the innovation is both capital-saving and product-replacing will the average period of production be shortened. This he dismissed as exceptional, citing the secular increase in physical capital per head as presumptive evidence of the greater frequency of time-increasing inventions: "Industrial experience will verify two propositions . . . first, that with the larger capitalistic equipment, the product per unit of labour increases; and, second, that this increase in product does not go on *pari passu* with the addition of capitalistic equipment." "The Positive Theory of Capital and its Critics", *Quarterly Journal of Economics* (January 1896), p.150. It is worth noting that Wicksell's famous discussion of the effect of inventions upon wages in the *Lectures on Political Economy* does not consider the possibility of capital-saving improvements.
23. *Capital*, III, pp.103 and 277.
24. See W. Fellner, "Marxism Hypotheses and Observable Trends Under Capitalism: A 'Modernized Interpretation', *Economic Journal* (March 1957); but see the elliptical comments of P.A.Samuelson, "Wages and Interest: A Modern Dissection of Marxian Economic Models", *American Economic Review* (December 1957), pp.893-4.
25. In other words, the demand for capital is *less* elastic in the long run than in the short run: all savings come out of profits and the capital stock is used to capacity; hence, a lower profit rate depresses savings not because it affects the willingness to save and invest but because it affects the ability to do so.
26. Innovations may be conveniently classified in terms of their effect upon relative shares (see Fellner, *loc. cit.*, pp.212-13). A capital-saving innovation raises labour's share and, of course, tends to lower the capital-output ratio; the effect upon the rate of profit, however, depends upon which of the two consequences predominate. A spate of capital-saving innovations occurring together will engender commodity-substitution towards capital-intensive goods which fall in relative price; this stimulates the demand for capital and the capital/output ratio may actually rise. Indeed, to predict the effect of an innovation upon rates of return and upon relative shares it would be necessary to know the elasticity of demand for every product and the elasticity of supply of every factor-input in addition to the changes in the marginal rates of substitution of factors.
27. See *ibid.*, pp.220-2. Professor Fellner notes that under conditions of monopsony, in which the firm necessarily affects the price of the input it purchases, producers are made directly aware of relative factor scarcities by the respective gaps between average and marginal factor costs.
28. See A.A.Alchian, "Uncertainty, Evolution and Economic Theory", *Journal of Political Economy* (June 1950).

10 Another Look at the Labour Reduction Problem in Marx

When Ronald Meek published his *Studies in the Labour Theory of Value* in 1956, its undogmatic tone, its obvious depth of knowledge in the history of economic thought, and its heroic attempt to bring Marx up to date in relation to problems of monopoly immediately placed it among the two or three best expositions of Marxian economics in the English language. The book was republished in 1973 with a new and long introduction, which gave striking witness to the stimulating impact of Sraffa on orthodox Marxism. Ronald Meek never ceased to be a Marxist, but in this introduction he candidly admitted that there were serious, unsolved problems in the standard versions of Marx. Among the many unsolved problems he included the so-called "skilled labour reduction problem":

I would now be rather more critical of certain aspects of Marx's treatment of the quantitative side of the value problem. His treatment of the unskilled labour problem ... although suggestive enough, is rather fragmentary and incomplete, and there seems little doubt that he underestimated the importance of the problem (Meek, 1973, p. xvi).

This is all Meek said and we are left wondering what would constitute a complete, satisfactory treatment of the reduction problem from the Marxian standpoint.

Marx's treatment of the problem of differentiated labour has frequently been criticised by Marxists and anti-Marxists alike[1] but the prevailing view among modern Marxists is that, whatever Marx himself may have said, the labour reduction problem is capable of being solved, at least in principle, in the general spirit of the Marxian system. Such, I am sure, was Ronald Meek's own view, even in the later years of his life. Critics of Marx, however, generally regard the labour reduction problem as the Achilles Heel of Marxian economics and they would heatedly deny that the standard solutions of the problem can be reconciled with other leading features of the Marxian system. I share that view. My only justification for writing this essay is not to restate objections long familiar to Marxologists but, I hope, to throw fresh light on the nature of the difficulties.

197

I STATING THE PROBLEM

Marx argued that the value of commodities is determined by the "socially necessary" labour-time required to produce them and that these labour costs are countable in units of common, abstract labour, skilled labour being treated as so many multiples of common labour. These multiples must be construed as purely technical conversion coefficients and not simply as earnings differentials between different types of labour, because it is obviously illegitimate to invoke wage rates in what, after all, purports to be an explanation of how prices are determined. So long as labour is only differentiated in terms of acquired skills, there is no problem: we can assume that such skills are produced in a private "training industry" at cost-covering prices, in which case labour skills are simply means of production, like machines, that are produced and reproduced at the going rate of profit. In other words, the time-consuming production of skilled labour raises no separate difficulties for the labour theory of value that are not also raised by the time-consuming production of machines.

The argument breaks down, however, the moment we concede that labour is also differentiated in terms of "ability", regardless of whether those ability differences are innate or whether they are due entirely to family rearing. Such "ability" differences simply cannot be interpreted as given technical coefficients in a notional industry called the "family", producing an output in accordance with the principle of equal profit-ability. We could, of course, argue that all differences in native ability are randomly distributed among individuals, who in turn are randomly distributed among industries, in consequence of which these differences have no impact on the relative prices of commodities produced by different industries. Insofar as there are industries with high concentrations of exceptionally talented individuals (sports, the performing arts, and perhaps even education), these industries must then be set aside as frank exceptions to the labour theory of value on the same grounds as non-reproducible goods in general. Marx himself never employed this argument, and indeed virtually ignored the problem of ability differences, but modern Marxists[2] have frequently adopted this escape route, in effect treating different types of labour as differing only in certain cognitive skills that have been acquired in a training course.

There is a third difficulty in the standard interpretation of the labour reduction problem which is rarely given its proper due in the Marxian literature (but see Howard and King, 1975, pp. 130-2): it is that jobs within and between industries differ not only in their pecuniary but also in their non-pecuniary attributes, and that individual workers cannot be assumed to be totally indifferent about the various mixes of these attributes associated with particular jobs. Indeed, in a famous chapter of Book I of *The Wealth of Nations*, Adam Smith argued that some jobs require more manual or mental skill, more endurance, more risk of injuries, more indifference to routine, and more irksome responsibility than others; in addition, jobs also differ in "agreeableness" and in the variance of both earnings and full-time opportunities which they offer. For that reason, he denied that a competitive labour market tends to equalise the rate of wages for labour regarded as homogeneous by employers; what it equalises are the "net advantages" of different jobs to individual workers. Be that as it may, we must either argue that workers lack the power to make occupational choices, or that the non-pecuniary fringe benefits of different jobs are more or less uniformly distributed among the major sectors of the economy. Insofar as there are industries like agriculture that do rely more heavily on payments in kind rather than payments in money, we must once again treat them openly as exceptions to the labour theory of value.

Marx made at least oblique references to all three of the difficulties in the labour reduction problem, and in the opening chapter of Volume I of *Capital* he so much as implied that skilled labour-time is simply the sum of unskilled labour-time plus the total labour-time expended on training unskilled workers, including the labour embodied in the output of trainees forgone (Marx, 1976, pp. 135, 305, 435; also Marx 1909, pp. 168-9). Unfortunately, he also said that "Experience shows that this reduction [of skilled to unskilled labour time] is constantly being made" and that such reductions are established by "a social process that goes on behind the backs of the producers", appearing to them as something "handed down by tradition" (Marx, 1976, p. 135; also pp. 276, 294-5). A footnote on the same page explains that the reduction has nothing to do with relative wages, that, in short, it is a genuine physical decomposition of skilled labour into its historic unskilled labour costs. But what is this *social* process of reducing skilled to unskilled labour in physical terms? Why should either capitalists or workers care about the value-calculus in terms of labour-time?[3]

Moreover, in a later portion of Volume I, (1976, p. 305) Marx suddenly announces the "thesis of the increasing homogenisation of labour" under capitalism: the distinction between skilled and unskilled labour is simply an illusion fostered by custom, which is shortly to disappear; indeed elsewhere he said that it already had disappeared in America, "the most modern form of bourgeois society" (Marx, 1970, p. 210). In other words, labour may have been heterogeneous in the past but capitalism tends constantly to erode all differences between types of labour by the introduction of skill-saving processes, so that purely homogeneous, common labour represents the appropriate abstraction that corresponds to capitalism at its highest stage of development. Thus the "social process" that permits heterogeneous labour to be commensurable in physical terms at early stages of capitalist development is destined to be eroded by the very process of capital accumulation. If this "thesis of the increasing homogen-isation of labour" is to be taken seriously, it amounts in effect to the prediction that earnings differentials will gradually narrow and eventually disappear under capitalism.

Now, undoubtedly, factor substitution acts constantly to overcome shortages of skilled labour by a process of deskilling, but, on the other hand, technical progress frequently acts in the opposite direction by raising the skill requirements of new products and processes. It is a moot question whether the labour force has in fact become more or less physically differentiated in the process of industrialisation, but certainly the educat-ional explosion of the last thirty-five years and the relative constancy of inter-occupational wage differentials in advanced countries over the last fifty and even one hundred years suggest the very opposite of Marx's belief in the increasing homogenisation of labour.[4] This is not a question we can settle here, but certainly Marx's treatment of the labour reduction prob-lem leaves many loose ends that he never tied together.

Is it really true that "ability" differences are only important in certain restricted areas of economic activity that can be safely ignored at the high level of abstraction of the labour theory of value? Are workers really indifferent between different kinds of work, or compelled to suppress the differences they do care about because of the fear of unemployment? Is occupational mobility simply a vestige of the past, a sign of underdevelop-ment? But if so, how are we to account for the undeniable fact that there is always wage dispersion even for unskilled labour in a single geographical labour market?

Let us take these two sets of questions in reverse order.

II THE OCCUPATIONAL MOBILITY OF WORKERS

Marxists usually ignore the Smithian theorem of the equalisation of "net advantages" in labour markets, assuming implicitly that the elasticity of supply of every type of labour is infinite, thus eliminating the influence of demand on the determination of relative wages. When they do recognise the fact that different workers have different preferences for the pecuniary and non-pecuniary aspects of work, they usually rely on the concept of "the industrial reserve army" to get rid of the difficulty.[5] In so doing, however, they only avoid Scylla by encountering Charybdis. The labour theory of value requires the assumption that workers move freely between different jobs so as to equalise both the rate of wages of the same type of labour and certain non-pecuniary attributes of the jobs taken up, such as the intensity of effort and the length of the day over which the effort is expended. Without this assumption, there is no warrant for the fundamental Marxist belief that every "productive" worker generates surplus value at a rate that is uniform throughout all industries and all occupations.

The argument goes like this: if labour is homogeneous in quality, there will be one ruling wage rate in the economy; and if workers prefer a shorter to a longer working day, and if they care nothing about the other aspects of a job, they will choose jobs and firms in such a way that the length of the working day is everywhere equalised; finally, according to the labour theory of value, a given quantity of homogeneous labour always produces an equal quantity of value; it follows that every "productive" worker in the economy must spend the same number of hours reproducing the value of his wage bundle and hence the same number of hours working to produce a surplus value for the capitalist who employs him; thus, as a by-product of competition in the labour market on the part of both capitalists and workers, the rate of surplus value is equalised throughout the economy. QED.

The "theorem of the uniform rate of surplus value" has been expounded by a large number of Marxist commentators,[6] but its origins go back to Marx himself.[7] Clearly, it calls for workers willing and able to move between jobs in search of the highest wage and the shortest working day, which is as much as to say that there is at least one non-pecuniary characteristic of jobs that makes workers "vote with their feet". It follows that the price of different types of labour does to that extent depend on both supply and demand, rather than simply on ratios of labour embodied in the production of vocational skills, and, hence, that the labour reduction problem cannot be solved along traditional lines. To put it in a nutshell: the "theorem of the uniform rate of surplus value" requires effective occupational mobility, but effective occupational mobility contradicts the standard solution to the labour reduction problem, according to which relative wages reflect only the relative labour-times embodied in the production of vocational skills (see Wolfson, 1966, pp. 49-56, 80-2; Morishima, 1973, pp. 180, 191-3).

Alternatively, of course, we could give up the "theorem of the uniform rate of surplus value", allowing the rate of surplus value to differ either between industries or between stated categories of workers. But if we allow it to differ between industries, we would have to know precisely how it varied between industries in order to calculate the total mass of surplus values that is said by Marx to mark an upper boundary on the total profits that can be earned by capitalists. Moreover, if we admit that these unequal rates of surplus value in different industries are in any way functionally related to the varying amount of machinery that workers are equipped with — a conclusion that would be difficult to resist once we have abandoned the "theorem of the uniform rate of surplus value" — we threaten Marx's still more fundamental theorem that attributes surplus value solely to living labour, irrespective of the amount of "dead labour" with which it is combined.[8]

If, on the other hand, we permit the rate of surplus value to differ, not between industries but between stated categories of workers, we may easily encounter circumstances in which the rate for some categories is actually negative, meaning that these workers exploit capitalists rather than the other way around, and, in general, it will be true in this case that a certain proportion of workers will be exploited by other workers as well as by capitalists. However, some radical American economists with Marxist leanings have not been deterred by these uncomfortable implications and have claimed that, indeed, the labour market under capitalism is always segmented into non-competing sexual, racial and ethnic groups, so that there are as many rates of surplus value as there are separate segments in the labour markets, in consequence of which some workers end up exploiting others (Bowles and Gintis, 1977).

In this latter version of Marx, the Marxian theory of profits as surplus value created by living labour is reduced to the innocuous theorem that the rate of profit is positive if and only if at least one rate of surplus value of a particular labour segment is positive (Bowles and Gintis, 1977, p. 190; see also Bowles and Gintis, 1978), which in turn implies nothing more than that at least one labour segment produces a positive net physical product which is not entirely handed over to workers. Even Morishima (1978), whose sympathy for Marx's ideas is, to say the least, ambiguous, finds the notion of unequal rates of surplus value across different labour segments too radical a departure from both the spirit and the letter of Marx to be acceptable as a way round the labour reduction problem.

It is important to note that Bowles and Gintis simply bypass the reduction problem because they deduce the set of equilibrium prices directly from a physical specification of the input-output matrix and an exogenously given vector of wage rates for heterogeneous labour without going through the intervening Marxian value system defined in terms of direct labour-time. In short, they follow Sraffa rather than Marx, as a result of which they end up with a Marxism that is shorn of the labour theory of value. What meaning, then, can be assigned to expressions involving "the rate of surplus value" is anybody's guess; labour-time in a Sraffian treatment of Marx is simply a unit of social accounting and nothing whatever can be deduced about the nature of profits from an accounting convention, as some Sraffian Marxists are the first to admit (Steedman, 1977, pp. 59, 206). Suffice it to say that there simply is no labour reduction problem in Sraffa (Steedman, 1977, pp. 91-3, 204-5).

III ABILITY DIFFERENCES BETWEEN WORKERS

We turn back now to the problem of ability differences, which have long been recognised by Marxists as creating exceptions to the labour theory of value. The outstanding question is whether they can in fact be ignored for an analysis focusing on commodities produced in the manufacturing "heartland" of a capitalist economy. The Marxian literature abounds in statements which assert the unimportance of ability differences among workers in most industries and the constant tendency of mechanisation to eliminate such differences as still exist. Unfortunately, the only "abilities" that appear to be recognised are those involving physical strength, manual dexterity, and vocationally specific cognitive and artistic skills.[9] This is very odd because other Marxists, such as Edwards (1976) and Gintis (1971) have shown fairly conclusively that psycho-motor and cognitive skills do not explain much of the differences in pay between workers in the same industry; these differences seem to depend principally on differences in the affective behavioural traits of workers, such as docility, compliance, initiative, achievement-drive, etc., which are probably the joint result of their home background and the schooling they have received. There is, however, absolutely no evidence that these kinds of affective "abilities" are becoming any less significant as time passes, or that their incidence is confined to certain exceptional service and entertainment industries. Indeed, it is precisely for that reason that Bowles and Gintis reject the traditional Marxian procedure of reducing differences among workers to differences in the amount of labour embodied in the production of acquired skills.[10] As a matter of fact, the standard Marxian solution of the labour reduction problem bears an amazing likeness to certain extreme versions of human-capital theory in orthodox economics in which all wage differences are regarded as being solely due to education-cum-training costs.

I say advisedly "certain extreme versions" because, on balance, recent work in human-capital theory will not sustain the thesis that "abilities do not matter" for purposes of explaining the pay structure (see Blaug, 1976, pp. 842-3). Now, it is perfectly true that Marx did not intend to explain wage differences and that the labour reduction problem deliberately avoids reference to wage rates. Nevertheless, evidence about the distribution of abilities, and about the nature of these abilities, forms an essential element in the research programme of human-capital theorists and it is to this evidence that we must look for an answer to the question of the significance of ability differences.

When Böhm-Bawerk and Hilferding debated the labour reduction problem at the turn of the last century, very little was known about the structure of relative wages, and particularly the personal characteristics of workers in relation to differential rates of pay. Thus Böhm-Bawerk (1949, p. 85) boldly asserted that earnings differentials cannot in fact be explained solely by differences in the costs of training, which is perfectly true, but he had no basis other than casual empiricism for making that statement. But since then the rise of human-capital theory has generated a vast body of evidence about the determinants of the distribution of earnings in terms of such individual characteristics as age, years of work experience, length of schooling, quality of schooling, occupational status, community of residence, family origins, and even measured IQ at an early age. And yet when we examine the numerous writings of Marxists in recent years on the labour reduction problem we do not find a single reference to this new source of data with which to test the hypothesis that differences in the abilities of different workers make no difference whatsoever either to job performance or to wage rates in such sectors as manufacturing, transportation, services, etc. Moreover, the new data strongly suggest that the implicit private rate of return to the "training industry", which of course includes the whole of the formal education system, is not in fact equalised with the rate of profit on business capital (Blaug, 1976, pp. 838-9), implying that vocationally useful skills are not simply produced like "peculiar machines" at the going rate of profit; in short, even if we disregard ability differences between workers, the labour reduction problem is only solved in the abstract. Besides, as I said, these ability differences, whether due to nature or to nurture, show up as significant in all the "earnings functions" that have poured out of the human-capital research programme, which is a further reason for doubting the classic solution to the labour reduction problem.

It will not do to argue that all this is irrelevant because the Marxian argument refers only to "productive" labour, whereas the earnings function of human-capital theory refer to all labour earning either weekly wages or monthly salaries. It is a simple matter to extract from the literature a set of functions for wage-earners in manufacturing, all of whom necessarily fall within the Marxian category of "productive labour", and even these show that wage differentials are, at least in part, due to ability differences even within the same occupational category. Nor can it be argued that these ability differences may mean something for pay differentials but that they are irrelevant for the production of real output; whenever physical measures of job performance are employed, it turns out once again that different workers perform at different rates in carrying out the same tasks and that these differences are best explained by differences in their behavioural traits (Gintis, 1971).

IV CONCLUSIONS

The labour reduction problem can only be solved at a stratospheric level of abstraction that totally ignores real-world evidence about the determinants of relative wages, the rates of return to educational and training activities, and the patterns of occupational mobility. Indeed, what stands out about the entire debate surrounding the reduction problem is the facility with which the participants in that debate switch between levels of discourse at various stages in their argument: one moment we are adding farm labourers to coal miners in terms of their embodied labour-hours and in the next breath we are justifying this exercise by pontifical pronouncements about the effects of automation in basic industry; sometimes we are told that workers differ only in certain acquired skills, and a minute later we are assured that exceptions to that rule are largely confined to the peripheries of the economic system; for some purposes, workers are seen to choose between occupations in accordance with their different inclinations, and for others it is denied that they have any choice at all; and so forth. Such confusions are a manifestation of the fact that the labour reduction problem has gradually become a purely formal puzzle in the working out of the Marxian paradigm, while all the interesting historical and empirical questions about labour markets have been allowed to become the exclusive province of orthodox economists. What determines relative wages? Why are inter-industrial and inter-occupational pay differentials so remarkably stable over time? Why is labour training so valued that workers are frequently willing to pay for it themselves via lower wages during the training period? Why is formal schooling capable of raising a worker's earning potential? What governs the mobility of workers between occupations? And why is technical progress sometimes skill-using rather than skill-replacing? Marxists have been so busy solving analytical brainteasers (like the labour reduction problem) which they have themselves created that they have sorely neglected the task of studying how capitalist economies actually work.

NOTES

1. For reference to the history of the debate, see Rowthorn (1974, fn. 1) and Roncaglia (1974, fnn. 10-12).
2. See, for example, Meek (1973, pp. 172-3), Rowthorn (1974, p. 40) and Howard and King (1975, pp. 130-2).
3. Morris and Lewin (1973-4) interpret the "social process" to be a traditional

sense of the justice of the inherited pay structure which is then translated into "an objective social system of occupational equalization forces" defined in terms of labour time. No doubt, there is such a sense of the justice of past earnings differentials but they never explain why these should come to be converted by anybody into a "job evaluation" system of reckoning in units of common labour.

4. Braverman (1974) documents the remorseless process of deskilling in the history of the American economy and, by blandly ignoring the forces that act in the opposite direction, implies the historical validity of the "thesis of the increasing homogenisation of labour".

5. Thus Howard and King (1975, p. 132) declare: "the weight of the industrial reserve army is sufficient, in all normal circumstances, to ensure the suppression of individual preferences. Thus workers take jobs which they actively dislike (at the prevailing wage) in order to exist. Marx himself noted that the reduction of skilled to unskilled labour requires, *inter alia*, "indifference of the labourer to the nature of his labour', and 'the elimination of all vocational prejudices among labourers'.... And according to his theory of alienation, workers in capitalist society 'shun work like the plague', as much because it entails subordination of the labourer to the capitalist as because of the intrinsic characteristic of specific jobs. Within very broad limits, men shun *all* types of work equally."

6. See, for example, Wolfson (1971, pp. 19, 21), Morishima (1973, p. 52), Baumol (1974, p. 55n), Howard and King (1975, p. 26) and Harris (1978, p. 84).

7. "If capitalists employing unequal amounts of living labour are to produce unequal amounts of surplus-value, it must be assumed, at least to a certain degree, that the intensity of exploitation, or the rate of surplus-value, are the same, or that any existing differences in them are balanced by real or imaginary (conventional) elements of compulsion. This would presuppose a competition among the labourers and equilibration by means of their continual migration from one sphere of production to another. Such a general rate of surplus-value — as a tendency, like all other economic laws — has been assumed by us for the sake of theoretical simplification. But in reality it is an actual premise of the capitalist mode of production" (Marx, 1909, p. 206).

8. It is not clear that this implication is fully appreciated by some Marxist writers (Rosdolsky, 1977, pp. 539-41; Desai, 1979, p. 51) who are perfectly willing to give up the "theorem of the uniform rate of surplus value".

9. Thus Sweezy (1942, p. 44) writes: "So far as the vast majority of productive workers is concerned, specialized talents are not of great importance; the qualities which make a good worker — strength, dexterity, and intelligence — do not differ greatly from one occupation to another. No more than this need be granted to establish the essential commensurability of simple and skilled labour." Similarly, Rowthorn (1974, p. 40) declares: "Mechanisation, automation and other changes in methods of production have already reduced dramatically the importance of such special capabilities as great physical strength or manual dexterity, and further changes in this direction will continue to occur in the future. Specific intellectual and artistic natural ability will doubtless remain important in certain restricted areas of economic activity. But their overall significance is not and probably never was very great." Roncaglia (1974, pp. 9-10) endorses Rowthorn and adds: "the reality of mass production undoubtedly confirms Marx's approach [of assuming a random distribution of abilities among workers and industries] as we

remember that all wage labourers are in substantially the same position as they face capital". (Marx, incidentally, did not assume a random distribution of abilities among workers and industries — he simply said nothing about ability differences.)

10. "A wide variety of statistical evidence suggests that skills, at least as conventionally measured by training and cognitive achievement scores, are a weak determinant of occupational position, job performance and income. The importance of age, race and sex differences has been quite widely demonstrated .... We have shown that even the higher income and privileged job assignments enjoyed by more schooled workers, though much celebrated by the human capital school, cannot be explained by the cognitive skills or on-the-job training associated with higher levels of education and longer job experience" (Bowles and Gintis, 1977, p. 180).

REFERENCES

Baumol, W.J. (1974), "The transformation of values: what Marx 'really' meant (an interpretation)", *Journal of Economic Literature*, No. 1, pp. 51-62.

Blaug, M. (1976), "The empirical status of human capital theory: a slightly jaundiced survey", *Journal of Economic Literature*, No. 3, pp. 827-55.

Böhm-Bawerk, E. Von (1949), *Karl Marx and the Close of His System*, ed. P.M. Sweezy (New York).

Bowles, S. and Gintis, H. (1977), "The Marxian theory of value and heterogeneous labour: a critique and reformulation", *Cambridge Journal of Economics*, 1, pp. 173-92.

—— (1978), "Professor Morshima on heterogeneous labour and Marxian value theory", *Cambridge Journal of Economics*, 2, pp. 311-14.

Braverman, H. (1974), *Labour and Monopoly Capital* (New York).

Desai, M. (1979), *Marxian Economics*, 2nd edn. (Oxford).

Edwards, R. C. (1976), "Individual traits and organizational incentives: what makes a 'good' worker?", *Journal of Human Resources*, 11, pp. 51-68.

Gintis, H. (1971), "Education, technology and the characteristics of worker productivity", *American Economic Review*, 61, pp. 266-79.

Harris, D.J. (1978), *Capital, Accumulation and Income Distribution* (London).

Howard, M.C. and King J.E. (1975), *The Political Economy of Marx* (London).

Marx, K. (1909), *Capital, Volume III*, ed. F. Engels, trans. E. Untermann (Chicago)

—— (1970), "Introduction", in *A Contribution to the Critique of Political Economy*, ed. M. Dobb, trans. S. W. Ryazanskaya (Moscow).

—— (1976), *Capital, Volume I*, intro. E. Mandel, trans. B. Fowkes (Harmondsworth).

Meek, R. L. (1973), *Studies in the Labour Theory of Value*, 2nd edn. (London).

Morishima, M. (1973), *Marx's Economics: A Dual Theory of Value and Growth* Cambridge).

—— (1978), "S. Bowles and H. Gintis on the Marxian theory of value and heterogeneous labour", *Cambridge Journal of Economics*, 2, pp. 305-9.

Morris, J. and Lewin, H. (1973-4), "The skilled labour reduction problem", *Science and Society*, 37, pp. 454-72

Roncaglia, A. (1974), "The reduction of complex labour to simple labour", *Bulletin of the Conference of Socialist Economists*, 9, pp. 1-12.

Rosdolsky, R. (1977), *The Making of Marx's "Capital" (London)*.
Rowthorn, B.(1974), "Skilled labour in the Marxist system", *Bulletin of the Conference of Socialist Economists*, 8, pp.25-45.
Steedman, I.(1977), *Marx After Sraffa* (London).
Sweezy, P.M.(1942), *Theory of Capitalist Development* (New York).
Wolfson, M.(1966), *A Reappraisal of Marxian Economics* (New York).
    (1971), *Karl Marx*, Columbia Essays on Great Economists 3 (New York).

11   Was There a Marginal Revolution?

I

The term "marginal revolution" is usually taken to refer to the nearly simultaneous but completely independent discovery in the early 1870s by Jevons, Menger, and Walras of the principle of diminishing marginal utility as the fundamental building block of a new kind of static micro-economics. It constitutes, so the argument goes, one of the best examples of multiple discoveries in the history of economic thought, which simply cries out for some sort of historical explanation: it is too much to believe that three men working at nearly the same time in such vastly different intellectual climates as those of Manchester, Vienna, and Lausanne could have hit by accident on the same idea; it must be due to some common cause, which it is the job of the intellectual historian to identify. The only trouble is that none of the standard explanations are convincing.[1] The levels of economic development of England, Austria, and France were so different in the 1860s that all crypto-Marxian explanations in terms of changes in the structure of production, or in the relationship between social classes, tend to strain our credulity. Likewise, the Utilitarian-empiricist tradition of British philosophy, the neo-Kantian philosophical climate of Austria, and the Cartesian philosophical climate of France simply had no elements in common that could have provoked a utility revolution in economics. In matters of economic policy, there was in fact continuity with classical thinking, and when Jevons and Walras wrote on policy questions, as they did, there was little or no connection between practical recommendations and their views on value theory. As for an alleged "need" to defend the capitalist system, there was hardly anything more suitable than the old wages-population mechanism of classical economics or the writings of Bastiat, which owed nothing to marginal utility. Lastly, there was no real sense of intellectual crisis in the 1860s either in England or on the Continent which might have encouraged a search for alternative economic models; besides, historicism was such an alternative model which continued to gain new adherents after 1860, not only in Germany but also in England. In short, the simultaneous discovery of marginal utility may call for an explanation, but none of the available explanations is satisfactory.

Perhaps the difficulty is that the idea of a "marginal revolution" is the sort of "rational reconstruction" of the history of economic thought, like the concept of "mercantilism" or that of "classical economics" as defined by Keynes, that is bound to generate spurious historical puzzles. This is a large part of the problem, I think, but it is not the whole of it. The debate over the marginal revolution so-called has in fact confused two quite different things: the explanation of the origins of the revolution (if revolution it was) and the explanation of its eventual triumph. Some carelessness in the use of the concept of "explanation" in intellectual history has further clouded the debate.

II

A useful way to begin is to ask ourselves whether the discovery of marginal utility by Jevons, Menger, and Walras was in fact a "multiple," in Robert Merton's sense of the term.[2] After an intensive investigation of hundreds of multiple discoveries in the history of science, Merton concluded that "all scientific discoveries are in principle multiples, including those that on the surface appear to be singletons" (p. 477). Lest this should appear to be "a self-sealing hypothesis, immune to investigation," Merton conceded that it was only true of certain kinds of science at certain stages of their development: "A great variety of evidence ... testifies then to the hypothesis that, once science has become institutionalized, and significant numbers of men are at work on scientific investigation, the same discoveries will be made independently more than once and that singletons can be conceived of as forestalled multiples" (p. 482). Although two-thirds of his 264 intensively investigated multiples involved an interval of ten years or less, Merton refused to confine the concept of multiples to nearly simultaneous discoveries: "Even discoveries far removed from one another in calendrical time may be instructively construed as 'simultaneous' or nearly so in social and cultural time, depending upon the accumulated state of knowledge in the several cultures and the structures of the several societies in which they appear" (p. 486). Enough has now been said to indicate that the concept of "multiples" is difficult to interpret, particularly in fields less professionalised than the natural sciences. The gist of the argument, however, seems to be that "mature science" is characterised by cumulative, continuous progress such as to make the next leap forward, if not absolutely inevitable, at least highly predictable.[3]

We may now ask: Was the state of economic science in the 1860s such as to make the eventual emergence of the marginal utility principle a perfectly predictable phenomenon, in which case it is hardly surprising that Jevons, Menger and Walras discovered it at just about the same time? The answer to that question must surely be No.

First of all, it is highly doubtful that we can speak of one economic science in the 1860s as if it were a heritage shared between economists all over the world, studying the same treatises, reading the same journals and employing a common set of tools in the analysis of a similar range of problems. A glance at Hutchison's terse accounts of the state of economic thought around 1870 in England, Germany, Austria, France and the United States will show that there were at least two, if not three or four, "models" of economic science extant at that time.[4] Although Jevons struggled against the tyranny of Mill's influence, German economists had long since rejected "Smithianismus" and all Ricardian varieties thereof, while French economists for their part never exhibited much interest either in the analytical features of English classical political economy or in the rallying cries of the German historical school. The insularity of British economics and the lack of communication between economists in different countries right up to the 1890s[5] is perfectly exemplified by the fact that Jevons, a leading economic bibliophile, died in 1882 without realising that a man called Menger had written a book on economics which would one day be likened to his own *Theory of Political Economy*. Secondly, the notion that economic science as such was inexorably moving towards the discovery of marginal utility somewhere around the middle of the century is simply a rationalisation after the fact. Surely, the much more likely next step in English classical economics in the 1860s was either the generalisation of the marginal concept in Ricardian rent theory to all factors of production, that is, the breakthrough to a marginal productivity theory of factor pricing, or perhaps the further refinement of Ricardian value theory into something like linear input-output analysis? But as we know, the former came only belatedly in the 1890s among the generation that succeeded our marginal utility trio, and the latter has only emerged in the twentieth century.

What of the counter-argument, however, that marginal utility was not discovered but only rediscovered in the 1870s? Lloyd and Longfield had developed the distinction between total and marginal utility in 1834, followed soon after by Senior (I ignore Bernoulli in the eighteenth century as an "outlier"). If Jevons, Menger and Walras do not constitute a "multiple," perhaps Lloyd, Longfield and Senior deserve the title. But Lloyd, Longfield and Senior made little substantive use of marginal utility and thus only illustrate Whitehead's adage that everything new has been said before by someone who did not discover it. The same objection does not apply to Dupuit (1844), Gossen (1854), and Jennings (1855), all of whom not only rediscovered marginal utility but employed it to analyse consumer behaviour (and Gossen did so with all the confidence and revolutionary ardour of Jevons and Walras). Nevertheless, the same argument that applied to Jevons, Menger and Walras applies now to

Dupuit, Gossen and Jennings: they struck on the law of diminishing marginal utility at about the same time, but in response to totally different intellectual pressures and without the benefit of an inherited corpus of similar economic ideas.

We have now collected three trios, nine names in all, of economists who between 1834 and 1874 seized on the idea of marginal utility, four of whom saw it indeed as the stock from which a new economics could be evolved. If we deny that this constitutes a Mertonian "multiple," are we not splitting hairs?

It is clear how we might escape the dilemma. Recall Merton's own words: "Even discoveries far removed from one another in calendrical time may be instructively construed as 'simultaneous' ... depending upon the accumulated state of knowledge in the several cultures and the structures of the several societies in which they appear." Thus, from the fact that marginal utility was independently discovered over and over again in different countries between 1834 and 1874, we might argue that there must have been a core of economic ideas which was held in common by economists all over the world, whose inner logic would eventually dictate the exploration of consumers' demand with the tools of utility theory. In other words, we can infer the state of the science from the existence of a multiple, instead of the other way around. But that is to deprive the theory of multiples of its most attractive feature, namely, the idea that the development of a science is to some extent predictable. So long as we take Merton's argument seriously as providing something more than an inductive generalisation with many exceptions, we must deny that even nine names necessarily make a "multiple." The point is very simple: if communication between scientists were perfect, all multiples would be forestalled and we would only observe singletons; at the other end of the spectrum, if there were no communication whatsoever between scientists, multiples would have no more significance than the fact that lightning does occasionally strike twice in the same place; thus, multiples are only interesting phenomena if there is a high but nevertheless imperfect degree of communication between the practitioners of a discipline.

It is true that classical economics had no theory of demand and that its theory of price determination would sooner or later strike someone as peculiarly asymmetrical. But as the example of Cournot shows, it would have been perfectly possible to repair this deficiency without introducing utility considerations. It is also true that marginal utility was "in the air" throughout the nineteenth century and kept turning up afresh every ten years or so: Lloyd and Longfield, 1834; Dupuit, 1844; Gossen, 1854; Jennings, 1855; Jevons, 1862 (the date at which he first publicly proclaimed his theory); Menger, 1871; and Walras, 1874. But that is a far cry from saying that marginal utility economics was, in some sense, inevitable.

We might as well say that the emergence of macroeconomics in the 1930s was inevitable because certain Swedish economists were thinking along the same lines in the 1920s as Robertson and Keynes. *Post hoc ergo propter hoc* is a perennial temptation in intellectual history.

III

Howey's *Rise of the Marginal Utility School, 1870-1889* has taught us that the "marginal revolution," like the Industrial Revolution, went unrecognised by those who lived through it. The now standard version, which dates the revolution near 1871 and links together the names of Jevons, Menger and Walras as having written essentially about the same thing, was first announced in the late 1880s and (despite Marshall's endorsement in 1890) did not become a regular feature of histories of economic thought until well past the turn of the century.[6] The long-delayed acceptance of the marginal utility theory of value, which went hand in hand with the delayed acceptance of a rational account of its history, is perhaps the best indication we can have that it was indeed an anomaly which did not emanate logically from classical economics. This suggests, in other words, that the last quarter of the nineteenth century was one of those revolutionary phases in the history of economics when, in the language of Thomas Kuhn, economists adopted a new "paradigm" to guide their work.

Unfortunately, there appears to be no agreement as to just what the new paradigm was that Jevons, Menger and Walras put forward. Was it a new emphasis on demand rather than supply, on consumer utility rather than on production costs?[7] Was it something as ambitious as a subjective theory of value, which was to supplant the objective labour-cost theories of the past?[8] Was it rather the extension of the principle of maximisation from business firms to households, making the consumer and not the entrepreneur the epitome of rational action?[9] Was it perhaps the equimarginal principle, enshrined in the proportionality of marginal utilities to prices as the condition of consumer equilibrium?[10] Was it instead, as Schumpeter like to say, the explicit or implicit discovery of general equilibrium analysis?[11] Or lastly, was it simply the first conscious recognition of constrained maximisation as the archetype of all economic reasoning? Whichever version we adopt, it is difficult to sustain the thesis that Jevons, Menger and Walras were really preoccupied with the same paradigm.

Menger is in any case the odd man out: he was not self-consciously aware, as Jevons and Walras were, of being a revolutionary; he eschewed mathematical formulations and hence the pure logic of extremum problems; he only formulated "Gossen's third law" in words and certainly did not emphasise it; he certainly rejected cost theories of value, but on the other hand he was deeply suspicious of all determinate theory of pricing and he underlined discontinuities, uncertainties, and bargaining around the market price.[12] In other words, there is a great deal more to be said for coupling Jevons and Walras with Gossen than with Menger, and the only reason for the standard version is that Menger's name was continually invoked by his disciples Wieser and Böhm-Bawerk, both of whom were determined to persuade the profession that Austrian economics was a differentiated product. Similarly, it takes hindsight to see much in common between Jevons — a precisely formulated theory of barter exchange, an explicit mathematical statement of "Gossen's third law," a theory of the short-run supply schedule of labour, and some grandiose but unfulfilled promises of a new kind of utility economics — and Walras, who really did derive demand curves from utility schedules, struggled likewise to derive supply curves from marginal productivity considerations, worked out a theory of market pricing, and wove all the elements together with a general equilibrium framework.

The whole question is made more difficult by the ironic fate which history visited on the founders. In the end, what proved important about marginal utility was "the adjective rather than the noun."[13] Utility theory was gradually deprived of all its bite, to end up as merely "revealed preferences"; cost theories of value were shown not to be wrong, but only valid as a special case; and general equilibrium virtually disappeared, only to be revived in the 1930s by Hicks and Samuelson as "everybody's economics." Could anyone have foreseen in 1871 the tortuous path by which marginal utility economics led via Paretian welfare economics to cost-benefit analysis and dynamic programming? Not for nothing do we speak of a "marginal revolution" and not a "marginal utility revolution," but marginalism as a paradigm of economic reasoning is a twentieth-century invention; there is as much marginalism in Ricardo as in Jevons or Walras, but it is applied to different things.

IV

The term "paradigm" as a self-authenticated viewpoint no doubt raises as many questions as it answers,[14] but if we equate it loosely with Schumpeter's Vision — "a preanalytic cognitive act that supplies the raw material for the analytic effort" — we may describe the last quarter of the nineteenth century as a period when economists did develop a new view of their research agenda. A brief way of describing this new Vision is to say that pricing and resource allocation with fixed supplies of the factors of production became *the* economic problem, setting aside all questions about changes in the quantity and quality of productive resources through time. Whether we want to describe this shift as a "revolutionary phase," given the fact that it took at least twenty to thirty years and in some sense is still going on, is a matter of words. Jevons, Menger and Walras are not the founders of this new way of looking at economic problems, but they are important landmarks in the early stages of the shift of emphasis. That they published nearly simultaneously is a pure coincidence, because their reflections on the problem are actually separated by more than a decade. Only biographical data can tell us why Jevons and Walras (and Gossen) each insisted on the novelty of his ideas, whereas Menger (and Lloyd and Longfield and Jenkin) did not.[15] Therefore, to try to explain the origin of the marginal utility revolution in the 1870s is doomed to failure: it was not a marginal *utility* revolution; it was not an abrupt change, but only a gradual transformation in which the old ideas were never definitively rejected; and it did not happen in the 1870s.

V

The fact that Jevons, Menger and Walras all published their works within the span of three years, while a coincidence, was not an insignificant coincidence; it encouraged the acceptance of marginal utility economics, or at any rate greatly increased the probability of its early acceptance. Nevertheless, the new economics still failed to make much headway for at least a generation, despite the fact that all three founders were academic economists with established reputations, who argued their case persuasively and subsequently spared no efforts to push their ideas. The historical problem, therefore, is to explain, not the point in time at which the marginal concept was applied to utility, but rather the delayed victory of marginal utility economics.

This is not a difficult problem provided we do not insist that historians "retrodict" in essentially the same way that scientists predict; in other words, that historical explanations can be regarded as valid only if they take the form of counterfactual hypotheses based on some general "covering law." What historians do is to make past events intelligible — they illuminate rather than explain — and in the nature of the case, therefore, there can be no hard and fast rules on whether A caused B or was merely associated with B.[16] It is, therefore, fruitless to argue whether the diffusion of marginal utility economics, as distinct from its genesis, was largely the result of endogenous or of exogenous influences. It is precisely in this period that economics began to emerge as a professional discipline with its own network of associations and journals, the dilettante amateur of the past giving way for the first time to the specialist earning his livelihood under the title of "economist." A professionalised science necessarily develops its own momentum, the impact of external events being confined to the shell and not reaching the core of the subject.[17] But in 1870, or 1880, or even 1890, core and shell were still deeply intertwined. To argue, therefore, as Stigler does, that the retarded adoption of utility theory in economics can *only* be explained by "the rise of new values as the discipline became increasingly academic"[18] is merely to throw back the problem one stage further: Why did economics become professionalised in the last quarter of the nineteenth century and why should a professionalised science of economics find the truth of utility theory so self-evident that resistance to it becomes impossible?

It seems clear that no monocausal explanation can do justice to the long uphill struggle of the marginal revolution. One is struck in reading the treatises of the 1870s and 1880s by the bewildering variety of attitudes adopted towards the principal tenets of classical economics, such as the labour theory of value, the quantity theory of money, the Ricardian theory of differential rent, etcetera. Jevons, Menger and Walras each in his own way emphasised the methodological advantages of abstracting from historical and institutional considerations in the interest of obtaining perfectly general results from the minimum number of assumptions. But such considerations had little appeal to most contemporary economists, who still cared more about relevance than about rigour. As far as applied problems were concerned, marginal utility was, as we have said above, largely irrelevant, and the methodological problem that troubled most economists in the critical decade of the 1880s was the issue of induction versus deduction, the conflict between fact gathering and model building. Wherever there was a historicist bias — a pervasive bias in Germany and a widespread one in England — marginal utility economics was dismissed, together with English classical political economy, as excessively abstract and permeated with implausible assumptions about human behaviour. The fact that Jevons and Walras chose to express themselves in mathematical terms was undoubtedly responsible for further resistance to their ideas; the notion of reducing social phenomena to mathematical equations was still new and profoundly disturbing to nineteenth-century readers. It was the rise of Marxism and Fabianism in the 1880s and 1890s that finally made subjective value theory socially and politically relevant; as the new economics began to furnish effective intellectual ammunition against Marx and Henry George, the view that value theory really did not matter became more difficult to sustain. Furthermore, the addition of marginal productivity to marginal utility in the 1890s related the new economics to the problem of distribution, making it virtually impossible to deny a logical conflict between the ideas of Jevons, Menger and Walras and those of Smith, Ricardo and Mill. In 1891 Marshall provided a reconciliation between marginal utility economics and classical economics which made the new ideas palatable by showing that they could be fitted together into a wider context. But even at this late stage, the Marshallian integration was not immediately accepted on the Continent, and the three interlocking "revolutions" that had characterised the last two decades of the nineteenth century — the marginal utility revolution in England and America, the subjectivist revolution in Austria, and the general equilibrium revolution in Switzerland and Italy — continued well into the twentieth century.

VI

It may be convenient to seize on 1871 as marking the date from which all this started. But that date has no more special claim on our attention as historians of economic thought than any other. Classical political economy did not begin in 1776, and the birth of marginal utility economics — marginalism, modern economics, by whatever name we choose to characterise it — similarly, cannot be pinned down to any particular date. To sum up: (1) the "marginal revolution" was a process, not an event; (2) there was no "multiple" discovery of marginal utility, but only the temporal coincidence of three or more singletons; and (3) the success of the marginal revolution is intimately associated with the professionalisation of economics in the last quarter of the nineteenth century, and it is this which constitutes the problem that must be, and to some extent has been, explained by historians of economic thought.

NOTES

1. I canvassed the various explanations in my *Economic Theory in Retrospect*, 2d edn. (Homewood, Ill., 1968), pp. 303-8. The present note is an attempt to rethink the issue raised in those pages.
2. R. K. Merton, "Singletons and Multiples in Scientific Discovery: A Chapter in the Sociology of Science," *Proceedings of the American Philosophical Society*, 105, No. 5 (1961).
3. Merton guards himself against misinterpretation by denying that his thesis implies that "all discoveries are inevitable in the sense that, come what may, they will be made, at the time and the place, if not by the individual(s) who in fact made them" (p. 485). For a similar qualification, see his "Resistance to the Systematic Study of Multiple Discoveries in Science," *European Journal of Sociology*, 4, No. 2 (1963) p. 246.
4. T. W. Hutchison, *A Review of Economic Doctrines, 1870-1929* (Oxford, 1953), Chs. 1, 8, 12, and 16; see also the writers cited by Jevons, Menger, and Walras in their treatises, with hardly a name in common. R. S. Howey, *The Rise of the Marginal Utility School, 1870-1889* (Lawrence, Kans., 1960), Chs. 1-5.

5. See T. W. Hutchison, "The 'Marginal Revolution' and the Decline and Fall of English Classical Political Economy," in *The Marginal Revolution in Economics*, eds. R. D. Collison Black, A. W. Coats and C. D. W. Goodwin (Durham, North Carolina, 1973) (referred to hereafter as *Marginal Revolution).*

6. Howey, Chs. 26 and 27.

7. See A. W. Coats, "The Economic and Social Context of the Marginal Revolution of the 1870s," in *Marginal Revolution.*

8. See R. L. Meek, "Marginalism and Marxism," in *Marginal Revolution.*

9. *Ibid.* It is worth noting that Adam Smith's theory of occupational choice certainly treats individual workers as maximisers. There was nothing new in the idea of extending the sphere of rational action to households, but the notion of extending it to consumer behaviour was new.

10. Blaug, *Economic Theory in Retrospect*, pp. 301-2.

11. A. Schumpeter, *History of Economic Analysis* (New York, 1954), p. 918.

12. For a somewhat extreme statement of this argument, see E. Streissler, "To What Extent Was the Austrian School Marginalist?", in *Marginal Revolution.*

13. Hutchison, *Review of Economic Doctrines*, p. 16.

14. Masterman has counted twenty-one different definitions of "paradigm" in Kuhn's *Structure of Scientific Revolutions*, ranging from "a universally recognized scientific achievement" to a "general metaphysical viewpoint." M. Masterman, "The Nature of a Paradigm," in *Criticism and the Growth of Knowledge*, ed. I. Lakatos and A. Musgrave (London, 1970), pp. 61-5. Without precisely defining his sense of the term, Coats has argued that economics "has been dominated throughout its history by a single paradigm — the theory of economic equilibrium via the market mechanism." A. W. Coats, "Is There a 'Structure of Scientific Revolutions' in Economics'?" *Kyklos*, 22 (1969) p. 292. Similarly, Bronfenbrenner first defines a paradigm as a "mode of framework of thought and language" and then gives instances of paradigms, such as the demand-and-supply cross, the equation of exchange, and Hicksian IS-LM curves, which are much more specific than a mode or a framework. M. Bronfenbrenner, "The 'Structure of Revolutions' in Economic Thought," *History of Political Economy*, 3 (Spring 1971) p. 150.

15. For some convincing biographical evidence, see R. D. Collison Black, "W. S. Jevons and the Foundation of Modern Economics," and W. Jaffé, "Léon Walras's Role in the 'Marginal Revolution' of the 1870s," in *Marginal Revolution*. As N. B. de Marchi argues, Mill and Cairnes were actually in possession of all the pieces required to make the breakthrough to marginal utility economics, but could not do so because of their Ricardian blinkers: "Mill and Cairnes and the Emergence of Marginalism in England," in *Marginal Revolution.*

16. I am making tacit reference to a great debate that was started in the 1940s with an article by C. G. Hempel. See P. Gardiner, ed., *Theories of History* (Glencoe, Ill., 1959); and S. Hook, ed., *Philosophy and History: A Symposium* (New York, 1963).

17. For this useful distinction, see J. J. Spengler, "Exogenous and Endogenous Influences in the Formation of Post-1870 Economic Thought: A Sociology of Knowledge Approach," in *Events, Ideology, and Economic Theory*, ed. R. V. Eagly (Detroit, 1968).

18. G. J. Stigler, "The Adoption of the Marginal Utility Theory," in *Marginal Revolution.*

12   Entrepreneurship Before and After Schumpeter

Capitalism is usually defined as an economic system in which the means of production are privately held. But private ownership of the means of production may involve a number of separate functions: the provision of financial capital, the employment and co-ordination of the factors of production, the management and administration of the entire enterprise, and the ultimate power of making strategic decisions about investment. The existence of capital markets and the invention of the principle of limited liability makes it possible completely to separate the supply of financial capital from all the other functions. Likewise, the hiring of inputs and the functions of routine management and administration can be almost completely delegated to salaried employees. That leaves the power of making the fundamental decisions to invest or not to invest, to enter a new market or to leave an old one, etcetera, as the only function that cannot be hived off: a businessman need not to be a "capitalist" or "manager" but he must be a decision-maker, whether he liked it or not. It is his function and this function along that deserves the title of "entrepreneurship".

Given the vital role of entrepreneurship in an economic system characterised by private ownership of capital, the analysis of entrepreneurship must, surely, occupy a central role in the investigations of economists? Or so one might have thought before studying the subject! However, when we open any current textbook of elementary economics, we discover that entrepreneurship is hardly mentioned, or mentioned only in passing. Is this some sinister conspiracy of silence, or are economists so confused about the nature of economics as to ignore what is staring them in the face?

It was not always thus: the strange disappearance of the entrepreneur from the centre of the stage of economic debate has a long history. Adam Smith in *The Wealth of Nations* (1776) clearly separated the functions of the capitalist from those of the manager, and he emphasised the fact that "profits" of the capitalist exclude the "wages" of management as a payment for "the labour of inspection and direction". However, Adam Smith did not distinguish in any way between the capitalist as the provider of the "stock" of the enterprise and the entrepreneur as the ultimate decision-maker. He did use the terms "projector" and "undertaker" as the English equivalents of the French word "entrepreneur" but only as synonyms for the business proprietor. This failure to isolate the entrepreneurial function from that of pure ownership of capital became the standard practice of all the English classical economists. Thus, the term "entrepreneur" or any of its English equivalents is totally absent in the writings of David Ricardo and so is the concept of the businessman as the principal agent of economic change.

Some would argue that the English classical economists may be forgiven for having amalgamated the functions of the capitalist and the entrepreneur. Of course, the corporate form of business organisation, in which the capitalist role of the stockholders is sharply distinguished from the decision-making role of managers and entrepreneurs, had been invented centuries before. Nevertheless, until the "railway mania" of the 1840s, trading on the British stock exchange was largely confined to government bonds and public utility stocks and the prevalent form of business ownership in the heyday of the Industrial Revolution was the small to medium-sized family firm, the capital funds being provided by the owner, his relatives, or his friends. No wonder then that the classical economists failed to highlight the distinctive character of the entrepreneurial function.

On further reflection, however, this historical explanation of the neglect of entrepreneurship in English classical political economy appears somewhat unconvincing. The fact of the matter is that the concept of the entrepreneur as having a function quite distinct from that of both the capitalist and the manager had already been formalised by a remarkable French economist of the eighteenth century, Richard Cantillon, writing some twenty years before Adam Smith.

Richard Cantillon had the remarkable insight that discrepancies between demand and supply in a market create opportunities for someone to buy cheap and to sell dear and that it is precisely this sort of arbitrage which brings competitive markets into equilibrium. He named people who take advantage of these unrealised profit opportunities "entrepreneurs", that is, those who are willing "to buy at a certain price and sell at an uncertain price". Moreover, he noted that action of this kind need not involve manufacture and need not absorb the personal funds of the entrepreneur, although it frequently did. In short, for Cantillon entrepreneurship is a matter of foresight and willingness to assume risk, which is not necessarily connected with the employment of labour in some productive process. Cantillon therefore left no doubt of the difference between the functions of the entrepreneur and the capitalist.[1]

Adam Smith read Cantillon but took no notice of his analysis of entrepreneurship. Similarly, David Ricardo had the benefit of Jean Baptiste Say's writings, which leaned heavily on Cantillon in distinguishing between the provision of capital to a business enterprise, on the one hand, and the function of superintendence, direction, control, and judgment, on the other (Hébert and Link, 1982, pp. 29-35). Nevertheless, there is not so much as a hint of the special role of entrepreneurship in Ricardo. It is evident that Ricardo, and for that matter virtually all the other leading English classical economists, regarded production and the investment of capital as a more or less automatic process, involving no critical decision-making and certainly no risky judgment or imagination of any kind. Ricardo recognised that the first capitalist to introduce a novel improvement such as a new machine is liable to reap extra returns but this did not lead him to single out the capacity to innovate as the feature which distinguished one capitalist from another.

And exactly the same thing is true of Marx. Despite his emphasis on the constant accumulation of capital, on the remorseless pressure under competition to introduce labour-saving machinery to keep ahead of rivals, on the need under capitalism to innovate or to perish, Marx too treated the business process as virtually automatic once the required capital was forthcoming.[2] The only aspect of production that was problematic for Marx was what he called "the labour process", the control and direction of the work force so as to secure the intensity of human effort that could never be properly specified in the written employment contract. According to Marx, squeezing the work force to make greater efforts is one of the two principal sources of extra profits for capitalists, the other being the introduction of new machinery. But there is never any problem in Marx about which new machines the capitalist is to introduce; likewise in Marx, there appear to be no choices to make about the size of the business, or the number of products to manufacture, or the type of market to penetrate. The businessman in Marx is simply capital personified as the "despot" of the work place. In other words, Marx, like all economists before him and since him, realised that the action of competition requires differences in behaviour among economic agents (after all, if they all acted exactly the same in the face of the same circumstances, economic change and progress would be impossible to explain). Nevertheless, Marx took no interest in these individual differences among capitalists that alone account for the dynamic evolution of the capitalist system.

Marx knew perfectly well that capitalists can borrow all their capital from banks, which is why he regarded "interest" on capital as a deduction from the "profits" of the enterprise. He also knew that the special skills of managers, including the skills of monitoring and supervising the labour force, can be hired on the labour market. But he never considered whether the residual income left over after paying the interest on borrowed capital and the wages of management corresponds to any particular economic function, for example, the function of buying inputs at certain prices and selling the output at uncertain prices, as a result of which there may be losses rather than profits. He must have thought either that decision-making under uncertainty, which is what is involved in operating a business enterprise, entails no risks, or that if it does, there is an unlimited supply of people in a capitalist economy willing to take such risks. At any rate, Marx simply conflated the functions of the capitalist and the entrepreneur and in that sense simply carried on where Adam Smith and David Ricardo left off. In short, Marx, who claimed to be alone in truly analysing the "laws of motion" of capitalism, had simply no explanation to give of the actual source of the acknowledged technical dynamism of capitalism.

For the first entirely adequate statement of the entrepreneurial role, we must go not to Marx, or even to Cantillon or Say, but to the nineteenth-century German economist, Johann von Thünen. His remarkable but hopelessly obscure book, *The Isolated State*, Volume II (1850), defines the gains of the entrepreneur as being that which is left over from the gross profits of a business operation after paying (1) the actual or imputed interest on invested capital, (2) the wages of management, and (3) the insurance premium against the calculable risk of losses. The rewards of the entrepreneur, Thünen went on the say, are therefore the returns for incurring those risks which no insurance company will cover because they are unpredictable. Since novel action is precisely the condition under which it is impossible to predict the probability of gain or loss, the entrepreneur is "inventor and explorer in his field" *par excellence* (Hébert and Link, 1982, pp.45-7). Notice: this masterful grasp of the entrepreneur as the residual income claimant of a risky, unpredictable income, typified by but not confined to the innovative entrepreneur, predates the publication of Marx's *Capital* by seventeen years! Moreover, Marx had read Thünen's *Isolated State*. In short, let us not say that Marx identified the entrepreneur and the capitalist because he could not have known better.

John Stuart Mill's *Principles of Economics* (1848) popularised the term "entrepreneur" among English economists but failed to break the hold of the Smith-Ricardo tradition of the entrepreneur as simply a multifaceted capitalist. Soon thereafter, the new economic analysis that increasingly came to characterise professional economics after 1870 shifted attention away from the internal organisation of the business enterprise, thus eliminating the role of both the capitalist and the entrepreneur. The general equilibrium theory of Léon Walras, a central figure in the marginal revolution which ushered in the era of the neoclassical economics, provides a perfect example of how the new microeconomics caused the entrepreneur, as it were, to disappear. Every productive agent in a competitive economy, Walras tells us, is rewarded according to his marginal product, that is, the increment of output which is contributed by the marginal unit of that agent. Now suppose some economic agent hires others to produce a certain product; the hiring agent will be forced by competition to pay all the agents whom he employs their marginal product; this may leave him with something over and above the marginal product of his own services; if so, this merely induces the hired agents themselves to become the hiring agent, thus eliminating the positive residual; if, on the other hand, the residual proves to be negative, the hiring agent ceases to be a residual income recipient and rents the use of his services to others at the value of its marginal product; in either case, the residual always tends to become zero. The hiring agent is, of course, our friend the entrepreneur but Walras assumed that entrepreneurship is not itself a factor of production but rather a function that can be carried on by any agent, say, the capitalist or the salaried manager. In any case, with a zero residual income, the total product is, as neoclassical economists were fond of saying, exactly "exhausted" when all productive agents are paid their marginal products. When perfect competition has done its work, when we have reached short-run and long-run equilibrium, labour receives "wages" in accordance with the marginal product of labour, capital receives "interest" in accordance with the marginal product of capital goods, but "profits" have been eliminated and the entrepreneur, as Walras said, "neither benefits, nor loses" (Hébert and Link, 1982, pp. 63-4).

We are now at the heart of the question with which we began: why do modern economists neglect entrepreneurship? So long as economic analysis is preoccupied with the nature of static equilibrium under conditions of perfect competition, there is simply no room either for a theory of entrepreneurship or a theory of profits as the residual income-claim of persons who assume the risks associated with uncertainty. What the older classical economists had called "profits", or what Marx called "surplus value", is now said to be "interest" and of course perfect competition produces a positive rate of interest even in stationary equilibrium. But a permanent, positive residual over and above wages and interest can only be the result of constant technical progress disrupting the stationary state and the new neoclassical economics has little to say about the circumstances governing technical progress.

The growing popularity of general equilibrium theory set the seal on the possibility of theorising about entrepreneurship. As a matter of fact, static equilibrium analysis increasingly came to typify the study of economics as the nineteenth century gave way to the twentieth. And even in the 1930s when Keynesian macroeconomics arrived on the scene, Walrasian static equilibrium analysis was refurbished, a process which reached even greater stages of refinement in the 1950s. Despite valiant attempts to dynamise microeconomics, large parts of modern economics remain trapped in a static framework. Worse than that is the fact that modern economics lacks any true theory of the competitive *process*; what it actually possesses is the theory of the outcome of that process in an equilibrium *state*. In short, it emphasises equilibrium at the expense of disequilibrium. By assuming that all economic agents have free access to all the information they require for taking decisions, decision-making in modern economics is largely trivialised into the mechanical application of mathematical rules for optimisation. No wonder then that the elementary textbook of today is rich in the treatment of consumer behaviour, the profit-maximising decisions of business firms (in short-run equilibrium), the theory of wages, the theory of interest, the theory of international trade, etcetera, but poor in the analysis of technical change, the growth of big business, the causes of the wealth and poverty of nations — and the theory of entrepreneurship.[3]

This is the more remarkable in that this virtual consensus about the unimportance of entrepreneurship has been seriously questioned on at least two notable occasions in the twentieth century. The first occasion came with the publication of Frank Knight's *Risk, Uncertainty and Profit* (1921), an acknowledged classic of modern economics.

Knight began by elaborating on Thünen's distinction between "risk" and "uncertainty". Many uncertainties of economic life are like the chances of dying at a certain age: their objective probability can be calculated and to that extent they can be shifted via insurance to the shoulders of others. Such risks thus become an element in the costs of production, a deduction from and not a cause of profits or losses. There are other uncertainties, however, which can never be reduced to objective measurement because they involve unprecedented situations. "The only 'risk' which leads to profit", Knight remarked, "is a unique uncertainty resulting from an exercise of ultimate responsibility which in its very nature cannot be insured nor capitalized nor salaried" (quoted by Hébert and Link, 1982, p. 71).

The beauty of Knight's argument was to show that the presence of true "uncertainty" about the future may allow entrepreneurs to earn positive profits despite perfect competition, long-run equilibrium and "product exhaustation". Production takes place in anticipation of consumption, and since the demand for factors of production is derived from the expected demand of consumers for output, the entrepreneur is forced to speculate on the price of his final product. But it is impossible to determine the price of the final product without knowing what payments are being made to the factors of production. The entrepreneur resolves this dilemma by guessing the price at which output will sell, thereby translating the *known* marginal physical products of the factors of production into their *anticipated* marginal value products. Although the factors are hired on a contractual basis and therefore must be paid their anticipated marginal value product, the entrepreneur as a residual, non-contractual income-claimant may make a windfall gain if actual receipts prove greater than forecasted receipts.

Knight denied that this uncertainty theory of profits provides some sort of social justification for profits as a type of personal income. The argument is a subtle one: we cannot describe this non-contractual, windfall gain as a necessary price that must be paid for the performance of a specific service, the "painful" cost of bearing uncertainty, for that would imply a definite connection between the level of profit and the burden of bearing uncertainty. But no such definite connection exists. If it did exist, uncertainty-bearing would have all the characteristics of a productive factor and marginal productivity theory would apply to it: profits would equal the marginal product of entrepreneurship and would therefore constitute a standard charge on production. But profits are the windfall difference between the expected and realised returns of an enterprise and as such would cease to exist in a stationary economy in which all future events could be perfectly foreseen. So, it is not that profits are justified under capitalism but that capitalism is one way of ensuring that someone is willing to assume the "gamble" of undertaking production under uncertainty. This "gamble" can be socialised by collective ownership of the means of production and we can then ask: which system is better at generating successful "gambles"?; what we cannot do is to deny that production under any social system necessarily involves a "gamble".

Knight's book, although published over sixty years ago, has withstood criticism remarkably well. There was little problem about assimilating his contributions to orthodox economic ideas because Knight did not question static economic analysis so far as it went. Unfortunately, he failed to persuade orthodox economics that the uncertainty theory of profits was anything more than a footnote to mainstream analysis, tying together some loose ends that had been left lying around ever since Adam Smith. Economics was now provided with a satisfactory explanation of profits and entrepreneurship but, of course, the main focus of analysis continued to be the pricing of factors of production in accordance with marginal productivity principles under stationary conditions.

Ten years before the appearance of Knight's book, the young Schumpeter had contributed a wholly different view of *the* economic problem in *The Theory of Economic Development* (1911). In this book, entrepreneurship and its connection with dynamic uncertainty is placed at the centre of economic inquiry.[4] Schumpeter developed his argument by constructing a model of an economy in which technical change of any kind is absent. Such an economy, he contended, would settle down to a repetitive and perfectly routine economic process in which there is no uncertainty about the future. Hence, there would be no profits in such an economy and, moreover, even the rate of interest would fall to zero. In short, competitive long-run stationary equilibrium as visualised in traditional theory rules out both profit and interest. Schumpeter's claim that only technical innovations and dynamic change can produce a positive rate of interest has been hotly disputed (see Haberler, 1951; Samuelson, 1981) but at the expense of considering his associated views on innovation and enterprise. Distinguishing between "invention" and "innovation" — the discovery of new technical knowledge and its practical application to industry — and defining "innovations" broadly as the introduction of new technical methods, new products, new sources of supply, and new forms of industrial organisation, Schumpeter traced all disrupting economic change to innovations and identified the innovator with the entrepreneur. The entrepreneur is the source of all dynamic change in an economy and for Schumpeter (1942, Chs. 7, 12) the capitalist system cannot be understood except in terms of the conditions giving rise to entrepreneurship.

As in all the previous theories of entrepreneurship, the entrepreneur in Schumpeter is a functional role which is not necessarily embodied in a single physical person and certainly not in a well-defined group of people. The entrepreneur may be a capitalist or even a corporate manager but whether all these different functions are combined in one or more persons depends on the nature of capital markets and on the forms of industrial organisation. But Schumpeter went even further than his predecessors in recognising that the same person may be an entrepreneur when he is an innovating businessman, only to lose that character as soon as he has built up his business and settled down to running it along routine lines. Thus, the actual population of entrepreneurs in a capitalist economy is constantly changing because the function of entrepreneurship is typically mixed up with other kinds of activity.

Schumpeter's influence on entrepreneurial theory has been overwhelming and subsequent writers on entrepreneurship have usually defined their own position by contrasting it with his. In the meanwhile, however, mainstream economic theory has continued to neglect Schumpeter's writings on entrepreneurship as it continues to neglect Knight's theory of profits because neither fits in with static equilibrium analysis. The theory of entrepreneurship has, however, been given a new lease of life by the modern Austrian school, descending from Ludwig von Mises and Friedrich Hayek. In two closely reasoned books, *Competition and Entrepreneurship* (1973) and *Perception, Opportunity and Profit* (1979), a student of von Mises, Israel Kirzner, has sought once again to persuade his fellow economists that the properties of disequilibrium states deserve as much attention as those of equilibrium states. Disequilibria are due to intertemporal and interspatial differences in demand and supply and hence give rise to unrealised profit opportunities. The essence of entrepreneurship, for Cantillon as much as for Kirzner, consists in the personal alertness to such potential sources of gain. There is a subtle change of emphasis in Kirzner's discussion of entrepreneurship from that of Schumpeter's: Schumpeter always portrayed the entrepreneur-innovator as a disequilibrating force disturbing a previous equilibrium, whereas Kirzner (1973, pp. 72-4, 79-81, 126-31; 1979, Ch. 7) depicts him as seizing upon a disequilibrium situation and working to restore equilibrium. But not too much should be made of this change of emphasis, which is no doubt a reflection of the state of contemporary economic theory in 1911 and 1973: in the days before World War I, economists needed convincing that an achieved state of general equilibrium is the exception and not the rule, whereas nowadays economists need convincing that the process of arriving at general equilibrium has never been satisfactorily explained.

Unfortunately, the new Austrian theory of entrepreneurship reduces entrepreneurship to any kind of arbitrage and in so doing wipes out most of the crucial questions that have been posed about entrepreneurship. The popular stereotype of the entrepreneur as a swashbuckling business tycoon may take too narrow a view of entrepreneurship but, on the other hand, the Austrian conception of the entrepreneur as anyone who buys cheap and sells dear is so general as to dissolve practically all the questions one cares to ask about entrepreneurship. As Demsetz has said (in Ronen, 1983, p. 277) entrepreneurship in new Austrian theory is "little more than profit maximization in a context in which knowledge is costly and imitation is not instantaneous". A more promising approach to the theory of entrepreneurship is offered in a recent study by Mark Casson who synthesises and extends previous work by Knight, Schumpeter, Kirzner and many others. Casson defines an entrepreneur as "someone who specializes in taking judgmental decisions about the coordination of scarce resources" (Casson, 1982, p. 23), every term in this definition being carefully chosen to highlight the specific content of the entrepreneurial role. The entrepreneur is a person, not a team, committee or organisation, and he is someone who has a comparative advantage in making decisions; moreover, he reaches a different decision from other people in the face of identical circumstances either because of access to better information or because of a different interpretation of the same information. The entrepreneurial function is, in principle, performed in all societies by individuals whose judgment differs from the norm, and military and political life may provide as much scope for entrepreneurship as the economic one. Capitalism then is simply an economic system that harnesses entrepreneurship to industrial decisions. Even economic entrepreneurship under capitalism, however, may range from pure arbitrage or financial speculation to the non-routine decisions of salaried managers and the daring innovations of self-employed businessmen. It is true, as Schumpeter argued, that ownership and entrepreneurship are conceptually separate functions and that one can be an entrepreneur without being a capitalist. Nevertheless, entrepreneurship in practice is likely to be packaged together with asset ownership because financial intermediaries are reluctant to lend to an entrepreneur precisely because the entrepreneur's assessment of a situation necessarily differs from everybody else's assessment, including that of the lender. In other words, personal wealth, or at least the wealth of friends and relatives, is in fact a major constraint on the scale of entrepreneurial activity and bank credit has only a limited role to play.

Casson's theory throws new light on the long-lived reluctance in economic thought to divorce proprietorship from entrepreneurship, thus identifying the capitalist with the entrepreneur. The industrial entrepreneur frequently was and still is a capitalist, and this association between the two roles is not accidental but stems from the very nature of entrepreneurship as consisting of an eccentric evaluation of economic events which other people are unwilling to support. Casson's theory also clears up another longstanding bone of contention in the history of entrepreneurship (see Kanbur, 1980; Ronen, 1983, pp. 147-9). Schumpeter (1951, pp. 251-2; 1954, p. 556) always insisted paradoxically that risk-bearing is not an entrepreneurial function and that all the risks of an enterprise are borne by the capitalist. Even accepting the Knightian distinction between risk and uncertainty, Schumpeter agreed with Knight that profits cannot be construed simply as an earned reward for the psychic pain of bearing uncertainty in the sense that smaller profits would discourage people from becoming entrepreneurs; it might or it might not, depending entirely on the number of risk-averters in a society. If we taxed away the profits of entrepreneurship or cut off industrial entrepreneurship by collectivising the means of production, all we might do, according to Schumpeter, is to drive entrepreneurship into non-economic activity. Casson (1982, Ch. 17) argues, however, that the profits of entrepreneurship are "earned income" in the true sense of the term. In the short run, the entrepreneur's reward is a "rent of ability", a temporary monopoly rent to superior judgment, and in the long run, it is in fact a necessary compensation for the time and effort involved in identifying and making judgmental decisions and obtaining financial backing to undertake the search for information. Since it is frequently the entrepreneur's own wealth that supports his activity, the entrepreneur risks his own capital but, in addition, he always risks the opportunity cost of his time and effort and the value of his "good will" for future operations.

Be that as it may, private ownership of the means of production and private entitlement to the profits of entrepreneurship do not lack economic justification. Entrepreneurship may be a universal feature of all society but capitalism provides a unique institutional setting to release the entrepreneurial spirit. The technical dynamism of capitalism, which Marx attributed to the organisational invention of the factory, the despotic control of the workers by capitalists, and the restless urge of the bourgeoisie to save and invest, must instead be credited in large part to the institution of private property rights, which channels the entrepreneurial spirit into productive outlets where previously it remained locked into speculative and purely merchandising activity. If we fully understood the nature of industrial entrepreneurship and the conditions under which is flourishes, and I do not claim that we have done more than scratch the surface of that subject, we would at long last be near to answering the great question with which economics began: what *are* the causes of the wealth of nations?

I do believe that Schumpeter in some respects takes us further towards an answer to this great question than does Marx. The entrepreneurial function is central to the workings of a capitalist society and yet there is no entrepreneurial function in Marx. Ah, Marxists will say, where is the entrepreneur without capitalist backing and without capitalist control of "the labour process"? Why label the entrepreneurial function the principal agent of economic change when the entrepreneur is in practice frequently capitalist and manager as well? I can only imagine how Schumpeter might have answered that question. Yes, he might have said, without control of the work force, without the constant monitoring of job performance, there are no profits and there is no growth. But is this a specifically capitalist phenomenon? Would a socialist society be able to dispense with the "labour process"? Yes, if labour-managed enterprises are feasible (as Marx thought they were) and No otherwise.[5] In short, Schumpeter would have said, any industrialised society must somehow get workers to work effectively. But industrial entrepreneurship — an individual taking a chance to introduce a new method or a new product — is specifically capitalist: it cannot be collectivised without being destroyed. That is why the growth of the large corporation is worrying because it may erode the institutional basis of dynamic entrepreneurship.

Let us call a halt to this imaginary dialogue and return to the main subject at hand: the neglect of entrepreneurship in modern, mainstream economics. Surely, this neglect must give us pause? It is a scandal that nowadays students of economics can spend years in the study of the subject before hearing the term "entrepreneur", that courses in economic development provide exhaustive lists of all the factors impeding or accelerating economic growth without mentioning the conditions under which entrepreneurship languishes or flourishes, and that learned comparisons between "socialism" and "capitalism" are virtually silent about the role of entrepreneurship under regimes of collective rather than private ownership.

NOTES

1. See the detailed treatment of Cantillon in Hébert and Link (1982, Ch. 3).
2. I am not the first to have noticed this. As Schumpeter (1954, p.556) said: "Ricardo, the Ricardians and also Senior ... almost accomplished what I have described as an impossible feat, namely, the exclusion of the figure of the entrepreneur completely. For them — as well as for Marx — the business process runs substantially by itself, the one thing needful to make it run being an adequate supply of capital". See also Schumpeter (1951, p.250) and Kirzner (1979, Ch. 3).
3. Again, this has been said before by others (e.g. Baumol, 1968; Leff, 1979; Kirzner, 1979, Ch. 7).
4. Even twenty-three years later, when Schumpeter (1934, p. xi) wrote a preface to the English translation of his book, he found himself moved to exclaim that the arguments of his book "might usefully be contrasted with the theory of [static] equilibrium, which explicitly or implicitly always has been and still is the centre of traditional theory".
5. In this respect, see the interesting discussion by A. Bergson of the innovatory process in Yugoslavian labour-managed enterprises (Ronen, 1983, Ch. 8).

REFERENCES

Baumol, W. (1968), "Entrepreneurship in Economic Theory", *American Economic Review*, 58, No. 2 (May 1968).

Casson, M. (1982), *The Entrepreneur. An Economic Theory* (Oxford).

Haberler, G. (1951), "Schumpeter's Theory of Interest", in *Schumpeter; Social Scientist*, ed. S. Harris (Cambridge, Mass.).

Hébert, R.F., Link, A.N. (1982), *The Entrepreneur. Mainstream Views and Radical Critiques* (New York).

Kanbur, S.M. (1980), "A Note on Risk Taking, Entrepreneurship, and Schumpeter", *History of Political Economy,* 12, No. 4, (Winter).

Kirzner, I. (1973), *Competition and Entrepreneurship* (Chicago).

—— (1979), *Perception, Opportunity, and Profit. Studies in the Theory of Entrepreneurship* (Chicago).

Leff, N. H. (1979), "Entrepreneurship and Development: The Problem Revisited", *Journal of Economic Literature* 17, No. 1 (March 1979).

Ronen, J. ed. (1983), *Entrepreneurship* (Lexington, Mass.).

Samuelson, P. A. (1981), "Schumpeter as an Economic Theorist", in *Schumpeterian Economics*, ed. H. Frisch (New York).

Schumpeter, J. A. (1934), *The Theory of Economic Development* (Boston, Mass.).

—— (1942), *Capitalism, Socialism, and Democracy* (New York).

—— (1951), *Essays of Joseph A. Schumpeter*, ed. R. V. Clemence (Cambridge, Mass.)

—— (1954), *History of Economic Analysis* (New York).

Part III
Methodology

13 Kuhn versus Lakatos, or Paradigms versus Research Programmes in the History of Economics *

In the 1950s and 1960s economists learned their methodology from Popper. Not that many of them read Popper. Instead, they read Friedman, and perhaps few of them realised that Friedman is simply Popper-with-a-twist applied to economics. To be sure, Friedman was criticised, but the "Essay on the Methodology of Positive Economics" nevertheless survived to become the one article on methodology that virtually every economist has read at some stage in his career. The idea that unrealistic "assumptions" are nothing to worry about, provided that the theory deduced from them culminates in falsifiable predictions, carried conviction to economists long inclined by habit and tradition to take a purely instrumentalist view of their subject.

All that is almost ancient history, however. The new wave is not Popper's "falsifiability" but Kuhn's "paradigms." Again, it is unlikely that many economists read *The Structure of Scientific Revolutions* (1962). Nevertheless, appeal to paradigmatic reasoning quickly became a regular feature of controversies in economics and "paradigm" is now the byword of every historian of economic thought.[1] Recently, however, some commentators have expressed misgivings about Kuhnian methodology applied to economics, throwing doubt in particular on the view that "scientific revolutions" characterise the history of economic thought.[2] With these doubts I heartily concur. I will argue that the term "paradigm" ought to be banished from economic literature, unless surrounded by inverted commas. Suitably qualified, however, the term retains a function in the historical exposition of economic doctrines as a reminder of the fallacy of trying to appraise particular theories without invoking the wider metaphysical framework in which they are embedded. This notion that theories come to us, not one at a time, but linked together in a more or less integrated network of ideas, is however better conveyed by Lakatos'

* An earlier version of this chapter was presented as a paper at the History of Economic Thought Society Conference in London, September 1974. I wish to express my thanks to A. W. Coats, N. de Marchi, J. Hicks, S. J. Latsis, D. P. O'Brien, R. Towse, and D. Winch for comments on this earlier draft and to the participants in the London conference for a helpful discussion of its contents.

233

"methodology of scientific research programmes." The main aim of my article is indeed to explore Lakatos' ideas in application to the history of economics.[3]

The task is not an easy one. Lakatos is a difficult author to pin down. His tendency to make vital points in footnotes, to proliferate labels for different intellectual positions, and to refer back and forth to his own writings — as if it were impossible to understand any part of them without understanding the whole — stands in the way of ready comprehension. In a series of papers, largely published between 1968 and 1971, Lakatos developed and extended Popper's philosophy of science into a critical tool of historical research, virtually resolving a long-standing puzzle about the relationship between positive history of science and normative methodology for scientists. The puzzle is this. To believe that it is possible to write a history of science "wie es eigentlich gewesen" without in any way revealing our concept of sound scientific practice or how "good" science differs from "bad" is to commit the Inductive Fallacy in the field of intellectual history; by telling the story of past developments one way rather than another we necessarily disclose our view of the nature of scientific explanation. On the other hand, to preach the virtues of *the* scientific method while utterly ignoring the question of whether scientists now or in the past have actually practised that method seems arbitrary and metaphysical. We are thus caught in a vicious circle, implying the impossibility both of a value-free, descriptive historiography of science and an ahistorical, prescriptive methodology of science.[4] From this vicious circle there is, I believe, no real escape, but what Lakatos has done is to hold out the hope that the circle may eventually be converted into a virtuous one.

Enough said by way of introduction. Let us look briefly at Popper and Kuhn, before putting Lakatos' "methodology of scientific research programmes" to work in a field such as economics.

1 FROM POPPER TO KUHN TO LAKATOS

Popper's principal problem in *The Logic of Scientific Discovery* (1965) was to find a purely logical demarcation rule for distinguishing science from non-science. He repudiated the Vienna circle's principle of verifiability and replaced it by the principle of falsifiability as the universal *a priori* test of a genuinely scientific hypothesis. The shift of emphasis from verification to falsification is not as innocent as appears at first glance, involving as it does a fundamental asymmetry between proof and disproof. From this modest starting point, Popper has gradually evolved over the years a powerful anti-inductionist view of science as an endless dialectical sequence of "conjectures and refutations."[5]

A hasty reading of *The Logic of Scientific Discovery* suggests the view that a single refutation is sufficient to overthrow a scientific theory; in other words, it convicts Popper of what Lakatos has called "naive falsificationism" (Lakatos and Musgrave, 1970, pp. 116, 181; Lakatos, 1971, pp. 109-14). But a moment's reflection reminds us that many physical and virtually all social phenomena are stochastic in nature, in which case an adverse result implies the improbability of the hypothesis being true, not the certainty that it is false. To discard a theory after a single failure to pass a statistical test would, therefore, amount to intellectual nihilism. Patently, nothing less than a whole series of refutations is likely to discourage the adherents of a probabilistic theory. A careful reading of Popper's work, however, reveals that he was perfectly aware of the so-called "principle of tenacity" — the tendency of scientists to evade falsification of their theories by the introduction of suitable *ad hoc* auxiliary hypotheses — and he even recognised the functional value of such dogmatic stratagems in certain circumstances.[6] Popper, in other words, is a "sophisticated falsificationist," not a "naive" one.[7]

In general, however, Popper deplores the tendency to immunise theories against criticism and instead advocates a bold commitment to falsifiable predictions, coupled with a willingness and indeed eagerness to abandon theories that have failed to survive efforts to refute them. His methodology is thus plainly a normative one, prescribing sound practice in science, possibly but not necessarily in the light of the best science of the past; it is an "aggressive" rather than a "defensive" methodology because it cannot be refuted by showing that most, and indeed even all, scientists have failed to obey its precepts.[8]

In Kuhn's *Structure of Scientific Revolutions*, the emphasis shifts from normative methodology to positive history: the "principle of tenacity," which for Popper presents something of an exception to best-practice science, becomes the central issue in Kuhn's explanation of scientific behaviour. "Normal science," or problem-solving activity in the context of an accepted theoretical framework, is said to be the rule, and "revolutionary science," or the overthrow of one "paradigm" by another in consequence of repeated refutations and mounting anomalies, the exception in the history of science. It is tempting to say that for Popper science is always in a state of "permanent revolution," the history of science being the history of continuous "conjectures and refutations"; for Kuhn, the history of science is marked by long periods of steady refinement, interrupted on occasions by *discontinuous* jumps from one ruling "paradigm" to another with no bridge for communicating between them.[9]

The judge a dispute such as this, we must begin by defining terms. In the first edition of his book, Kuhn frequently employed the term "paradigm" in a dictionary sense to stand for certain exemplary instances of scientific achievement in the past. But he also employed the term in quite a different sense to denote both the choice of problems and the set of techniques for analysing them, in places going so far as to give "paradigm" a still wider meaning as a general metaphysical *Weltanschauung*; the last sense of the term is, in fact, what most readers take away from the book. The second edition of *The Structure of Scientific Revolutions* (1970) admitted to terminological imprecision in the earlier version[10] and suggested that the term "paradigm" be replaced by "disciplinary matrix"; "disciplinary" because it refers to the common possession of the practitioners of a particular discipline; "matrix" because it is composed of ordered elements of various sorts, each requiring further specification" (Kuhn, 1970, p. 182). But whatever language is employed, the focus of his argument remained that of "the entire constellation of beliefs, values, techniques and so on shared by the members of a given community," and he went on to say that if he were to write his book again, he would start with a discussion of the professionalisation of science before examining the shared "paradigms" or "disciplinary matrices" of scientists (p. 173).

These are not fatal concessions for the simple reason that the distinctive feature of Kuhn's methodology is not the concept of paradigms that everyone has seized on, but rather that of "scientific revolutions" as sharp breaks in the development of science, and particularly the notion of a pervasive failure of communications during periods of "revolutionary crises." Let us remind ourselves of the building bricks of Kuhn's argument: the practitioners of "normal science," although widely scattered, form an "invisible college" in the sense that they are in agreement both on the "puzzles" that require solution and on the general form that the solution will take; moreover, only the judgment of colleagues is regarded as relevant in defining problems and solutions, in consequence of which "normal science" is a self-sustaining, cumulative process of puzzle solving within the context of a common analytical framework; the breakdown of "normal science" is heralded by a proliferation of theories and the appearance of methodological controversy; the new framework offers a decisive solution to hitherto neglected "puzzles" and this solution turns out in retrospect to have long been recognised but previously ignored; the old and new generations talk past each other as "puzzles" in the old framework becomes "counterexamples" in the new; conversion to the new approach takes on the nature of a religious experience, involving a "gestalt switch"; and the new framework conquers in a few decades, to become in turn the "normal science" of the next generation.

The reader who is acquainted with the history of science thinks immediately of the Copernican revolution, the Newtonian revolution, or the Einstein-Planck revolution. The so-called Copernican revolution, however, took a hundred and fifty years to complete and was argued out every step of the way; even the Newtonian revolution took more than a generation to win acceptance throughout the scientific circles of Europe, during which time the Cartesians, Leibnizians, and Newtonians engaged in bitter disputes over every aspect of the new theory; likewise, the switch in the twentieth century from classical to relativistic and quantum physics involved neither mutual incomprehension nor quasi-religious conversions, at least if the scientists directly involved in the "crisis of modern physics" are to be believed.[11] It is hardly necessary, however, to argue these points, because in the second edition of his book Kuhn candidly admits that his earlier description of "scientific revolutions" suffered from rhetorical exaggeration: paradigm changes during "scientific revolutions" do not imply absolute discontinuities in scientific debate, that is, a choice between competing but totally incommensurate theories; mutual incomprehension between scientists during a period of intellectual crisis is only a matter of degree; and the only point of calling paradigm changes "revolutions" is to underline the fact that the arguments that are advanced to support a new paradigm always contain ideological elements that go beyond logical or mathematical proof (Kuhn, 1970, pp.199-200).[12] As if this were not enough, he goes on to complain that his theory of "scientific revolutions" was misunderstood as referring solely to major revolutions, such as the Copernican, Newtonian, Darwinian, or Einsteinian; he now insists that the schema was just as much directed at minor changes in particular scientific fields, which might not seem to be revolutionary at all to those outside "a single community [of scientists], consisting perhaps of fewer than twenty-five people directly involved in it" (pp.180-1).

In short, in this later version of Kuhn, any period of scientific development is marked by a large number of overlapping and inter-penetrating "paradigms"; some of these may be incommensurable but certainly not all of them are; "paradigms" do not replace each other immediately and, in any case, new "paradigms" do not spring up full-blown but instead emerge as victorious in a long process of intellectual competition. It is evident that these concessions considerably dilute the apparently dramatic import of Kuhn's original message, and in this final version the argument is difficult to distinguish from the average historian's account of the history of science. What remains, I suppose, is the emphasis on the role of values in scientific judgments, particularly in respect of the choice between competing approaches to science, together with a vaguely formulated but deeply held suspicion of cognitive factors like epistemo-logical rationality, rather than sociological factors like authority, hier-archy, and reference groups, as determinants of scientific behaviour. What Kuhn has really done is to conflate prescription and description, deducing his methodology from history, rather than to criticise history with the aid of a methodology. Kuhn does his best, of course, to defend himself against the charge of relativism and to explain "the sense in which I am a convinced believer in scientific progress" (Kuhn, 1970, pp. 205-7), but the defence is not altogether convincing. Actually, a wholly convincing defence would reduce his account of "scientific revolutions" to a nonsense.

Which brings us to Lakatos.[13] As I read him, Lakatos is as much appalled by Kuhn's lapses into relativism as he is by Popper's ahistorical if not antihistorical standpoint.[14] The result is a compromise between the "aggressive methodology" of Popper and the "defensive methodology" of Kuhn, but a compromise which stays within the Popperian camp;[15] Lakatos is "softer" on science than Popper, but a great deal "harder" than Kuhn, and he is more inclined to criticise bad science with the aid of good methodology than temper methodological speculations by an appeal to scientific practice. For Lakatos, as for Popper, methodology has nothing to do with laying down standard procedures for tackling scientific problems; it is concerned with the "logic of appraisal," that is, the normative problem of providing criteria of scientific progress. Where Lakatos differs from Popper is that this "logic of appraisal" is then employed at one and the same time as a historical theory which purports to retrodict the development of science. As a normative methodology of science, it is empirically irrefutable because it is a definition. But as a historical theory, implying the scientists in the past did in fact behave in accordance with the methodology of falsifiability, it is perfectly refutable. If history fits the normative methodology, we have reasons additional to logical ones for subscribing to fallibilism. If it fails to do so, we are furnished with possible reasons for abandoning our methodology. No doubt, Hume's Guillotine tells us that we cannot logically deduce ought from is or is from ought. We can, however, influence ought by is and vice versa: moral judgments may be altered by the presentation of facts, and facts are theory-laden so that a change of values may alter our perception of the facts. But all these problems lie in the future. The first task is to re-examine the history of science with the aid of explicit falsificationist methodology to see if indeed there is any conflict to resolve.

Lakatos begins by denying that isolated theories are the appropriate units of appraisal; what ought to be appraised are clusters of inter-connected theories or "scientific research programmes" (SRP). Duhem and Poincaré had argued long ago that no individual scientific hypothesis is conclusively verifiable or falsifiable, because we always test the particular hypothesis in conjunction with auxiliary statements and therefore can never be sure whether we have confirmed or refuted the hypothesis itself. Since any hypothesis, if supplemented with suitable auxiliary assumptions, can be maintained in the face of contrary evidence, its acceptance is merely conventional. Popper met this "conventionalist" argument by distinguishing between "*ad-hoc*" and "*non-ad-hoc*" auxiliary assumptions; it is perfectly permissible to rescue a falsified theory by means of a change in one of its auxiliary assumptions, if such a change increases the empirical content of the theory by augmenting the number of its observational consequences; it is only changes which fail to do this that Popper dismissed as "*ad hoc*".[16] Lakatos generalises this Popperian argument by distinguishing between "progressive and degenerating problem shifts." A particular research strategy or SRP is said to be "*theoretically progressive*" if a successive formulation of the programme contains "excess empirical content" over its predecessor, "that is, . . . predicts some novel, hitherto unexpected fact"; it is "empirically progressive if this excess empirical content is corroborated" (Lakatos and Musgrave, 1970, p. 118), Contrariwise, if the programme is characterised by the endless addition of *ad hoc* adjustments that merely accommodate whatever new facts become available, it is labelled "degenerating."

These are relative, not absolute distinctions. Moreover, they are applicable, not at a given point in time, but over a period of time. The forward-looking character of a research strategy, as distinct from a theory, defies instant appraisal.[17] For Lakatos, therefore, an SRP is not "scientific" once and for all; it may cease to be scientific as time passes, slipping from the status of being "progressive" to that of being "degenerating" (astrology is an example), but the reverse may also happen (parapsychology?). We thus have a demarcation rule between science and non-science which is itself historical, involving the evolution of ideas over time as one of its necessary elements.

The argument is now extended by dividing the components of an SRP into rigid parts and flexible parts. "The history of science," Lakatos observes, "is the history of research programmes rather than of theories," and "all scientific research programmes may be characterized by their 'hard core,' surrounded by a protective belt of auxiliary hypotheses which has to bear the brunt of tests." The "hard core" is irrefutable by "the methodological decision of its protagonists" — shades of Kuhn's "paradigm"! — and it contains, besides purely metaphysical beliefs, a "positive heuristic" consisting of "a partially articulated set of suggestions or hints on how to change, develop the 'refutable variants' of the research-programme, how to modify, sophisticate, the 'refutable' protective belt" (Lakatos and Musgrave, 1970, pp. 132-5).[18] The "protective belt," however, contains the flexible parts of an SRP, and it is here that the "hard core" is combined with auxiliary assumptions to form the specific testable theories with which the SRP earns its scientific reputation.

If the concept of SRP is faintly reminiscent of Kuhn's "paradigms," the fact is that Lakatos' picture of scientific activity is much richer than Kuhn's. Furthermore, it begins to provide insight as to why "paradigms" are ever replaced, a mystery which is one of the central weaknesses of

Kuhn's work. "Can there be any objective (as opposed to socio-psychological) reason to reject a programme, that is, to eliminate its hard core and its programme for constructing protective belts?" Lakatos asks. His answer, in outline, is that "such an objective reason is provided by a rival research programme which explains the previous success of its rival and supersedes it by a further display of heuristic power" (Lakatos and Musgrave, 1970, p. 155; also Lakatos, 1971, pp. 104-5). He illustrates the argument by analysing Newton's gravitational theory — "probably the most successful research programme ever" — and then traces the tendency of physicists after 1905 to join the camp of relativity theory, which subsumed Newton's theory as a special case.[19] The claim is that this move from one SRP to another was "objective," because most scientists acted as if they believed in the normative "methodology of scientific research programmes" (MSRP). Lakatos goes on to advance the startling claim that all history of science can be similarly described; he defines any attempt to do so as "internal history" (Lakatos, 1971, pp. 91-2).[20] "External history," in contrast, is not just all the normal pressures of the social and political environment that we usually associate with the word "external," but any failure of scientists to act according to MSRP, as, for example, preferring a degenerating SRP to a progressive SRP on the grounds that the former is more "elegant" than the latter, possibly accompanied by the denial that it is degenerating.[21] The claim that all history of science can be depicted as "internal" may of course be difficult to sustain in the light of historical evidence, but Lakatos recommends that we give priority to "internal history" before resorting to "external history." Alternatively, what we can do is "to relate the internal history *in the text*, and indicate in the footnotes how actual history 'misbehaved' in the light of its rational reconstruction" (Lakatos, 1971, p. 107), advice which Lakatos himself followed in his famous Platonic dialogue on the history of Euler's Conjecture on Polyhedrons (Lakatos, 1964).

In reply to Lakatos, Kuhn minimised the differences between them: "Though his terminology is different, his analytic apparatus is as close to mine as need be: hard core, work in the protective belt, and degenerating phase are close parallels for my paradigms, normal science, and crisis (Lakatos and Musgrave, 1970, p. 256). Kuhn insisted, however, that "what Lakatos conceives as history is not history at all but philosophy fabricating examples. Done in that way, history could not in principle have the slightest effect on the prior philosophical position which exclusively shaped it" (Kuhn, 1970, p. 143). This seems to ignore Lakatos' deliberate attempt to keep history as such separate from "philosophy fabricating examples" and provides no resolution of the dilemma which surrounds the historiography of science: either we infer our scientific methodology from the history of science, which commits the fallacy of induction, or we preach our methodology and rewrite history accordingly, which smacks of "false consciousness." [22]

Lakatos, replying to Kuhn, tries to score a logical victory for his own approach to the historiography of science by claiming that it is perfectly capable of postdicting novel historical facts, unexpected in the light of the extant approaches of historians of science. In that sense, the "methodology of historiographical research programmes" may be vindicated by MSRP itself: it will prove "progressive" if and only if it leads to the discovery of novel historical facts (Lakatos 1971, pp. 116-20). The proof of the pudding is therefore in the eating. It remains to be seen whether the history of a science, whether natural or social, is more fruitfully conceived, not as steady progress punctured every few hundred years by a scientific revolution, but as a succession of progressive research programmes constantly superseding one another with theories of ever-increasing empirical content. [23]

2 SCIENTIFIC REVOLUTIONS IN ECONOMICS

Both Kuhn and Lakatos jeer at modern psychology and sociology as pre-paradigmatic, proto-sciences, and although economics seems to be exempted from the charge, Lakatos seems to think that even economists have never seriously committed themselves to the principle of falsifiability: "The reluctance of economists and other social scientists to accept Popper's methodology may have been partly due to the destructive effect of naive falsificationism on budding research programmes" (Lakatos and Musgrave, 1970, p. 179 n). It is perfectly true that a dogmatic application of Popper to economics would leave virtually nothing standing, but it is a historical travesty to assert that economists have been hostile to Popper's methodology, at least in its more sophisticated versions. What is the central message of Friedman's "as-if" methodology if not commitment to the idea of testable predictions? And indeed, the pronouncements of nineteenth-century economists on methodology, summed up in John Neville Keynes' magisterial treatise *The Scope and Method of Political Economy* (1891), are squarely in the same tradition even if the language is that of verification rather than falsification plus or minus a naive Baconian appeal to "realistic" assumptions. The real question is whether the "principle of tenacity" does not figure much more heavily in the hstory of economics than in the history of, say, physics. [24] Analytical elegance, economy of theoretical means, and generality obtained by ever more "heroic" assumptions have always meant more to economists than relevance and predictability. They have in fact rarely practised the methodology to which they have explicitly subscribed, and that, it seems to me, is one of the neglected keys to the history of economics. The philosophy of science of economists, ever since the days of Senior and Mill, is aptly described as "innocuous falsificationism".[25]

Let us begin by reviewing the attempts to apply Kuhn's methodology to economics. What are the ruling "paradigms" in the history of economic thought? According to Gordon, "Smith's postulate of the maximizing individual in a relatively free market . . . is our basic paradigm"; "economics has never had a major revolution; its basic maximizing model has never been replaced . . . it is, I think, remarkable when compared to the physical sciences that an economist's fundamental way of viewing the world has remained unchanged since the eighteenth century" (Gordon, 1965, pp. 123, 124). Likewise, Coats asserts that economics has been "dominated throughout its history by a single paradigm — the theory of economic equilibrium via the market mechanism," but, unlike Gordon, Coats singles out the so-called Keynesian revolution as a paradigm change, a Kuhnian "scientific revolution," and subsequently he has claimed almost as much for the so-called marginal revolution of the 1870s (Coats, 1969, pp. 292, 293; Black, Coats, and Goodwin, 1973, p. 38; but see p. 337). Benjamin Ward, a firm believer in Kuhn's methodology, also dubs the Keynesian revolution a Kuhnian one, and furthermore he claims that the recent post-war period has witnessed a "formalist revolution" involving the growing prestige of mathematical economics and econometrics, which leaves him wondering why such a radical change should have made so little substantive difference to the nature of economics (Ward, 1972, pp. 34-48). Lastly, Bronfenbrenner, after defining a "paradigm" as "a mode or framework of thought and language," goes on to cite Keynesian macroeconomics, the emergence of radical political economy, the recent revival of the quantity theory of money, and the substitution of the Hicksian IS-LM cross for the Marshallian demand-and-supply cross as cases in point, a procedure which falls into the trap set by Kuhn himself (Bronfenbrenner, 1971, pp. 137-8). Bronfenbrenner identifies three revolutions in the history of economic thought: "a laissez-faire revolution," dating from Hume's *Political Discourses* in 1752; the marginal revolution of the 1870s as a "second possible revolution"; and the Keynesian revolution of 1936.

If we had not previously recognised the inherent ambiguities in Kuhn's concepts, this brief review would suffice to make the point. Be that as it may, it appears that if economics provides any examples at all of Kuhnian "scientific revolutions," the favourite example seems to be the Keynesian revolution, which at any rate has all the superficial appearance of a paradigm change. It is perfectly obvious, however, that the age-old paradigm of "economic equilibrium via the market mechanism," which Keynes is supposed to have supplanted, is actually a network of interconnected subparadigms; in short, it is best regarded as a Lakatosian SRP. It is made up, first of all, of the principle of constrained maximisation,

"Smith's postulate of the maximizing individual in a relatively free market," or what Friedman calls for short the "maximization-of-returns hypothesis." The principle of maximising behaviour subject to constraints is then joined to the notion of general equilibrium in self-regulating competitive markets to produce the method of comparative statics, which is the economist's principal device for generating qualitative predictions of the signs rather than the magnitudes of his critical variables. The "hard core" or metaphysical part of this programme consists of weak versions of what is otherwise known as the "assumptions" of competitive theory, namely, rational economic calculations, constant tastes, independence of decision-making, perfect knowledge, perfect certainty, perfect mobility of factors, etcetera. If they are not stated weakly, they become refutable by casual inspection and cannot, therefore, be held as true *a priori*. The "positive heuristic" of the programme consists of such practical advice as (1) divide markets into buyers and sellers, or producers and consumers; (2) specify the market structure; (3) create "ideal type" definitions of the behavioural assumptions so as to get sharp results; (4) set out the relevant *ceteris paribus* conditions; (5) translate the situation into an extreme problem and examine first- and second-order conditions; etcetera. It is evident that the marginalists after 1870 adopted the "hard core" of classical political economy, but they altered its "positive heuristic" and provided it with a different "protective belt."

Keynes went still further in tampering with the "hard core" that had been handed down since the time of Adam Smith. First of all, Keynes departed from the principle of "methodological individualism," that is, of reducing all economic phenomena to manifestations of individual behaviour. Some of his basic constructs, like the propensity to consume, were simply plucked out of the air. To be sure, he felt impelled by tradition to speak of a "fundamental psychological law," but the fact is that the consumption function in Keynes is not derived from individual maximising behaviour; it is instead a bold inference based on the known, or at that time suspected, relationship between aggregate consumer expenditure and national income. On the other hand, the marginal efficiency of capital and the liquidity-preference theory of the demand for money are clearly if not rigorously derived from the maximising activity of atomistic economic agents. Similarly, and despite what Leijonhufvud would have us believe, Keynes leaned heavily on the concepts of general equilibrium, perfect competition, and comparative statics, making an exception only for the labour market, which he seems to have regarded as being inherently imperfect and hence always in a state, not so much of disequilibrium as of equilibrium of a special kind.[26]

The real novel aspects of Keynes, however, are, first of all, the tendency to work with aggregates and indeed to reduce the entire economy to three interrelated markets for goods, bonds, and labour; secondly, to concentrate on the short period and to confine analysis of the long period, which had been the principal analytical focus of his predecessors, to asides about the likelihood of secular stagnation; and thirdly, to throw the entire weight of adjustments to changing economic conditions on output rather than prices. Equilibrium for the economy as a whole now involved "underemployment equilibrium," and the introduction of this conjunction, an apparent contradiction in terms, involved a profound change in the "hard core" of nineteenth-century economics, which undoubtedly included the faith that competitive forces drive an economy towards a steady state of full employment. Furthermore, the classical and neoclassical "hard core" had always contained the idea of rational economic calculation, involving the existence of certainty equivalents for each uncertain future outcome of current decisions. Keynes introduced pervasive uncertainty and the possibility of destabilising expectations, not just in the "protective belt" but in the "hard core" of his programme. The Keynesian "hard core," therefore, really is a new "hard core" in economics. The Keynesian "protective belt" likewise bristled with new auxiliary hypotheses: the consumption function, the multiplier, the concept of autonomous expenditures, and speculative demand for money, contributing to stickiness in long-term interest rates. It is arguable, however, whether there was anything new in the marginal efficiency of capital and the saving-investment equality. Keynesian theory also had a strong "positive heuristic" of its own, point the way to national income accounting and statistical estimation of both the consumption function and the period multiplier. There is hardly any doubt, therefore, that Keynesian economics marked the appearance of a new SRP in the history of economics.

Furthermore, the Keynesian research programme not only contained "novel facts" but it also made novel predictions about familiar facts: it was a "progressive research programme" in the sense of Lakatos. Its principal novel prediction was the chronic tendency of competitive market economies to generate unemployment. Now, the fact that there was unemployment in the 1930s was not itself in dispute. Orthodox economists had no difficulty in explaining the persistence of unemployment. The government budget in both the United States and Britain was in surplus during most years in the 1930s. It did not need Keynes to tell economists that this was deflationary. It was also well known that monetary policy between 1929 and 1932 was more often tight than easy; at any rate, neither the United States nor the United Kingdom pursued a consistent expansionary monetary policy. Furthermore, the breakdown of the international gold standard aggravated the crisis. There was, in other words, no lack of explanations for the failure of the slump to turn into a boom, but the point is that these explanations were all "*ad hoc*," leaving intact the full-employment-equilibrium implications of standard theory. The tendency of economists to join the rank of the Keynesians in increasing numbers after 1936 was therefore perfectly rational; it was a switch from a "degenerating" to a "progressive" research programme, which had little to do with contentious issues of public policy.

This assertion is likely to arouse consternation because we all have been taken in, to a greater or lesser extent, by the mythology which has come to surround the Keynesian revolution. According to the Walt Disney version of inter-war economics, the neoclassical contemporaries of Keynes are supposed to have believed that wage cutting, balanced budgets, and an easy-money policy would soon cure the Great Depression. It comes as a great surprise to learn from Stein (1969) and Davis (1971) that no American economist between 1929 and 1936 advocated a policy of wage cutting; the leaders of the American profession strongly supported a programme of public works and specifically attacked the shibboleth of a balanced budget. A long list of names, including Slichter, Taussig, Schultz, Yntema, Simons, Gayer, Knight, Viner, Douglas and J. M. Clark, concentrated mainly at the universities of Chicago and Columbia but with allies in other universities, research foundations, and government and banking circles, declared themselves in print well before 1936 in favour of policies that we would today call Keynesian. Similarly, in England, as Hutchison (1968) has shown, names such as Pigou, Layton, Stamp, Harrod, Gaitskell, Meade, E.A.G. and J. Robinson came out publicly in favour of compensatory public spending. If there were any anti-Keynesians on questions of policy, it was Cannan, Robbins, and possibly Hawtrey, but definitely not Pigou, the bogeyman of the *General Theory*.[27] This, by the way, explains the reactions of most American and British reviewers of the *General Theory*: they questioned the new theoretical concepts, but dismissed the policy conclusions of the book as "old hat."

A fair way of summarising the evidence is to say that most economists, at least in the English-speaking countries, were united in respect of practical measures for dealing with the Depression, but utterly disunited in respect of the theory that lay behind these policy conclusions. What orthodoxy there was in theoretical matters extended only so far as microeconomics. Pre-Keynesian macroeconomics in the spirit of the quantity theory of money presented an incoherent mélange of ideas culled from Fisher, Wicksell, Robertson, Keynes of the *Treatise*, and Continental writers on the trade cycle. In a sense then the Keynesian theory succeeded because it produced the policy conclusions most economists wanted to advocate anyway, but it produced these as logical inferences from a tightly knit theory and not as endless epicycles on a full-employment model of the economy.[28]

It would seem that certain puzzles about the Keynesian revolution dissolve when it is viewed through Lakatosian spectacles. The attempt to give a Kuhnian account of the Keynesian revolution, on the other hand, creates the image of a whole generation of economists dumbfounded by the persistence of the Great Depression, unwilling to entertain the obvious remedies of expansionary fiscal and monetary policy, unable to find even a language with which to communicate with the Keynesians, and, finally, in despair, abandoning their old beliefs in an instant conversion to the new paradigm. These fabrications are unnecessary if instead we see the Keynesian revolution as the replacement of a "degenerating" research programme by a "progressive" one with "excess empirical content." Moreover, in this perspective, we gain a new insight into the post-war history of Keynesian economics, a history of steady "degeneration" as the Keynesian prediction of chronic unemployment begins to lose its plausibility. In the 1950s, the contradiction between cross-section and time-series evidence of the savings-income ratio, the former yielding a declining and the latter a constant average propensity to save, spawned a series of revisions in the Keynesian research programme, from Duesenberry's relative income hypothesis to Friedman's permanent income hypothesis to Modigliani's life-cycle theory of saving. Simultaneously, Harrod and Domar converted static Keynesian analysis into a primitive theory of growth, a development which discarded principal elements in the Keynesian "protective belt" and more or less the whole of the "hard core" of the original Keynesian programme. Friedman's monetarist counter-revolution went a good deal further, and for a few years in the late 1960s it almost looked as if Keynes had been decisively repudiated. The efforts of Patinkin, Clower and Leijonhufvud to give a disequilibrium interpretation of Keynesian economics, and thus to integrate Keynesian theory into a more general neoclassical framework with still greater "excess empirical content," would seem to constitute a "progressive" research programme, superseded both static pre-Keynesian microeconomics and static Keynesian macroeconomics. Keynes' *General Theory* is now a special case, and this is scientific progress in economics, perfectly analogous to the absorption of Newton as a special case in the general theory of relativity.

It is possible to give a similar "internalist" account of the so-called marginal revolution as further demonstration of the applicability of MSRP to economics. The difficulties in the standard notion that marginalism was a new "paradigm" in economics were thoroughly thrashed out at the Bellagio Conference (see Black, Coats and Goodwin, 1973) and it is only necessary to add that the innovations of Menger, Jevons, and Walras are more suitably described, not as a new SRP, but as a "progressive problem shift" in the older research programme of classical political economy. As frequently happens in such cases, there was "loss of content" as well as gain. What was lost, such as theories of population growth and capital accumulation, had become by the 1860s an incoherent body of ideas, virtually empty of empirical implications. The reaction against the classical school was more a reaction against Ricardo than against Adam Smith. The Ricardian system was itself a "progressive problem shift" in the Smithian research programme, motivated by the experiences of the Napoleonic wars and designed to predict the "novel fact" of the rising price of corn, leading in turn to rising rents per acre and a declining rate of profit. The "hard core" of Ricardo is indistinguishable from that of Adam Smith, but the "positive heuristic" contains elements which would certainly have surprised Adam Smith, and this explains the difficulties that many commentators have experienced in identifying disciples of Ricardo who were not also disciples of Adam Smith.[29]

I once argued that the distinctive feature of the Ricardian system was, not the labour theory of value, not Say's law, not even the inverse relation between wages and profits, but "the proposition that the yield of wheat per acre of land governs the general rate of return on invested capital as well as the secular changes in the distributive shares" (Blaug, 1958, p. 3). The notion that Ricardo is at one and the same time the heir of Adam Smith and his principal critic can be conveyed succinctly in the language of MSRP. All the leading British classical economists up to Jevons and even up to Sidgwick subscribed to the basic Ricardian link between the productivity of agriculture and the rate of capital accumulation, and it is in this sense that we can speak of a dominant Ricardian influence on British economic thought throughout the half-century from Waterloo to the Paris Commune. There are unmistakable signs after 1848 of "degeneration" in the Ricardian research programme, marked by the proliferation of "*ad hoc*" assumptions to protect the theory against the evidence that repeal of the Corn Laws in 1848 had failed to bring about the effects predicted by Ricardo (Blaug, 1968, pp. 227-8).[30] On the other hand, the Ricardian research programme was by no means dead by 1850 or even 1860. Cairnes' work on the Australian gold discoveries and Jevons' study *The Coal Question* (1865) showed that there was still unrealised potential in the Ricardian system. Nevertheless, Mill's "recantation" of the wages fund theory in 1859 expressed a widely felt malaise, typical of those who find themselves working within a steadily degenerating SRP.

The trouble with this line of argument is that Ricardo did not exert a preponderant influence on Continental economic thought. There is absolutely no evidence of any widespread sense of increasing discomfort in France or Germany around 1870 with classical economic doctrine, conceived broadly on the lines of Adam Smith rather than of Ricardo. What was missing in the British tradition, it was felt, was the utility theory of value, which had roots on the Continent going back to Condillac, Galiani, and even Aristotle. What we see in Menger and even more in Walras, therefore, is the attempt to concentrate attention on the problem of price determination at the expense of what Baumol has called the "magnificent dynamics" in Smith, Ricardo and Mill, in the course of which due emphasis was given to the neglected demand side. This could be seen, and indeed was seen, as an improvement rather than an outright rejection of Adam Smith. There was no room in this schema for the specifically Ricardian elements, except in afterthoughts about long-run tendencies. In the Continental perspective, that is, the whole of the Ricardian episode in British classical political economy was regarded as something of a detour from the research programme laid down by Adam Smith. In other words, whatever we say about Jevons and the British scene, there was no marginal revolution on the Continent: there was a "problem shift," possibly even a "progressive problem shift," if predictions about "the price of an egg" may be regarded as more testable than predictions about the effects of giving free rein to the workings of "the invisible hand."

Clearly, economists after 1870, or rather 1890, reassessed the nature of the facts that economics ought to be concerned with. It is conceivable that this "gestalt switch" can only be explained in terms of "external history." If so, and particularly if we lack any independent corroboration for this historical explanation, we have a refutation of MSRP as a metahistorical research programme. I have been arguing, however, that an "internalist" account makes it unnecessary to resort to "external factors." It would be premature, however, to arrive at that conclusion on the basis of my crude sketch of historical developments. Only a series of detailed case studies of the spread of marginalism on the Continent after 1870 could settle that question.[31] What I want to insist here is simply that MSRP gives us a powerful handle for attacking these problems.

3   THE THEORY OF THE FIRM AS A CASE IN POINT

It is tempting to bring the story forward and to ask whether MSRP is capable of shedding light on the apparent "degeneration" of the Marshallian research programme in the first two decades of the twentieth century, culminating in the debate on "empty economic boxes" and the emergence of the theory of monopolistic or imperfect competition; or the less controversial "degeneration" of the Austrian theory of capital after Wicksell's failure to resolve certain outstanding anomalies in the concept of an "average period of production"; or the startling failure of the Walrasian programme to make much progress until Hicks' *Value and Capital* (1939) and Samuelson's *Foundations* (1948) provided it with a new "positive heuristic"; and so forth and so forth. But I will resist these temptations[32] and turn instead to an examination of Latsis' indictment of the traditional theory of the firm, the first attempt in the literature to provide a case study of MSRP in economics.

Latsis argues convincingly that theories of perfect and imperfect competition may be considered together as forming part of the same neoclassical research programme in business behaviour with one identifiable "hard core," one "protective belt," and one "positive heuristic." The "hard core" is made up of "(1) profit-maximisation, (2) perfect knowledge, (3) independence of decisions, and (4) perfect markets".[33] The "protective belt" includes several auxiliary assumptions: "(1) product homogeneity, (2) large numbers, and (3) free entry and exit." The "positive heuristic" consists of "the analysis of equilibrium conditions as well as comparative statics" (Latsis, 1972, pp. 209, 212). This research programme is labelled "situational determinism" because "under the conditions characterising perfect competition the decision-maker's discretion in choosing among alternative courses of action is reduced simply to whether or not to remain in business" (Latsis, 1972, p. 209).[34] This seems to ignore the fact that, apart from remaining in business, the competitive firm also has to decide what output to produce. But the nub of the argument is that the firm either produces the profit-maximising level of output or no output at all: "I shall call situations where the obvious course of action (for a wide range of conceptions of rational behaviour) is determined uniquely by objective conditions (cost, demand, technology, numbers, etc.), *'single exit'* or 'straightjacket' situations" (Latsis, 1972, p. 211).

In other words, once an independent decision-maker with a well-ordered utility map in a perfect competitive market is given perfect information about the situation he faces, there is nothing left for him to do, according to neoclassical theory, but to produce a unique level of output, or else to go out of business. There is no "decision process," no "information search," no rules for dealing with ignorance and uncertainty in the theory: the problem of choice among alternative lines of action is so reduced that the assumption of profit maximisation automatically singles out one best course of action. The motivational assumptions of "orthodox theory," Latsis concludes, could be "weakened from profit maximisation to bankruptcy avoidance," without affecting its prediction (Latsis, 1972, p. 223).

But what are these predictions? The "positive heuristic" of the research programme is directed at such questions as "(1) Why do commodities exchange at given prices?; (2) What are the effects of changes in parameters (say demand) on the variables of our model once adjustment has taken place?" (Latsis, 1972, pp. 212-13). But Latsis spends little time considering the specific predictions of neoclassical theory under given circumstances. For example, a standard prediction of the traditional theory of the firm is that a change in the corporate income tax, being a change in a proportionate tax on business income, does not affect the level of output of a competitive firm in the short run because it does not alter the level of output at which profits are maximised; for that reason the theory predicts that the tax will not be shifted. There is a considerable literature which tends to refute that prediction (Ward, 1972, p. 18), and this is relevant, although not necessarily clinching, evidence against traditional theory and, by the way, in favour of the sales-maximisation hypothesis. Latsis largely ignores these and other refutations. At various points he does refer to evidence indicating that hightly competitive industries sometimes fail to behave in the way predicted by the theory (Latsis, 1972, pp. 219-20), but for the most part he takes it for granted that traditional theory has a poor predictive record.[35]

He has little difficulty in showing that the habitual appeal to conditions of perfect competition as an "ideal type" fails to specify the limits of applicability of the traditional theory of profit maximisation, so that even the behaviour of oligopolists has come to be analysed with the same tools. But such "immanent criticism" tells us nothing about "the degree of corroboration" of a theory. For that we need a report on the past performance of the theory in terms of the severity of the tests it has faced and the extent to which it has passed or failed these tests.[36] Latsis provides no such report. In part, this is because his central argument is that all the programme's successive versions have failed to generate empirical results. But the fact of the matter is that they were thought to do so. For example, the Chamberlin tangency solution was supposed to predict excess capacity in the case of many sellers with differentiated products. Similarly, theories of joint profit maximisation under conditions of oligopoly were supposed to predict price rigidities. We cannot avoid asking, therefore, whether these predictions are borne out by the evidence.

Thus, it is difficult to escape the conclusion that Latsis' characterisation of the neoclassical theory of the firm as "degenerating" (Latsis, 1972, p. 234) is actually based on an examination of the theory's assumptions rather than its testable implictions. This conclusion is strengthened by considering his discussion of "economic behaviouralism" in the writings of Simon, Cyert and March, Williamson, and Baumol as a rival research programme in business behaviour. He usefully distinguishes "behaviouralism" from "organisationalism," the former emphasising learning and "slack" in a fluid and only partially known environment, the latter emphasising the survival needs of organisations; "behaviouralism" is applicable to a single decision-maker but "organisationalism" denies that there are such animals and insists that the objectives of decision-makers should not be postulated *a priori* but ascertained *a posteriori* by observation of decision-making in the real world. Traditional theory turns the decision-maker into a cypher, whereas both behavioural and organisational theories focus attention on the nature and characteristics of the decision-making agent or agents; they do so by repudiating all "hard core" concepts of optimisation, rejecting even the notion of general analytical solutions applicable to all business firms facing the same market situation.

It would be premature, Latsis argues, to attempt an appraisal of "behaviouralism" as a budding research programme. The approach may have potential for problems to which the traditional theory is unsuited but "neoclassical theory gives some simple answers to questions which we cannot even start asking in terms of behaviouralism (namely, in the domain of market structure and behaviour)" (Latsis, 1972, p. 233). Likewise, behaviouralism has not "successfully predicted any unexpected novel fact" and "as a research programme, it is much less rich and much less coherent than its neoclassical opponent" (Latsis, 1972, p. 234). But lest this imply the superiority of traditional theory, Latsis hastens to add that these are uncommensurable research programmes: "the two approaches are, in my view, importantly different and mutually exclusive over an extensive area" (Latsis, 1972, p. 233).[37] In other words, the neoclassical research programme is condemned as "degenerating" although it has no rival in its own domain, and furthermore, the condemnation is based on the logic of single-exit determinism and not on its record of repeated refutations. In the final analysis, therefore, Latsis denies the normative "hard core" of MSRP: neoclassical theory is primarily rejected because it is theoretically sterile and only secondarily because it fails to be empirically corroborated. There is nothing wrong with such a criticism, but it is less than might have been expected from an application of MSRP to economics.

There is a further point. One of the promising features of Lakatos' methodology is the insistence that we literally cannot appraise single theories: we test theories, but we appraise research programmes. The neoclassical research programme is much more than a theory of the firm; it is also a theory of the determination of wage rates and interest rates, and it includes, and some would say it starts with, a theory of consumer behaviour. If the neoclassical research programme in the economics of industry is to be written of as "degenerating," the rot should show up in the theory of factor pricing and in the theory of demand. One can sympathise with an author who declines to review the whole of microeconomics in order to assess its "degree of corroboration," but that is no excuse for not mentioning the entire research programme. It is certainly impossible to understand the tenacious defence of marginalism in the field of business behaviour without recognition of the fact that what is at stake is the whole of price theory.[38] Here, as elsewhere, Latsis seems to me to do less than justice to Lakatos' methodology.

4 DO ECONOMISTS PRACTISE WHAT THEY PREACH?

Having said that much, it only remains for me to do what I criticise Latsis for not doing, namely, to appraise the whole of neoclassical economics with the aid of Lakatos' methodology. But I am not equal to that task. What I will do is to voice some misgivings about the applicability of any philosophy of science grounded in the history of the physical science to a social science like economics. I express these misgivings tentatively. If they are widely shared, so much the worse for the prospect of writing an entirely "internalist" history of economic thought.

I begin by quoting Machlup, who in his long career has returned repeatedly to problems of the methodology of economics:

When the economist's prediction is *conditional*, that is, based upon specified conditions, but where it is not possible to check the fulfilment of all the conditions stipulated, the underlying theory cannot be disconfirmed whatever the outcome observed. Nor is it possible to disconfirm a theory where the prediction is made with a stated *probability* value of less than 100 per cent; for if an event is predicted with, say, 70 per cent probability, any kind of outcome is consistent with the prediction. Only if the same "case" were to occur hundreds of times could we verify the stated probability by the frequency of "hits" and "misses." This does not mean complete frustration of all attempts to verify our economic theory. But it does mean that the tests of most of our theories will be more nearly of the character of *illustrations* than of verifications of the kind possible in relation with repeatable controlled experiments or with recurring fully-identified situations. And this implies that our tests cannot be convincing enough to compel acceptance, even when a majority of reasonable men in the field should be prepared to accept them as conclusive, and to approve the theory so tested as "not disconfirmed" (Machlup, 1955, p. 19).[39]

This passage may be read as a criticism of "naive falsificationism," but it may also be read as a plea for still more "sophisticated falsificationism." It is precisely because tests of economic theories are "more nearly of the character of illustrations than of verifications" (I would prefer to say "falsifications") that we need as many "illustrations" as possible. But that implies that we concentrate our intellectual resources on the task of producing well-specified falsifiable predictions; in other words, we give less priority to such standard criteria of appraisal as simplicity, elegance and generality, and more priority to such criteria as predictability and empirical fruitfulness. It is my impression, however, that most modern economists would order their priorities precisely the other way round.

Ward's book asks *What's Wrong with Economics?* and his answer in brief is that economics is basically a normative policy science travelling in the false disguise of a positive one. Insofar as it is a positive science, however, he agrees that "the desire systematically to confront the theory with fact has not been a notable feature of the discipline," although that, he contends, "is not the central difficulty with modern economics" (Ward, 1972, p. 173). What I want to argue, by way of contrast, is that the central weakness of modern economics is in fact the reluctance to produce theories which yield unambiguously refutable implications.

When, in the long process of refining and extending the neoclassical research programme over the last hundred years, have we ever worried about "excess empirical content," much less "corroborated excess empirical content"? Consider, for example, the preoccupation since 1945 of some of the best brains in modern economics with problems of growth theory, when even practitioners of the art admit that modern growth theory is all about "shadows of real problems, dressed up in such a way that by pure logic we can find solutions for them" (Hicks, 1965, p. 183). But that example is too easy. Take rather that part of the neoclassical research programme which comes closest in matching the rigour and elegance of quantum physics, the modern theory of consumer behaviour, based on axiomatic utility theory, to which a long line of economists from Fisher, Pareto, Slutsky and Johnson, to Hicks, Allen, Samuelson and Houthakker have devoted their most intense efforts. There is little sign that these prodigious labours have had a substantive impact on household budget studies or on the literature dealing with statistical demand curves. Or to switch fields, consider the endless arguments in textbooks on labour economics about the assumptions that underlie the misnamed "marginal productivity theory of wages" at the expense of space devoted to considering what the theory actually predicts and how well it has fared. If this is not misplaced emphasis, what is? We all recognise that misplaced emphasis at least implicitly, which is why Lipsey's textbook was so well received when it first appeared: to this day, its relative emphasis on empirical testing stands out among the current textbooks on elementary economics.

But surely economists engage massively in empirical research? Certainly they do, but much empirical work in economics is like "playing tennis with the net down": instead of attempting to refute testable predictions, economists spend much of their time showing that the real world bears out their predictions, thus replacing falsification, which is difficult, with confirmation, which is easy. A single example must suffice. Ever since Solow's celebrated article of 1957, estimation of aggregate Cobb-Douglas production functions for purposes of measuring the sources of economic growth and drawing inferences about the nature of technical progress has become a widespread practice in economic research. Ostensibly, such work tests the prediction that production functions in the aggregate obey the condition of constant returns to scale and that individual markets, despite trade unions and despite monopolies, impute prices to factors in accordance with the theory of perfect competition. More than a decade passed before Fisher (1971) showed conclusively that it is perfectly possible to obtain a good fit of an aggregate Cobb-Douglas production function even if the underlying pricing mechanism is anything but competitive. But long before that, several econometricians had argued convincingly that the concept of aggregate production functions, as distinct from microproduction functions, lacks a firm theoretical foundation.[40] If the advice was ignored, it was because most economists are delighted with puzzle-solving activity of an empirical kind even if it is virtually tantamount to "measurement without theory." Marshall used to say that "explanation is prediction written backwards." Many economists forget that prediction is not necessarily explanation written forwards.[41] It is only too easy to engage in empirical works that fail utterly to discriminate between competing explanations and which consist largely of mindless "instrumentalism."

Those who explicitly revolt against orthodoxy are often infected by the same disease. So-called Cambridge controversies in the theory of capital, which actually are controversies about the theory of functional income distribution, have raged on for twenty years without so much as a reference to anything but stylised facts, such as the constancy of the capital-output ratio and the constancy of labour's relative share, which turn out on examination not to be facts at all. The fundamental issue at stake between Cambridge U.K. and Cambridge U.S., we are told by no less an authority on the debate than Joan Robinson, is not so much the famous problem of how to measure capital as it is the question of whether saving determines investment instead of investment determining saving.[42] That issue depends in turn on the question of whether the world is better described by full employment or by underemployment equilibrium. Inasmuch as the entire debate is carried out in the context of steady-state growth theory, and as everyone agrees that steady-state growth is never even approximated in real economics, there is no reason whatever for refusing to operate with both models, depending on the problem at hand. Neither model has any predictive power, and Cambridge controversies, therefore, are incapable of being resolved by empirical research. This has not, however, prevented either side from battling over the issues with redoubled fury. Protagonists in both camps have described the controversy as a war of "paradigms," but in fact the two "paradigms" intersect and indeed overlap almost entirely.

Even the radical political economists in the United States have spent most of their efforts on "telling a new story": the same old facts are given a different interpretation around the "paradigm" of power conflict in contrast to the "paradigm" of utility maximisation in mainstream economics (see Worland, 1972). What little empirical work has appeared in the *Review of Radical Political Economy* on race and sex discrimination, the financial returns to education, and patterns of social mobility in the United States has lacked discriminating, well-articulated hypotheses that could distinguish between orthodox and radical predictions (see Bronfenbrenner, 1970). But the movement does at least have the excuse of explicitly announcing its preference for social and political relevance over simplicity, generality and falsifiability as characteristics of "good" theory.[43]

Neoclassical economists do not have the same excuse. They preach the importance of submitting theories to empirical tests, but their practice suggests that what they have in mind is merely "innocuous falsificationism." Of all the great modern economists who have advocated a falsificationist methodology — Harrod, Koopmans, Friedman, Samuelson, Baumol and Boulding — Friedman is almost the only one whose analysis and research exemplify his own precepts. His work on Marshallian demand curves, on the expected-utility hypothesis, on flexible exchange rates, and particularly on the permanent-income hypothesis is marked by a constant search for refutable predictions. *The Theory of the Consumption Function* (1957) is surely one of the most masterly treatments of the relationship between theory and data in the whole of the economic literature. But even Friedman produced his "theoretical framework for monetary analysis" long after making dramatic claims of direct empirical evidence in favour of the quantity theory of money (see Friedman, 1970). As a monetarist, even Friedman has failed to live up to his own methodology.[44]

I have left to the last the issue of welfare economics, where of course no questions of testable implications can arise. Here the Lakatos methodology is helpless because there is nothing in the physical sciences that corresponds to theories which deduce the nature of a social optimum from certain fundamental value judgments. Economists have talked a great deal of nonsense about "value-free" welfare economics on the curious argument that the standard value judgments that underlie the concept of a Pareto optimum — every individual is the best judge of his own welfare; social welfare is defined only in terms of the welfare of individuals; and the welfare of individuals may not be compared — command wide assent and this consensus somehow renders them "objective." They have also swallowed whole the untenable thesis that "normative" as distinct from "methodological" value judgments are not subject to rational discourse and have thus denied themselves a fruitful area of analysis.[45] But these issues apart, the intimate relationship between normative and positive economics has been a potent source of "ad hoccery" in economics, the effort to retain theories at all costs by the addition of assumptions that lack testable implications.

No doubt, welfare economics and positive economics are separable in principle. However, practical policy recommendations typically violate the logical separability of the two. Decision-makers demand as much advice on their objectives as on the means to achieve these objectives, and the supply of advice naturally responds accordingly. Besides, as Samuelson said in the *Foundations*: "At least from the time of the physiocrats and Adam Smith, there has never been absent from the main body of economic literature the feeling that in some sense perfect competition represented an optimal situation." The modern Invisible Hand theorem provides a rigorous demonstration of that feeling: every long-run perfectly competitive equilibrium yields an optimal allocation of resources, and every optimum allocation of resources is a long-run perfectly competitive equilibrium. Of course, this leaves out the "justice" of the associated distribution of personal income; furthermore, "optimal allocation" is strictly defined with reference to the three basic value judgments of Paretian welfare economics. Nevertheless, every economist feels in his bones that the Invisible Hand theorem is almost as relevant to socialism as to capitalism, coming close indeed to a universal justification for the role of market mechanisms in any economy. It is hardly surprising, therefore, that economists fight tooth and nail when faced with an empirical refutation of a positive theory involving the assumption of perfect competition. For what is threatened is not just that particular theory but the entire conception of "efficiency" which gives raison d'être to the subject of economics. No wonder then that the "principle of tenacity" — the fear of an intellectual vacuum — looms so large in the history of economics.

The upshot of this long harangue is to suggest that MSRP may not fit the history of economics: economists may cling to "degenerating" research programmes in the presence of rival "progressive" research programmes, while denying that the "degenerating" programme is in need of resuscitation because they are suspicious of hard data, inclined to assign low priority to the discovery of novel facts, accustomed by long habit to deny the feedback of evidence on theory, or simply because they are deeply attached to the welfare implications of their theories. If this should prove to be the case after a detailed examination of twentieth-century economics with the aid of MSRP, it may tell us something more fundamental about the difference between natural and social science than the old saws about the unchanging universe of physics and the continually changing universe of economics.

5   CONCLUSIONS

Lakatos' metahistorical research programme has a "hard core" of its own: scientists are rational and accept or reject ideas for good intellectual reasons, the only problem being to determine what these are. The programme also has a "protective belt" which contains such propositions as these: scientists attach importance to the ability of theories to survive tests but they do not discard theories after a single failure; scientists appraise programmes, not theories; scientists appraise programmes historically as they evolve over time and continually revise their appraisals; lastly, scientists appraise programmes in competition with rivals and will retain a programme at any cost if no alternatives are available. The "positive heuristic" of the metahistorical research programme is equally obvious: collect theories into research programmes; spell out the "hard core," "the protective belt," and "the positive heuristic" of the respective programmes; examine the efforts that have been made to test theories, and trace the manner in which falsifications are dealt with in the programme; set out the anomalies that are recognised by practitioners of a programme and, if possible, the anomalies that have come to be forgotten; trace the standards by which the adherents of a research programme judge their predecessors and by which they hope to be judged by their followers, that is, analyse their methodological pronouncements; and, finally, highlight the novel facts which are discovered in the course of a programme. The object of the exercise is to show that most scientists join research programmes that have "excess empirical content" and desert research programmes that lack this characteristic. This is "internal history," and every other reason for joining one camp rather than another is "external." It was Lakatos' claim that the "rational reconstruction" of the history of science conceived in these terms would in fact need few footnotes referring to "external history."

Can the history of economics be written in this fashion? It is perfectly true that most externalist accounts of scientific progress are very persuasive — they are selected to be so. When certain theories become the ruling scientific ideas of their times for "good" internalist reasons, there are frequently also ideological reasons that make the theory palatable to vested interests and appealing to the man in the street. These can be invoked subsequently to argue that the theory was in fact accepted for external reasons (consider Malthus' theory of population, or Darwin's theory of natural selection). But such externalist explanations, while not wrong, are nevertheless redundant if we have regard to professional rather than popular opinion. To be convincing, the externalist thesis in the history of ideas must produce instances of (1) internally consistent, well corroborated, fruitful, and powerful scientific ideas which were rejected at specific dates in the history of a science because of specific external factors, or (2) incoherent, poorly corroborated, weak scientific ideas which were in fact accepted for specific external reasons. I can think of no unambiguous examples of either (1) or (2) in the history of economics and therefore conclude that a Lakatosian "rational reconstruction" would suffice to explain virtually all past successes and failures of economic research programmes.

NOTES

1. Similarly, sociologists have seized avidly on the Kuhnian apparatus: See, e.g., Ryan (1970), pp. 233-6, Martins (1972) and the collection of essays in Whitley (1974).
2. See Coats (1969), Bronfenbrenner (1971), and Kunin and Weaver (1971).

3. I dedicate this chapter to the memory of Imre Lakatos, Professor of Logic and the Philosophy of Science at the London School of Economics, who died suddenly at the age of fifty-one on February 2, 1974. We discussed an early draft of this paper a number of times in the winter of 1973 and, for the last time, the day before his death. He promised me a rebuttal, which now alas I will never read.
4. One of Lakatos' fundamental papers (1971, p.91) opens with a paraphrase of one of Kant's dictums, which perfectly expresses the dilemma in question: "Philosophy of science without history of science is empty: history of science without philosophy of science is blind."
5. Not to mention his formulation of a political philosophy, generated by the same conception. For a splendid, if somewhat hagiographic, introduction to the wide sweep of Popper's work, see Magee (1973).
6. For example: "In point of fact, no conclusive disproof of a theory can ever be produced; for it is always possible to say that the experimental results are not reliable, or that the discrepancies which are asserted to exist between the experimental results and the theory are only apparent and that they will disappear with the advance of our understanding" (Popper, 1965, p.50; see also pp.42, 82-3, 108); in the same spirit, see Popper (1962) II, pp.217-20, Popper (1972) p.30, and Popper in Schilpp (1974) I, p.82.
7. Economists will recognise immediately that Lipsey really was a "naive falsification in the first edition of his *Introduction to Positive Economics* and only adopted "sophisticated falsificationism" in the third edition of the book: see Lipsey (1966) pp.xx, 16-17.
8. I owe the vital distinction between "aggressive methodologies" and "defensive methodologies" to Latsis (1974). Popper does make references to the history of science, and clearly Einstein is his model of a great scientist. Nevertheless, he is always insistent on the metaphysical and hence irrefutable basis of the falsifiability principle (see, e.g. Schilpp, 1974, II, pp.1036-7).
9. See the revealing criticism of Popper by Kuhn and the equally revealing criticism of Kuhn by Popper (Lakatos and Musgrave, 1970, pp.14-15, 19, 52-5).
10. Masterman (Lakatos and Musgrave, 1970, pp.60-5) has in fact identified twenty-one different definitions of the term "paradigm" in Kuhn's 1962 book.
11. Toulmin (1972) pp.103-5. Of all the many critiques that Kuhn's book has received (Lakatos and Musgrave, 1970), and references cited by Kunin and Weaver, 1971), none is more devastating than that of Toulmin (1972, pp.98-117), who traces the history of Kuhn's methodology from its first announcement in 1961 to its final version in 1970. For an extraordinarily sympathetic but equally critical reading of Kuhn, see Suppe (1974) pp.135-51.
12. This is almost obvious because if two "paradigms" were truly incommensurable, they could be held simultaneously, in which case there would be no need for a "scientific revolution": the strong incommensurability thesis is logically self-contradictory (Achinstein, 1968, pp.91-106). What Kuhn must have meant is "incommensurability to some degree," and the new version is simply a belated attempt to specify the degree in question.
13. My sketch of recent developments in the philosophy of science omits discussion of such influential writers as Feyerabend, Hanson, Polanyi and Toulmin, who have each in their own ways challenged the traditional positivist account of the structure of scientific theories. But see Suppe (1974), whose masterful essay of book length covers all the names mentioned above. Lakatos, however, is deliberately omitted in Suppe's account (Suppe, 1974, p.166n.).
14. See the characteristic reaction of Popper to Kuhn: "to me the idea of turning

for enlightenment concerning the aims of science, and its possible progress, to sociology or to psychology (or ... to the history of science) is surprising and disappointing" (Lakatos and Musgrave, 1970, p.57).

15. Bloor (1971, p. 104) seems wide of the mark in characterising Lakatos' work as "a massive act of revision, amounting to a betrayal of the essentials of the Popperian approach, and a wholesale absorption of some of the most characteristic Kuhnian positions."

16. Although Popper's distinction succeeds in refuting "conventionalism," it tends to erode the fundamental asymmetry between verification and falsification which is the linchpin of his philosophy of science: see Grünbaum (1973) pp.569-629, 848-9. Archibald (1967) illustrates the problem of distinguishing *ad hoc* auxiliary assumptions in testing the Keynesian theory of income determination.

17. If the term "scientific research programmes" strikes some readers as vague, it must be remembered that the term "theory" is just as vague. It is in fact difficult to define "theory" precisely, even when the term is employed in a narrow sense: see Achinstein (1968) Ch. 4.

18. Lakatos' "hard core" expresses an idea similar to that conveyed by Schumpeter's notion of "Vision" — "the preanalytic cognitive act that supplies the raw material for the analytic effort" (Schumpeter, 1954, pp.41-3) — or Gouldner's "world hypotheses," which figure heavily in his explanation of why sociologists adopt certain theories and reject others (Gouldner, 1971, Ch. 2). Marx's theory of "ideology" may be read as a particular theory about the nature of the "hard core"; Marx was quite right in believing that "ideology" plays a role in scientific theorising but he was quite wrong in thinking that the class character of ideology was decisive for the acceptance or rejection of scientific theories.

19. However, he is not committed to the belief that every progressive SRP will be more general than the degenerate SRP which it replaces. There may well be a Kuhnian "loss of content" in the process of passing from one SRP to another, although typically the overlap between rival programmes will be larger than either the content-loss or content-gain.

20. This is what Suppe (1974, pp.53-6) has called the "thesis of development by reduction," namely, that scientific progress comes largely, and even exclusively, by the succession of more comprehensive theories which include earlier theories as special cases. The thesis, even in its weaker version, has been hotly debated by philosophers of science for many years.

21. Lakatos holds that one cannot rationally criticise a scientist who sticks to a degenerating programme if, recognising it is degenerating, he is determined to resuscitate it. This is somewhat contradictory. Feyerabend (1975, pp.185-6) seizes on this weakness and others in a penetrating but sympathetic critique of Lakatos from the standpoint of epistemological anarchism (*ibid.*, Ch. 16, pp.181-220).

22. The dilemma in question is widely recognised by philosophers of science, as well as historians of science: see, e.g., Lakatos and Musgrave (1970) pp.46, 50, 198, 233, 236-8; Achinstein's comments on Suppe (Suppe, 1974, pp.350-61); and Hesse's essay in Teich and Young (1973).

23. Contrast Kuhn (1957) and Lakatos and Zahar (1978) on the so-called Copernican revolution. See also Zahar (1973) and Feyerabend (1974) on the Einsteinian revolution and Urbach (1974) on the IQ debate. For several other case studies applying Lakatos' MSRP to the history of physics, chemistry, and economics, presented at the Nafplion Colloquium on Research Programmes in

Physics and Economics, September 1974, see Howson, 1976; Latsis, 1976. For the only published application to economics to date, see Latsis (1972) discussed below.

24. "It may be said without qualification," Keynes wrote in *Scope and Method*, "that political economy, whether having recourse to the deductive method or not, must begin with observation and end with observation ... the economist has recourse to observation in order to illustrate, test, and confirm his deductive inferences" (Keynes, 1955, pp. 227, 232). But it is characteristic that most of Chapters 6 and 7, from which these sentences are drawn, is about the difficulties of verifying deductive inferences by empirical observations; we are never told when we may reject an economic theory in the light of the evidence or indeed whether any economic theory was ever so rejected.

25. I owe this happy phrase to an unpublished paper by A. Coddington.

26. The best single piece of evidence for this statement is Keynes' reaction to Hicks' famous paper, "Mr. Keynes and the Classics." "I found it very interesting," he wrote to Hicks, "and really have next to nothing to say by way of criticism." Since Hicks' IS-LM diagram ignores the labour market, the reaction is hardly surprising. On Leijonhufvud's reading of Keynes, see Blaug (1975) and the references cited there.

27. I ignore the Stockholm school, which developed, independently of any clearly discernible influence from Keynes, most of the concepts and insights of Keynesian macroeconomics before the publication of either *The General Theory* (1936) or *The Means of Prosperity* (1933): see Uhr (1973). For Ohlin's recollections of the impact of Keynes of the Stockholm theorists, see Ohlin (1974) pp. 892-4.

28. Keynes himself put it in a nutshell. Writing to Kahn in 1937 with reference to D. H. Robertson and Pigou, he observed: "when it comes to practice, there is really extremely little between us. Why do they insist on maintaining theories from which their own practical conclusions cannot possibly follow? It is a sort of Society for the Preservation of Ancient Monuments' (Keynes, 1973, p. 259). A hint of the same argument is found in *The General Theory*: a footnote in the first chapter refers to Robbins as the one contemporary economist to maintain "a consistent scheme of thought, his practical recommendations belonging to the same system as his theory."

29. See, e.g., O'Brien (1970), who shows that even John Ramsay McCulloch, Ricardo's leading disciple, never succeeded in resolving the conflict in his mind between Smith and Ricardo.

30. In an illuminating paper on Ricardo's and John Stuart Mill's treatment of the relationship between theory and facts, de Marchi (1970) argues that Mill did not, as I have alleged, evade refutations of Ricardo's predictions by retreating into an unspecified *ceteris paribus* clause; he was simply careless with facts and declined to reject an attractive theory merely because it predicted poorly. The issue between us is one of subtle distinctions and, as I am going to argue later on, these distinctions still plague modern economics. Suffice it to say that a defensive attitude to the Ricardian system is increasingly felt in successive editions of the *Principles* and even more in the writings of Cairnes and Fawcett (Blaug, 1958, pp. 213-20).

31. Black, Coats, and Goodwin (1973) provide a few such case studies which seem to me to strengthen the internalist thesis.

32. I will also resist the temptation to apply MSRP to Marxian economics, which began badly to "degenerate" in the first decade of this century when the German Marxists failed to respond creatively to Bernstein's revisionism, and

which has continued to "degenerate" ever since, the unmistakable signs of which are endless regurgitation of the same materials, the continual substitution of appeals to authority for analysis, and a persistently negative attitude to empirical research.

33. This formulation strikes me as being too strong to constitute the irrefutable metaphysic of the neoclassical research programme, which only shows that two Lakatosians need not agree on how to apply MSRP to a particular case in question.

34. The phrase "situational determinism" is derived from Popper's *Open Society*, where *the* method of economic theory is described as "analysis of the situation, the situational logic" (cited in Latsis, 1972, p. 224).

35. In the same way, Friedman simply takes it for granted that traditional theory has a splendid predictive record: "An even more important body of evidence for the maximation-of-returns hypothesis is experience from countless applications of the hypothesis to specific problems and the repeated failure of its implications to be contradicted. This evidence is extremely hard to document; it is scattered in numerous memorandums, articles and monographs concerned primarily with specific concrete problems rather than with submitting the hypothesis to test. Yet the continued use and acceptance of the hypothesis over a long period, and the failure of any coherent, self-consistent alternative to be developed and widely accepted, is strong indirect testimony to its worth" (Friedman, 1953, p. 23). This is without doubt the most controversial passage of an otherwise persuasive essay because it is unaccompanied by even a single instance of these "countless applications." No doubt, when the price of strawberries rises during a dry summer, when an oil crisis is accompanied by a sharp rise in the price of oil, when share prices tumble after a deflationary budget, we may take comfort in the fact that the implications of the maximisation-of-return hypothesis have once again failed to be refuted. However, given the multiplicity of hypothesis that could account for the same phenomena, we can never be sure that the repeated failure to produce refutations is not a sign of the reluctance of economists to develop and test unorthodox hypotheses. It would be far more convincing to be told what economic events are excluded by the maximisation-of-returns hypothesis, or better still, what events, if they occurred, would impel us to abandon the hypothesis.

36. In Popper's words: "By the degree of corroboration of a theory I mean a concise report evaluating the state (at a certain time t) of the critical discussion of a theory, with respect to the way it solves its problems; its degree of testability; the severity of the tests it has undergone; and the way it has stood up to these tests. Corroboration (or degre of corroboration) is thus an evaluating *report of past performance*" (Popper, 1972, p. 18).

37. Loasby (1971) reaches the same conclusions, using Kuhn's methodology; like Latsis, he views profit maximisation as irrefutable because it is not a hypothesis but a "paradigm." In reply to Latsis, Machlup (1974) has seized eagerly on the admission of incommensurability between behaviouralism and marginalism, claiming that "a research programme designed to result in theories that explain and predict the actions of particular firms can never compete with the simplicity and generality of the marginalist theory, which, being based on the constructs of a fictitious profit-maximiser, cannot have the ambition to explain the behaviour of actual firms in the real world."

38. As Krupp has so aptly observed: "The degree of conformation of an entire theory is highly intertwined with value judgements which reflect, among other things, the selection of its constituent hypothesis. It is not coincidental, there-

fore, that the advocates of the theories of competitive price will simultaneously defend diminishing returns to scale, a low measure of economic concentration, the demand-pull explanation of inflation, a high consumption function, the effectiveness of monetary policies on full employment, the insignificance of externalities, and the general pervasiveness of substitution rather than complementarity as a basic relation of the economic system" (Krupp, 1966, p. 51).

39. In the same spirit, see Grunberg and Boulding in Krupp (1966).
40. For a fuller discussion, see Blaug (1974).
41. What I am denying is the well-known "thesis of the structural symmetry of explanation and prediction": see Hempel (1963) pp. 367-76 and Grünbaum (1973) Ch. 9.
42. For references and details, see Blaug (1974).
43. Franklin and Resnik (1974) pp. 73-4, provides a typical methodological pronouncement: "From a radical perspective, in which analysis is closely linked to advocacy of fundamental changes in the social order, an abstract model or category is not simply an aesthetic [sic] device. It is purposely designed to assist in the changes advocated, or in describing the nature of the barriers that must be broken down if the advocated changes are to occur."
44. The case of Friedman also illustrates the fact that agreement on falsificationism among modern economists disguises a significant spectrum of attitudes in respect of the type of test that is deemed appropriate in different circumstances. As Briefs (1961) argues, in an unduly neglected book, economists have always disagreed about the role of statistical significance tests versus that of historical analysis as alternative methods of refuting economic hypotheses; even supporters of statistical testing differ about the admissability of single-equation regressions in contrast to simultaneous equation estimates, depending in turn on whether the individual writer favours partial or general equilibrium analysis. Friedman's writings exemplify all three methods.
45. For the beginnings of such an analysis, see Sen (1970) pp. 58-64. The positive suggestions for reconstructing economics in Ward (1972) are along similar lines. It is worth noting that the failure to distinguish "methodological" and "normative" value judgments has been productive of much misunderstanding surrounding the value-fact dichotomy in social inquiry. Methodological judgments involve criteria for judging the validity of a theory, such as levels of statistical significance, selection of data and assessment of their reliability, adherence to the canons of formal logic, etcetera, which are indispensable in scientific work. Normative judgments, on the other hand, refer to ethical judgments about the desirability of certain kinds of behaviour and certain social outcomes. It is the latter which are said to be capable of being eliminated in positive science. See Nagel (1961) pp. 485-502, for almost the last word on this endlessly debated topic.

REFERENCES

Achinstein, P. (1968), *Concepts of Science* (Baltimore).

Archibald, G. C. (1967), "Refutation or Comparison?" *British Journal for the Philosophy of Science*, 17.

Black, R. D. C., A. W. Coats, and C. D. W. Goodwin, eds. (1973), *The Marginal Revolution in Economics: Interpretation and Evaluation* (Durham, N.C).

Blaug, M. (1958), *Ricardian Economics* (New Haven).

—— (1968), *Economic Theory in Retrospect*. 2nd edn. (Homewood, Ill).

—— (1974), *The Cambridge Revolution: Success or Failure?* (London).

—— (1975), "Comments on C.J. Bliss, 'Reappraisal of Keynesian Economics,'" in *Current Economic Problems: The Proceedings of the Association of University Teachers of Economics Conference, 1974*, eds. M. Parkin and A.R. Nobay (London).

Bloor, D. (1971), "Two Paradigms for Scientific Knowledge," *Science Studies*, 1.

Briefs, H.W. (1961), *Three Views of Method in Economics* (Washington).

Bronfenbrenner, M. (1970), "Radical Economics in America: A 1970 Survey," *Journal of Economic Literature*, 8 (September).

—— (1971), "The 'Structure of Revolutions' in Economic Thought," *History of Political Economy*, 3 (Spring).

Coats, A.W. (1969), "Is There a 'Structure of Scientific Revolutions' in Economics?" *Kyklos*, 22.

Davis, J.R. (1971), *The New Economics and the Old Economists* (Ames, Iowa).

de Marchi, N.B. (1970), "The Empirical Content and Longevity of Ricardian Economics," *Economica*, 37, (August).

Feyerabend, P.K. (1974), "Zahar on Einstein," *British Journal for the Philosophy of Science*, 25.

—— (1975), *Against Method. Outline of an Anarchistic Theory of Knowledge* (London).

Fisher, F.M. (1971), "Aggregate Production Functions and the Explanation of Wages: A Simulation Experiment," *Review of Economics and Statistics*, 53 (November).

Franklin, R.J., and S. Resnik (1974), *The Political Economy of Racism* (New York).

Friedman, M. (1953), *Essays in Positive Economics* (Chicago).

—— (1970), "A Theoretical Framework for Monetary Analysis," *Journal of Political Economy*, 78 (March/April).

Gordon, D.F. (1965), "The Role of the History of Economic Thought in the Understanding of Modern Economic Theory," *American Economic Review*, 55, (May).

Gouldner, A.W. (1971), *The Coming Crisis of Western Sociology* (London).

Grünbaum, A. (1973), *Philosophical Problems of Space and Time, Boston Studies in the Philosophy of Science*, ed. R.S. Cohen and M. Wartofsky (Dordrecht-Holland).

Hempel, C.G. (1963), *Aspects of Scientific Explanation* (New York).

Hicks, J. (1965), *Capital and Growth* (Oxford).

Howson, C. (1976), *Method and Appraisal in the Physical Sciences* (Cambridge).

Hutchison, T.W. (1968), *Economics and Economic Policy in Britain, 1964-1966* (London).

Keynes, J.M. (1973), *The Collected Writings of John Maynard Keynes: XIV. The General Theory and After*, Part II (London).

Keynes, J.N. (1955), *The Scope and Method of Political Economy*, 4th edn. (New York).

Krupp, R.S., ed. (1966), *The Structure of Economic Science: Essays on Methodology* (Englewood Cliffs, N.J.).

Kuhn, T.S. (1957), *The Copernican Revolution* (Cambridge, Mass).

—— (1970), *The Structure of Scientific Revolutions*, 2d edn. (Chicago).

Kunin, L., and F.S. Weaver (1971), "On the Structure of Scientific Revolutions in Economics," *History of Political Economy*, 3 (Fall).

Lakatos, I. (1964), "Proofs and Refutations, (I), (II), III), (IV)," *British Journal for the Philosophy of Science*, 14.

—— (1971), "History of Science and Its Rational Reconstruction," in *Boston Studies in Philosophy of Science*, VIII, ed. R. S. Cohen, and C. R. Buck.

—— and A. Musgrave, eds. (1970), *Criticism and the Growth of Knowledge* (London).

—— and E. Zahar (1978), "Why Did Copernicus' Programme Supersede Ptolemy's?" in *The Methodology of Scientific Research Programmes*, eds. J. Worrall and G. Currie (Cambridge, 1978), I.

Latsis, S. J. (1972), "Situational Determinism in Economics," *British Journal of the Philosophy of Science*, 23.

—— (1974) "Situational Determinism in Economics," Ph.D. Dissertation, University of London.

—— (1976), *Method and Appraisal in Economics* (Cambridge).

Lipsey, R. G. (1966), *An Introduction to Positive Economics* (London).

Loasby, B. J. (1971), "Hypothesis and Paradigm in the Theory of the Firm," *Economic Journal*, 81 (December).

Machlup, F. (1955), "The Problem of Verification in Economics," *Southern Economic Journal*, 22 (July).

—— (1974) "Situational Determinism in Economics," *British Journal of the Philosophy of Science*, 25

Magee, B. (1973), *Popper* (London).

Martins, H. (1972), "The Kuhnian Revolution and Its Implications for Sociology," in *Imagination and Precision in Political Analysis*, eds. A. H. Hanson, T. Nossiter and S. Rokkau (London).

Nagel, E. (1961), *The Structure of Science* (London).

O'Brien, D. P. (1970), *J. R. McCulloch: A Study in Classical Economics* (London).

Ohlin, B. (1974), "On the Slow Development of the 'Total Demand' Idea in Economic Theory: Reflections in Connection with Dr. Oppenheimer's Note," *Journal of Economic Literature*, 12, No. 3 (September).

Popper, K. R. (1962), *The Open Society and Its Enemies*, 4th edn. (London).

—— (1965), *The Logic of Scientific Discovery* (New York).

—— (1972), *Objective Knowledge: An Evolutionary Approach* (Oxford).

Ryan, A. (1970), *The Philosophy of the Social Sciences* (London).

Schilpp, P. A., ed. (1974), *The Philosophy of Karl Popper*. Library of Living Philosophers, 2 Vols (La Salle, Ill.).

Schumpeter, J. A. (1954), *History of Economic Analysis* (New York).

Sen, A. K. (1970), *Collective Choice and Social Welfare* (Edinburgh).

Stein, H. (1969), *The Fiscal Revolution in America* (Chicago).

Suppe, F. (1974), *The Structure of Scientific Theories* (Urbana, Ill.).

Teich, M., and R. Young, eds. (1973), *Changing Perspectives in the History of Science* (Dordrecht-Holland).

Toulmin, S. (1972), *Human Understanding* (Oxford).

Uhr, C. G. (1973), "The Emergence of the 'New Economics' in Sweden: A Review of a Study by Otto Steiger," *History of Political Economy*, 5 (Spring).

Urbach, P. (1974), "Progress and Degeneration in the 'IQ Debate' (I), (II)," *British Journal for the Philosophy of Science*, 25.

Ward, B. (1972), *What's Wrong with Economics?* (New York).

Whitley, R. (1974), *Social Processes and Scientific Development* (London).

Worland, S. T. (1972), "Radical Political Economy as a 'Scientific Revolution,'" *Southern Economic Journal*, 39 (October).

Zahar, E. (1973), "Why Did Einstein's Programme Supersede Lorentz's?" *British Journal for the Philosophy of Science*, 24.

14 Economic Methodology in One Easy Lesson

Someone has said: "Methodology is like medicine. We tolerate it because it is supposed to be good for us, but we secretly despise it". But despising methodology as they do, all economists nevertheless have their favourite home remedy for every theoretical illness; unfortunately, they rarely make it clear either to themselves or to others why they believe that these remedies will work. The point of the study in economic methodology is precisely to bring to the surface those rules and conventions that we constantly invoke to justify our own theories and to attack the theories of others. In short, when I say "economic methodology", I do *not* mean the methods and research techniques of economics. I mean "methodology" as it is properly defined: the study of the principles which we regularly employ to establish and validate economic theories.

Methodology, as I have said, is a subject that is not much liked by modern economists, who suffer from what Fritz Machlup has called "methodophobia", and widespread "methodophobia" has had the unfortunate consequence of turning most economists into bad methodologists. My object in this chapter is not so much to convert "methodophobia" into "methodophilia" but simply to demonstrate that some fundamental principles of methodology are easily learned and that, having learned them, we inevitably improve our capacity to appraise and compare competing economic theories.

1. SOME VITAL DISTINCTIONS

Whether we realise it or not, we have all encountered leading examples of certain well-known methodological positions. Surely, every living economist has at some point in his career read and reread Milton Friedman's famous essay, "The Methodology of Positive Economics"? What Friedman espouses in that essay is the methodology of "instrumentalism", namely, the view that scientific theories are merely instruments for making accurate predictions about natural or social phenomena and that all attempts to interpret them as more than that — say, explanations of cause and effect having definite truth-value — may be dismissed as naive. He

265

chose to express his point of view by denying the need to base economic theories on so-called "realistic" assumptions, asserting that "as-if" assumptions will meet all our purposes, and in so doing he disguised the somewhat old-fashioned character of his methodological prescriptions. The methodology of "instrumentalism" is a degenerate form of the methodology of "conventionalism" advocated almost sixty years earlier by such philosophers of science as Ernst Mach and Henri Poincaré, who insisted that scientific theories are not passive reflections of events that take place outside ourselves but free creations of the mind that simply summarise nature as conveniently as possible.

In reacting to Friedman's essay, Paul Samuelson likewise harked back to nineteenth-century "conventionalism". He rejected what he called the "F-twist", namely, Friedman's assertion that the lack of realism of a theory's assumptions is not relevant to its validity, but then spoiled his case by opting for the methodology of "descriptivism", which is simply another name for "conventionalism". Scientific explanations, Samuelson argued, are simply superior descriptions, and descriptions that accurately predict a wide range of observable events are all the "explanations" that we are ever likely to get here on earth. In the final analysis, therefore, both Friedman and Samuelson belong to the same methodological camp and what disagreements there are between them merely constitute a quarrel about language.

What is striking about "instrumentalism", "descriptivism", or simply "conventionalism", is its defensiveness. By emphasising, one might also say by overemphasising, predictive accuracy, it does concede that theories may be poor instruments, bad descriptions, and clumsy conventions; in short, it acknowledges that theories are refutable. But in all other respects, it seeks to protect theories from those who demand the provision of some sort of causal mechanism, linking the action of human agents and the operation of social institutions to the outcomes predicted by theories. It is not always appreciated how radically such "conventionalism" departs from what was not so long ago regarded as an indispensable element of all valid theorising in the social sciences. I mean the doctrine of *Verstehen* that was a standard feature of the methodological writings of the Austrian school, echoed in modern times in another methodological book that virtually every economist has read: *Essay on the Nature and Significance of Economic Science* (1932) by Lionel Robbins.

Verstehen doctrine asserts that theories in the social sciences, as opposed to theories in the natural sciences, must invoke causal motives in the human agents being studied that are understandable to us all in terms of our own intuition and imagination. Theories that fulfil this requirement are true *a priori*, although of course they may not be applicable to a given situation, being offset by disturbing causes outside the range of the theory.

But theories that do not fulfil the requirements of *verstehende* social science may be dismissed out-of-hand as meaningless.

Verstehen doctrine has few adherents today. The followers of Ludwig von Mises, who like to describe themselves as "modern Austrian economists", continue to insist on the methodological dualism that is implied by *Verstehen* doctrine: one methodology for the natural sciences and quite a different methodology for the social sciences. Fritz Machlup too reminds us in his numerous methodological essays of the valid role of introspection in appraising the motives that our theories assign to human actors. But even he does so *sotto voce* and more recently he has accepted the label of "conventionalism" as correctly depicting his own methodological position. Apart from such stalwarts, *Verstehen* doctrine has almost wholly passed out of economics and most modern economists hardly recognise the notions embodied in that doctrine, much less the standard label for such notions.

The dominant methodological doctrine of today is "conventionalism" in one or more of its varieties, whose purpose, as I have said, appears to be to ward off the demand of institutionalists for realism in theory construction. Ironically enough, some of those who today insist on what I will call a "defensive methodology" that can defend orthodox practice against its critics were themselves advocating an "aggressive methodology" only yesterday, that is, a methodology that threatens to deprive orthodoxy of some of its proudest possessions. Everyone who has read Samuelson's *Foundations of Economic Analysis* (1948), from which we all learned the fundamental distinction in economics between the "quantitative calculus" and the "qualitative calculus", will recall that one of Samuelson's central purposes in that book was to derive "operationally meaningful theorems" in economics, meaning hypotheses about economic reality which can conceivably be refuted by factual observations. It is rarely possible in economics to specify the *magnitude* of the change in the endogenous variables which results from a change in one or more of the exogenous variables — this is the "quantitative calculus" — but we must insist as a minimum requirement, Samuelson argued, that we can determine the algebraic sign of the change — this is the "qualitative calculus". Applying the criterion of the "qualitative calculus" to some of the main pillars of received theory, Samuelson concluded that there was little empirical content in the modern theory of consumer behaviour and he was equally sceptical about the principal tenets of the "new welfare economics" which purported to make meaningful statements about welfare without resorting to any interpersonal comparisons of utility.

We must notice, first of all, that the methodological views that Samuelson advances in the *Foundations* have actually nothing to do with "operationalism". "Operationalism", associated with the name of a physicist, Percy Bridgman, is fundamentally concerned with the construction of definite "correspondence rules" to connect the abstract concepts of scientific theories to the experimental operations of physical measurement. What Samuelson's definition of "operationally meaningful theorem" amounts to is rather Popper's methodology of "falsificationism" expressed in the language of the Vienna circle. Be that as it may, the point is that Samuelson's early brand of "operationalism" clearly ruled out some economics as bad economics, whereas his later "descriptivism" merely reinterpreted the whole of orthodox economics as methodologically unassailable. Perhaps it is all a matter of time: the *Foundations* was the work of a young man — although published in 1948, it was completed in 1939 — whereas the statements of the methodology of "descriptivism" were penned in 1965.

It is not to Samuelson's *Foundations*, however, that we owe the first explicit introduction of Popper's criterion of falsifiability into economic discussion. That honour goes to Terence Hutchison's *Significance and Basic Postulates of Economic Theory* (1938). Hutchison's principal target of attack in that book was "apriorism" of the Mises-Robbins kind, typically involving some version of *Verstehen* doctrine, that is, the methodological view that economics is essentially a system of pure deductions from a series of postulates derived from inner experience, which are not themselves open to external verification. Unfortunately, in attacking *apriorism* Hutchison overstated his case. He more or less implied that the bulk of economic theory consisted of "analytic" tautologies, when in fact it largely consisted, and to some extent still consists, of "synthetic" propositions so stated as to defy empirical testing. For example, Hutchison dismissed economic hypotheses accompanied by unspecified *ceteris paribus* clauses as tautologies, whereas in fact they are untestable assertions about the real world.

This may sound like hair-splitting but the distinction between tautologies and untestable propositions about the real world is vital for Hutchison's methodological prescriptions. His principal prescription was that economic inquiries should be confined to empirically testable statements. Because he muddled up untestable "synthetic" propositions with "analytic" ones, however, he was vague about the question whether the requirement of testability refers to the assumptions or to the predictions of economic theory. On balance, he seemed to emphasise the testing of postulates, or what we nowadays call "assumptions", and in many places he seemed to be proposing a research programme in economics that begins with facts and ends with facts. He subsequently denied this charge of "ultra-empiricism" but nevertheless the burden of the book points to the assumptions rather than the predictions of economic theory as the source of the malaise of modern economics. In so doing, he seemed to be demanding a reorientation of economics that would literally have wiped the slate clean all the way back to Adam Smith. Methodological prescriptions that are, or that appear to be, as nihilistic as this will always be resisted by working economists and so it was with Hutchison's prescriptions. His book fell into oblivion and yet it, together with Samuelson's *Foundations*, had brought Popperism firmly into economic methodology, from which it has indeed never been banished.

It reappears without acknowledgement in Friedman, and with acknowledgement in Machlup, and it also appears in an extreme form in Andreas Papandreou's *Economics as a Science* (1958). Papandreou operates with a basic distinction between "models" and "theories": for him, "models" cannot be refuted because their relevant "social space" is not adequately characterised and even "basic theories" have to be supplemented by auxiliary assumptions to become the "augmented theories" that are genuinely refutable. His indictment of current practice in economics is simply that economists rarely formulate "augmented theories" and instead are satisfied with "models" or with "basic theories", which are virtually irrefutable *ex post* explanatory schema. He gives no examples and seems to confine "augmented theories" to comparative static propositions of the quantitative kind, thus ignoring the much larger class of qualitative comparative static propositions. But is is never easy to decide just what he does mean because his entire argument is buried beneath mountains of a new set-theoretical apparatus for economics, which obscures rather than clarifies his meaning. The fact remains, however, that his acid test of acceptability throughout is "empirical meaningfulness", and to that extent he must be classed as an advocate of the Popperian methodology of "falsificationism".

This brings us to Richard Lipsey's popular textbook, *An Introduction to Positive Economics*, first published in 1963 and currently appearing in its sixth edition, whose opening chapters on scientific method have always amounted to a frank avowal of "falsificationism". To this day it remains the outstanding Popper-inspired introduction to elementary economics, continually emphasising throughout all its pages the need to assess competing economic theories in the light of the available empirical evidence. The "naive falsificationism" of the first edition has given way in subsequent editions to "sophisticated falsificationism", which is much closer to the spirit and even the letter of Popper himself: economic theories cannot be faulted by a single, decisive test but only by a whole series of empirical tests, and even the results of such a series must be weighed in the light of alternative theories purporting to explain the same range of events.

At this point, we may be tempted to echo Hutchison's recently expressed opinion that by now "Perhaps a majority of economists — but not all — would agree that improved predictions of economic behaviour or events is the main or primary task of the economist". And yet I wonder. There are plenty of indications that the majority, if it is a majority, represents no more than 51 per cent of modern economists: radical economists, Marxists and neo-Marxists, post-Keynesians and neo-Keynesians, institutionalists, and heterodox economists of all kind, who together constitute a sizeable proportion of the younger generation of living economists, certainly do not agree that economic theories must ultimately stand or fall on the basis of the predictions that they yield, that empirical testing of hypotheses constitutes, as it were, the Mecca of modern economics. Even Benjamin Ward's aggressive catalogue of *What's Wrong With Economics?* (1972) denies that the failure to emphasise the empirically falsifiable conse-quences of theories is one of the major flaws of modern economics. To show how far an anti-Popperian methodology actually prevails in some quarters of the profession, we need only mention a methodological work of Martin Hollis and Edward Nell, entitled *Rational Economic Man*, with a telling subtitle *A Philosophical Critique of Neo-Classical Economics* (1975).

This book examines what the authors take to be the unholy alliance between neoclassical economics and logical positivism and it manages to do so without even mentioning the name of Karl Popper. Logical posi-tivism, they argue, is a false philosophy and it must be replaced by "rationalism", by which they mean the demonstration that there are Kantian "synthetic" *a priori* truths, that is, truths about the real world that are somehow available to us before we begin to examine the world. A leading example of these "synthetic" *a priori* truths, they tell us, is the fact that economic systems must reproduce themselves; reproduction is there-fore *the* "essence" of economic systems, which alone can furnish a sound basis for economic theory. The trouble with neoclassical economics, they hold, is that there is nothing in the neoclassical approach that guarantees that firms and households will reconstitute themselves from period to period. After this, one might expect to learn that sound economic theory is growth theory, which of course is fundamentally concerned with the infinitely reproducible, steady-state properties of economic growth paths. But no, the only alternative to neoclassical economics that incorporates the essential fact of reproduction is what they call "Classical-Marxian economics", meaning neo-Ricardian economics that leans more heavily on the work of Piero Sraffa than on the work of Karl Marx.

Any mention of the "essence" of economic systems makes us prick up our ears. According to Aristotle, the "essence" of something is that element that makes a thing what it is, and there is no doubt that every attempt to provide a definition of an entity involves the attempt to pin down its essence. In other words, there is nothing wrong with "essentialism" as part of the logic of the science of taxonomy. But the notion that "rationalism" or "essentialism" can also furnish us with a philosophy of theorising in the social sciences has only to be stated explicitly to reveal its feebleness. How indeed are we to decide what are these "essences" of economic life that must be captured in our theories if we refuse to accept any empirical yardsticks for validating our theories? Even Hollis and Nell are forced to concede in the concluding chapter of their book that economic systems sometimes fail to reproduce themselves, a case in point being the capitalist economic system in time of business crises. Perhaps it would be better then not to base our economic theories entirely on the concept of constant reproduction? Now, whatever we think of that question, I doubt that we shall answer it by throwing away the whole of the heritage of positivism in favour of the ancient, Aristotelian way of thinking about scientific problems. At any rate, it is clear that the essentialist approach to economic knowledge leaves no role whatever for quantitative research. The book by Hollis and Nell simply wipes out all the advances in methodological thinking in post-war economics that Popperism has ushered in. One might almost say that if they had read Popper's many devastating comments on the philosophy of "essentialism", their book would never have been written.

Where does that leave us? Suffice it to say that nothing like an overwhelming consensus has emerged from our bird's-eye view of post-war economic methodology. But despite some blurring around the edges, it is possible to discern a mainstream view. Despite the embarrassment of the F-twist, Friedman and Machlup do seem to have persuaded most of their colleagues that direct verification of the assumptions of economic theory is both unnecessary and misleading; economic theories should be judged in the final analysis by their predictive implications for the phenomena which they are designed to explain. At the same time, it is held that economics is only a "box of tools" and that empirical testing can show, not so much whether particular models are true or false, but whether or not they are applicable in a given situation. The prevailing methodological mood is not only highly protective of received economic theory, it is also ultra-permissive within the limits of the "rules of the game": almost any model will do, provided it is rigorously formulated, elegantly constructed, and promising of potential relevance to real-world situations at some unknown date in the future. Modern economists frequently preach falsificationism but, as we shall see, they rarely practise it: their working philosophy of science is aptly described by the label "innocuous falsificationism".

2. A CRITICAL EXAMINATION OF METHODOLOGICAL VIEWS

The charge of "innocuous falsificationism" can only be substantiated by examining the status of some ruling economic theories. But a little of the flavour of what is meant is conveyed by taking a closer look at the methodological positions we have outlined above. Agreeing that Friedman is an "instrumentalist", that Samuelson is a "descriptivist", that Machlup is a "conventionalist", that Robbins is an "apriorist", so what? What is wrong with any or all of these positions and what is so wonderful about "falsificationism" that we should welcome its predominance in the methodological thinking of modern economists, decrying only that it is more preached than practised?

There is little need to criticise "apriorism", since it is a dead horse that needs no flogging. As we all know, Robbins thought that price theory could be built up purely deductively on the basis of a few fundamental postulates, such as the notion that individuals have consistent preference orderings among all the goods they wish to purchase and that the production function of goods is always subject to the principle of diminishing marginal productivity. These fundamental postulates, Robbins argued, are both *a priori* "analytic" truths, that is, logical implications of what we mean when we talk of demand and supply, and *a priori* "synthetic" truths, that is, elementary and indisputable facts of experience. "We do not need controlled experiments to establish their validity", he said; "they are so much the stuff of our everyday experience that they have only to be stated to be recognised as obvious". It is ironic to realise that Eugen Slutsky had in fact demonstrated seventeen years before Robbins wrote those words that something as fundamental as the universal "law" that demand curves are always negatively inclined cannot be based simply on the assumption that individuals have consistent and transitive preference orderings among goods. It is equally ironic to note that linear production models, which dispense with the principle of diminishing marginal productivity, had been part and parcel of the first statements of general equilibrium theory fifty years earlier. But irony apart, the point of Robbins' "apriorism" is to show that empirical research in economics is necessary only to demonstrate that particular theories are actually applicable to a given situation; the truth or validity of the theory is guaranteed by its intuitively obvious assumptions and by its tight, deductive structure. In short, economic theories can be shown not to apply but they cannot be empirically refuted.

If there is any part of Robbins' *Essay* that stands up even today, it is Chapter six, which denies the possibility of making objective interpersonal comparisons of utility. Again, it is highly ironic to notice that this impossibility theorem is based on the notion that we cannot verify statements of interpersonal comparisons of utility either by introspection or by observation. But if this much is granted, it applies just as much to *intra*personal comparisons of utility as a basis of demand theory as to *inter*personal comparisons of utility as a basis of welfare economics, thus contradicting the earlier chapters in the book. In other words, if we rely on introspection in formulating demand theory, we do so, surely, because we assume that other people have much the same psychology as ourselves? In that case, how can we deny the same sort of assumption in formulating propositions about welfare economics? Thus, Robbins himself supplies the key to what is wrong with "apriorism" in demand theory.

It is fortunate that in the case of Robbins we have for once a methodologist's afterthoughts on his own methodological pronouncements. In his *Autobiography* (1971), written almost forty years after the *Essay on the Nature and Significance of Economic Science*, he glanced back at the reception of his book. He remained unpersuaded by most of the criticisms that the book received but in retrospect he agreed that he paid too little attention to the problem of testing both the assumptions and the implications of economic theory: "the chapter on the nature of economic generalizations", he said, "smacked too much of what nowadays is called essentialism ... it was written before the star of Karl Popper had risen above our horizon. If I had known then of his path-breaking exhibition of scientific method ... this part of the book would have been phrased very differently".

I said earlier that "apriorism" is now a dead horse. But methodologies, like old soldiers, never die — they only fade away. While the economic profession as a whole has long discarded "apriorism", a small group of latter-day Austrian economists have returned to a more extreme version of it contained in Ludwig von Mises' *Human Action: A Treatis on Economics* (1949). Mises' statements of radical "apriorism' are so uncompromising that they have to be read to be believed. They go well beyond Robbins in rejecting anything that smacks of econometrics or quantitative testing of economic predictions, and they categorically deny the meaningfulness of any macroeconomic propositions that are not firmly grounded in purposive, individual behaviour. This school of so-called "modern Austrian economics" has interesting things to say about the study of competitive processes, as distinct from the properties of final equilibrium states, but its methodological ideas are a throwback to the Neanderthal "essentialism" of yesterday.

So much for "apriorism". "Instrumentalism" is not so easily dealt with. A good case can be made for the argument that all scientific explanations are really nothing more than successful engines for making predictions, and that every answer to a why?-question turns out on closer examination to be simply an answer to a how?-question. After all, even Newtonian celestial mechanics, the most successful scientific research programme in the history of science, lacks a push-and-pull mechanism to account for gravity and in that sense fails actually to "explain" the attraction between bodies in motion. In short, "instrumentalism" holds that all explanations are really predictions written backwards, and, likewise, all predictions are really explanations written forwards. The notion that there is nothing in logic that allows us to distinguish explanations from predictions has been dubbed, for obvious reasons, the "Symmetry Thesis" and the Symmetry Thesis is the heart of the matter in the methodology of "instrumentalism" or "descriptivism".

There are serious objections to the Symmetry Thesis, which perhaps strike social scientists even more readily than they do natural scientists. Problem number 1 is that the history of science contains a number of theories which appear to explain natural phenomena, without however predicting them even in a statistical sense. A leading example is the Darwinian theory of evolution, which seems to account for the survival of species after the fact but is powerless to predict the survival of any particular species before the fact. The Symmetry Thesis would imply that Darwinian theory cannot count as science, which must at least cause us to think again about the cogency of the Symmetry Thesis. Problem number 2 is that science, and particularly social science, abounds in rules-of-thumb that yield highly accurate predictions about both natural and social events despite the fact that we may have absolutely no idea why these rules-of-thumb work as well as they do. No economist has to be told that there is a world of difference between an extrapolated trend line that more or less accurately predicts the magnitude of a variable in the next period and a least squares regression that seeks to explain the variance of some dependent variable by means of a causal theory connecting the independent variables to the dependent variable. The difference lies precisely in what we do when a prediction lets us down: if we have simply extrapolated a trend line for the sake of making a prediction, any failure to predict accurately leaves us back at square one no wiser than before; on the other hand, if we have based our predictions on a particular theory about the relationship between the relevant variables, a failure to predict accurately sends us back to the theory to do a repair job. In other words, prediction is not simply explanation written backwards because it is all too easy to predict without explaining anything.

Still, it is better to predict accurately without being able to give reasons for our accuracy than to wait in silence for a true explanation that may some day be forthcoming. And in this trite observation lies the strength of "instrumentalism": it is a methodology of scientific modesty; it asks little of science and, hence, cannot be faulted on its own grounds. Do businessmen really have the requisite knowledge and information in a world of dynamic uncertainty to maximise profits? Can consumers plausibly be expected to have what John Maurice Clark called "an irrational passion for dispassionate calculations"? Don't ask such questions, says the "instrumentalist". Ask rather whether theories that assume that businessmen and consumers act as if they were rational maximisers make accurate predictions about economic phenomena. And, yes, accuracy of predictions is a principal test that all good theories must pass. But it is not the only test that they must pass.

It is not the only test that they must pass because the predictive record of theories is itself difficult to assess without introducing considerations of the scope and underlying structure of the theories in question. A famous philosopher of science, Pierre Duhem, argued at the turn of the last century that no scientific theory can ever be refuted decisively, because every refutation involves that theory plus the addition of certain auxiliary assumptions relating to measurement instruments, initial situation, boundary conditions, etcetera; any refutation can always be explained away as due to the absence of one of these auxiliary assumptions. If we are ever to refute the predictions of a theory, we can only do so in terms of a long series of experiments under a variety of circumstances and even then we have to agree in the end not to employ what Popper calls "immunizing stratagems" that endlessly protect the theory by *ad hoc* amendments. In other words, when assessing the predictive record of a theory, we have to be sure that we know where and when it applies, and that means that we have to examine its assumptions and not just its predictive implications.

All such questions are badly muddled in Friedman's notorious essay on the methodology of positive economics. That essay actually argues two quite distinct theses. On the one hand, it claims that economists should not worry at all if the assumptions of their theories are "unrealistic". On the other hand, it claims that neoclassical microeconomics, or what he calls "the maximization-of-returns hypothesis", has frequently been tested, that it has passed most of these tests with flying colours, and he explains this impressive achievement by what is in fact a new theory of competition. Competition, he tells us, represents a Darwinian process of survival that produces exactly the same results that would ensue if all business firms maximised their profits and all consumers maximised their utility. This, I repeat, is not a behaviourist reinterpretation of traditional theory but rather a new theory. Friedman presents these two theses as if one were the corollary of the other, although actually they have very little to do with each other.

Take first the thesis of the Irrelevance of Realistic Assumptions. As any number of commentators have pointed out, Friedman equivocates between three meanings of the concept of "unrealistic" assumptions, switching at different stages of his argument from one to the other without informing us that he is doing so. The assumptions of economic theory are sometimes said to be "unrealistic" because they are abstract, because they idealise the behaviour of economic agents, and because they simplify the relevant background variables. It is of course easy to show that absolutely any theory which is not an exact replica of reality abstracts, idealises and oversimplifies outrageously. If "good" theories explain much with little, they must be descriptively inaccurate or unrealistic in their assumptions — and that is an end to the matter.

There is a second sense in which the assumptions of economics may be said to be "unrealistic" — they may ascribe motives to economic actors that we, as fellow human beings, simply find incomprehensible. If we believe in *Verstehen* doctrine, we would rule out any theory that relied on assumptions that were unrealistic in this sense. Friedman, however, totally rejects *Verstehen* doctrine and he sees no problem about having a theory that requires economic agents to process information and to calculate its consequences with the speed of electronic computers; a Darwinian process of competitive rivalry guarantees that we will only observe survivors who actually maximise profits and all that matters for the theory is whether it correctly predicts this outcome.

But there is still a third sense in which the assumptions of theories may be said to be "unrealistic" and it is perhaps this interpretation which most of Friedman's critics have had in mind. It is the case where the assumptions are believed to be either false or highly improbable in the light of directly perceived evidence about economic behaviour; for example, business firms may be observed to commit themselves unalterably to fixed rules for pricing their products irrespective of economic circumstances, thus implying that they are not maximising profits. Friedman cleverly guards himself against this objections by conceding frankly that, in the example just given, we are probably applying the maximisation-of-return hypothesis incorrectly to a situation outside its proper domain. In other words, he is perfectly aware of the fact that one of the roles that assumptions play in theories is to specify the range of phenomena to which the theory is intended to apply; thus, every time we test the implications of a theory, we are in fact asking whether its assumptions are "realistic" in the sense of correctly specifying the circumstances under which it applies. Once we eliminate any reference to a theory's domain of application, we render it untestable, because every refutation can be countered by the argument that it has been incorrectly applied.

Having introduced this important methodological clarification about the role of assumptions in the testing of theories, Friedman immediately takes back with one hand what he has just given with the other by allowing, say, the theory of perfect competition to apply to any firm whatsoever even if that firm operates in a highly concentrated industry. There is no inconsistency, he asserts, in regarding the same firm as if it were a perfect competitor for one problem and a perfect monopolist for another, depending on what it is we wish to predict. In the final analysis, therefore, Friedman always reverts to an extreme "instrumentalist" interpretation of economic theory, according to which predictions and only predictions are all that matter.

The Big Bad Wolf in his essay is he who insists on direct verification of fundamental assumptions as the critical test of the validity of a theory in advance of, or independently from, a test of its predictions. But was there ever such a Bad Wolf? What the critics have argued is (1) that accurate predictions are not the only relevant test of the validity of a theory and if they were, it would be impossible to distinguish between genuine and spurious correlations; (2) that direct evidence about assumptions either of motivation or of overt behaviour is not necessarily more difficult to obtain than data about market outcomes which are regularly employed to test predictions; (3) that the attempt to test assumptions may yield important insights that help us to interpret the results of predictive tests; and (4) that if predictive testing with patently counterfactual assumptions is indeed all we can hope for in economics, we ought to demand that our theories be put to extremely severe tests.

To underline these points, let us spend a moment on what is meant by a "test" of an assumption about motivation. Now, it may be agreed that any attempt to interrogate businessmen as to whether they do or do not seek to maximise profits, or to equate marginal revenue and marginal costs, or to discount the returns from capital projects at the cost of capital to the firm, is bound to produce ambiguous answers whose interpretation will usually beg the very same questions that are being investigated. But other inquiries are possible: not "what are the bits of information that are actually collected before making strategic output and investment decisions?", or "how are such decisions actually made in the light of conflicts within the firm between the executives of different departments?" The traditional theory of the firm treats the firm as if it were a "black box" without specifying its internal decision-making machinery. An inquiry that seeks to throw light on the nature of the "black box" must, surely, illuminate the attempt to test the predictions of the black-box theory of business behaviour? In any case, without such an inquiry, the predictions of the theory are almost as difficult to test as are the assumptions.

Once we admit that there is nothing wrong with asking businessmen what they do and why they do it, and that we may even learn something from such questions, we are ready to contemplate the validity of the theory of competition as a Darwinian selection process — and not until. As I remarked earlier, this is not old wine in new bottles but rather new wine. By leaning heavily on a Darwinian interpretation of competitive outcomes, Friedman is in fact repudiating the "methodological individualism" that is embedded in the neoclassical approach to economic questions: instead of deriving testable predictions in-the-large from the rational action of individuals agents in-the-small, the predictions of microeconomics are instead derived from a new kind of causal mechanism, namely, a dynamic selection process that rewards those businessmen who, for whatever reasons, act "as if" they were rational maximisers, while penalising those who act in some other way by bankruptcy.

The reference to a *dynamic* selection process shows immediately what is wrong with the argument: traditional microeconomics is largely, if not entirely, a theory of timeless comparative statics, and, as such, it is strong on equilibrium outcomes but weak on the process whereby equilibrium is attained. To vindicate Friedman's argument, we need to be able to predict behaviour in disequilibrium situations, that is, we need to supplement the standard theory of the firm by a so-far missing theory of the appearance and disappearance of firms in the economic environment. Suppose there are increasing returns to scale, or any other technologically-based cost advantages; if a non-maximising firm gains an initial advantage over a maximiser, say, by entering the industry earlier in time, the scale advantage may allow that non-maximiser to grow faster than the maximiser and to do so irreversibly; in consequence, the only firms that we actually observe are firms that fail to maximise profits and that indeed carry "slack". Even the mere presence of differentiated products and associated advertising may produce a similar result. Now, of course, we can define a set of assumptions — constant returns to scale, identical products, perfect capital markets, reinvestment of all profits, etcetera — that will support the Darwinian theory of competition, but that procedure will only bring us back full circle to the question of the "realism" of assumptions. In a nutshell, the problem with the Darwinian theory of competition is the same as the problem of reading meaning into "the survival of the fittest" in Darwinian theory: to survive it is only necessary to be better adapted to the environment than one's rivals, and we can no more establish from natural selection that surviving species are perfect than we can establish from economic selection that surviving firms are profit-maximisers.

Have I covered the entire menu of possible economic methodologies? Some would say not. They discern in the writings of the American institutionalists a mode of explanation that is neither "apriorism", "conventionalism", "operationalism", "instrumentalism", "descriptivism", nor "falsificationism": it is what has been called "pattern modelling" because it seeks to explain events or actions by identifying their place in a pattern of relationships that is said to characterise the economic system as a whole. "Pattern modellers", we are told, reject all forms of "atomism" and refuse to abstract from any part of the whole system; their working hypotheses are relatively concrete and close to the system being described, and if they generalise at all, they do so by developing typologies; their explanations emphasise "understanding" rather than "predictions" and they view an explanation as contributing to understanding if new data fall into place according to the stated pattern.

I have no doubt that this is a more or less accurate description of the methods of some institutionalists, such as Thorstein Veblen, Clarence Ayres, and perhaps Gunnar Myrdal. But it is difficult to find anything like "pattern modelling" in the writings of John R. Commons, Wesley Clair Mitchell and John Kenneth Galbraith, whom some would regard as leading institutionalists. It is clear that all of these writers are united in some respects: none of them will have any truck with concepts of equilibrium, rational behaviour, instantaneous adjustments and perfect knowledge, and they all favour the idea of group behaviour under the influence of custom and habit, preferring to view the economic system more as a biological organism than as a machine. But that is a far cry from saying that they share a common methodology, that is, a common method of validating their explanations. There may be such a thing as a school of institutionalism but it clearly has no unique methodology denied to orthodox economists.

A much better description of the working methodology of institutionalists is what Benjamin Ward labels "storytelling", which he argues also describes much orthodox economics, particularly of the applied kind. Storytelling makes use of the method of what historians call "colligation", the binding together of facts, low-level generalisations, high-level theories, and value judgments in a coherent narrative, held together by a glue of implicit set of beliefs and attitudes that the author shares with his readers. In able hands, it can be extremely persuasive and yet it is never easy to explain afterwards why it has persuaded.

How does one validate a particular piece of storytelling? One asks, of course, if the facts are correctly stated; if other facts are omitted; if the lower-level generalisations are subject to counter-examples; and if one can find competing stories that will fit the facts. In short, one goes through a process identical to the one that we regularly employ to validate the hypothetico-deductive explanations of orthodox economics. However, because storytelling lacks rigour, lacks a definite logical structure, it is all too easy to verify and virtually impossible to falsify. It is, or can be, persuasive precisely because it never runs the risk of being wrong.

Perhaps economic problems are so intractable that storytelling is the best that we can do. But if such is the case it is odd that we should actually recommend the safe methodology of "storytelling" and deplore the risky methodology of "falsificationism". Surely, the more falsificationism, the better.

Index of Names

Index of Subjects